Our Lady of Victorian Feminism

OUR LADY OF

VICTORIAN FEMINISM

The Madonna in the Work of Anna Jameson,
Margaret Fuller, and George Eliot

Kimberly VanEsveld Adams

Ohio University Press
Athens

Ohio University Press, Athens, Ohio 45701
© 2001 by Kimberly VanEsveld Adams
Printed in the United States of America

Ohio University Press books are printed on acid-free paper ⊗™

09   08   07   06   05   04   03   02   01   5   4   3   2   1

Library of Congress Cataloging-in-Publication Data

Adams, Kimberly VanEsveld.
    Our Lady of Victorian Feminism : the Madonna in the work of Anna
Jameson, Margaret Fuller, and George Eliot / Kimberly VanEsveld
Adams.
        p. cm.
    Includes bibliographical references and index.
    ISBN 0-8214-1361-9 (alk. paper) — ISBN 0-8214-1362-7 (pbk.: alk.
paper)
        1. English prose literature—Women authors—History and criticism. 2.
Jameson, Mrs. (Anna), 1794–1860—Criticism and interpretation. 3. Women
and literature—Great Britain—History—19th century. 4. English prose
literature—19th century—History and criticism. 5. Fuller, Margaret,
1810–1850—Criticism and interpretation. 6. Eliot, George, 1819–1880—
Criticism and interpretation. 7. Christianity and literature—History—19th
century. 8. Feminism and literature—History—19th century. 9. Mary,
Blessed Virgin, Saint—In literature. 10. Mary, Blessed Virgin, Saint—Art.
11. Feminism in literature. 12. Women in literature. 13. Feminism in art.
14. Women in art. I. Title.
PR756.W65 A64 2000
823'.809351—dc21
                                                                                00-063680

To Johan and Maryclaire

Bishop John Sheets . . . said that the [pastoral letter] failed to "alert the faithful" to the dangers of feminists who see God as both male and female and deny the maleness of Jesus.
—Ari Goldman, *The New York Times* (June 19, 1992)

There she stands—the transfigured woman, at once completely human and completely divine, an abstraction of power, purity, and love.
—Anna Jameson, *Legends of the Madonna*

Where did your Christ come from? From God and a woman! Man had nothing to do with him.
—Sojourner Truth, "Ain't I a Woman?"

Would [Woman] but assume her inheritance, Mary would not be the only Virgin Mother.
—Margaret Fuller, *Woman in the Nineteenth Century*

Every day . . . the small flock of surviving villagers paid their visit to this cottage to see the Blessed Lady, and to bring her of their best as an offering—honey, fresh cakes, eggs, and polenta. . . . Many legends were afterwards told in that valley about the blessed Lady who came over the sea.
—George Eliot, *Romola*

Contents

Illustrations

Acknowledgments

I would first like to thank David Sanders and Nancy Basmajian at Ohio University Press for accepting the book and seeing it through the press. I would also like to express my gratitude to the following friends and colleagues: Kevin Van Anglen, for volunteering to edit and make cuts in the manuscript and providing donnish advice on my treatment of religious history; Betsy Bowden, Marie Cornelia, Sheila Cosminsky, Larry Davis, Rafey Habib, Robert Kiely, Andrew Lees, Mason Lowance, Timothy Martin, Robert Ryan, and Carol Singley, for reading various chapters and in some cases helping me obtain research support; the Five College Women's Studies Research Center, Mount Holyoke College, for giving me a research associateship that enabled me to finish the book; the University of Pennsylvania, the Philadelphia Free Library, Rutgers University, Harvard University, the Boston Public Library, the Massachusetts Historical Society, the Five Colleges consortium, the Beinecke Library, Yale University, and the Bodleian Library, Oxford, for allowing me access to their collections; K. C. Dietsch, for preparing the Jameson slides used in the book; Randi Eldevik, Maryclaire Moroney, Donald Mull, and Emily Sohmer Tai, for being wonderful scholars and dear friends; Johan de Jong, for editing drafts late at night, giving up things he wanted in support of my career, and loving me even at my crabbiest; and Scarlatti de Kat, for keeping me company in the study.

Parts of this book were published in slightly altered form in *Journal of Feminist Studies in Religion* 12, no. 1 (spring 1996): 41–70; *Women's Studies* 25 (1996): 385–405; and *Women's Theology in Nineteenth-Century Britain*, ed. Julie Melnyk (New York: Garland, 1998), 59–62. My thanks also go to Laurence Pollinger Limited and the Earl of Lytton for permission to quote from the Lovelace Papers.

Abbreviations

Dispatches	Fuller, *"These Sad But Glorious Days": Dispatches from Europe, 1846–1850*
Eliot Letters	*The George Eliot Letters*, ed. Gordon Haight
Fuller Letters	*The Letters of Margaret Fuller*, ed. Robert Hudspeth
Jameson, Letters	*Letters of Anna Jameson to Ottilie von Goethe*, ed. G. H. Needler
Madonna	Jameson, *Legends of the Madonna*
Monastic Orders	Jameson, *Legends of the Monastic Orders*
ODCC	*Oxford Dictionary of the Christian Church*
PLA	Fuller, *Papers on Literature and Art*
SE	*George Eliot: Selected Essays, Poems and Other Writings*, ed. A. S. Byatt and Nicholas Warren
SLA	Jameson, *Sacred and Legendary Art*
WNC	Fuller, *Woman in the Nineteenth Century*
WSSR	Jameson, *Winter Studies and Summer Rambles in Canada*

Our Lady of Victorian Feminism

Introduction

This book focuses on three nineteenth-century women: Anna Jameson (1794–1860), the Anglo-Irish art historian; Margaret Fuller (1810–1850), the American Transcendentalist essayist; and Marian Evans (1819–1880), the English novelist and lapsed Evangelical, who wrote under the name George Eliot. All three, Protestants by background and feminists by conviction, are curiously and crucially linked by their use of the Madonna in arguments designed to empower women. They are not the only Victorians to focus on this figure, but in their work the Madonna is not, as is customary in this period, abstracted from church tradition and used with literary license, usually in support of a constrictive domestic ideology; rather, she has a central role in a feminist biblical hermeneutics. Anna Jameson saw the Madonna historically as the feminine face of the divine, a figure whose glory and power are shared by women. Jameson also made the Madonna a human and inclusive figure; she noted ethnic and class variations in Marian portraiture and insisted on a Madonna who ages. Margaret Fuller and George Eliot focused instead on the Madonna as Virgin and Mother, seeing her as a figure at once intellectually self-reliant and fulfilled by her family relationships. As such, the Madonna represented the self-perfection and completion that ordinary women would achieve when freed from social restraints. Fuller also considered her a powerful symbol of the female artist, miraculously producing books, or "virgin births," with no man's aid. All three women explored the Virgin

2   Mother's likeness to the creative and destructive goddess-figures of the religions predating Christianity. The three writers form a significant group,
because they were quite unusual among their English-speaking and Protestant contemporaries in seeing feminist possibilities in the Madonna,[1] and
because they knew or knew of each other and frequently were influenced
by each other's work. More generally, they enable us to consider issues of
representation, the relations of nineteenth-century feminism and religious
thought, and cross-cultural and trans-Atlantic influences in our theorizing
about nineteenth-century culture.

My argument about Jameson, Fuller, Eliot, and the Madonna involves
placing the three writers in the context of the nineteenth-century women's
movement, in which they participated both as authors and as activists.
Many early feminists (e.g., Mary Wollstonecraft, Sarah Grimké, Lucretia
Mott, and Barbara Leigh Smith Bodichon) claimed that women are men's
spiritual equals and so should be their social and political equals as well.
Most nineteenth-century feminists (e.g., John Stuart Mill and Frances
Power Cobbe) argued, from necessity but usually also from conviction,
that woman's primary though not exclusive role was as wife and mother.
Some went farther and saw woman's "maternal character" as the source of
her strength and moral force. Yet most also praised the single state, for
making women self-reliant and free to act. Elizabeth Cady Stanton said of
her unmarried collaborator Susan B. Anthony:

> The world has ever had its vestal virgins, its holy women,
> mothers of ideas rather than of men, its Marys as well as its
> Marthas, who, rather than be busy housewives, preferred to sit
> at the feet of divine wisdom, and ponder the mysteries of the
> unknown. . . . All honor to the noble women who have devoted
> earnest lives to the intellectual and moral needs of mankind![2]

A notable achievement of Jameson, Fuller, and Eliot is their realization
that the *Madonna* might serve as a powerful symbol of all these feminist
concerns. Thus Jameson described the Madonna as "the transfigured
woman, at once completely human and completely divine," whose status
in heaven, as the equal or near-equal of her Son, reflects and reinforces the
status of women as the equals of men. Fuller's Virgin Mother represented a
woman's hope of being *both* the Mary and Martha of the biblical story, both
Minerva and Muse, and enjoying the male privilege of an intellectual
vocation as well as a family of her own. Eliot, more pessimistically, used

Madonna-figures, notably Dinah Morris in *Adam Bede*, to show the current impossibility of being simultaneously virgin and mother, because the mother could not escape the impediment imposed by the biological and social construction of the female body. Thus Eliot ironically suggested the benefits of sexual and psychic virginity: a woman could enjoy freedom and empowerment only in the virgin's state of physical and emotional self-denial. In later books, Eliot, like Jameson and Fuller, posited historical connections between sacred images and the power and status of actual women; women were more honored and valued, they suggested, in pre-modern European societies, which adored the Virgin and female saints. These writers' views anticipate the questions of modern feminist historians and theorists concerning the differing benefits of modernity for women and for men.

There is a second context for my discussion: the nineteenth-century Protestant assessments of Catholic belief and art. Jameson, Fuller, and Eliot encountered Catholicism both at home (in debates about the Irish Question, Irish immigration, and the restoration of the Catholic ecclesiastical hierarchy in England and its influence in America) and in their frequent travels abroad. They also encountered Mary in their solitary tours through art galleries or in Continental churches far from home. Moreover, they met her in books, from which they elevated her to a pantheon of personal heroes. As Protestants, the three writers came from religious backgrounds that acknowledged Mary's place in the Scriptures, as Joseph's wife and Jesus' mother, but did not venerate her. A Mary who was initially seen trailing no clouds of Catholic tradition and wearing no royal institutional robes could the more readily be appropriated by adult feminists and made to symbolize the power and freedom they were beginning to enjoy.

But the three writers balanced their freedom to appropriate or reject the religious past with a reverence for what previous generations had considered holy and precious. This regard for Catholic religious tradition distinguished them from feminists such as Wollstonecraft, Grimké, and Stanton. Stanton and her collaborators took something of a joyride through church history in the *Woman's Bible* (1895); one contributor said, for example, without consideration of the historical origins of the doctrine, that the Immaculate Conception was a slur on ordinary mothers, and that her own mother was as holy as Mary. In contrast, Jameson, Fuller, and Eliot looked back at the legends, liturgies, and sacred images of the past to find what they called the living spirit within the ancient beliefs and forms. And in a century marked by outbursts of anti-Catholic feeling, they were

4   sometimes remarkably open to reexamining, redefining, and even reviving concepts and practices such as celibacy, asceticism, and religious communities. In these respects, they shared the agenda (and even the audience) of the Oxford Movement, the Catholicizing reform movement within the Church of England led by Keble, Pusey, and Newman. But none of the women ever became Anglo-Catholic; they remained Protestants who saw the liberating possibilities of tradition but were also generally free from orthodox restraints. They went far beyond Newman, for example, in emphasizing the power of the Madonna of Catholic tradition by placing her in a line of ancient goddesses.

Finally, although all three writers tended to be reluctant commentators on current affairs (other than the Woman Question), their works were profoundly marked by the nineteenth-century "politics of Mary" (i.e., the uses of Mary as a political symbol, frequently by the supporters of royal and religious ancien regimes). For instance, Eliot's historical novel *Romola* (1862–63), set in Renaissance Florence, is engaged with Pre-Raphaelite and political questions of religious representation. Fuller eventually came to address the 1848 Italian struggle, and when she fully grasped the politics of Mary in Italy, the Madonna—earlier her symbol of female intellectual and spiritual self-reliance—was replaced by the Jesus of Protestantism, whom she considered an appropriate symbol of the *Risorgimento*. Jameson reacted to abuses of power by political and religious leaders by proclaiming spiritual rather than secular queenship as the model for female power. But unlike Fuller, she continued to see some liberatory potential in the Madonna, not least because this figure was the Holy Mother of the Catholics in Jameson's native Ireland during the decades of Irish resistance to British rule.

As the foregoing discussion indicates, this study examines Madonna-figures (primarily those favored by three women writers) in relation to Victorian views of feminism, religion and politics, and art and literature. Jameson, Fuller, and Eliot were innovators in their treatment of Marian images, but not in making them the subject of their work—for Madonna-figures appeared with some frequency in the art and literature found in Britain and the United States in the nineteenth century. There is, for example, the young wife, her sweet face encircled by a halo-like bonnet, sitting on shipboard beside her husband in Ford Madox Brown's Pre-Raphaelite painting *The Last of England* (1852–55). As Nina Auerbach notes, her rosy skin and steady eyes, the pink ribbon, and the clasped hand of the baby concealed under her cloak are signs of hope in a gray scene of immigrants departing (44–47). The photographer Julia Cameron had a parlor-maid, May Hillier, who was known locally as "Mary Madonna" because her employer so often posed her in that role (Trudgill, 258). Madonnas in Victorian literature—so labeled by narrators and readers because of their looks and their love and purity—include Dickens's Little Nell in *The Old Curiosity Shop* and Agnes in *David Copperfield*, Wilkie Collins's protagonist in *Hide and Seek*, Eliot's Milly Barton and later heroines, Harriet Beecher Stowe's Mary Scudder in *The Minister's Wooing*, and (in a challenge to Victorian moral codes) innocent or purified fallen mothers such as Gaskell's Ruth, Barrett Browning's Marian Erle, Hawthorne's Hester Prynne, and Hardy's Tess.[3] According to Sandra Gilbert and Susan Gubar, there is a "clear line of literary descent" from the Madonna in heaven to the Angel in the House, but the angel is the preferred representation of female purity in a more secular age (21; see also Auerbach, 63–88).

Victorian authors did not limit their focus to Madonnas, but frequently paired them with Magdalenes; they were especially interested in the interchangeability of the two figures. ("Magdalene," the name of the New Testament saint of repentant sexuality, was a nineteenth-century term for the fallen woman.) For instance, George Eliot in one of her reviews expressed her pleasure in taking up a historical novel by Charles Kingsley "after a surfeit of . . . Madonnas and Magdalens."[4] Yet her own fiction contributed to the supply: Dinah Morris and Hetty Sorrel, Maggie Tulliver (in both roles), perhaps Romola and Tessa. Most modern critics feel that the Magdalene has the more interesting role, since she possesses sexual energy and the power and freedom not just to be bad, but to be active at all. The Madonna's goodness is by contrast generally seen as involving restraints: she is contained within the household and subordinate rather than resistant to men, her life is centered around service to her husband and child, and her innocence is kept intact by limitations on her knowledge and experience of the world. To be sure, Nina Auerbach claims there is subversive potential in the domestic Madonna, calling her "the immobilized possessor of unprecedented spiritual power," and Elizabeth Langland challenges the narrow "angelic" interpretation of woman's domestic role. But most literary critics, like many of their counterparts in religious studies, have assumed that the Madonna is a figure ultimately under masculine control, rather than, as I claim, a contested symbol that many, including nineteenth-century feminists, have managed to appropriate and define.[5] In

6   addition, literary critics, while focusing on the reception of Madonna-figures by English-speaking Protestants, have not generally examined these Madonnas in relation to the religious debates of the age.

These general points can be illustrated with the work of the feminist scholars Marina Warner, Margaret Homans, Helena Michie, and Tricia Lootens. Warner's *Alone of All Her Sex: The Myth and the Cult of the Virgin Mary* (1976) is a rich and detailed study that has had a profound effect on literary discussions, because it provides a more holistic approach to the subject than perhaps any previous treatment. Warner surveys the Catholic Church's representations of Mary as Virgin, Queen, Bride, Mother, and Intercessor. Yet although she does not restrict herself to authorized texts—she draws on the New Testament, ancient Near Eastern myths, the writings of the Church Fathers, saints, and popes, popular religious beliefs, and her own experiences as a Catholic girl—she minimizes the ability of ordinary people or oppressed groups (especially women) to manipulate Marian images to their own benefit. Warner's is a feminist analysis that does not allow the possibility of empowering appropriations of the Virgin Mary; she argues instead that Marian images reflect the power of patriarchy.[6]

The literary critics Margaret Homans, Helena Michie, and Tricia Lootens, in their analyses of Mary as a symbol, follow Warner and reach similarly pessimistic conclusions about female agency and entrenched male power. Homans's *Bearing the Word* (1986) is a Lacanian analysis of dominant myths of language in nineteenth-century women's writing. Homans shows that the Virgin Mary was sometimes used as a model for literary motherhood, but this figure proved problematic, particularly for women writers with actual children, since she traditionally has functioned as the intact transmitter but not the author of the Word, has limitations on her use of language, and represents the denigration of the female body (29–32, 153–222). Michie, in *The Flesh Made Word* (1987), explores the association of the Christian Madonna and her delicate Victorian daughters with fasting as well as chastity; both forms of self-denial "obliterat[e] signs of sexuality" (20–21). Lootens, in *Lost Saints* (1996), argues that British Victorians considered Mary the personification of all that was most alien and monstrous in Roman Catholicism, but "Mary as a literal religious figure was one thing . . . ; Mary as a glorious model was another." Lootens claims that Marian virtue (specifically, Mary's unearthly purity, which is invulnerable to corruption or change, and her sanctity without spiritual struggle) was revered once it was "semisecularized" and refocused onto sentimental heroines, such as the beneficent domestic "Angel."[7]

Significantly, what these three important critics have in common is their focus on a single prominent image of the Virgin Mary: Mary as gentle, submissive, pure, and good (Warner, 335). They, like Warner, naturally doubt that imitation of this figure allows ordinary women much movement within language or society. Yet the nineteenth century had far more Marys than this. The three studies also point to a general tendency in literary scholarship: the relationship of Madonna-figures to Victorian religious beliefs is left largely unexplored, despite the theological controversies that marked this intensely (or at least overtly) religious age.[8] Problematic historical assumptions can be the result. For example, *would* Marian womanhood be fiercely rejected as religious belief and then accepted in literary form? In particular, *would* Protestant Victorians impose on themselves a model of Marian womanhood with what were to them the most untenable elements of Catholic Mariology, found, notably, in the dogma of the Immaculate Conception (1854)? If *we* notice such contradictions, should we assume our predecessors did not? A closer look at the Victorian religious landscape in fact shows that fierce anti-Romanists were likely to be Evangelicals suspicious of novel reading (and therefore unlikely to have literary Madonnas as household icons). Moreover, there was increasing support for Catholic civil rights, and interest in Catholic spirituality, particularly among the educated classes. In addition, the creator of the Angel in the House, Coventry Patmore, was strongly drawn to Catholicism even before his conversion; thus the highly popular domestic Madonna, often called a secularized or semisecularized figure, seems, to the contrary, rooted in Catholic thought.[9]

As these points indicate, an acknowledgment of the range of Victorian religious and political views allows a more complex picture of responses to Marian imagery, while also revealing the variations in Madonna-figures produced and appropriated in religious, artistic, and political debates.[10] This book offers brief sketches of this political and cultural landscape (as in the next chapter), while giving detailed representations of a few notable female figures. These women's attitudes were, however, representative of the intellectual circles in which they moved and lead us to rethink some prevalent critical assumptions. We see, for example, that Victorian Protestants, especially among the educated classes, often showed tolerance of Catholicism; that the figure of the Virgin Mary could be associated with

8   religious or political liberalism in this period, that Victorian religious tra-
ditionalism, as opposed to religious radicalism, was not necessarily antithetical to the feminist cause; and that the Madonnas that characterize the
period are not found just in the art and literature produced at home. We
should also be aware that Jameson, Fuller, and Eliot were engaged in debate with their influential (and often more conservative) contemporaries—
Carlyle, Emerson, Ruskin, and others. They remind us that women helped
shape the public and private discourse of their age and could give even
theological arguments a feminist edge.

How exactly might attention to the religious and feminist views of
prominent Victorian women, and to their lived experience, alter our perceptions of Victorian Madonna-figures? One might start by reconsidering
the common literary and critical pairing of Madonna and Magdalene, and
the recurrent emphasis on the Madonna as the circumscribed, powerless
domestic angel. These two categories, while important, prove insufficient
for characterizing the Madonnas of the period and of the three writers. For
Jameson, Fuller, and Eliot saw the Madonna not primarily as the product
of Victorian domestic ideology, but rather as a figure defined and redefined by the theology, art, and history of the Church. That means she seldom appears with the Magdalene—neither in religious art (where the two
are grouped together almost exclusively in scenes of the Crucifixion), nor
in the three writers' texts, where Mary appears repeatedly or at crucial
points in solitary splendor, colossal, queenly, "complete in her own perfections." When Jameson, Fuller, and Eliot do consider the Virgin Mother
as part of a pair, she is usually with the Son, as is customary in Christian
theology.[11] The three writers were particularly interested in presenting
Jesus and Mary as the masculine and feminine representations of the divine, signifying the spiritual equality of men and women. They thus bring
Mary into the orbit of Godhead, rather than linking her to a penitent
fallen woman; this move is simultaneously orthodox and radical, a high
claim for women's status and power.

Jameson, Fuller, and Eliot also call into question the assumptions of
many Victorian and modern critics in their treatment of purity—which is
almost invariably considered the most important attribute of the Christian
or the domestic Madonna. ("Above all, be pure," the Angel in the House
says to Virginia Woolf, as she seeks to guide the author's pen.) They
changed the terms of the argument by making purity characteristic of, or

at least a moral expectation for, men as well as women.[12] The three writers associated purity with godliness and cleanliness of mind as well as body; for Fuller, the pure mind was an unsullied crystal that lets the light of God shine through. Purity in their enlarged conception became a synonym of goodness and virtue. Eliot and Fuller were of course "fallen women" by conventional Victorian standards, since they engaged in sexual relations before or without being married. But it is intriguing that the unions they criticized as impure were not like their own, marked by mental and physical fidelity and in Eliot's case by intellectual partnership,[13] but instead contemporary marriages in which the men treated their wives like prostitutes, corrupting their minds, or the women prostituted themselves, treating their bodily integrity as a commodity and buying with it an unloved husband's wealth and status.[14]

The domestic Madonna's purity has been commonly thought to limit her sphere of action. But the three writers' work, and their lives and those of their friends, demonstrate that purity in fact tended to give women independence and the power to act, especially in unconventional ways. In Jameson's reading of the Gospel of Luke, the Virgin Mary's journey alone to see her cousin Elizabeth is contrary to oriental customs, but Mary has just been chosen as the pure mother of God, and miracles greet her on her arrival (*Madonna*, xxxix; Luke 2; Helsinger et al., 2:200–2). The Queen of Heaven, in Jameson's presentation, is a figure whose purity makes possible her acts of beneficence and power—in particular, what many see as her irresistible intercession with God. (In an interesting parallel, the critic Dorothy Mermin focuses attention on Lady Godiva as a woman so above reproach that when she rode naked through the streets of Coventry, a reformer on horseback, it was Peeping Tom who was struck blind.)[15] Barrett Browning noted that for a modern woman, the young American sculptor Harriet Hosmer, celibacy made an unconventional lifestyle possible:

> [Hosmer] emancipates the eccentric life of a perfectly "emancipated female" from all shadow of blame by the purity of her's. She lives here [in Rome] all alone (at twenty-two) as Gibson's pupil . . .—dines & breakfasts at the caffes precisely as a young man would,—works from six oclock in the morning till night, as a great artist must. (Sherwood, 97)

Likewise, Florence Nightingale's reputation as "The Lady with the Lamp," who made the Scutari hospitals "holy as a church," helped give her the

10   power to reform the Army medical corps afterward. George Eliot's Romola adopted Nightingale's profession, designated by religious dress, in fifteenth-century Florence, and for the first time was able to move freely about the city and share her substance with the sick and needy.

Contrary to the representations of many Victorian authors and modern critics, then, it was the pure Madonna who enjoyed freedom of movement, and it was the sexually "impure" woman who lacked social standing and had her sphere of action restricted. Fuller and Eliot, for example, freely chose their relationships and did not condemn themselves, but when the American writer found herself pregnant and unmarried in 1848, she had to exile herself from Rome and was forced to interrupt her reports on the revolution for the *New-York Tribune* (and forego her pay). She reemerged among expatriate circles with a husband and a baby not new born, causing much gossip (Blanchard, 290–98, 317–20). Eliot when she began housekeeping near London with Lewes experienced the lapse of her previous social life. Barbara Leigh Smith (later Bodichon), despite organizing the midcentury petition drive for married women's property rights, was not one of the official leaders of the group (Mary Howitt and Jameson were) because of her illegitimate birth as well as her radical ideas. Lack of purity could be an impediment to public action into the second generation.[16] The life experiences of Jameson, Fuller, Eliot, and their circle thus reveal the harshness of Victorian social mores as well as the ways realities do not always match modern critical assumptions (such as the posited disjunction between purity and freedom). In addition, the three writers' radical reconception of purity is emblematic of the ways they redefine the figure of the Madonna.

This study of Victorian Madonnas is informed by a number of general methodological assumptions about religion. These assumptions are that individuals as well as institutions shape religious traditions; that religion, like feminism, can be an empowering and liberating force in the lives of women and men, as well as (unfortunately) an instrument of oppression;[17] and that Victorian religious beliefs are central to our understanding of Victorian literature and culture. In formulating arguments based on these assumptions, I have benefited particularly from the work of religious scholars, art historians, and historians. The analyses of early Marian images and doctrines by Margaret Miles, Emile Mâle, Caroline Bynum, Hilda Graef, and Jaroslav Pelikan have facilitated identification of the images and ideas found in (and sometimes radically refashioned by) Victorian writers, both

Protestant and Catholic. The historians John Bossy, Edward Norman, Mary Heimann, and Ann Taves have sympathetically recorded the struggles of the resurgent Catholic Church and its members in Protestant England and America, while David Blackbourn, Sandra Zimdars-Swartz, and Jeanette Rodriguez have investigated Marian apparitions in Europe and the Americas. All have drawn attention to the centrality of Mary to both Catholic doctrine and popular devotion in the nineteenth and twentieth centuries; Blackbourn notes that *all* Catholic spiritual experience in this period "was increasingly likely to be cast in a Marian idiom" (26–33). The theologians Rosemary Radford Ruether, Mary Daly, and Elizabeth Johnson, along with feminist scholars in other fields, have raised a question important to this study: has the Virgin Mary served only as a distorted and repressive female ideal because of her close links to the practices and politics of a patriarchal church and male-dominated societies, or is she a symbol that can empower women?[18] Many feminists have answered this question negatively (their views will be discussed at various points); my study is more optimistic because of the links I have found between Victorian women's uses of the Madonna-figure and the contemporaneous feminist movement.

Ruether, Blackbourn, Rodriguez, and Miles are representative of scholars who focus on popular religious beliefs and the ideas of individuals who are not necessarily authorized voices of religious institutions. All four examine the political resonances of Marian phenomena while acknowledging, usually through attention to marginalized groups, the possibility of a liberating and even revolutionary "politics of Mary." A space for theorizing about Victorian Protestant and feminist appropriations of the Madonna is thus opened up. Ruether, for example, argues that the popular and individual dimension of religion is primary and essential:

> Human experience is the starting point and the ending point of the hermeneutical circle. . . . Received symbols, formulas, and laws are either authenticated or not through their ability to illuminate and interpret experience. Systems of authority try to reverse this relation and make received symbols dictate what can be experienced as well as the interpretation of that which is experienced. In reality, the relation is the opposite. If a symbol does not speak authentically to experience, it becomes dead or must be altered to provide a new meaning. . . . [Individual believers], in their local communities of faith, are always engaged in making their own selection from the patterns of

received tradition that fit or make sense in their lives. There is always an interaction between the patterns of faith proposed by teachers to individuals and the individuals' own appropriation of these patterns as interpretations of experience. (*Sexism and God-Talk*, 12–13, 15)

Ruether's theories make normative the reevaluation and appropriation of religious tradition practiced by individuals such as Jameson, Fuller, and Eliot. They evidently did what any religiously observant Victorian lady would do, but had the temerity to do it in public. Ruether, moreover, claims that experience is the ground of religious belief, and that individuals and communities shape religious traditions. Blackbourn and Rodriguez support this point by showing the constant yet often overlooked presence in Catholicism of "people's Madonnas"—sometimes conceived of in resistance to church authorities. For example, Blackbourn in his study of Marian apparitions in nineteenth-century Europe (only some of them accepted by the church) notes that the Virgin Mother usually appeared at times of economic hardship and political upheaval and was seen by believers as a responsive powerful protector; she was also regarded as a mother-figure by the poor, usually motherless young visionaries (7–27). Rodriguez contends that the Virgin of Guadalupe is an important figure in the lives of Mexican and Mexican-American women precisely as she has not been assimilated into the church's hierarchy. The Virgin, like these women, is socially marginal —*mestiza* and female—yet active, sympathetic, and powerful (48, 143–58). One thus sees the plausibility of related Madonna-formations by intellectual women outside the Catholic Church who were drawn to its images of the female divine and alienated to varying degrees from their own religious backgrounds.[19]

Miles draws attention to two important uses of sacred and secular images with similar relevance for my discussion. She says that memorable images *"express* a valued aspect or quality of our experience or they *compensate*, offer alternatives to, our individual experience. . . . We need images that express . . . what we are about, and we need images that represent—that make present—aspects of human possibility we have known, perhaps only momentarily." Miles's important point, that images can express what is yearned for and not yet realized, might be related to Ruether's feminist reinterpretation of a central concept in Christianity, the image of God as representing the ideal of humanity and affirming women's full humanity.[20]

Both insights would be appreciated by the three writers of this study, who
all proposed Mary as a sex-specific image of the divine, a vision of what
female nature can authentically be.

Finally, there is the question of the "politics of Mary." Ruether argues
that the "prophetic tradition of the Bible," which claims God is on the side
of the oppressed (the poor and women) against unjust power systems, can
and should be used to criticize the Bible itself and any "ideological defor-
mation" of religion, such as the transformation of Jesus' radically egalitarian and anti-authoritarian message into the patriarchal hierarchy of papacy
and empire. Mary's place in this prophetic tradition is to be a new model
of willing and active discipleship for both men and women, as well as a
new symbol of the liberated church (*Sexism and God-Talk*, 22–33, 152–58).
The biblical tradition identified by Ruether is one of the languages that
empowered nineteenth-century feminists such as the radical Grimké sisters, Jameson, and Fuller. Ruether also helps one see the possibility of a
"politics of Mary" not identified with the interests of power groups; and
Blackbourn and Rodriguez indeed describe Mary-centered popular challenges, even in the "Age of Mary," to the authority of the state and the official theology of the church. The women writers of my study take matters
a step farther, allowing one an unexpected glimpse of nineteenth-century
Madonna-figures embraced by both popular Catholic nationalist movements and liberal Protestant feminists who gave such movements their
support.

This brief look at Marian scholarship and methodologies in the fields
of modern literature, art, religion, and history allows us to start identifying
a gallery of nineteenth-century Madonna-figures, some familiar, some new.
There is a prominent popular Madonna found in historians' work: the commanding yet comforting Mother of the modern apparitions, who requires a
return to ritual observances ("Pray the Rosary") and grants humble people's
prayers. There is the Protestant (and patriarchal) Madonna-figure of Victorian studies, the sweet-faced, silent little bourgeois housewife, content in
her role as "*his* lady," perhaps extending a merciful hand to her fallen sister.
There are important theological Madonnas: Our Lady of the Immaculate
Conception, proclaimed in 1854, and the "New Eve" of the Church Fathers,
rediscovered by John Henry Newman. And there are political Madonnas,
notably the *Mater Ecclesia* who protects nineteenth-century popes against

14   the forces of revolution and modernity. Jameson, Eliot, and Fuller, however, were drawn to different Madonna-figures. Instead of the apparitional Madonnas of popular piety, they sought the exquisite heavenly Queens of medieval art; instead of the domestic Madonna, the solitary intellectual Virgin and the redefined Virgin Mother; instead of the New Eve, the Christian Goddess who succeeded the Great Mothers of the ancient world; instead of the *Mater Ecclesia*, the Roman revolutionaries' *Mater Dolorosa*. Such rediscovered images became part of a new conception of the Madonna: the figure I have called Our Lady of Victorian Feminism.

Intellectual and Cultural Contexts

Jameson, Fuller, and Eliot may seem to constitute a peculiar trio for an investigation of the Virgin Mary and Victorian feminism. What do an art historian and a novelist, a Transcendentalist and an agnostic, an Anglo-Irishwoman and an American have in common? And what can explain their remarkable responses to the figure of the Madonna, so often seen in Britain and America in the limited roles accorded her by Protestantism and domestic fiction? This chapter will begin to answer these questions by focusing on the lives of the three writers, the connections among them, and the most important contexts for their work. The three writers were of their time in their awareness of nineteenth-century Catholicism, their interest in European religious art, and their advocacy of feminist ideas. They were singular, though, in their ability to synthesize their unusually extensive knowledge and see the feminist potential of Marian images, which many of their contemporaries still regarded with suspicion. The chapter will be historical in its approach, because particular events prove central to explaining the achievement of the three writers: the growth of both Catholicism and religious toleration in Britain and America; the emergence of a Catholicizing movement within the Anglican church; Britain's new enjoyment of artistic treasures unmatched in her former colony; and the rise of a women's movement that shared a number of ideas about woman's nature with its conservative adversaries.

Anna Brownell Murphy Jameson, probably the least familiar of the three writers of this study, was an Irish-born Englishwoman whose histories of medieval and Renaissance art were respected by her contemporaries and often reprinted in England and America. She also produced popular lives of queens and poets' consorts, Shakespeare criticism, and accounts of her travels in France, Italy, Germany, and North America. Jameson was an honored adviser to the Langham Place feminists, a London-based group led by Barbara Bodichon, Bessie Parkes, and Emily Faithfull. She was active in some of their campaigns, and her art-historical scholarship was cited as testimony to the high abilities of women. The Langham Place advocacy of female self-sufficiency had personal relevance for Jameson. For much of her adult life, she supported her parents, two sisters, and a niece while she lived apart from her husband, Robert Jameson, an emotionally cold alcoholic who failed to provide the financial settlement he promised or leave her any legacy. Jameson's marriage was the more painful because she was a very sociable woman, a noted conversationalist with a gift for friendship. Lady Byron, Goethe's daughter-in-law Ottilie, the great stage actresses Fanny Kemble and Adelaide Kemble Sartoris, and the writers Robert and Elizabeth Barrett Browning, Harriet Martineau, Maria Edgeworth, and Joanna Baillie were all among her friends and correspondents.

Margaret Fuller, the eldest child of a Boston lawyer and congressman, was given an education similar to John Stuart Mill's by her father, who evidently wanted not just an infant prodigy but an intellectual companion. He changed his mind when she grew older and sent her to a school for young ladies, which made her aware of the conflicts between "masculine" intellectualism and femininity. Fuller became a friend of Emerson and the other New England Transcendentalists and for two years edited the group's journal, the *Dial* (1840–44). A two-part article she wrote for the *Dial*, "The Great Lawsuit," was expanded into a book, *Woman in the Nineteenth Century* (1845), and earned her a position with Horace Greeley's *New-York Tribune*. Fuller had taught herself several European languages and read and reviewed Continental literature, but the death of her father in 1835 had forced her to cancel a trip to Europe. She at last had her chance to go overseas as Greeley's correspondent, and after traveling through Britain and France she arrived in Italy in time for the 1848 uprising against papal and foreign rule. She fell in love with one of the Roman revolutionaries, the aristocrat Giovanni Angelo Ossoli, whom she married after the birth of their son. Seeing no prospects in Italy, the family took ship for the United States and drowned at the end of the voyage, in sight of Fire Island.

George Eliot was born Marian Evans, the youngest child of an estate steward in Nuneaton, near Coventry, England. She received a good education at area schools and went on to teach herself ancient and modern languages (Latin, Greek, Hebrew, French, German, Italian, Spanish). Her essays in the *Westminster Review* and other London periodicals give an idea of her intellectual range: English, American, and Continental literature, Greek drama, religion and theology, philosophy, classical and modern art, the natural and social sciences. As an adolescent, Eliot was an Evangelical (a Calvinist Anglican), but in her early twenties she abandoned religious orthodoxy. Her first books were translations of two works of German higher criticism: *The Life of Jesus*, by D. F. Strauss, and *The Essence of Christianity*, by Ludwig Feuerbach. The start of her relationship with George Henry Lewes (a biographer of Goethe and writer on philosophy and science) gave her, so she said, the happiness and confidence necessary to turn from journalism to fiction writing, though the irregularity of their union caused family members and friends to shun her. Her works discussed in this study of the Madonna are the novels *Adam Bede* (1859), *Romola* (1863), *Middlemarch* (1871–72), and *Daniel Deronda* (1876) and the dramatic poem *The Spanish Gypsy* (1868).

Jameson, the eldest of the three women, was the first established as a writer. Her first book, *Diary of an Ennuyée* (1826), sold well, and *Characteristics of Women* (or *Shakespeare's Heroines*, 1832) was her entree into intellectual circles in Britain, Germany, and North America, where she traveled to join her husband, a Canadian official, in a last attempt to save their unhappy marriage. She spent some time in Massachusetts, where she met members of Margaret Fuller's circle, notably the Unitarian minister William Ellery Channing. Fuller was then teaching in Providence and attempting a biography of Goethe, but she was handicapped by both a lack of documents (she eventually had to give up this book-length project) and her male friends' reticence on the known details of Goethe's love affairs. She knew that Jameson had described her close relationship with the surviving members of his family, notably his daughter-in-law Ottilie, in an account of her travels in Germany, and the author was then visiting Boston and New York. Fuller wrote her a letter that expressed her feelings of being entrapped in New England and cut off from European intellectual life, but it probably struck the recipient as both impertinent and desperate:

[Dr. Channing said] that you seemed to feel a natural delicacy about any new disclosures [about Goethe]. But oh! if I could but see you I am persuaded that you would tell me all I wish to know—Is it quite impossible for me to see you? How I wish I was famous or could paint beautiful pictures and then you would not be willing to go without seeing me. But now—I know not how to interest you,—the miserable frigid letter within will not interest you—Yet I am worthy to know you, and be known by you, and if you could see me you would soon believe it, and now I need you so very much. (*Fuller Letters*, 22 Dec. 1837, 1:318; see also 2:60)

There was no reply (Erskine, 158–59).

Fuller's first published work was a translation of Eckermann's *Conversations with Goethe*, which she noted Jameson had begun to translate (during her miserable winter in Toronto) but had given up as too German for a general British audience. Jameson did produce a travel book about her North American stay, which Fuller obtained before her own journey through the Great Lakes and farther west. She cited Jameson, usually not very admiringly (the lack of response to her letter may have rankled), in *Summer on the Lakes*. But one of the most arresting images in her feminist masterpiece *Woman in the Nineteenth Century*, the Indian girl betrothed to the sun, was taken from Jameson's travel book, and she praised the older writer as advancing the cause of women, particularly through her courageous discussion of prostitution.[1]

Jameson's acknowledgments of Fuller are much less extensive. After her trip to New England, she told a friend about an essay in the *Dial*, which she sensed could not be by Emerson. Her criticisms of the style ("such good & often profound thoughts . . . so ill put together and so obscurely expressed . . . every now & then the meaning drops out of sight, like a dim star") resemble the frequent complaints of contemporaries about Fuller's writing.[2] In an 1845 letter Jameson said she planned to purchase a copy of *Woman in the Nineteenth Century*, which was just out; the numerous references to herself should have made it irresistible, but she instead expressed her fears (that letter again?) that the cause of women might be handled "coarsely and in bad taste" (Macpherson, 214). In her published writings Jameson cited Fuller only once, in her *Commonplace Book*, published in 1854.[3] The two women finally met in Rome, where Jameson consented to introduce Fuller to Ottilie von Goethe, too late to benefit Fuller's work. In a letter to Frau von Goethe, written after Fuller's death, Jameson reminded her of the meeting and mentioned Fuller's *Memoirs*, which she described ungraciously as "a very curious and remarkable book, only *too much* of it" (Macpherson, 186).

George Eliot, like Margaret Fuller, longed to meet Anna Jameson, who with Harriet Martineau and Mary Howitt was one of the few notable women writers in the 1830s and early 1840s and an inspiration to younger women. The two were introduced through mutual friends and dined together, evidently several times, in the early 1850s. Eliot was then the associate editor of the *Westminster Review*, and Jameson may well have read Eliot's (unsigned) articles in that periodical knowing who wrote them, the information coming from the author herself or Jameson's own well-connected friends (*Eliot Letters*, 8:96; Haight, 106). Any possibility of friendship between the women must have ended, however, when Jameson's friend Robert Noel met Miss Evans and George Henry Lewes (a married man) on their way to Germany; indeed, it was Jameson who helped spread the news of this adulterous relationship: "The story of Lewes and his Wife is true, I fear. The lady who is with him I have seen before her (known) liaison with him. She is first-rate in point of intellect and science and attainments of every kind, but considered also as very *free* in all her opinions as to morals and religion" (Jameson, *Letters*, 209). Jameson's attitude, beyond the clear relish of good gossip, is hard to pin down, since she was not a consistent prude; she supported her friend Ottilie through a pregnancy by a lover and allowed the short-lived child to be named Anna. Eliot used Jameson's series on religious art to research her novels, but there is no record of another meeting. She would have been aware of some of Jameson's activities, though, through their mutual friends Bessie Parkes and Barbara Bodichon. Jameson purchased Lewes's biography of Goethe ("earnest admiration of Goethe, . . . great vigour, but also some vulgarity of style"), and before her death in 1860 she read the first of Eliot's novels, the "admirable" *Adam Bede*, but she did not know who the author was (Jameson, *Letters*, 209, 225). Bodichon guessed, but she promised to keep the secret.

As for Fuller and Eliot, Fuller could not have been familiar with her English counterpart's writings, because she died in 1850, before Eliot had published in a journal bigger than the *Coventry Herald*.[4] But Eliot met Emerson during the American's visit to Coventry in 1848, and she earlier read Emerson's essays and Fuller's *Woman in the Nineteenth Century*, according to her young friend Mary Sibree (*Eliot Letters*, 1:270; Cross, 1:82, 87). The

20   influence of Emerson and Fuller seems responsible for some uncharacteris-
tic statements that Eliot makes during what Bernard Paris calls her "pan-
theistic period," shortly after her repudiation of Christianity.[5] Eliot
positively reviewed Fuller's *Woman in the Nineteenth Century* in the *Westminster
Review* (along with Wollstonecraft's neglected *Vindication*), and Gordon
Haight attributes to her other short notices of Fuller's work.

    The links among the three women, and their mutual friends, raise the
question of whether any of them influenced the others' work on the
Madonna. Jameson's and Fuller's clear impact on Eliot's treatment of the
Virgin Mary will be the subject of later chapters. The connections between
Jameson's and Fuller's texts are more complicated. While Fuller frequently
cites the older woman, who was usually the prior writer on a topic (e.g.,
Goethe and Eckermann, North American Indian women, prostitution),
Fuller's most important analysis of the Madonna, in *Woman in the Nineteenth
Century*, predates Jameson's *Legends of the Madonna*. Jameson, however, rarely
credits any modern source (even the art historian Rio) in her series *Sacred
and Legendary Art*, and that pattern of omission makes any direct influence
hard to ascertain. There are parallels, though, in their treatment of the Virgin Mother, notably their emphasis on her as the solitary powerful goddess
of Christianity.

    The lives and links of the three writers explain, in part, why they have
been chosen for examination here. But this study also focuses more
broadly on the common backgrounds of the three writers, the nineteenth-
century intellectual and cultural contexts of their work: their exposure to
Catholicism in England and America and on the Continent, their knowledge of the art collected and produced in this era, and their place in
nineteenth-century feminism. To be sure, the participation of Jameson,
Fuller, and Eliot in a rising network of female intellectuals lends particular
cultural credence to their views, including those on the Madonna. Yet they
were almost alone in giving the Madonna a prominent place in their
Protestant and feminist arguments. The historical contexts will provide
some explanations of their work, but readers must be aware, too, of a matter of temperament. The three women were all notable for their restless-
ness, inquisitiveness, and flexibility: they never stopped traveling; they
never stopped looking, conversing, and reading; and they did not merely
tolerate but absorbed the best of "foreign" wisdom and culture.

    Scholars have often seen the Victorian era as anticipating our era: it
was the Age of Empire, or Industrialization, or Darwin, Douglass, and

Susan B. Anthony. But we need also to stress the ways an era differs from ours, so that our pictures of the past are not subtly distorted—and that involves, as David Blackbourn and Jenny Franchot point out, giving due attention to the religious phenomena that characterize even the modern period (Blackbourn, xxxiii; Franchot, 834–37). With these aims in mind, I will consider the nineteenth century not as the Age of Marx, but as the Age of Mary.

The "Age of Mary" is a name frequently given to Continental Europe during this era—more precisely, the years 1854 (dogma of the Immaculate Conception) to 1950 (declaration of the Assumption of the Virgin)—because of the great revival in Marian devotion. There had been Marian apparitions at the Rue du Bac in Paris in 1830 (which led in 1832 to the striking of the Miraculous Medal honoring Mary immaculate), at La Salette in 1846, and at Lourdes in 1858. Later sightings of Mary occurred at Pontmain (1871), at Marpingen in Germany (1876–77), at Knock in Ireland (1879), and at Fatima in Spain (1917). The Immaculate Conception (the belief that the Virgin Mary was conceived free from original sin), which had long been taught and popularly accepted (as in the apparitions), was proclaimed as dogma by Pope Pius IX in 1854. The Immaculate Conception prepared the way for the declaration of a second dogma, Papal Infallibility, at the Vatican Council of 1870. Marian devotion increased, and many Catholics went on pilgrimages to Marian shrines, in particular Lourdes (Zola's novel *Lourdes* is a critical account of the touristy commercialization of the site by the 1890s). Religious orders dedicated to the Virgin and lay confraternities honoring her were founded.[6]

In England, Mary and Marian devotion were becoming publicly visible during the nineteenth century. For example, after the Irish Catholic leader Daniel O'Connell became an M.P. in 1829, he often said the Rosary in the vicinity of the Parliament buildings before important votes—a sight quite unlikely since 1688 and guaranteed to perturb the unsuccessful opponents of Catholic emancipation (O'Dwyer, 259–62). In Coventry (the home of Marian Evans) in the 1840s, Sister Margaret Hallahan instituted Rosary evenings and combated the rowdy annual celebration of Lady Godiva's ride by having an image of the Virgin Mary taken in procession around the church (Norman, *English Catholic Church*, 163–64). John Henry Newman says of the religious opinions he held as an Anglican priest, before his conversion in 1845: "I had a secret longing love of Rome the Mother of English Christianity, and I had a true devotion to the Blessed Virgin, in whose College I lived, whose Altar I served, and whose Immaculate Purity I had in one of my earliest printed Sermons made much of"

22   (*Apologia pro Vita Sua* [1864, 1886], 133). Frederick W. Faber, who followed
Newman into the Catholic Church and priesthood, was known for his
emotional preaching and extravagant Mariology; his *All for Jesus* (1853),
which sometimes honors the Mother over the Son, had sold 100,000
copies by 1869 (Norman, *English Catholic Church*, 231–34). Dante Gabriel
Rossetti's *Ecce Ancilla Domini*, shown to hostile viewers at the Portland
Gallery in 1850, and Annibale Carracci's *The Three Maries*, one of the most
popular works in the Manchester exhibition of 1857, were among the
paintings introducing Marian iconography to new audiences in Britain
(Rose, 40; Haskell, 98–99).

   The Catholic Emancipation Act of 1829 helped make possible the expansion of the Roman Catholic Church in England and Ireland, after more
than two centuries of penal laws.[7] The repeal of the Test and Corporation
Acts in 1828 and the Catholic Emancipation Act in 1829 gave civil rights
to Catholics in the united kingdom of Great Britain and Ireland; the vic-
tory showed the political power of Daniel O'Connell and his Catholic Association.[8] The Catholic ecclesiastical hierarchy was restored in England
in 1850, and Nicholas Wiseman became a cardinal and the first archbishop
of Westminster. He and his successors, Cardinals Manning and Vaughan
(all trained for the priesthood in Rome), ushered in a long period of Ultramontanist dominance and conflict with the English "Old Catholics,"
whose quiet piety and necessary past exercise of lay authority had made
them in important respects resemble their Protestant neighbors.[9] It was the
Ultramontanist bishops and priests who promoted the kind of Marian devotions widespread on the Continent. Edward Norman says of Cardinal
Wiseman, for example, that

> it was [his] highest task to revivify English devotional life, and
> that he did. The revival was centred in his own personal devo-
> tion to the Virgin and to the Counter-Reformation saints. The
> Forty Hours' Devotion was introduced, and the Rosary—"the
> devotion so little understood, nay, often so much slighted, even
> by good people in our country"—was encouraged by the foun-
> dation of rosary confraternities. Wiseman himself wrote two
> books of popular devotions for the laity, in furtherance of his
> conviction that existing Catholic prayers needed to be replaced
> because they were tainted with Protestantism.

This Ultramontanist view of "English Catholic" deficiency in devotion, accepted by Norman and other historians, has been called into question by

John Bossy and Mary Heimann, who point out that "English Catholics" 23
had their own well-established devotional tradition, defined by Richard
Challoner's *Garden of the Soul*, first published in 1740.[10] The common ground
among these historians seems to be that there was a heightened religious
commitment (or "Second Spring" or "new piety") in the English Catholic
Church from 1840 or 1850, and Marian devotion was both encouraged by
the leadership and practiced, even enthusiastically, in a rapidly growing
church. Mary, therefore, was becoming more visible both inside and outside English Catholicism.

Although anti-Catholicism, like anti-Semitism, can exist even without the
presence of members of the disliked group, the recurrent public outcries of
"No Popery!" in the nineteenth century were spurred by the clear signs of
Catholic expansion: Catholic Emancipation, Irish immigration to England,
the growth of religious orders and the introduction of new ones, the
restoration of the Catholic hierarchy (called "Papal Aggression"), and the
1870 Vatican Council, attended by the English hierarchy, at which papal
infallibility was declared.[11] Groups antipathetic to Catholicism included
many members of the English working classes, who were in economic
competition with the Irish immigrants willing to work for low wages; To-
ries, who opposed Catholic emancipation as a threat to the British consti-
tution and the Established Church; and Liberals like William Gladstone,
who wrote a pamphlet against the Vatican Council decrees in which he
voiced his suspicions about Rome and Catholic loyalty to the British
crown. A number of middle-class and working-class Protestants, particularly Evangelicals inside and outside the Church of England, were members of anti-Catholic organizations, including Orange Lodges.[12] The
father of Emily Davies (the future women's-rights activist and founder of
Girton College) was an Anglican clergyman who wrote little besides pam-
phlets against popery and Puseyism; he favored an Evangelical newspaper
with the same views (Caine, 61, 66 n. 29). Marian Evans herself, during her
adolescent Evangelical period, referred to the Catholic Church as "carrying on her brow the prophetical epithets applied by St. John to the Scar-
let beast, the Mystery of iniquity" (*Eliot Letters*, 1:26, 20 May [1839]).
Indeed, given the times, Anna Jameson was fortunate in the reviewer of
several of her books in *Blackwood's Magazine*, John Eagles, who rarely missed
an opportunity to denigrate "the Romish Church" but distinguished it from
the early and medieval church, which he regarded as unafflicted with "priestcraft and Popery." He thus could recommend ("Protestant reader, be not
alarmed") Jameson's series of books on medieval and early Renaissance art.[13]

24   Not every social group in Britain was antipathetic to Catholicism, however. The historians Owen Chadwick and Linda Colley point out that for the first two decades of the nineteenth century, a sizeable group in the House of Commons (Chadwick claims a constant small majority) steadily supported Catholic relief measures, despite the opposition of Tory governments. Chadwick adds that some bishops voted for Catholic Emancipation, and the liberal Churchman Thomas Arnold wrote in favor of it, on the grounds of "Christian duty" and justice.[14] Colley, Edward Norman, and K. S. Inglis make even larger claims; in Colley's words, "Toleration of Roman Catholicism and acquiescence in the civic claims of British Catholics had been increasing for some time across the social spectrum."[15] Focusing on the early nineteenth century, Colley explains this phenomenon by pointing to the end of military threats from Catholic powers after Waterloo and the growth in British strength (332). Norman emphasizes the links between Catholic Emancipation and subsequent reform bills; such liberal measures showed the growing acceptance of free institutions and the extension of legal rights and protections to more and more groups in the population (*English Catholic Church*, 22). All three historians stress the tolerant attitudes toward Catholicism prevalent among the educated and governing classes and reformers. Manufacturers and merchants, too, became more accepting of "Popery" as their trade with Catholic countries increased.

Anti-Catholicism was certainly not characteristic of the liberal and intellectual circles in which Jameson and Eliot moved in London. As one would expect, there were many Dissenters, particularly Unitarians and Quakers, among the progressives they knew, and Dissenters had common ground with English and Irish Catholics in their opposition to the established Anglican church (though of course the Catholic Church was the established church in much of Europe and taught the union of church and state). The Quaker and Radical politician William Howitt, for example, wrote a book criticizing "priestcraft" in all its forms but supported Catholic religious freedom, especially in Ireland.[16] Furthermore, a surprising number of women in Jameson's and Eliot's circles eventually converted to Catholicism, among them the popular poet Adelaide Procter, the women's-rights activist Bessie Parkes, and the author Mary Howitt (wife of William) and her daughter Meggie. (The elder daughter, Anna Mary Howitt, was affectionately described by friends as "one of the cracked people of the world" and "as good as a Catholic" [Herstein, 21, 98, 102].) Many of these women found themselves drawn to Catholicism because of the dryness of

Dissent and the deadness of the Established Church. Their first prolonged exposure to Catholicism tended to occur during travels on the Continent. Mary Howitt, for example, searched throughout her life for a true spirituality that emphasized love for others and was not form-bound. She disliked the insularity and orthodoxy of the Quakers, and while teaching her children certain Quaker beliefs, such as pacifism and religious and political liberty, she raised them as Christians, not as Friends (Howitt, 1:151–52, 259–63, 290–91). In Germany in the early 1840s, Mrs. Howitt, like other Romantics, was moved by the simple Catholic piety of the people: "There were little images of the Virgin in niches on the front of the cottages, which, although wretched plaster figures gaudily coloured, indicated much devotion." She found in the primitive valley chapel and Cologne Cathedral "the same spirit of sanctity and prayer" (1:314–15). (The wayside shrines and crucifixes she describes also appear in Jameson's travel writing [1838] and Eliot's *Adam Bede* [1859].)[17] Back in England, Mrs. Howitt and her husband left their Quaker meeting and tried Unitarianism and then spiritualism (Howitt, 2:4–13, 68, 142). Not long after her husband's death in 1879, she became a Catholic. Her Catholicism was not the sophisticated creed of Newman, but the "pure, simple Christian practice" she saw around her in her retirement home in the Tyrol and had first associated with the peasants of Germany (2:305).[18]

One of the more unexpected Victorian "converts" to Catholic devotion, though not Catholic belief, was John Ruskin. He was "the great Protestant of Modern Art," according to George Eliot, and in this capacity he made some anti-Roman remarks.[19] But in his autobiography, Ruskin says that when he acquired a fourteenth-century *Hours of the Virgin* in 1850 or 1851, "then followed, of course, the discovery that all beautiful prayers were Catholic,—all wise interpretations of the Bible Catholic;—and every manner of Protestant written services whatsoever either insolently altered corruptions, or washed-out and ground-down ages and debris of the great Catholic collects, litanies, and songs of praise" (*Praeterita* [1885–89], 398–99). Ruskin also tells a story about hearing a dull and merciless Protestant preacher in Turin and then "walk[ing] back into the condemned city, and up into the gallery, where Paul Veronese's Solomon and The Queen of Sheba glowed in full afternoon light." The scene taught him to trust the aesthetic pleasure found in the great paintings of the Church over Protestant doctrine: "things done delightfully and rightly, were always done by the help and in the Spirit of God" (*Praeterita*, 401–2).

26   Jameson's and Eliot's keen interest in Catholicism past and present can be readily demonstrated. Both followed the coverage of Catholic politics in the British newspapers and periodicals (Eliot was, after all, associate editor of the *Westminster Review* and a contributor to the *Leader*). Jameson was particularly concerned with the news from Ireland, her birthplace, which she visited during the famine years. She wrote an almost hysterical letter to Robert Peel, then Prime Minister, asking him to do something about the widespread starvation and death she had witnessed, and she supported the campaigns of the Irish politician Daniel O'Connell for Irish Catholic rights.[20] Eliot in Coventry may have lived at "ground zero" of the Catholic revival. John Bossy notes that Father Ullathorne's Catholic mission in Coventry, begun in 1841, was extraordinarily successful: in the 1851 survey of English church attendance, thirteen percent of all churchgoers in the town were at morning mass, and an estimated one hundred people converted each year (318–19). The Methodist-style mass revivals of Luigi Gentili, which drew many, including Protestants, into the Catholic Church, were held near Coventry in 1845 (Norman, *English Catholic Church*, 163, 226–30). One wonders if only memories of a Methodist aunt were behind Eliot's portrayal of Dinah Morris. Charles Newdegate, the local squire and M.P., was alarmed by such events in his district and led the anti-Catholic campaign in Parliament for many years. He lived at Arbury Hall near Nuneaton from 1835 to his death in 1887, and employed Eliot's father Robert Evans and later her brother Isaac as estate steward.[21]

Neither Eliot, who abandoned religious orthodoxy in 1842, nor Jameson, an Anglican, ever considered following the example of their London friends and becoming a Catholic. Jameson did exhibit occasional sectarian loyalty in her writings, and in one of her chancy books with a Protestant audience, *Legends of the Monastic Orders*, she took care to identify herself as non-Catholic and distance herself from extreme ascetic practices (xiv, xix–xxi). But these statements must be set against her support of Irish Catholic rights and her sympathetic interest in Catholic forms of belief (not to mention her night of drinking whiskey punch with Irish Dominican monks! [Erskine, 252]). Both Jameson and Eliot described how they were moved by masses they attended (Jameson, *Commonplace Book*, 154–57; *Eliot Letters*, 2:451–52), and Eliot wrote very sympathetically to Bessie Parkes at the news of her conversion.[22] It is equally important to note, in establishing the writers' relationship to Catholicism, that both made the history and art of the Church central to their careers. Eliot conducted ex-

tensive research in these areas for *Romola* and *The Spanish Gypsy*, both set in   27
the fifteenth century, and she incorporated saints' lives in many of her fic-
tions (using Jameson as one of her sources). Jameson's life work might be
described as introducing the valuable aspects of Catholicism to Protestants: Catholic art and art criticism; Catholic legends and beliefs; and religious sisterhoods, which she proposed as models for British women's
charitable work in two lectures delivered shortly after Nightingale's return
from the Crimea, where she was assisted by Catholic Sisters of Charity.

Of some relevance to this discussion are Eliot's reactions to Positivism
(the scientific, social, and religious theories of Auguste Comte), which
have been extensively studied by critics, some of whom have analyzed her
treatment of the Madonna in relation to Comte's Ideal Woman.[23] Yet this
comparison raises two questions about Eliot and Comte: first, whether
Catholicism may not have had an equal or greater impact on Eliot's religious and visual imagination; and second, whether Positivism, particularly
in its English form, really placed an emphasis on feminine images and examples. Comte's Religion of Humanity was derived from Catholicism, with
Comte as high priest, and his mother, his beloved Clothilde de Vaux, and
a younger friend serving as models of the Ideal Woman (Mother, Wife, and
Daughter), who is the object of worship (Standley, 24–27). But Eliot and
Lewes did not accept Positivism as a religion—Comte's *Catéchisme positive*,
published in 1852, cost him many English followers—and she was not active in the Positivist Society, founded in 1867, although she gave small do-
nations (Haight, 299–302; *Eliot Letters*, 1:lxii; 7:260 n.). The London centers
for positivist activities, Chapel Street and Newton Hall, were not established until 1870 and 1881, respectively (Eliot died in 1880), and the
prominent female image in Newton Hall, the *Sistine Madonna*, would have
been long familiar to her from Catholic art.[24] Critics have noted the presence of eminent and "holy" women in the *Positivist Calendar*, which was published in England by Eliot's friend Frederic Harrison. But the novelist's own
transcription of the calendar makes clear how badly the women were out-
numbered by the men; fewer than twenty days a year were to be devoted
to them.[25]

Frederic Harrison resisted all suggestions that the Positivist Society
was a "church" or a "religion" in any conventional sense.[26] But he did at one
point suggest the Positivist Society introduce a form of Congregational
worship (Harrison, 2:258), and Newton Hall certainly had its rituals, such
as the pilgrimages to the homes or tombs of great men, many of them

28   outspoken Protestants ("Chaucer, Shakespeare, Milton, Cromwell, Newton, Bacon, Harvey, Penn, Darwin").[27] These rituals, as well as the *Positivist
Calendar,* suggest that despite its origins in Catholic France and its memories of the Madonna, Positivism in England had a Protestantized as well as
a masculinized form.

The Church of England had its own Catholicizing movement, the Oxford
Movement (1833–45), led by John Keble, John Henry Newman, and E. B.
Pusey. The Oxford Movement, or Tractarianism, combined an impulse toward personal holiness and perfection with a program to revitalize the
Church of England by having it return to the beliefs and practices of the
patristic and medieval Church, long thought "Roman property." Newman's
call for the revival of Marian veneration is part of this agenda:

> I considered that . . . the Anglican Church must have a ceremo-
> nial, a ritual, and a fulness of doctrine and devotion, which it
> had not at present, if it were to compete with the Roman
> Church with any prospect of success. Such Additions would not
> remove it from its proper basis, but would merely strengthen
> and beautify it: such, for instance, would be confraternities, par-
> ticular devotions, reverence for the blessed Virgin, prayers for
> the dead, beautiful churches, munificent offerings to them and in
> them, monastic houses, and many other observances and institu-
> tions, which I used to say belonged to us as much as to Rome,
> though Rome had appropriated them and boasted of them, by
> reason of our having let them slip from us. . . . She [Rome]
> alone, with all the errors and evils of her practical system, has
> given free scope to the feelings of awe, mystery, tenderness, rev-
> erence, devotedness, and other feelings which may be especially
> called Catholic. (*Apologia pro Vita Sua,* 134–35)

In 1827 Keble published *The Christian Year,* a cycle of poems based on the
Anglican liturgical calendar, which has several poems honoring the Virgin:
"The Annunciation of the Blessed Virgin Mary," "The Purification of St.
Mary the Virgin," and "The Churching of Women" (309–12, 316–19,
389–90). The collection was so well received that Keble (though he
thought himself unworthy) became Professor of Poetry at Oxford from
1831 to 1841.[28] In the 1830s and 1840s Newman preached sermons at Ox-

ford honoring Mary as "the pattern of faith" and a model of sanctification   29
in the private life.[29] (After his conversion, he wrote *Certain Difficulties Felt by Anglicans in Catholic Teaching*, an important defence of Catholic Mariology, in reply to Pusey's *Eirenicon*.)[30]

Newman's desire for "beautiful churches" and "munificent offerings to them" points to another way that the Oxford Movement had a significant impact on the Anglican Church. The revival of Gothic architecture—associated on the Continent with Catholic Romantics such as Chateaubriand—became a hallmark of Tractarianism, whose priests needed appropriate ecclesiastical settings in which to practice the old rituals.[31] The modern use of Gothic for English churches actually began with the Church Building Act of 1818. But the combined influence of the Oxford Movement and the Camden Society, formed at Cambridge University in 1839 to study church architecture, decoration, and ritual, helped ensure that almost every Anglican church built for the next fifty years was in the Gothic style, and many existing churches fell victim to Gothicizing improvements.[32]

There was, however, resistance to such aesthetic and theological initiatives, which were criticized as "Romanism,"[33] even though the Tractarians saw themselves as defenders of the national church (the movement began with Keble's assize sermon on this topic). The group's opponents included the Prime Minister, Lord John Russell, who had a letter published in the *Times* in response to the 1850 restoration of the Catholic hierarchy: "There is a danger . . . which alarms me much more than any aggression of a foreign sovereign. . . . Clergymen of our own Church, who have subscribed the Thirty-Nine Articles and acknowledged in explicit terms the Queen's supremacy, have been most forward in leading their flocks 'step by step to the very verge of the precipice'" (Norman, *Anti-Catholicism*, 160). Newman would be the fearful example of a cleric who had gone over the edge and fallen down to Rome.

George Eliot and Anna Jameson both paid close attention to the Oxford Movement. Eliot as a young Evangelical Anglican criticized the *Tracts for the Times* when they appeared in the 1830s (*Eliot Letters*, 1:25–26, 46), but later she gave Maggie Tulliver *The Christian Year* to read, and (having long since lost her antagonism toward any sincere religious belief), she could not put down Newman's *Apologia* in 1864: "[It] affects me as the revelation of a life—how different in form from one's own, yet with how close a fellowship in its needs and burthens—I mean spiritual needs and

30   burthens." She took Newman's side against Kingsley (3:230–31; 4:158–59). Anna Jameson was well aware that the market for her art histories on Mary and the saints included the "Puseyites," whom the savvy novelist Maria Edgeworth sized up for her as "a vast class of purchasers"—"You ought to have 1,000 [pounds] from them nett" (letter to Jameson, 14 Nov. 1848, in Erskine, 255). But Jameson, as an Anglican but not a Tractarian, differed significantly from Newman; their Mariologies will be compared later.

The history of the Roman Catholic Church in the United States parallels in many ways the history of the church in England (as one might expect, given the origins of many early settlers). The three American colonies with large numbers of Catholics were Maryland, Pennsylvania, and New York. These colonies originally guaranteed freedom of religion, but from the time of the "Glorious Revolution" in England until American independence, Maryland and New York imposed on Catholics the American version of "Penal Laws," though they were not always enforced.[34] Independence from Britain brought legal relief to American Catholics, though not a suspension of suspicions against them, which were rooted in what the historian Sydney Ahlstrom calls "nativism and an old tradition of anti-popery" (547). After the Louisiana Purchase of 1803 greatly increased the Catholic population of the United States and its territories, there were periodic outbreaks of anti-Catholicism. In the 1820s and 1830s, evangelical preachers such as Horace Bushnell and Lyman Beecher preached against "popery"; they were influenced in part by the campaign against Catholic Emancipation in England. Anti-Catholic attacks were particularly directed against Irish immigrants beginning in the 1830s. The Ursuline convent in Boston was burned by a mob in 1834, and there were three days of anti-Catholic rioting in Philadelphia in 1844. The nativist and anti-Catholic Know-Nothing Party was a great power in American politics for a brief period, from 1852 to 1856 (in 1854, for example, the party had seventy-five members elected to Congress and controlled the Massachusetts legislature). Interestingly, however, these anti-Catholic attitudes did not generally characterize the American expatriates living in Italy. Margaret Fuller, for instance, who supported the Roman revolutionaries in 1848, was disgusted that so many of her fellow citizens supported democracy at home but authoritarian rule abroad, siding with the pope.

Catholic devotional practices in the English-speaking parts of the United States were similar to those in England, due in large part to the

popularity of English devotional books and the presence of missionary orders also found in England, such as the Jesuits and the Redemptorists.[35]
Historian Ann Taves shows that many of the popular devotions in America, especially from the mid-nineteenth century, were centered around
Mary: the Rosary, the Immaculate Conception (which was made the pa-
tronal feast of the United States in 1846), the Miraculous Medal, the Sacred Heart of Mary (promoted by the Jesuits), and most scapulars.[36] Mary
was dearly loved as the ever-present Mother in the "household of faith," a
popular nineteenth-century image suggesting the believer's familial relationship with Mary, Jesus, and the saints (Taves, 47–51). But from the early
years of the Republic the Virgin Mother was also assimilated to the ever
pious and obedient True Woman, and in this guise she was a limiting role
model for Catholic women (Kenneally, 13–59). Colleen McDannell (using
examples from the late nineteenth and early twentieth centuries) explains
Mary's domestication as a deliberate attempt to strip her of her traditional
supernatural and regal powers: "No longer the queen of the universe, Mary
became a Hebrew housewife who looked after the needs of husband and
child. 'The Blessed Virgin,' explained an 1887 article in the *Catholic Home*,
'was beyond all measure superior in dignity to St. Joseph, but it is not she
who guides and rules in this model family'" (McDannell, 60–61). Catholic
nuns in America provided a contrary example of what women could do
and be; Rosemary Radford Ruether calls them "the most independent
women professionals in nineteenth-century America" (Ruether and Keller,
21). They were educated, financially independent, and free from the authority of fathers, husbands, and even bishops, whom they often fought
tooth and nail in order to maintain authority over their own orders. They
built missions on the bare banks of western rivers and established schools,
orphanages, and hospitals, where their nursing during epidemics earned
them rare praise from contemporaneous feminist journals (Ruether and
Keller, 19–31; Kenneally, 43–59, 76–79). But even the female religious
tended to uphold the values of young ladyhood and Marian domesticity in
their academies for American girls (Kenneally, 56–59).

Margaret Fuller refers to such a wide range of Catholic figures in her writings (e.g., St. Theresa, Isabella of Castile, French Catholic missionaries
to the Indians, Manzoni, and Daniel O'Connell) that one should never
underestimate her knowledge of the church's history and politics.[37] But before she moved to New York City in late 1844, she had only limited direct

32   encounters with this religion and its adherents.[38] Almost all the Catholics she knew in New England seem to have been converts,[39] for she was separated by class and ethnicity from most "born" Catholics, who in Boston were primarily Irish, although she was aware of anti-Catholic and anti-Irish prejudice.[40] Fuller did meet Catholic immigrants as a newspaper writer in New York City. But even here she seems to have used earlier frameworks to interpret what she learned; Catholic couples, for example, became an example of the kind of "holy marriage" celebrated in *Woman in the Nineteenth Century*.[41] Fuller did not fully experience a Catholic culture until the late 1840s when she was in Italy, covering the Roman revolution for the *New-York Tribune*, and then her treatment of Catholicism and her attitude toward the Virgin Mary markedly changed.

    What chiefly differentiates Fuller from Jameson and Eliot is the extent to which she depended on literary sources for her religious ideas, particularly about the Madonna. Her British counterparts, of course, had their Continental travels to draw on, whereas Fuller before her move to New York and trip to Europe had fairly limited exposure to any religious group other than Unitarians. But she also seems to have had limited interest, because she was impatient with sectarianism. For example, she writes in one of her essays:

> We see dawning here and there a light that predicts a better day—a day when sects and parties shall be regarded only as schools of thought and life, and while a man prefers one for his own instruction, he may yet believe it is more profitable for his brethren differently constituted to be in others. God takes too good care of his children to suffer all truth to be confined to any one church establishment, age, or constellation of minds. ("Methodism at the Fountain," *PLA* [1846], 2:172–73)

Anti-sectarianism also informs her rather critical comments on the Oxford Movement.[42] Fuller valued far above sects the religious insights of other exceptional souls, seekers, and visionaries; she cited and described *individuals* in her writings: Dante, Manzoni, the Seer of Prevorst, John Wesley, Mother Ann Lee, the Indian girl betrothed to the sun. These were the sources for her own religious ideas and her work on the Madonna; these were the members of *her* "universal church" (see *PLA*, 2:173).

    It is possible that Fuller never would have written about the Madonna in *Woman in the Nineteenth Century* and her other texts on women if she had been exposed more to American Catholicism and the Catholicizing Oxford Movement. To be sure, the Catholic art she glimpsed in engravings and finally saw in Europe did give the Virgin Mary new visual resonances for her. But she hardly would have found much liberatory potential in a Madonna had she not first seen her as the glorious mother and queen of Dante, Petrarch, and Goethe—a figure far removed from the domesticated little wife of much American Catholic writing.

Twentieth-century feminist theologians and biblical scholars, many of them from Catholic backgrounds, have addressed the Virgin Mary's historical function in the patriarchal church as a symbol of perfect womanhood, and the possibility of feminist "redemption" of this figure. For instance, Mary Daly in *Beyond God the Father* (1973) identifies certain potentially liberatory aspects of Mary a patriarchal Church has not been able to repress altogether. Mary's perpetual virginity suggests her likeness to earlier goddess-figures who stand independent and alone, not defined by their biology or their relationships; this important reinterpretation of Mary is also found in Jameson, Fuller, and Eliot. Daly, furthermore, contends that the Immaculate Conception and the Assumption threaten male supremacy by potentially negating the myth of carnal feminine evil represented by Eve (*Beyond God the Father*, 81–95). But Daly's reading of Mary in *Gyn/ecology* (1978) is considerably more negative, although she says she still agrees with the major theses of the earlier work (*Beyond God the Father*, 1985 reintroduction, xiii n). In *Gyn/ecology* Daly claims to glimpse the "mythic presence of the Goddess" in the faint and distorted theological image of Mary. But the Goddess herself is desired; the Virgin Mary—"a pale derivative symbol," "a void waiting to be made by the male," the "Total Rape Victim"—does not seem worth recovering (xi, 83–89).

In *Sexism and God-Talk* (1983), Rosemary Radford Ruether (more optimistic than Daly) shows that women can have an ongoing and fruitful engagement with the Bible because of its prophetic tradition, which has and can be used to condemn oppressive and sexist religious traditions and social structures (22–33). Like Daly, Ruether criticizes the Church's Christology, its personality cult of a male savior, and its ecclesiastical Mariology, in which Mary represents a Church conceived in patriarchal terms as passive, receptive, and antithetical to sexuality and the body. She finds in the Gospels a Jesus who is the "kenosis of patriarchy" and a figure compatible with feminism, and a Mary who exemplifies willing faith and liberatory activity for women and men. This is Ruether's "Liberation Mariology" for a

34   Church that is "Humanity Redeemed from Sexism."[43] Elizabeth Johnson joins Ruether in criticizing received images of Mary and proposing ways to make her a positive symbol for modern believers, especially women. For example, Mary can be a real mother rather than the exceptional Virgo Perpetua; she can be recognized as the female face of God. But Johnson cites a number of feminist writers—Patricia Noone, Kari Borresen, Elisabeth Schussler Fiorenza, Mary Gordon, and Simone de Beauvoir—who see almost no empowering possibilities in this historically church- and male-controlled figure.[44]

    Jameson, Fuller, and Eliot knew the Catholic Marian tradition, particularly as it emerges in art (which tends to be subordinated to doctrine in discussions by modern feminist theologians). But they emphasized that tradition's medieval rather than its nineteenth-century aspects—Mary as the heavenly queen, rather than the "maid mild," picking up after Joseph. Because the conservative Mariology associated with Pio Nono was still developing during their writing careers (this pope outlived Fuller by twenty-eight and Jameson by eighteen years), they were probably less affected by it than modern Catholic feminists are; their Madonnas were still defined by Chartres and Notre Dame de Paris and not by Sacre Coeur. Moreover, the three writers combined their knowledge of Catholicism with the Protestant tenet of the spiritual equality of men and women, which helps ensure that a borrowed Madonna need not function as a symbol of female subordination. But claims of equality can coexist with assumptions of difference. The three writers' Mariologies are also marked by their feminist belief (characteristic of the nineteenth century) in certain essential and enduring differences between the sexes. Essentialist feminism (which is rejected by many modern feminists) may have limited the three writers' challenges to traditional images of Christ, but it fostered their most radical claims for Mary, as the necessary *female* face of the divine.

    Indeed, these three nineteenth-century writers are the unsung predecessors of feminist theologians such as Ruether, Johnson, and Daly (*Beyond God the Father*). They, too, saw feminist potential in images of Mary as the Virgin Goddess and the apotheosized Queen of Heaven, and they also put her in a tradition older than and encompassing the Catholic. Fuller linked Mary to the Great Goddesses, especially the virgin-mother Ceres. Eliot's Madonna-figure Dinah, white-robed in her moon-drenched chamber, resembles the goddess Diana, as critics have noted. And in a later novel Romola is worshipped by Mediterranean peasants as "the Lady from over the sea," the Virgin Mother, who is here closely associated with the Great

Mother in her various forms. Jameson claimed that devotion to the Madonna and to the mother-goddesses who precede her is "an acknowledgement of a higher as well as gentler power than that of the strong hand and the might that makes the right" (*Madonna*, xix). But these interpreters, in contrast to many of their modern counterparts, considered the Madonna to be not the deathly-pale reflection of the Goddess, but the culturally available Christian version, and even a figure representing the culmination of the earlier mythologies.

The art known and produced in the nineteenth century is a context as important as the religion or literature of the period for interpreting the work of Jameson, Eliot, and Fuller—and for understanding why they merit attention as feminists and Mariologists. Francis Haskell's account of art collecting in England and France from 1790 to 1870 makes clear the extent to which English public and private collections were built up because of the Napoleonic wars, which put loot from occupied Italy and the heirlooms of impoverished families on the international art market (24–33, 37). The consequence in Great Britain, according to Haskell, was that connoisseurs like Joshua Reynolds and the collectors they advised put a renewed emphasis on High Renaissance and Baroque masters, whose works were now so numerous and affordable: "Titians and Raphaels, Correggios, Rubenses and Guidos joined the odd family portrait or hunting scene that until then had constituted the sum total of [aristocratic] artistic possessions" (27–29, 37).

But earlier art also had its advocates. Friedrich Schlegel's praise of late-medieval and early Renaissance painters, including the Northern masters, when he saw the war-enriched collections of the Louvre in 1802–4, had a profound impact on German Romanticism.[45] Motivated by religious (often Catholic) and nationalistic beliefs, collectors such as the Boisserée brothers and painters such as Franz Pforr, Friedrich Overbeck (later head of the Rome-based "Nazarene" painters), and Caspar David Friedrich valued German and Flemish "primitives" and Gothic architecture over the sensual art of the High Renaissance and Baroque periods and (in some cases) the classicism associated with France. John Ruskin is probably the best-known advocate of the art predating Raphael—and the Victorian imitators of this art—in Britain. But he had several important predecessors: Francis Palgrave, author of a popular travel guide on northern Italy first published in 1823; A. W. Pugin, the Gothic architect; and A. F. Rio, a French Catholic

36 art historian. Rio in his *De la Poésie chrétienne* (1836, revised edition 1861–67) used religious sincerity rather than artistic achievement as his primary criterion for evaluating European paintings and on this basis argued for the superiority of the early Italian painters, particularly Giotto, Fra Angelico, Perugino, and the early Raphael. Rio's charm and capacity for self-promotion during his visits to England (he had a Welsh wife, Apollonia Jones), aided by some positive reviews and the interest of influential connoisseurs and Tractarians, made his book widely read even before its translation into English in 1854.[46] Jameson regarded Rio as something of a mentor, though her art histories differ from his in their plan and other important respects.[47] She wrote from Paris to her sister in 1841: "The great event of my life here has been the meeting with Rio. . . . I have twice been at the Louvre with [him] and De Triqueti [an admired sculptor friend] at my elbow, and have profited accordingly."[48] These gallery tours were preparation for the popular *Sacred and Legendary Art;* Francis Haskell (though repeating some spurious criticism of Jameson's abilities) identifies her as "probably second only to [Ruskin] in furthering the cult of the 'primitives'" in England (106).

The interest of all three women writers of this study—not just Jameson—in art and art criticism cannot be overestimated. All three, for example, were familiar with the aesthetic theories of German Romanticism, and they developed the distinctions made by Friedrich Schiller and Friedrich and A. W. Schlegel between naive and sentimental poetry, between classicism and romanticism, and between classical and Christian art.[49] Jameson, in addition to her works on medieval and Renaissance art, wrote several guidebooks on public and private British collections and travel books and articles dealing with contemporary painting and sculpture.[50] It seems that wherever English-speaking Victorians went (the National Gallery in London, the Royal Academy show, the Crystal Palace, the museums in Munich, the artists' studios in Rome), their taste would be shaped by this popular and prolific writer.

The full range of Eliot's writing on art during her years as a journalist has sometimes been missed, because most of this work is available only in Joseph Wiesenfarth's edition of her notebooks and uncollected writings. The Wiesenfarth edition contains two reviews of Ruskin plus a long journal entry on *The Stones of Venice*, a notice of Lessing's *Laocoon*, and three reviews of A. W. Stahr's *Torso*, a lengthy work on ancient Greek art and architecture. Eliot's comments on Stahr show her familiarity with the aesthetic theories of Winckelmann and other German classicists. Her indebt-

edness to Ruskin's theories of realism and truth in art has been discussed
by several scholars.[51] Eliot and Lewes indefatigably visited galleries and
churches during their numerous trips to Germany, the Low Countries,
France, Italy, and even Spain. It is possible that she sought out certain
works of art during her first trip to Germany—the *Sistine Madonna* and contemporary monumental sculpture—because of descriptions in German
travel books like Jameson's and Mary Howitt's. Her taste in art was broad,
but her preferences were for portraiture and High Renaissance painting
(Witemeyer, 21–24). Eliot saw as many art exhibits as she could in England, and she visited the studios of the Pre-Raphaelite painters; Hugh
Witemeyer shows that she was influenced by the Christian iconography of
their paintings.[52] The writer had a good visual memory, as Eliot scholars
have noted. For example, Norma Jean David and Bernard Richards have
found that a painting by Gerard Dou, the *Betende Spinnerin* in Munich, is
vividly evoked by a description in *Adam Bede*.[53] As I will show, Eliot models
Dinah Morris after the *Sistine Madonna* seen in Dresden, and Romola Bardi
after her friend Barbara Bodichon and one of Fra Angelico's Madonnas,
which Lewes had copied at Florence to hang before her as she wrote
(Haight, 326). Dorothea in *Middlemarch* is compared to several female
saints and a Virgin Mary who "look[s] down with those clear eyes at the
poor mortals who pray to her," and Mirah, the Jewish heroine of *Daniel
Deronda*, sits amid a "cloud of witnesses," the Madonna and cherubs on the
walls of the Meyricks' home, in this novel about the "separateness with
connection" of Judaism and Christianity (*Middlemarch*, 826; *Daniel Deronda*,
178–79).

Margaret Fuller, according to the art historians Corlette Walker and
Adele Holcomb, was the first or one of the first Americans to achieve competence in the field of aesthetic criticism, and she deserves credit as the editor of the *Dial* for the number of articles on art published in this
transcendentalist journal (Walker and Holcomb, 124, 131–32). Her 1839
review of paintings by the American artist Washington Allston shows she
had a keen eye and an evocative style, reminding one of Ruskin (though
predating *Modern Painters*).[54] Fuller's assessments of Allston differ tellingly
from those of Anna Jameson, who saw his paintings during her visit to the
United States in 1837–38 (she had earlier received verses from the artist,
who admired her *Diary of an Ennuyée* [Thomas, 124, 167]). Fuller, for instance,
could not be brought to admire Allston's Madonna and Child, with its "air
of got up naivete and delicacy," which "persons of better taste than I

38   like"—notably Jameson, who called it "a beautiful little picture, . . . in its
truly Italian and yet original treatment."[55] One senses here the sentimen-
tality of which Fuller often accused the older writer.

What makes Fuller's achievement as an art critic remarkable is the very
limited number of original art works on view in Boston. In addition to Allston's works, she saw a few modern paintings and sculptures by Thorwald-
sen, Powers, and others, which were in private collections and annually
put on display for the community.[56] But her exposure to art seems otherwise to have been restricted to the plaster casts of classical sculptures in
the Boston Athenaeum, books, and the (black-and-white) engravings of
paintings that her friend Samuel Gray Ward brought back from Europe.[57]
In *Summer on the Lakes*, she is reminded of Titian's *Venus and Adonis* by the wild
red roses of Wisconsin, and she quotes a lengthy description of this painting
—which she had never seen, at least not in color, since all the versions
were in Europe.[58]

The experience of the American novelist Nathaniel Hawthorne is also
telling. According to Haskell, when Hawthorne was the United States con-
sul for Liverpool, he used the great 1857 Manchester exhibition to educate
himself about paintings. After two weeks, he could distinguish Rembrandt
from Rubens, but he most admired Dou's *Woman Cleaning a Saucepan* and the
seventeenth-century Dutch still lives, which he described in his journal as
"such life-like representations of cabbages, onions, turnips, cauliflowers,
and peas" (*English Notebooks*, 556 [9 Aug.1857], quoted by Haskell, 99). In
Rome Hawthorne toured the galleries and churches under the guidance of
Jameson, but her niece says he "preferr[ed] to maintain intact his own very
singular impressions and opinions as to art, ancient and modern" (Macpherson, 302). Just a few years later, the man so recently a novice wrote *The Marble Faun* (1860), his novel about art and artists in Rome, in which he praised
the American sculptor Harriet Hosmer and the Virgin Mary–like copyist
Hilda, with their "pure" genius, at the expense of the passionate Fuller-like
character Miriam (43–44, 51–63, 120–25). Hawthorne's portrait of Hilda
subtly puts down the professional art historian who had been his *cicerone*.
Hilda is called a superb judge of art, but she supposedly grasps the excel-
lences of a painting through self-surrendering feeling and instinct, rather
than through knowledge and a creative and critical mind, qualities of males
like the sculptor Kenyon; the abilities of women in artistic fields are thus
called into question (56–57, 117–27). Hawthorne denigrates Christian
Rome, which Jameson preferred, in comparison with the classical city:
"Everywhere, some fragment of ruin, suggesting the magnificence of a for-

mer epoch; everywhere, moreover, a Cross—and nastiness at the foot of it." He also criticizes some of Jameson's favorite artists: Giotto and Cimabue, whose faded frescoes at Assisi are said to reflect a dead faith; and the modern sculptor John Gibson, a friend of hers (110–11, 123–24, 134, 303). But the female expertise Hawthorne earlier dismissed seems to have become necessary for his novel: several of his longer descriptions of paintings closely resemble Jameson's published assessments of Raphael, Fra Angelico, and portrait Madonnas (337–39).

The example of Hawthorne prepares us to consider the American feminists who were his contemporaries, most of whom had even less exposure to European art. The consequence, I argue, is that they lacked interest in the Madonna and had no sense of her possibilities for feminism. Sarah Grimké and Elizabeth Cady Stanton illustrate this point, because both produced lengthy analyses of women in the Bible that deal—or fail to deal—with the figure of Mary. Grimké was the author of *Letters on the Equality of the Sexes* (1838), and Stanton the instigator and principal contributor to the *Woman's Bible* (1895–98).[59] Both developed a feminist biblical hermeneutics because they saw religious arguments against women's rights as the most formidable to overcome.

Neither Grimké nor Stanton had much exposure to European culture and art. Grimké seems never to have been outside the United States, and Stanton made three trips to Great Britain, Ireland, and France (in 1840 and the 1880s), but her negative comments on monasticism and the Mass suggest her hostility toward Catholic culture. The two women probably had few glimpses of the Madonna, or of any European religious art, at home in America. Grimké was a Quaker, while Stanton, a Presbyterian by birth, came under the influence of Quaker and Unitarian beliefs, and none of these religious traditions used visual art in worship; the Quaker meetinghouse that Grimké attended in the 1830s still stands in Philadelphia, and it has bare walls. The major art museums in the East Coast cities where the two women lived were all established after the Civil War.[60] Until the late nineteenth century, European and European-style religious paintings in America were almost exclusively in private collections or Catholic churches. Stanton does mention visiting art galleries and museums during her trips to Europe. But an anecdote in Margaret Hope Bacon's biography of Lucretia Mott seems more in character: when Stanton was in London in 1840, she asked Mott so many questions about abolitionism and women's rights that the two did not get beyond the entrance of the British Museum (Bacon, 98). The liturgical experiences of Grimké and Stanton, combined

40   with the aesthetic barrenness of their young country, account for the almost complete absence of references to visual art in their work.

Grimké's and Stanton's circumscribed awareness of the glorious images of Mary in religious art affected their analysis of women in the Bible. Grimké in *Letters on the Equality of the Sexes* celebrates the female prophets of the Old and New Testaments in order to argue that women like herself, the present-day "prophetic daughters," should be allowed to preach and teach (85–95). Yet the Virgin Mary is excluded from Grimké's gallery of heroic women (biblical prophets and ministers, secular queens and intellectuals), even though, as Jameson points out, the Church has historically represented Mary as "poetess and prophetess," the divine Mother of Wisdom, and Queen of Heaven.[61] Grimké in a later unpublished essay, "Sisters of Charity" (the title taken from Jameson), offers a powerful vision of what woman should be: "Hitherto . . . the majesty of her being has been obscured, and the uprising of her nature is but the effort to give to her whole being the opportunity to expand into all its essential nobility."[62] But it is Jameson, Fuller, and Eliot, and not Grimké, who give this majestic figure the name of Mary.

In Stanton's *Woman's Bible,* the New Testament section contains only brief and desacralizing comments on the Virgin Mary, which are credited to Mrs. Stanton and Anonymous (who may conceal her identity because she sounds so much like the notorious Mrs. S). Both Stanton and her collaborator reject the Virgin Birth (which they sometimes confuse with the Immaculate Conception); Anonymous adds that the Virgin Birth is a slur on "natural motherhood," and her own mother was as holy as Mary.[63] Stanton's hostility toward Marian doctrines extends to all aspects of Catholicism; in her account of her travels in southern France, she refers to "the fallacies of Romanism" and describes the Catholic churches and rituals as from the "Dark Ages" (*Eighty Years,* 342, 346).

The quite different experiences and attitudes of Quakers and Unitarians in England may be illustrated by Mary Howitt, who shared not only Grimké's religion but also her commitment to slaves' and women's rights; she met Stanton at the World's Anti-Slavery Convention in London in 1840.[64] Howitt felt deprived of art and literature as the child of Friends; she had to take aesthetic comfort in Wedgwood teapots and inkwells and plaster mantelpieces, and sneak novels and poetry (Howitt, 1:95–96, 103, 107). But as an adult she became familiar with religious art from Raphael to Rossetti on her trips to Germany and Italy and through her friendships with the Pre-Raphaelite painters in London. And as noted earlier, her ex-

posure to Catholic piety on the Continent led late in life to her conversion
to that faith and her embrace of the Virgin Mary. The younger generation
in Howitt's Unitarian and Quaker circle included several artists: her daughter Anna Mary, who studied art in Germany, and Barbara Bodichon and
Bessie Parkes, both feminist activists; the three went on painting holidays
together (Cherry, 47–48). Parkes saw the religious art of Rome with her
friend Jameson in 1857, a few years before converting to Catholicism
(Macpherson, 297).

Although this examination has been limited to a handful of English
and American feminists, it does suggest a crucial difference between the
two feminist movements: the Englishwomen had a far more extensive
knowledge of European art and culture. One can see how Britain produced
a Jameson, ready to place the Virgin Mary at the heart of her feminist theology and at the head of her female heroes; one wonders how America
ever produced a Fuller. What would Grimké's *Letters on the Equality of the Sexes*
and Stanton's *Woman's Bible* have been like if these American Dissenters had
written under the daily inspiration of the Madonnas in the churches of
Italy or the National Gallery of London? What would American feminism
have been like?[65]

Karen Offen's broad definition of feminism, drawn from the writings
of nineteenth- and twentieth-century European and American women, is a
useful starting point for categorizing Victorian views on women's rights,
particularly the views of Jameson, Eliot, and Fuller. According to Offen,
women and men who are feminists acknowledge the validity of women's
own experience and values; they recognize the institutionalized unjust
treatment of women as a group by men as a group in a given society; and
they challenge the ideas, institutions, and power structures that uphold
male privilege in that society (152). This formulation is quite similar to the
historian Gerda Lerner's definition of "feminist consciousness."[66] Offen's
definition brings together two important strands of feminism, which she
calls individualist feminism and relational feminism. The former strand emphasizes individual rights and takes adult male citizenship as the standard
for equality, while the latter strand defines women relationally (the relationship is usually marriage or the male-female dyad) and bases claims for
greater rights on women's assumed essential nature (e.g., their capacities
for childbearing and nurturing) and their distinctive contributions to
society, which begin at the level of the family (134–37). Offen brings out

42   the ways such essentialist arguments, usually considered the property of
the opposition, have been appropriated for feminist ends.

Barbara Caine's narrower and more historicized study of feminism in
Victorian Britain reinforces Offen's categorizations. Where Offen speaks
of "individualist" and "relational" feminism, Caine identifies "liberalism"
and "domestic ideology" as the two forces shaping Victorian feminist
thought, and notes that the importance of the latter has long been under-
estimated:

> Where once feminism was defined as a belief in the need for
> equal rights between women and men, there is now a wide-
> spread recognition of the importance Victorian feminists at-
> tached to establishing and maintaining sexual differences
> between men and women. The idea that the English women's
> movement was concerned primarily, even exclusively, with gain-
> ing access for women to the public sphere, has given way to an
> ever-increasing recognition of the extent of Victorian feminist
> concern with the oppression of women in domestic life, in mar-
> riage, and in all forms of sexual relations. (2)

Caine explains these essentialist and domestic emphases by pointing to the
limitations of liberal thought for Victorian women. From the seventeenth
century, she says, liberalism confirmed the power, freedom, and privileges
(including sexual privileges) of the *man*, as head of the household and as
citizen. Others—women, the workers who called him "master"—existed to
serve him; liberalism left unchanged their political and economic subordination, in particular women's assignment to the domestic rather than
public sphere. Classicism, the "language" used in Victorian public life, confirmed the gendering of the public sphere; it was a language women did
not know, and it made ancient Greece (a society in which women were
even more disadvantaged) the model of democracy. In this situation, according to Caine, Victorian women needed a weapon *against* liberalism.
They turned to domestic ideology, seeing arguments about sexual difference as the only way to address their sexual oppression and to redefine
their supposed marks of inferiority as virtues (38–41, 53). But Caine, like
Offen, notes that mixed arguments were common; in fact, she says, "it is
[women's] use of both outlooks"—liberalism and domestic ideology—
"which defines and characterizes Victorian feminism."[67]

Two American feminist historians—Nancy Cott and Ellen Carol DuBois

—have challenged Offen's (and by extension Caine's) definitions of feminism. Cott argues that the term "feminism," first used in the early twentieth century to describe a particular individualist ideology, cannot legitimately be applied to earlier and especially markedly different movements and modes of thought.[68] Both Cott and DuBois raise questions about the value of relational feminism,[69] with Cott contending that such essentialist or domestic arguments have no place in any feminist movement:

> What [Offen] has not acknowledged sufficiently is how fully the underpinnings of this view of women's position—with its acceptance of sexual dualism, belief in the complementarity of the sexes, and reliance on the nuclear family as the basic unit of social organization—composed the standard, conservative, status quo view of women's position, rather than anything remotely feminist. . . . My point is that relational feminists' views on gender shared everything with non-feminist or traditionalists *except* the point that arbitrary male domination should not be tolerated. Why therefore, call their entire approach "feminist"—even with the "relational" modifier? (Cott, *Signs*, 204)

The debate within academic feminism is not confined to historians. For example, the literary critics Deirdre David and Tricia Lootens criticize essentialism as inconsistent with feminism, seeing it as reinforcing the limiting category of the feminine and placing women outside the historical realm of activity and change (David, 177–96; Lootens, 95–115).

I consider Cott's strictures regarding use of the term "feminism" problematic for several reasons. First, the use of this word to describe intellectuals and activists before the twentieth century is well established.[70] Cott's distinction is meaningful to modern historians, but it has not been found useful by many scholars in other fields and periods. Also, it would be hard to find a word to take the place of "feminism"; "woman movement," the term used by nineteenth-century American activists, according to Cott, is awkward and has no adjectival form. Finally, it is common historical and scholarly practice, as Barbara Caine points out in reply to Cott, to apply terms retrospectively in order to show continuities of thought and practice; Caine's examples are "liberal" and "socialist" (5–7), but one might add "medieval" and "Renaissance."

The second issue that Cott and DuBois raise concerns whether essentialist and domestic arguments are empowering or even feminist at all.

44   Many theorists see two dominant strands or tendencies in nineteenth-century feminism, which generally correspond to Caine's "liberal" and "domestic" feminism and Offen's analogous types. For example, Josephine Donovan speaks of "Enlightenment Liberal feminism" and "cultural feminism,"[71] and Maggie McFadden of the "minimizing" and "maximizing" strains of feminism. McFadden identifies Wollstonecraft, Mill, and Susan B. Anthony as figures who minimize male-female differences, and her "maximizers" include maternalists and cultural feminists (495–504). A number of historians—for example, Philippa Levine and Christine Bolt—join Barbara Caine in acknowledging the importance of "domestic feminism" in nineteenth-century Britain and America. Levine writes, "For many women committed to the fight for women's rights, the most effective weapon was not the total rejection of [domestic] ideology but rather a manipulation of its fundamental values." She notes that these women frequently claimed their purity made them morally superior to men and thus justified their greater involvement in public life.[72] The historian Gerda Lerner explores how women from medieval to modern times used their roles as mothers to gain authority and even to claim equality with men. From the nineteenth century, they also saw possibilities in organized "sisterhood."[73]

The crucial difference between feminist scholars such as Caine, Offen, Levine, and Lerner and the historians Cott and DuBois seems to be that the former focus on European and British figures instead of or in addition to American feminists. The leaders of the American women's-rights movement (Lucretia Mott, Elizabeth Cady Stanton, Susan B. Anthony) tended to be far more radical than their mid-century British counterparts (e.g., Bessie Parkes and Emily Davies), and prominent American spokeswomen for domesticity, such as Catharine Beecher and Emma Willard, were hardly feminist. If one's norm for nineteenth-century feminism is Stanton, who forged the thunderbolts, and Anthony, who threw them, one will probably find few fireworks on the domestic hearth.

The issues to consider now are what evidence supports the contention that Jameson, Fuller, and Eliot were "feminists," and what kind of feminist each might be; full discussions of each writer's views will appear in the following chapters. This topic is a controversial one, particularly among Eliot scholars, who often differ in their interpretations of the same evidence. My analysis will build on Barbara Caine's demonstration that essentialist ideas and selective support of causes were integral rather than antithetical to Victorian feminism.

The commitment of Jameson, Fuller, and Eliot to the cause of women's rights is revealed most clearly in their views on education. As scholars and professional writers who struggled to teach themselves classical and modern languages, history, and religion and theology, they believed that women should be "educated equally with men" (*Eliot Letters*, 4:366). Jameson delivered public lectures on women's need for better education and job training; Eliot gave advice and a financial contribution to Emily Davies, founder of Girton College for women; and Fuller organized educational Conversations for groups of women in Boston. Eliot thought that education for women would promote harmony between the sexes, because while certain valuable essential differences between the sexes would be manifested, men and women would come to reason in the same ways and share the same beliefs and judgments.[74]

Eliot and Jameson also worked for political change. They signed and circulated the Langham Place group's 1856 petition for married women's property rights, which were finally guaranteed by parliamentary acts in 1870 and 1882 (see Lacey, 4–5; *Eliot Letters*, 2:225–27). To be sure, Eliot discouraged her friend Sara Hennell, a governess and religion scholar, from campaigning for women's suffrage, but only because she feared that such activism, though manageable for nonworking women, would demand too much of Hennell's time. Still, she did support the cause and praised Mill's speeches in Parliament, seeing the vote as enabling women to protect themselves from "the exercise of any unrighteous power" (*Eliot Letters*, 4:390, 366–67). She felt, though, that her relationship with Lewes would undermine her public advocacy of feminist causes.

The three writers' publications are the most extensive evidence of their positions on the Woman Question. Jameson advocated expanded rights for women not only in her published lectures but also in her travel book *Winter Studies and Summer Rambles in Canada* and her art histories, as her nineteenth-century readers and modern critics such as Dorothy Mermin, John Killham, and Judith Johnston have noted.[75] After Fuller finished *Woman in the Nineteenth Century*, in which she urged that "every arbitrary barrier" to woman's progress be thrown down, specifying legal, economic, and educational barriers (*WNC*, 255–61), she became a writer for Horace Greeley's *New-York Tribune*, reporting on conditions in state women's institutions. Most modern surveys of nineteenth-century American feminism give Fuller a prominent place; her religious thought influenced Elizabeth Cady Stanton's.[76] Eliot protested restrictions on women and celebrated women's intellectual achievements in her reviews "Woman in France:

46 Madame de Sablé," "Margaret Fuller and Mary Wollstonecraft," and "Life and Opinions of Milton" (on his divorce tracts), and she was sympathetically engaged with the Woman Question in her novels, particularly *The Mill on the Floss* (education) and *Middlemarch* (education, vocation, and marriage).[77] Given the three writers' sustained advocacy of women's rights, if they are denied the label "feminist," they are most likely being judged according to the standards of our time rather than their own.

Jameson, Fuller, and Eliot all made the mixture of liberal and domestic arguments that Caine calls typical of Victorian feminism, and they are also representative in their selective support of causes (Caine, 4–8, 53). The three writers thought women are men's equals, as souls and as citizens, and should therefore have the same political, economic, intellectual, and moral rights and responsibilities. But they let others lead the campaign for these rights; as intellectuals and authors, they (like many of their modern counterparts in universities, as Booth points out [*Greatness Engendered*, 23–25]) emphasized individual development and literary achievement over political activism. This choice was understood and appreciated by the Langham Place feminists, who strategically praised the achievements of a female elite ("See what Mrs. Browning and Rosa Bonheur can do!") while working to improve the conditions of ordinary women.

But Fuller's and Eliot's awareness of the singularity of their achievement did limit their feelings of solidarity with less gifted women. Some scholars have consequently questioned their commitment to feminism. Fuller claimed to know no one who was her mental equal, and organized her women's Conversations as "uplift" (Blanchard, 166, 144–53). Eliot criticized the work of other women writers ("Silly Novels by Lady Novelists") and, as often noted, treated her heroines differently from herself, giving *their* intellectual and artistic energies only a narrow outlet, perhaps because of her belief that only a few women, or men, could do well the kind of work she undertook (*Eliot Letters*, 4:425). Jameson took the opposite tack from Fuller and Eliot and early in her career accepted the role of "lady writer," which facilitated her hesitant entry into the profession. She had a "feminine" style, described by Mermin as "perfectly spontaneous, artlessly responsive to the emotions it conveys, a brilliant enactment of the characteristics attributed to women writers" (Mermin, 88), and her first books were on "ladies' topics": famous queens, the consorts of poets, Shakespeare's heroines. With this profile, she has sometimes been perceived as reluctant to challenge the ideology of separate spheres and as being merely proto-feminist, despite her involvement in mid-century activism.

Such criticisms of both the exceptional and the ladylike woman writer indicate the difficulties feminist scholars face in theorizing about female and feminist authorship in the nineteenth century and earlier periods. The two dominant models of authorship in studies so far have been the unusually talented Victorian woman writer struggling against patriarchal language and institutions (see Deirdre David, Margaret Homans, and Sandra Gilbert and Susan Gubar) and the woman writer finding a place in a female tradition (see Dorothy Mermin, Elaine Showalter, Nina Auerbach [1978], and Ellen Moers). The models themselves are frequently interrogated. For example, Alison Booth, in *Greatness Engendered*, shows that since the Great Writer has been defined by masculine norms, women have had to overcome somehow the impediment of sex to attain this status (Booth, 1–7). Eliot's "greatness" was indicated by her inclusion in the *English Men of Letters* series, and Edgar Allan Poe praised his contemporary by saying, "There are men, women, and Margaret Fuller." Booth's study reexamines both this masculinist conception of authorship and the related model of the solitary woman writer's struggle against patriarchy. Tricia Lootens shows the drawbacks inherent in the second model, female tradition. Canonization of Victorian women writers, she argues, has had a deadening effect, turning them into forgettable plaster saints. While my study focuses on ideas and influence more than on authorial or intellectual roles, I do analyze Jameson, Fuller, and Eliot as feminist and religious intellectuals. My study follows the "tradition" and "communal" model of authorship, and I hope to contribute to the discussions of female authorship by grounding the three writers in the nineteenth-century feminist movements, which have been receiving relatively little attention in recent feminist literary criticism.[78] I will also draw attention to the links between English and American writers and artists (e.g., between Jameson and the American sculptor Harriet Hosmer), which facilitated a surprisingly extensive transatlantic traffic in feminist and religious ideas.

As I have indicated, literary critics are also divided on the question of whether essentialist ideas disqualify a Victorian writer from the category of feminist. Booth, Mermin, and Auerbach have emphasized the need to historicize our understandings of feminism and to realize that ideas of woman's nature and influence could be manipulated and resonate in unexpected ways. Jameson, Fuller, and Eliot argued for the fundamental equality of the sexes. But they did see certain essential differences, such as woman's physical and assumed psychological capacity for maternity, which give her a distinctive role and contribution to society. All three, however, pointed out that there are differences between woman's nature and man's understanding of woman's nature; woman has, for example, an intellect of her own and is not merely the "heart" of a marriage (*WNC*, 256). Yet it is not clear that the essentialism of these writers places woman outside history and change in a realm of the "eternal feminine," as David and Lootens have suggested (David on Eliot, 177–96; Lootens on Jameson and others, 95–115). For Jameson and Fuller, the "idea of woman" changes over time; woman's powers and abilities and the social understanding of her nature will all expand. Eliot (even before Darwin) put discussions of human nature into an evolutionary context: the organism and its natural and social environment change, little by little, in reaction to each other (reviews in *SE*, 127, 337).

The three writers thought that woman should not be bound by arguments about female nature, because such arguments can be misused by men, and "Nature seems to delight in varying the arrangements. . . [N]o need to clip the wings of any bird that wants to soar and sing, or finds in itself the strength of pinion for a migratory flight unusual to its kind. The difference would be that *all* need not be constrained to employments for which *some* are unfit." This is Fuller's statement, quoted approvingly by Eliot in her review and used to good purpose when she created the character of Maggie Tulliver a few years later ("Margaret Fuller and Mary Wollstonecraft," in *SE*, 335–36). Jameson was aware of another problem with arguments from nature: they tend to make normative the experience of certain privileged groups, such as white middle-class married women, and to marginalize other groups (self-sufficient women, working-class women, nonwhite women), sometimes to the extent that members of these groups are considered "unwomanly" and subhuman. She drew attention to such biased norms, particularly among the opposition, when she sarcastically observed that women who did hard manual labor somehow fell outside the category of "Woman," a creature supposedly suited for only light domestic tasks ("Woman's Mission," 221–22).

While my own position is that most differences between men and women are due to social conditioning (i.e., almost all differences are "gender" differences, not "sex" differences), I think we should take essentialist arguments seriously, because of their historical importance, which is demonstrated above, and because of their centrality to feminist spirituality. Important claims can be advanced using essentialist arguments, such as the claim that maternity involves power: the power to bring forth life or, in the case of Mary, the power to bring forth God. It is the three writers' essentialist beliefs that support their most radical arguments about Mary and women. Jameson, for example, makes the "apocalyptic feminist" claim that Mary and the women made in her image have the power to transform the earth, ushering in an era of peace (see Helsinger et al., 2:199–206). Eliot and Fuller suggest that the Virgin Mother is the feminine element of God or a symbol of the divine within women; when women are seen as men's equals, God no longer bears the likeness only of the Son of Man. Feminists who disagree with essentialist views are likely basing their arguments on the specifically Western political assumptions of bourgeois liberalism or Marxist materialism.[79] Recent studies of the universal powerful figure of the mother-goddess (examples of which sometimes include the Christian Queen of Heaven) suggest we need at least to be open to the possibility that women in cultures and eras other than our own have owed the power and prestige they have enjoyed to essentialist assumptions about female nature.[80] Adrienne Rich, in *Of Woman Born*, uses the figure of the Great Goddess to explore the difference between woman's wondrous biological capacity to bear and nourish children and the crippling institution of motherhood. She argues for the imaginative and perhaps someday realized benefits of a feminism centered on woman's maternal power: "I have come to believe . . . that female biology . . . has far more radical implications than we have yet come to appreciate" (xv, 21). The religion scholar Marilyn Massey, reminding us that the nineteenth century had gendered notions of the soul as well as of the body, contends that the idea of "feminine soul," anathema to many of her colleagues, in fact sometimes enabled women to reconceive deity in their own image and to seek more power and freedom for themselves in their families and in society (*Feminine Soul*, 23–25, 163–88). It is in these contexts that the feminism of Jameson, Fuller, and Eliot and their claims for the Madonna resonate.

Legends of a Feminist Madonna

CHAPTER TWO

Anna Brownell Murphy Jameson (1794–1860) was a practitioner of feminist scholarship influential in her century and a respected and versatile professional writer, whose books were reviewed in the major British periodicals. Yet she has just begun to attract scholarly attention. The fullest discussion to date is Judith Johnston's biography, which explores Jameson's development as a feminist "woman of letters" and analyzes the various nonfictional forms of her work.[1] Jameson's Shakespeare criticism and travel writing have also been the subject of critical articles.[2] But only a few scholars so far—chief among them Johnston and Adele Holcomb—have shown much interest in Jameson as an art historian, and the connections between her works on religious art and her own religious beliefs have hardly been examined.[3] This oversight is surprising, given Jameson's importance for our understanding of nineteenth-century art criticism, literature, and women's history. Jameson's scholarship was remarkably cohesive; her historical, religious, and art-historical writings informed and were shaped by her activism on behalf of women, and she made an important feminist contribution to the debates of her day. The Victorians listened to Jameson as well as to Carlyle, Ruskin, Newman, and Patmore; it is time for her voice to be represented in studies of this period.

Jameson's major work was the four-volume series *Sacred and Legendary Art*, which was designed to help Britons and Americans (particularly Protestants) touring the galleries and

Figure 1. Anna Brownell Jameson, 1848 (photograph by David Octavius Hill). Courtesy of the National Portrait Gallery, London.

52   churches of Europe understand what they saw.[4] In *Legends of the Madonna* (1852), the third title in the series, Jameson categorized and explained the various representations of Mary found in medieval and Renaissance art. But the book was not merely a guidebook; Jameson used the Marian art she described to advance the cause of women. Like Fuller and Eliot, Jameson favored images of Mary as the solitary, contemplative Virgin and the powerful Queen, and she stressed Mary's role as the Christian goddess. She continued the practice that Fuller evidently initiated (*Woman in the Nineteenth Century* predated *Legends of the Madonna* by seven years) of using Mary to bring out the "idea of Woman."[5] The Virgin Mother was not, in Jameson's view, "alone of all her sex," as the Church Fathers and modern feminist critics have said, but instead the empowering ideal of what women could become.[6]

Jameson did not neglect the humbler representations of Mary as a wife and homemaker. She interpreted this art as giving value to the productive work of women, particularly peasant women; the domestic Madonna of Victorian literature was, in contrast, a bourgeois ideal. But Jameson joined Fuller and Eliot in resisting efforts to limit women to domestic roles. Furthermore (as I show in chapter 4), although modern critics have often assumed that the Angel in the House was a secularized figure or at least a Protestant ideal detached from Catholic forms of belief, the writings of Coventry Patmore, John Henry Newman, and John Ruskin in fact suggest that this domestic Madonna was directly or indirectly shaped by patristic theology. Jameson could refigure Mary in empowering ways—as the Queen of Heaven rather than queen of the household—in large part because her Mariology was drawn from alternative Catholic sources.

Jameson, like Fuller and Eliot, was an unusually learned woman, able to write confidently about Catholic doctrine and history, European art, German literature, and contemporary political and women's issues. But whereas Eliot is known principally as a novelist and Fuller as an essayist *sui generis*, Jameson's primary achievements were as an art historian and a feminist theologian. As I argue in chapter 3, her art histories offer a theory of the development of European art and also contain an original aesthetic in which sacred images (including images of Mary) are seen as repositories of received and individual truth and lead the viewer into the presence of God. In creating this aesthetic, Jameson produced not just readings of Mary but a full-fledged Mariology responsive to Catholic history, Anglican doctrine, and her own and other women's needs and beliefs. Jameson's contributions have not heretofore been realized because the religious thought of male

Victorians (e.g., Newman, Hopkins, and in America Emerson) has received most of the attention, and because the scholars who have analyzed her art histories have too readily accepted her disclaimer that her approach was aesthetic rather than religious.[7] Although Jameson's Marian aesthetic developed in relation to her feminist views, her most innovative ideas and radical claims were rooted in what seems to us her conservatism. Her essentialist feminist beliefs led her to pair Mary and Jesus as equals or near-equals, the feminine and masculine faces of the divine. Paradoxically, it was Jameson's high regard for tradition that allowed her to recognize and emphasize Marian images that could communicate the intellectual and social equality of men and women.

Jameson's achievement as an art historian is all the more impressive when one remembers that she was writing for an audience that was neither Catholic nor feminist nor particularly art-loving. *Legends of the Madonna* shows her deftness in persuading a Protestant audience to accept Marian images, particularly those consonant with the author's feminist views. In this work, Jameson divides her discussion of artistic representations of Mary into two parts: first, Devotional Subjects, which illustrate a dogma, such as the Coronation of the Virgin, the *Mater Dolorosa*, or the Immaculate Conception, and which appeal to the "faith and piety" of the viewer; and second, Historical Subjects, which are dramatic treatments of biblical and legendary incidents from the life of the Virgin (liii–lv). It is primarily in the devotional section of *Legends of the Madonna* that we see Mary as Jameson describes her in the general introduction to the book: "an impersonation in the feminine character of beneficence, purity, and power, standing between an offended Deity and poor, sinning, suffering humanity" (xvii). "Beneficence, purity, and power": the key word in this phrase is the last. Even allowing for the extravagances of late-medieval piety, we can see that Jameson selects and praises devotional images of the Madonna that emphasize her spiritual power, which is often exercised independently of her Son's (see, e.g., figure 2). For instance, Jameson in her opening chapter on the Virgin without the Child describes the earliest representations of the solitary Virgin as "female figure[s] of colossal dimensions, . . . stand[ing] immediately beneath some figure or emblem representing almighty power," "grand and mysterious," "wonderfully majestic and simple" (4; see figure 3). Mary is here "not merely the mother of Christ" but also "the second Eve, the mother of all suffering humanity; THE WOMAN of the primaeval

54   prophecy whose issue was to bruise the head of the Serpent"; the type of the Church triumphant and crowned in heaven; "the most glorious, most pure, most pious, most clement, most sacred Queen and Mother, Virgin of Virgins" (4). These titles for Mary come from patristic and medieval Mariology; yet Jameson's emotional responses to the heavenly Queen and Virgin go far beyond mere reporting.

Jameson describes numerous examples of the Coronation of the Virgin (*Madonna*, 13–26), but she chooses to provide sketches of the images that maximize the Virgin's power and status. Four of her six sketches are of the Virgin seated on the same throne as Christ, receiving her crown. In Jameson's first, admittedly singular, example, a twelfth-century mosaic, the

Figure 2. Enthroned Virgin of the Campo Santo. Drawing by Anna Jameson from *Legends of the Madonna* (1852). Photo courtesy of K. C. Dietsch.

Figure 3. The solitary, powerful Virgin of San Venanzio, in the Lateran (mosaic, A.D. 642). Drawing by Anna Jameson from *Legends of the Madonna* (1852). Photo courtesy of K. C. Dietsch.

Virgin is "seated at [Christ's] right hand, at the same elevation, and alto-   55
gether as his equal" (figure 4). Jameson's remaining two sketches show the
Virgin kneeling rather than sitting on the throne, being crowned by the
Father himself and the other members of the Trinity.

Jameson also chooses to emphasize Mary's equality or near-equality
with Christ in her discussions of the Virgin of Mercy, "the most powerful
of intercessors," who is frequently shown in late-medieval art pleading for
sinners before Christ the stern judge. Jameson observes that the Virgin of
Mercy is usually seated on the same level as Christ or at least at his right
hand (26–27). A painting by Martin Schoen (or Schoengauer, fifteenth
century) shows the Father as judge, armed with a sword and javelins, and
the Son standing beside him, with the Virgin in the foreground, "looking

Figure 4. The Virgin and Christ enthroned: she is shown "altogether as his equal."
Santa Maria Trastevere (mosaic, A.D. 1130–43). Drawing by Anna Jameson from
Legends of the Madonna (1852). Photo courtesy of K. C. Dietsch.

56   up to her Son with an expression of tender supplication," while the "im-
ploring looks" of sinners "are directed to *her*" (28). The Virgin as dispenser
of mercy on earth, in Jameson's description, is a huge figure, the folds of
whose robe protect men, women, and children, kings, nobles, and
priests—in other words, all of Christendom (29–30; see figures 5 and 6).

Jameson stresses the Virgin's independence as well as her power.
Among devotional images of the Virgin without the Child, one of the latest Jameson analyzes is the Immaculate Conception, a favorite subject of
the seventeenth-century (Counter-Reformation) painters Guido and
Murillo. While the Virgin's mercy toward suffering humanity, as Jameson
notes, is thought to be an expression of her maternal character, in the Immaculate Conception "the maternal character is set aside, and she stands
alone, absolute in herself, and complete in her own perfections" (xxxvi).

On turning to devotional images of the Virgin *with* the Child, Jameson
herself seems frequently moved to worship:

Figures 5 and 6. The Madonna of Mercy, sheltering petitioners under her robe. Examples from
the Scuola (Brotherhood) of Charity, Venice (bas relief), and by Piero della Francesca,
painted for the hospital of Borgo San Sepolcro in the Apennines. Drawings by Anna Jameson from *Legends of the Madonna* (1852). Photos courtesy of K. C. Dietsch.

> When the glorified type of what is purest, loftiest, holiest in
> womanhood, stands before us, arrayed in all the majesty and
> beauty that accomplished Art, inspired by faith and love, could
> lend her, and bearing her divine Son, rather enthroned than sus-
> tained on her maternal bosom, "we look, and the heart is in
> heaven!" and it is difficult, very difficult, to refrain from an *Ora
> pro Nobis*. (58; see also 73–76)

The Madonna who worships her Son is herself his throne, and she is
adored by attendant angels, saints, and men and women crying "Salve
Regina!" to the being "so human, so maternal, and yet so unearthly" (73,
102–3). Jameson here celebrates the maternal character, which she (like
many Victorians, including feminists) sees as present in all women (Jameson, *Letters*, 234). Fathers, divine and human, are unnecessary in these
paintings; God is not shown, and Jameson notes that Mary's father Joachim
and Joseph are often omitted from votive groups that include Mary's
mother Anna (*Madonna*, 80). Even the Son may be overlooked in the exal-
tation of the divine mother:

> the Virgins of the old Italians. . . . look so divinely ethereal that
> they seem uplifted by their own spirituality: not even the air-
> borne clouds are needed to sustain them. They have no touch of
> earth or earth's material beyond the human form; their proper
> place is the seventh heaven; and there they repose, a presence
> and a power—a personification of infinite mercy sublimated by
> innocence and purity; and thence they look down on their wor-
> shippers and attendants, while these gaze upwards "with looks
> commercing with the skies." (76)

Jameson most likely read Fuller's *Woman in the Nineteenth Century* (1845)
before she wrote *Legends of the Madonna*, and while she does not cite the
American writer, her discussion of the Virgin Mother in the first sections
of her book has pronounced similarities to Fuller's analyses. Jameson, like
Fuller, focuses on the Virgin Mary as "bringing out the idea of woman" and
uses testimony from ancient religious thinkers and modern poets in support of this argument. Both writers emphasize Mary's role as a powerful
solitary Virgin, and they place her in the ancient line of Mediterranean
goddess-figures.

⸻❦⸻

58   It is with reluctance that Jameson moves on from the devotional representations of the Madonna in the first part of *Legends of the Madonna* to the historical subjects, those drawn from the Gospel stories and legends about
her life (*Madonna*, 133–34). One reason for Jameson's comparative lack of
enthusiasm seems to be that the historical paintings are generally not by
her favorite "old Italians" but by late-sixteenth-century and seventeenth-
century artists—Titian, Tintoretto, Correggio, Poussin, Rubens, Vandyck,
Rembrandt—whom she sometimes discerningly praises but more often
criticizes as coarse, violent, showy, materialistic, and lacking in religious
feeling.[8] But a more important reason is that Jameson clearly prefers the
devotional images of "the sovereign lady of Christendom" to the historical
representations of Mary as "mere woman" (133–34; contra Johnston,
204–5). It is also the case that Mary is no longer the primary focus of the
historical paintings, which instead depict *events* in which she, usually Jesus,
and others are involved (e.g., the marriage at Cana). Jameson consequently
must spend less time contemplating and praising Mary and more time explaining the legends and the theological points behind the paintings (e.g.,
the nativity of the Virgin, the death of Joseph), many of which would be
unfamiliar to her Protestant and Bible-centered readers.

But the "mere woman" is a useful figure nonetheless. Jameson argues
that our humanity is reflected in the earthly Mary of the Gospels and legends: our maternal experiences are made sacred by her loving gaze at her
first-born son, our losses are solaced by her grief over the death of her husband and child, and our work is given value when Jesus' mother is shown
cooking, spinning, sewing, and washing the holy family's clothes.[9] Mary
also has an important function in Jameson's social commentaries on the
condition of women and children—for example, their victimization by
men. Jameson says of the Magi:

> They had come, perhaps, from some far-distant savage land, or
> from some nation calling itself civilised, where innocence had
> never been accounted sacred, where society had as yet taken no
> heed of the defenceless woman, no care for the helpless child;
> where the one was enslaved, and the other perverted: and here,
> under the form of womanhood and childhood, they were called
> upon to worship the promise of that brighter future, when peace
> should inherit the earth, and righteousness prevail over deceit,
> and gentleness with wisdom reign for ever and ever! (212)

The nations purporting to be civilized are here the ancient pagan East, but could also include the American South, in this book written by an anti-slavery sympathizer, or the England of the factory slaves, some just children, or Jameson's mother-country Ireland, suffering from famine and political oppression and so often on her mind (see "Woman's Mission," 196–207; Clara Thomas, 183–86). The author later, in her discussion of the outpouring of the Holy Spirit at Pentecost, argues that as this divine and empowering gift descended upon both men and women, the sexes are equally called upon to do the Lord's work of loving, serving, acting, and suffering (*Madonna*, 304; similarly, S. Grimké, *Letters*, 89–92).

Jameson, then, is generally calmly approving rather than enthusiastic in her analyses of the humanized mother of Jesus. But her commentaries on the various biblical and legendary images strengthen the links she establishes between Mary and ordinary women. In the devotional section, the Madonna is a divinized representative of womankind. In the historical section, she experiences all women's earthly joys and sorrows. Both linkages have political resonances and feminist implications.

It could be said—indeed, the art historian Adele Holcomb has said—that Jameson is merely *describing* the religious art of the Middle Ages and Renaissance, without indicating her own artistic preferences or religious views ("Sacred Art," 111). But internal evidence from *Legends of the Madonna* and other volumes of *Sacred and Legendary Art* calls this interpretation into question. Jameson carefully selects *powerful* representations of Mary to discuss in *Madonna*, and her approach to religious subjects and paintings is often far from neutral. Jameson is quite ready to criticize even the greatest of painters and paintings—for example, Rubens for his "daring bad taste" in a Last Judgment, and Michelangelo for his degraded Christology (*Madonna*, 29). She also singles out works for praise on both artistic and religious grounds—the Transfiguration of Raphael, for example, the often-criticized but, to her mind, the only gloriously successful representation of this most difficult subject (*History of Our Lord*, 1:341–46). Jameson, moreover, does not distance herself or her readers from the Marian representations she describes by citing Protestant doctrinal differences. For example, she says that the various titles given to Mary (such as Our Lady of Mercy, Refuge of Sinners, Our Lady of Wisdom, Our Lady of the Rosary) express the wants and sorrows of "poor suffering humanity" or the "divine attributes from which they hope to find aid and consolation" (*Madonna*, lxiv–v).

60   She does not note that "humanity" here includes very few Protestants, who are usually taught to abhor such names and claims for Mary.[10] Jameson's reluctance to articulate Protestant doctrinal positions in *Madonna* is significant, because it implies that the Madonna in her full historical development—the physical and moral and theological type—is a figure all can accept. This point is reinforced by the verses of English poets (Wordsworth, Shelley, and Browning), which Jameson cites as addressed to or evocative of the celestial Virgin Mother worthy of worship (xlii–xliii).

    The arrangement of *Legends of the Madonna* is also evidence that Jameson was not merely describing Marian art but advancing an argument of her own. The organization is primarily artistic and topical: Jameson begins with devotional subjects (the Virgin without the Child, the Virgin with the Child, Votive Images, and so on) and then presents the biblical and legendary scenes of Mary's life, from the Immaculate Conception and the Annunciation to her Assumption into heaven. The discussion only roughly follows the history of Christian doctrine, although doctrinal changes lead to the emergence of new Marian images.[11] Jameson's plan of organization thus means she begins with representations of Mary at her most powerful and independent: "Queen of Heaven, Virgin of Virgins!" She accordingly reinforces the message of the general introduction, that Mary is the goddess of Christianity, powerful, solitary, and divine, rather than just the simple maid of Galilee.

    For a truly Protestant and sectarian approach to religious art, one need only look at *History of Our Lord* (the final volume in the series), which was begun by Jameson and completed after her death by Elizabeth Eastlake.[12] Eastlake imposed on Jameson's materials a chronological organization that reflected the Protestant understanding of providential history (the Fall, the foreshadowings of the Redemption, the Redemption, the Last Judgment).[13] She also made a Protestant discrimination between Holy Scripture, considered the source of inspired information about Jesus, and the apocryphal and legendary sources, which she called far less worthy and reliable.[14] Eastlake went so far as to criticize paintings of the Passion that showed Mary swooning (rather than quietly standing) by the cross "and thus diverting the attention both of the actors in the scene and the spectators of the picture from the one awful object" (*History of Our Lord*, 1:6). The author of *Legends of the Madonna* would hardly have concurred in this reading of the Blessed Virgin's attention-getting behavior and inappropriate centrality to the scene (see *Madonna*, 284, 289–96).

Eastlake's evaluations of religious art seem ultimately to be based on sectarian rather than aesthetic criteria. Good art, in her view, instructs and edifies believers with materials derivable from Scripture; in other words, it conforms to the doctrines of the Reformation.[15] Jameson, in contrast, thought that historians' and critics' sympathy with earlier minds should guide their evaluations of art, and even though her preferences in art were often similar to Eastlake's, she provided aesthetic rather than primarily theological criteria for her judgments. If Eastlake had been given the same editorial control over *Legends of the Madonna* that she exercised over *History of Our Lord*, the book would have been organized around the New Testament account of the life of Mary, and Nativity scenes no doubt would have predominated. The Queen of Heaven would not have been allowed to be the type that informs the whole.

Jameson's high claims for Mary, found throughout the four volumes of *Sacred and Legendary Art*, are integrally related to her feminist and religious understanding of the essential equality of men and women. An appropriate starting point for an examination of these views is an 1847 "credo" that appears several times in her writings and contains ideas reiterated throughout her work. Here Jameson states her fundamental belief: that God created man and woman equal in reason, in freedom, in their responsibility to develop their God-given capacities, and in their immortal destiny.[16] There is no difference in the virtues and vices of the sexes—"whatever is morally wrong, is equally wrong in men and in women and no virtue is to be cultivated in one sex that is not equally required by the other"—nor in their marital responsibilities of "mutual truth," fidelity to the sacred vow, "self-controul," and "purity of heart" (Jameson, *Letters*, 233–34). Like Margaret Fuller and George Eliot, Jameson does, however, see certain essential differences in men's and women's "endowments," specifying the "maternal organisation" common to all women, whether or not they are mothers. In her view, women's "sacred province" is consequently the home, while men administer the affairs of the larger community (234).

This statement of beliefs is significant, first, for its form, the credo. Although much of Jameson's work deals with Christian doctrine as represented in art, she nowhere in her public or private writings discusses at length the creeds of the Church and only once states her own agreement or disagreement with them (*SLA*, 1:339). Instead, she writes her own creed, showing which belief is most important to her: male-female equality. Yet

62   Jameson bases her claims on the highest religious authorities: the creation order of God as described in Genesis, "the Gospel of Christ," "the eternal law of justice," and natural law (Jameson, *Letters*, 233–34). Like her predecessor Mary Wollstonecraft and her contemporaries Sarah and Angelina Grimké and Margaret Fuller, Jameson makes her starting point the sameness of men and women as "souls" or "moral natures," in order to demonstrate that her feminist beliefs are not contradictory to but founded on religious beliefs, specifically those of Christianity. And like her younger friend, the women's-rights activist Barbara Leigh Smith Bodichon, Jameson utilizes the traditional form of the credo to give her statements religious authority and power.[17]

     Jameson's reference in her creed to women's domestic role—"the ordering of domestic life is our sacred province indissolubly linked with the privileges, pleasures, and duties of maternity"—may seem to twentieth-century feminists to be a troubling slip into "True Woman" mode (Jameson, *Letters*, 234). But one must remember that for Jameson, as for many single or separated women of her day, home was a *privilege*. She left the house her husband Robert Jameson built for her in Toronto because of the impossibility of living in Canada—to her, the North Pole—or of sharing the place with him. For years she maintained a tiny "nest" for her invalid father, her mother, and her unmarried sisters only by writing and traveling incessantly, gathering material for her books. Moreover, Jameson's compressed statement about women's domestic responsibilities is developed and clarified in her essays on women's work, written about the same time as her statement of beliefs. For instance, in "'Woman's Mission,' and Woman's Position" (1846), Jameson points out the contradiction between the "assumed condition" of women—that they are all happy in their domestic sphere—and the real conditions of working women's lives. After describing the value of the domestic work women do, she notes the cost to working-class families of the loss of home. When a wife and mother is turned into a wage slave, she often lacks the energy after her hard day's labor, or the skills ordinarily learned in girlhood, to make the family's lodging a safe, clean, and welcoming place, where children are nurtured and cherished, and men are "refine[d] and comforte[d]" ("Woman's Mission," 196–207). Jameson is somewhat patronizing in her middle-class expectations of working-class women, but she does offer perhaps compensatory sympathy for the working women who, then as now, struggled under the double burden of paid work and housework. Jameson insists that working-class as well as middle-class women take jobs only out of necessity, to support themselves and feed their families. They are impeded by the reluctance of men to open more positions to them, to pay them adequately, and to allow them appropriate training. One of Jameson's examples is male opposition to a female School of Design recently opened by the government at Somerset House:

> The first expression of opinion which this just and benevolent project elicited, was a petition drawn up by the artists employed in wood engraving, praying that the women might not be taught, at the expense of the government, arts which would "interfere with the employment of men, and take the bread out of their mouths"; and further "tempt the women to forego those household employments more befitting their sex." (No petitions were presented on the part of men against young women let out in gangs to break stones and dig potatoes.) (221–22)

Jameson concludes that men should either live up to their rhetoric about "woman's sphere" and protect and fully provide for women, or else "play fair" and get out of the way (223–24; see also Johnston, 208–14).

In *Sisters of Charity and the Communion of Labor,* two lectures that Jameson delivered and then published in the mid-1850s, she more positively emphasizes the common obligation of men and women to *work* and to contribute to the welfare of the community, and she uses this obligation (which, like the earlier creed, draws on the "creation order" of Genesis 1–3) to authorize new roles for women (*Sisters of Charity,* 26–31). A comparison of Jameson's *Sisters of Charity* and Ruskin's famous lecture "Of Queens' Gardens" (1865), which may very well depend without acknowledgment on the earlier work,[18] will make clear the differences between Jameson's position and an antifeminist position. Jameson argues that men and women are by nature "mutually dependent, mutually helpful," and that this "communion" extends to every possible relationship between the sexes:

> Thus, for instance, a man, in the first place, merely sustains and defends his home; then he works to sustain and defend the community or the nation he belongs to: and so of woman; she begins by being the nurse, the teacher, the cherisher of her home, through her greater tenderness and purer moral sentiments; then she uses these qualities and sympathies on a larger scale, to cherish and purify society. (26–29)

64   Ruskin, proceeding from the idea of the complementarity of the sexes, makes much the same argument about man's defensive role, though woman's nurturing role becomes more ornamental:

> Generally, we are under an impression that a man's duties are public, and a woman's private. But this is not altogether so. . . .
>
> Now the man's work for his home is, as has been said, to secure its maintenance, progress, and defence; the woman's to secure its order, comfort, and loveliness.
>
> Expand both these functions. The man's duty as a member of a commonwealth, is to assist in the maintenance, in the advance, in the defence of the state. The woman's duty, as a member of the commonwealth, is to assist in the ordering, in the comforting, and in the beautiful adornment of the state. ("Of Queens' Gardens," 18:136)[19]

Despite these similarities in argument, the distance between Jameson and Ruskin soon becomes apparent. Jameson, as indicated by her creed, thinks men and women are equal in reason, in freedom, in talent, and in moral responsibility. In contrast, Ruskin's stated belief in complementarity ("Each [sex] has what the other has not: each completes the other") turns out to be doublespeak. As a number of feminist critics have noted,[20] when he divides up human qualities between the sexes, he offers an affirmation of male superiority and male privilege:

> The man's power is active, progressive, defensive. He is eminently the doer, the creator, the discoverer, the defender. His intellect is for speculation and invention; his energy for adventure, for war, and for conquest, wherever war is just, wherever conquest necessary. But the woman's power is for rule, not for battle,—and her intellect is not for invention or creation, but for sweet ordering, arrangement, and decision. She sees the qualities of things, their claims, and their places. Her great function is Praise [of the man, no doubt!]. (18:121–22)

If man acts, discovers, speculates, and creates, what worthwhile portion of the world's work is left for woman?

"Communion" and "complementarity"—or perhaps more accurately, "complimentarity"—have practical consequences for the two writers. Jameson demands the public recognition of "the woman's privilege to share in the communion of labor at her own free choice, and the foundation of institutions which shall train her to do her work well" (*Sisters of Charity*, 32). Women have the energy, intelligence, and natural capabilities to work alongside men in improving their society; it is the cowardice and short-sightedness of legislators that has prevented them (30–32). Ruskin, however, thinks men need assistants, not partners, and proposes training young women accordingly: "[A] man ought to know any language or science he learns, thoroughly—while a woman ought to know the same language, or science, only so far as may enable her to sympathise in her husband's pleasures, and in those of his best friends" ("Of Queens' Gardens," 18:128). The only freedom a young woman needs is to be turned loose in the library, "as you do a fawn in a field," so that she may nibble at the great books, but surely not swallow them whole (18:130–31). This kind of "toy-box" education for girls (in George Eliot's phrase)—superficial, unsystematic, unsynthesized, and easily forgotten—is, as Wollstonecraft, Fuller, Eliot, Florence Nightingale, and many other nineteenth-century women writers pointed out, the best way to ensure that girls do not grow up to rival boys as the doers, creators, discoverers, and inventors. Although Ruskin begins his lecture with confident definitions of female traits and bases on them his proposals for female education and adult roles, he claims here that girls grow up mysteriously and naturally, like other subhuman creatures—a fawn, a delicate flower. Female education therefore need not foster self-development; it should instead encourage selflessness. Such arguments, Florence Nightingale says bitterly in her essay *Cassandra*, show the slight value accorded the female self (30–43).

The main difference between Jameson's feminist position and Ruskin's antifeminist position is her assertion of male-female equality in the areas that really matter: reason and strength of character; social rights and responsibilities; the right to education and employment; and legal protections, especially of women's property. The midcentury campaigns for married women's property rights by British and American feminists show their concern to improve the domestic position of their sex even as they pushed for increased opportunities in the areas of education and employment.[21] For Jameson, as for other nineteenth-century feminists, the household is not the border for woman's ambition, as it ultimately is with Ruskin, but first base.[22]

66 Jameson's feminism informs and reinforces her Mariology in several significant ways. In her texts on the Woman Question she calls attention to the
importance of woman's maternal role, and in her art histories she admires
representations of the *Mater Amabilis*, who is shown not as a goddess but
simply as the loving earthly mother of the Redeemer. Like many young
mothers, Mary is preoccupied with her first-born child, caressing him,
gazing fondly on him, hanging in adoration over his cradle (*Madonna*,
114–15, 200). But woman's contributions to the "communion of labor"
must not be limited to her at-home services as a wife and mother, Jameson
says (*Sisters of Charity*, 26–29). And accordingly, Mary's "maternal character"
is sometimes set aside, and she appears in other roles—which have obvious though unstated relevance for nineteenth-century women. She is "poetess and prophetess." She is shown with a book as the *Virgo Sapientissima*,
"the Most Wise Virgin." She represents perfect purity, notably as the Immaculate Conception. And she exercises spiritual power as the "empress of
heaven" (*Madonna*, xxxvi, xli, 69–70, 134; Holcomb, "Sacred Art," 114).

Jameson's feminism is also reflected in the inclusiveness of her Mariology. Throughout her well-traveled life she shows a keen interest in the
condition of women of different classes and races (though rarely without
arriving at the comfortable conclusion that Englishwomen of her class
are the best off, although their position still needs improvement). For
example, she reports on the benefits of active religious sisterhoods—
especially the Sisters of Charity—for the women involved and the sick and
poor people they help. Like Margaret Fuller later, she analyzes the ways
that contact with European settlers lowered the status of Indian women in
North America.[23] Jameson's art histories place a comparable emphasis on
Mary as a symbol not just of Woman but of women in all their diversity.
She notes the ethnic variations in Marian portraiture—there are Madonnas with the features of Greek, Florentine, Milanese, Venetian, Spanish,
and Flemish women—and she adds, "I never looked round me in a room-
ful of German girls without thinking of Albert Durer's Virgins" (*Madonna*,
xxxviii). Jameson's taste is not for representations of Mary with peasant
features (see, for example, 115), though she can recognize the power of
the great Northern painters. But in her discussions of historical subjects,
she considers both accurate and moving many of the paintings and legends
that emphasize Mary's humble social status. Mary is shown giving birth in
a "poor stable" or "rough rocky cave," and she is serenaded, in paintings
from the Campagna and Calabria, by piping shepherds with sheepskin

jackets and ragged hats (200, 209). During her flight into Egypt, a refugee from political violence, Mary greets a gipsy fortuneteller as "Sister" (242–45). As the wife of a carpenter and housebuilder who trains their son in his craft, Mary is appropriately shown with her own tools, the work basket and distaff. She is not only the symbol of female industry but also a figure with whom the "poor artisan" can identify (177–78, 193, 267–69).

Jameson also insists on a Madonna who ages. Criticizing the inappropriate youthfulness that sometimes afflicts Marian images—a young sentimental *Mater Dolorosa* whose mourning over her dead Son seems to be what a dead sparrow would elicit—she says Mary should be a young woman from fifteen to seventeen in the subjects preceding her return from Egypt, but "a matron between forty and fifty, . . . still of a sweet and gracious aspect," during her Son's ministry and Passion (1). And on the authority of "all the most ancient effigies" in the catacombs and early mosaics, Jameson indicates that the Virgin after the Resurrection should be shown alone as "a majestic woman of mature age"—much like the author herself, a stout woman in her late fifties at the time she wrote *Legends of the Madonna.* Such expressions from a woman who was early separated from her husband and never had children of her own cannot be considered dispassionate scholarship, but are consistent with the author's feminism. The Madonna should represent all women (single, widowed, grieving, glorified in old age) and not just the Victorian ideal of that "'holiest thing alive,'" a young mother adoring her baby 115).

Finally, Jameson, on historical in addition to aesthetic grounds, links the status of Mary to the status of ordinary women. Jameson's preference for the "chaste and sacred" Madonnas of the Middle Ages, which she considers reverently drawn and conducive to worship, over the more skillfully drawn but often sensual and secular Madonnas of the Renaissance is typical of Romantic taste.[24] But it is also closely linked to her understanding of the historical condition of women. In her lecture *The Communion of Labor*, she notes that the early and medieval Church adored the Virgin and canonized superior women as saints. In contrast, the misogynistic Reformers "had repudiated angels and saints, but . . . still devoutly believed in devils and witches"; they attributed showings of female superiority not to God but to Satan and burned women at the stake. "All the women who perished by judicial condemnation for heresy in the days of the inquisition," Jameson says, "did not equal the number of women condemned judicially as witches, —hanged, tortured, burned, drowned like mad dogs" (282–83). Jameson's

68   conclusion is that medieval societies, which reverently and appropriately
honored the Madonna, also honored female nature and female accom-
plishments. She often associates the Renaissance (in its Catholic and classical as well as Protestant aspects) with images of women that are
"secularised, materialised, and shockingly degraded," not to mention
deadly (*Madonna*, 165–66; see also xxx–xxxv; 183–84).

This Victorian art critic, by reevaluating European history from the
perspective of women, is an important feminist precursor of modern historians such as Joan Kelly, Margaret King, and Merry Wiesner. King, like
Jameson, argues that the conventual life of celibacy and productive work
"offered the greatest scope for autonomy and dignity to the women of
Christian Europe" during the Middle Ages and early Renaissance, though
she adds that this life was available only to the privileged. King also shows
that devotion to the Virgin and female saints increased along with the
power of female religious leaders until the eve of the Reformation. Wiesner in her study of witchcraft in the sixteenth and seventeenth centuries
contends that women accused of witchcraft were treated much more
harshly in the Protestant North than under the Roman and Spanish Inqui-
sitions, which rarely burned witches. Wiesner's explanation parallels Jameson's argument about the Reformation: in the North, accused witches were
punished for who they were rather than for what they did, and therefore
"witch" was an ontological category attached to the category of "woman."[25]

Jameson's highest claim for Mary is that the Mother, as the representative of woman, is equal to the Son, the representative of man. Jameson
as a feminist writer generally emphasizes the sameness of the sexes, but she
does posit some enduring differences, and it is this essentialist emphasis on
difference that enables her to make her most radical statements about the
Virgin Mother.

At the start of *Legends of the Madonna*, Jameson explains the history of
Marian thought in this way:

> With Christianity came the want of a new type of womanly
> perfection, combining all the attributes of the ancient female di-
> vinities with others altogether new. Christ, as the model man,
> united the virtues of the two sexes, till the idea that there are es-
> sentially masculine and feminine virtues intruded itself on the
> higher Christian conception, and seems to have necessitated the
> female type. (xx)

Jameson here claims that Christian thought began with sameness: since virtues and vices were considered the same for men and women, Christ served as the model of moral perfection for both sexes. But in time Christians began to want a female divinity, because they desired a successor to the mother-goddesses of the ancient world, and because they began to believe that men and women have different virtues and therefore need different moral representatives, that is, Jesus and Mary. Jameson, as shown earlier, disagrees with this idea and considers it a step down from the "higher Christian conception" of moral sameness. Nonetheless, she presents difference as the initial reason for the emergence of Mary in Christianity. What happened next, according to Jameson, is that as Christian ideas about Jesus began to develop, Mary was raised with him: she became the *Theotokos*, the Queen of Heaven, and so on. Sameness again became predominant—Mary and Jesus must have the same status, similar powers— and sameness makes the Mother and Son equals or near-equals. Jameson does, however, note some enduring measure of complementarity or difference: for example, when in the Middle Ages Jesus was characterized as the avenging judge, Mary became the Mother of Mercy, interceding with him on behalf of sinners (*Madonna*, 27).

This, then, is Jameson's historical argument about the development of Mariology. Her own views of Mary, as presented in her *Commonplace Book* (5, 77–78, 83), are strikingly parallel.[26] Jameson again begins with sameness—that is, with claims that the virtues and vices of the two sexes, and the moral standards, are the same. Jesus is the moral exemplar for both men and women, and individual characters approximate perfection as they approach his (77–78). Yet Jameson also admits difference into this argument. She says the two sexes do not differ in the "quality" of their virtues and vices, but in "the modification of the quality" (77–78). An example might be gentleness and affectionateness. Jameson thinks that these qualities should be considered human virtues, not just feminine ones (78). Yet elsewhere she argues for woman's essential maternal role as the cherisher, nourisher, teacher, and refiner of her family and household ("Woman's Mission," 196–97; *Sisters of Charity*, 26–29). One might conclude that gentleness and affectionateness are virtues for both sexes but are appropriately more dominant in woman than in man because of her maternal role.[27]

By extending this argument about difference, Jameson posits a role for Mary:

> It might seem, that where we reject the distinction be-
> tween masculine and feminine virtue, one and the same type of

perfection should suffice for the two sexes; yet it is clear that *the moment we come to consider the personality, the same type will not suffice*: and it is worth consideration that when we place before us the highest type of manhood, as exemplified in Christ, we do not imagine him as the father, but as the son; and if we think of the most perfect type of womanhood, we never can exclude the mother. (*Commonplace Book*, 83, emphasis added)

"Personality" here seems to mean "person-ness" or "individual nature" (i.e., the qualities that make up one person; the individuating traits of a human being plus the traits he or she shares with other members of the same sex). Woman's maternal personality (her psychical and physical capacity for motherhood) means her model for perfection cannot be Jesus, but must be a woman, specifically a mother. And who but Mary is Jameson's "most perfect type of womanhood"? Reinforcement for this reading is Jameson's claim (common in the nineteenth century) that "the highest type of manhood" is Jesus, in his role as Son (83).

Jameson's emphasis on the Son rather than the Father as the perfect type of manhood allows two inferences. First, a son presumably resembles his mother, physically as well as psychologically, and is guided by her. And as Jameson points out, Mary's son must have borne the likeness of his mother, his only human parent (*Madonna*, xl–xli; Elizabeth Cady Stanton also makes this point). Thus even though in the history of doctrine Christology defines Mariology (the doctrinal characterization of Jesus determines that of Mary), Jameson suggests that in the Holy Family the Mother has certain kinds of priority, bearing and caring for a Son in *her* image. The second inference is that the Son represents perfect manhood because in him the masculine capacity for violence is not fully developed, as it is in the Father (who is a warlike figure in many Old Testament accounts). Support for this interpretation is Jameson's close association of Christianity and the feminine character with peace, the secular power and masculinity with violence. She writes in *Legends of the Madonna*, for example:

[Some say ideas represented by earlier goddesses] which were afterwards gathered into the pure, dignified, tender image of the Madonna, were but as the voice of a mighty prophecy, sounded through all the generations of men, even from the beginning of time, of the coming moral regeneration, and complete and harmonious development of the whole human race, by the estab-

lishment, on a higher basis, of what has been called the "feminine element" in society. And let me at least speak for myself. In
the perpetual iteration of that beautiful image of THE WOMAN
highly blessed—*there*, where others saw only pictures or statues, I
have seen this great hope standing like a spirit beside the visible
form: in the fervent worship once universally given to that gracious presence, I have beheld an acknowledgment of a higher as
well as gentler power than that of the strong hand and the
might that makes the right,—and in every earnest votary, one
who, as he knelt, was in this sense pious beyond the reach of his
own thought, and "devout beyond the meaning of his
will."(xix)[28]

In this quotation, the phrase "a higher as well as gentler power than that
of the strong hand and the might that makes the right" seems to refer to
the power of women ("the feminine element in society"), as represented by
Mary, and also to the power of Christianity. Both these forces for good can
transform a world where a "masculine element" is evidently responsible for
the domination of the violent and the strong. This radical feminist statement has the untenable consequence of making only men responsible for
the world's oppression and violence. But it does contain a remarkable assertion of women's social and religious role: the spirit of Christianity is best
represented by the feminine form of the Virgin Mother, the Queen of
Peace, who gave her likeness to the Prince of Peace, and women rather
than men will bring about the "moral regeneration" of the race. The critic
Marina Warner describes Western paintings in which the serpent in the
garden has Eve's features (58–59). Now the Savior is remade in the image
of his Mother. But the remaining question, for feminist Protestants like
Jameson, is whether the spiritual power of this Queen can be recognized
within their own religious traditions.

Representing Mary within the
Edifice of Anglicanism

CHAPTER THREE

Although Jameson's credo and her comments on the relationship of the Virgin Mother and the Son help us analyze the connections between her feminism and her treatment of Marian art, a full reconstruction of the author's religious views is difficult, because she—perhaps deliberately—left no extended statement of them. That impedes scholarly efforts to relate her Mariology to her own Anglican tradition. Jameson has no lengthy essays on religion comparable to those on women's issues. Instead, the main sources are her *Commonplace Book,* her letters, which are usually affectionate notes to friends and family members rather than (like much of Fuller's and Eliot's correspondence) essays in epistolary form; her travel writings, which contain some relevant material; and most importantly, the series *Sacred and Legendary Art.* Jameson frequently gave her own religious opinions in this series, but her aim was to avoid rather than to provoke religious controversy, in part because of her concern for sales[1] and her respect for the beliefs of others. The general introduction to *Legends of the Madonna* provides valuable insights into Jameson's Mariology, but her Christology is harder to reconstruct; she died before she could complete *History of Our Lord,* and though she had written most of the New Testament section, the important general introduction is by Lady Eastlake.

The difficulties a Victorian woman writer faced in claiming authority complicated Jameson's treatment of religious subjects. Gerardine Bates Macpherson recorded her aunt's

dignified enjoyment of the social homage that her work won for her (242). 73
Yet in the first volume of *Sacred and Legendary Art*, Jameson claimed to be un-
learned and unambitious, producing books only for her own pleasure. She
even posed as a child-guide to the "Eden" of art, who runs back and forth
to encourage her playfellows to come and see (1:vii, 38). She is a good example of a female intellectual who played down her expertise largely to
satisfy the expectations of the critics.[2]

Despite Jameson's reluctance to claim authority and the sometimes
frustrating nature of the sources, a fairly complete reconstruction of her religious views is indeed possible, for four reasons. First, Jameson throughout her writings emphasized certain religious beliefs and values, such as
religious tolerance, individual freedom, and nonviolence, as fundamental
and essential. Second, although she tried to avoid theological controversies in *Sacred and Legendary Art*, her writing was never impersonal.[3] In the art
histories as well as in the letters, travel journals, and *Commonplace Book*, one
frequently finds the "I," the personal reaction, the evaluation based on the
author's own articulated religious and artistic standards. Such evaluations
are particularly noticeable in Jameson's *Commonplace Book*, a collection of
statements on religion and other topics that she found sympathetic or an-
tagonistic and which "became a part of the individual mind" (preface, 3–5).
Third, Jameson noted that her *Commonplace Book* contained the material left
over from "the volumes on Shakespeare's Women, on Sacred and Legendary Art, and various other productions" (preface, 4). Thus the observa-
tions in the *Commonplace Book* are a vital addition to the often more cautious
statements on religion made in the art histories, and, in fact, her writings
on religion, art, travel, and current social issues form a continuous argument. Finally, as Jameson appropriated the religious form of the credo to
state her fundamental feminist beliefs about men and women, so in turn
she used the key terms of her feminism—sameness and difference—in her
most extensive statements about religion, particularly in her *Commonplace
Book*. Jameson's feminist and religious beliefs do not merely reinforce each
other but are at a fundamental level identical. This creativity and independence of thought become clear as she prepares a place for feminism
and for Mary within the edifice of Anglicanism.

Jameson stated her religious identity as Protestant and Anglican.[4] She
positioned herself as a religious moderate, criticizing both fanatics (the
vindictive Milton, the Reformers, and "ultra-religionists and puseyites")

74 and freethinkers (specifically including Harriet Martineau and George Eliot).[5] Yet while this may sound like the *via media* and latitudinarianism of the Church of England, Anglicanism was only one strand in Jameson's religious thought. She did not challenge Anglican orthodoxy (contra Adele Holcomb's view), but it was not the summation of her religious beliefs.

Jameson's theological balancing act is visible in many of her statements. For instance, she was highly critical of "the Voltairian creed, or No-creed" offered as an alternative to Christianity (Jameson, *Letters*, 175), yet she, like a number of her contemporaries, considered the Athanasian creed "a stumbling-block in Christendom" (*SLA*, 1:339). Overall, she indicated belief in the central Christian doctrines. For example, she called the crucifix an emblem of *"our* faith in a crucified Saviour" (*Madonna*, 37, emphasis added), and she used orthodox titles for Jesus: "our Lord," "our Saviour," "the Redeemer" (*History of Our Lord*, 1:335, 339). Gerardine Bates Macpherson, who worked closely with her aunt on the art histories, referred to the last volume, *History of Our Lord*, as "the crown of the undertaking" and noted Jameson's "devotional admiration of the Divine excellence" of Christ (Macpherson, 305–6).

Jameson showed a typical Anglican caution (or perhaps ambivalence) in many of her statements regarding Mary's position in Christianity, if not in her reactions to Marian images. For example, she warned against worshipping Mary, "the first of all created beings," as though she were the Creator (*Madonna*, xviii, xl). It is unlikely that Jameson accepted literally the doctrines of Mary's Immaculate Conception or heavenly queenship. Yet, evidently to make the Virgin less foreign to her Protestant readers, she showed the rootedness of these beliefs in the first six centuries of the Church, the "common ground" of East and West, and Catholics and Protestants (Moorman, 70–79, 102–11). Similarly, while Jameson celebrated representations of Mary as the heavenly intercessor, she did not herself express any belief in the intercessory powers of the Virgin and the Saints. Here she was in accord with the Anglican Thirty-Nine Articles and the Book of Common Prayer, which proscribe the "invocation of the Saints." In her work, as in the prayerbook, the saints are treated only as emblems or examples for believers.[6] For example, Jameson admired St. Sebastian as a figure combining youthful beauty with the inspired faith and enthusiasm of the martyr, and she called Mary Magdalene the representative of the penitent and forgiven sinner, particularly the fallen woman. In her stress on forgiveness, Jameson differs from many of her contemporaries, who saw a Magdalene's sexual fall from virtue as irrevocable (*SLA*, 2:415, 421; 1:343–44, 393–94; see also Johnston, 180–207).

Jameson, then, was an Anglican whose measured statements, particularly in the series *Sacred and Legendary Art*, seem not to have departed from orthodoxy. Yet the above description is not a sufficient explanation of what she believed. In particular, it does not explain her enthusiastic and even worshipful responses to religious art that reflects the highest mariological beliefs—responses common to Fuller and Eliot as well. Jameson's autobiographical account "A Revelation of Childhood," found in her *Commonplace Book* (104–31), provides a key to her reaction. As a child, Jameson says, she thought Jesus came down to tell people stories and make them good; this belief in the power of narrative, rather than doctrines, which she often misunderstood, was the basis of her juvenile religion (126–29). While Jameson as an adult writer proved herself capable of theological explanation, what persists in her work is her emphasis on the crucial religious function of narrative (specifically, the biblical stories and legends visually represented in sacred art). Words and pictures that tell a story and the individual's reaction to them are the original basis of religion, in Jameson's version of Christian history and in her own life. The religious aesthetic she developed, which was based on her responses to the legends and images of art, enabled her to appropriate Mary in ways not stipulated by, but in her view not in violation of, Anglican doctrine.

In her *Commonplace Book* Jameson defined religion as "the comprehension and acknowledgment of an unseen spiritual power and the soul's allegiance to it" (57). Christianity (in her Unitarian-sounding phrase) is "the comprehension and appreciation of the personal character of Christ, and the heart's allegiance to that" (57). The first definition, of religion, stresses the difference and distance between God and human beings, while the definition of Christianity emphasizes likeness and nearness: Christianity is the cult of a being with a "character," a lovable and perfect *man* (57, 83). The dual emphasis is characteristic of Jameson, who saw religion—her example almost always was Christianity—as a collaborative project: the spirit of Christianity is from God, and the response and forms are from human beings.[7] Human beings respond differently to the spirit of Christianity in different times and places (hence the rise and decline of monasticism in western Europe). In particular, the *forms* of human response—liturgies, images, even doctrines—vary. One example she cites is historic changes in

76   the representation of Mary, such as the new and widespread practice in thirteenth-century Europe of painting her with an expressive face sympathetically responding to the worshipper (*Madonna*, xxv). Another example is the doctrine of the Immaculate Conception (the sinless state of Mary from the moment of her own conception), which Jameson traced back to the fifth-century Nestorian controversy. Christians felt that Mary, recently proclaimed as the Mother of God, must herself be an inviolate "temple" fit for God to dwell in. Jameson commented, "Such was the reasoning of our forefathers; and, the premises granted, who shall call it illogical or irreverent?" (43). She thus indicated her sympathy with these early Christians, if probably not her acceptance of the doctrine, soon (1854) to become Catholic dogma. Jameson's understanding of religion as collaboration further informs her use of the terms "divine" and "holy" to designate either qualities attributed to God or the gods, or qualities seen as worthy of worship. The sacred in her work becomes primarily a human category of perception (see, for example, 57–58).

Concern with forms was common in the nineteenth century, a period of religious renewal. It is found, for example, in the writings of Mary Howitt, Ralph Waldo Emerson, and Margaret Fuller, who criticized the practices of their Quaker or Unitarian backgrounds. Yet Jameson was no iconoclast, either literally or metaphorically. In her view, forms are necessary in order for religion to express "'the invisible grace and majesty of spiritual truth,'" to reach human sympathies, and to have a social influence (*Commonplace Book*, 147; similarly 148–51). Contrary to the English Puritans and many religious liberals of her own day, she saw the forms of the past as an invaluable inheritance: "All reaction is destructive—all progress conservative. When we have destroyed that which the past built up, what reward have we?—we are forced to fall back, and have to begin anew" (*Commonplace Book*, 37, 39; similarly *SLA*, 1:6). But she felt that beliefs could become superstitions, and forms empty or idolatrous relics; this, too, was the emphasis of Howitt and Fuller. Jameson's criteria for such distinctions seem to have been her own religious values, many of which were also bourgeois liberal values: religious tolerance, individual freedom, moderation, nonviolence, and a privileging of the spiritual and transcendent aspects of religion over the material and time-bound.[8] One might criticize Jameson for not readily seeing her own beliefs as time-bound, as not necessarily part of the "spirit" of Christianity but a form of thought the spirit will move beyond. Yet how welcome her religious tolerance and balanced

opinions were, especially during a period of anti-Popery spasms in England.

Jameson's attitude toward forms was, furthermore, part of a carefully
and clearly worked-out religious aesthetic. She defended the uses of art in
worship: "Music, painting, sculpture,—if these are a means of lifting up the
heart to God, it is a proof that He intends us to use such means." For similar reasons, she saw no conflict between cathedral wealth and the Gospel,
calling churches the "patrimonial palace[s]" of both rich and poor ("Some
Thoughts on Art," in Macpherson, 353–54). She was careful, though, to
distinguish good religious art from bad. In her view, good art—her examples
were usually medieval—lifts us from contemplation of the material to the
spiritual; it appeals to our best self, "the best of our faculties and affections," and sometimes allows us to transcend the self altogether and be lost
in the divine: "'We look, and the heart is in heaven!'" (*Madonna*, xviii).

Jameson's aesthetic views, which were influenced by Friedrich
Schlegel and A. F. Rio, prompted her frequent criticisms of Renaissance art.
She observed that the revival of classical learning toward the end of the fifteenth century had positive effects on the "externals" of Christian art, giving it "added dignity and grace, a more free and correct drawing, a truer
feeling for harmony of proportion and all that constitutes elegance"
(*Madonna*, xxxi). But "the craving for mere beauty" became "dangerous" in
this period. Jameson regarded the values of Greek mythology—the worship of beauty, immortality, and power—as antithetical to the values of
Christian mythology, and she consequently deplored its desacralizing effect on the subject matter of religious art (*Madonna*, xxxi; *Commonplace Book*,
147). For this reason she criticized Michelangelo for making the Apostles
in his Last Judgment (1540) resemble Titans holding a council of war, and
she did not spare even her favorite Raphael, calling his St. Paul a Jupiter
Ammon and as such a fashion-following representation that the eye but not
the conscience could approve (*SLA*, 1:180, 225–26). Jameson was particularly appalled by the Renaissance "portrait Madonnas," devotional images
with the beautiful but recognizable features of a particular woman, such as
the painter's wife or the Pope's mistress. Citing Savonarola, martyred for his
protests, she noted that such portraits, confusing carnal with spiritual love,
were a kind of idolatry injurious to the faith of the simple (*Madonna*,
xxxi–xxxii). They could also function as a form of containment: the Virgin,
like Andrea del Sarto's Lucrezia or Robert Browning's "Last Duchess," becomes a woman belonging to and framed by one man. Jameson's arguments

78   prepared the way for Eliot's work: Savonarola is an important character in
      Romola, and portrait Madonnas are connected with issues of male control
      in this novel and *Middlemarch*.[9]

      Jameson's insistence on the contemplative purpose and the legibility
of sacred images[10] led her to identify two groups as the enemies of religious art and artists: the iconoclasts of various periods, and the connoisseurs. The iconoclasts included Emperor Leo III, an "ignorant, merciless
barbarian," who in the eighth century destroyed ancient images of the
Madonna and the saints and also persecuted those devoted to them
(*Madonna*, xxiii). Jameson was particularly caustic in her description of the
Tudors and Puritans who smashed their way through England's monasteries and churches:

> Many of the English Benedictines were, as individual characters,
> so interesting and remarkable, that I wish heartily they had re-
> mained to our time conspicuous as subjects of art. We should
> have found them so, had not the rapacity of Henry VIII and his
> minions, followed afterwards by the blind fanaticism of the Puri-
> tans, swept from the face of our land almost every memorial,
> every effigy of these old ecclesiastical worthies, which was ei-
> ther convertible into money or within reach of the sacrilegious
> hand. . . . When I recall the history of the ecclesiastical poten-
> tates of Italy in the 16th century, I could almost turn Puritan my-
> self: but when I think of all the wondrous and beautiful
> productions of human skill, all the memorials of the great and
> gifted men of old, the humanizers and civilizers of our country,
> which once existed, and of which our great cathedrals—noble
> and glorious as they are even now—are but the remains, it is
> with a very cordial hatred of the profane savage ignorance
> which destroyed and desecrated them. (*Monastic Orders*, 39)

Jameson's anger against the Reformers was not solely directed at their
iconoclasm; as noted earlier, she saw links between their violence against
images of the Madonna and female saints and their violence against
women (*Communion of Labor*, 282–84).

      The second group Jameson identified as enemies of religious art, the
connoisseurs, most notably Sir Joshua Reynolds, ushered in the nineteenth-
century reign of taste. They committed violence as art critics by removing

sacred art from the church to the drawing room or dressing room, where   79
it lost its religious context and became unreadable and religiously null.
Jameson complained:

> That Magdalene, weeping amid her hair, who once spoke com-
> fort to the soul of the fallen sinner,—that Sebastian, arrow-
> pierced, whose upward ardent glance spoke of courage and hope
> to the tyrant-ridden serf,—that poor tortured slave, to whose aid
> St. Mark comes sweeping down from above,—can they speak to
> *us* of nothing save flowing lines and correct drawing and gor-
> geous colour? Must we be told that one is a Titian, the other a
> Guido, the third a Tintoret, before we dare to melt in compas-
> sion or admiration?—or the moment we refer to their ancient re-
> ligious signification and influence, must it be with disdain or
> with pity? (*SLA*, 1:8)

This is not iconoclasm but (to coin a phrase) icono-aphasia: the evaluation
of sacred images forgetful of their religious meanings, their historical context, and the intentions of the artist. Jameson, however, used a much
stronger term: atheism (*Madonna*, lxviii). And with her usual (perhaps Anglican) skill for marking out a middle way (this time between "idolatry" and
godlessness), she defended her approach to religious art as both rational
and reverent. Like Carlyle, who pointed out how unfamiliar "Monk Latin"
was in comparison with Ciceronian Latin (*Past and Present*, 46), Jameson
noted that viewers of the newly popular medieval art needed background
knowledge comparable to that which they brought to classical art (*SLA*,
1:8–10). With her analysis of the way religious art lifted one to contemplation of the divine, she delicately suggested the reintroduction of sacred
images into English individuals' devotions—interpretation of those images
no doubt to be influenced by the progressive religious and feminist beliefs
of *Sacred and Legendary Art*.

As some of the passages cited above imply, Jameson's understanding of
the spirit and forms of Christianity and her religious aesthetic apply specifically to her treatment of Mary in belief and art. In the introduction to *Legends of the Madonna*, for instance, she briefly surveys the history of Marian
representation in order to show the building up of the Church's understanding of Mary. To the Biblical portrait of Mary (the "scriptural type" or
representation) was added the testimony purportedly of eyewitnesses

80   about Mary's physical appearance (the "literal type"). The Church initially emphasized Mary's human perfections (she was "the most perfect moral type of the intellectual, tender, simple, and heroic woman that ever was placed before us for our edification and example"). But from the fifth century the "moral type" began to be transformed into the "theological type," as Mary's part in the scheme of Redemption was elaborated and she was increasingly seen as supernatural and divine. Jameson considered the scriptural + literal + moral + theological type the complete portrait of Mary (*Madonna*, xxxvii–xli).

This could be taken as the impartial view of the art historian. But Jameson acknowledged variation in the types of Madonnas that individuals chose to revere: "Of course we each form to ourselves some notion of what we require; and these requirements will be as diverse as our natures and our habits of thought." And then she unexpectedly admitted her own ideal, realized only once—in Raphael's *Sistine Madonna*: "There she stands— the transfigured woman, at once completely human and completely divine, . . . looking out . . . quite through the universe, to the end and consummation of all things" (xli–xlii; see figure 7). This painting in the art gallery at Dresden caused the Anglican art historian to realize her own emotional need for Mary as *Goddess*, her need to worship woman as divine.

Jameson had aesthetic as well as emotional reasons for wanting a Mary who was divine as well as human. She thought that representations of Mary as either the "mere woman" or the stern embodiment of a dogma were inadequate, because they inspired affection or awe but not both. She also criticized classical statues of Mary that made her a Greco-Roman goddess, perfectly beautiful in face and form, but lacking what Jameson considered her distinctive Christian traits of purity and spiritual loveliness (*Madonna*, xli; *Commonplace Book*, 147, 278–79, 288–91). Jameson insisted that religious art should take us beyond the material to the spiritual; evidently only a glorified Virgin Mother, a Mary who was at once the scriptural, literal, moral, and theological type, would do.

Jameson, finally, had religious grounds for requiring a divinized Madonna, even though such a figure did not accord with Anglicanism. She constructed a sophisticated theory of the relation between visual representation and religious truth. Jameson was especially concerned that good religious art carry Christians beyond the material to the spiritual, so that they did not worship the image itself as an idol. But this idea was complicated by the strong suggestion in her work that the holy personages of the Bible, in particular, Jesus and Mary, are known through representations

Figure 7. Raphael, *The Sistine Madonna* (1513–14). Courtesy of the Gemaldegalerie Alte Meister, Staatliche Kunstsammlungen, Dresden.

82   (i.e., verbal characterizations and visual images). The implication is that Christians do not have direct knowledge of Jesus and Mary as historical persons, but know only others' representations of them. Even the most authoritative representation of Mary, the Lukan "portrait" in the New Testament, is attributed to an *individual* (the Evangelist, whom Jameson only provisionally identified with a painter named Luca), who is said to give us "scattered, artless, unintentional notices of conduct and character," rather than a full and inspired picture of the Virgin (*Madonna*, xxxix–xl). There are also the images and descriptions of the holy personages provided by the early Church, which reflect the *development* of Christian thought (*Madonna*, xl–xlii). Issues of mediation and interpretation are thus raised, which are particularly problematic for a Protestant like Jameson: the representation comes between us and the reality, and we may not be able to tell whether it accurately reflects that reality. Indeed, Jameson here approaches the dangerous territory of D. F. Strauss, who in his *Life of Jesus* (1835–36; trans. G. Eliot 1846) made the radical argument that the Gospels give us the mind of the early Church, not a historically reliable biography of Jesus.[11]

Jameson herself did not directly raise the issue of New Testament reliability. But she had a (typically nineteenth-century) way of dealing with it: an emphasis on the emotional grounds of faith. She showed that religious knowledge comes through representations—the most important being those of the Scriptures. But it also comes more directly. Jameson wrote in two entries in her *Commonplace Book*:

> [P]assions existed before principles; they came into the world with us; principles are superinduced. . . . Good principles derive life, and strength, and warmth from high and good passions; but principles do not give life, they only bind up life into a consistent whole. (46)
>
> Out of the attempt to harmonise our actual life with our aspirations, our experience with our faith, we make poetry,—or, it may be, religion. (26)

In the first observation, Jameson, an able psychologist, suggests that feelings are the vital element not only of principles and doctrines, but also of *religion*—for religion means, literally, a "rule" or a "binding up." The second quotation accords with Jameson's definitions of religion (*Commonplace Book*, 57); she considers the basis of religion to be the human longing for God and the human desire for completion and perfection, which are realized only in the divine. It is notable that she says nothing here about the Scriptures, or doctrines, or priests, or the Church, as necessary paths to the divine. Instead, human longing will lead to knowledge of God—to "the comprehension and acknowledgment of an unseen spiritual power" (57).

God is, however, never fully knowable. Yet instincts and "the aspiration after the high and beautiful" cannot have been given to humankind in vain (Jameson, *Letters*, 154). Jameson accordingly considered religious art important as the expression of human beings' ideas about God and their emotional needs and fears. For example, the representation of Mary as a beneficent intercessor shows the need for a merciful Mother standing between humankind and an offended Father (*Madonna*, xvii, lxiv, 26–28). Jameson's treatment of Christianity as collaboration therefore answers a central question about the "accuracy" of such representations: in her view, they express human responses to the eternal and progressive spirit of Christianity. They can be called true to the Spirit. Jameson also manages to define a Christianity that exists apart from revelation and doctrine: the encounter of the aspiring soul and the eternal spirit. The purity of this encounter is suggested by Jameson's occasional juxtaposition of "religion" and "the Church"; the Spirit is not identical with even the institutions that call Jesus their founder.

Jameson's self-designation as an Anglican, then, is a revealing but not a sufficient explanation of her religious beliefs. Her writings suggest her intellectual acceptance of Anglican teachings on Mary but also reveal the emotional and spiritual longing of this nineteenth-century feminist for a goddess-figure barely glimpsed in Anglicanism. By positing the human longing for the divine as the basis of religion, Jameson legitimized an emotional response to represented beliefs one might not intellectually hold. We make our religion, she says, rather than our religion making us. Feminine images of the divine are an appropriate response to the spirit of Christianity and will lead one to contemplation of God.[12]

This discussion of Jameson's religious aesthetic is not intended to suggest it was *sui generis*. Her love for medieval art was awakened by Romantic figures such as Friedrich Schlegel, and her criticisms of Sir Joshua Reynolds's influence on art and taste had an echo in the Pre-Raphaelites' condemnation of "Sir Sloshua." She shared with contemporaries such as Carlyle, Newman, and Pusey an interest in England's ancient cathedrals and monastic past—an interest that was taking form in stone, in the

84   Gothic Revival structures of A. W. Pugin and other architects. Jameson's general emphasis on the "spirit" rather than the "forms" of religion was widespread in an age that saw the religious revivalism of the Second Great Awakening and the emergence of Unitarianism and Transcendentalism in America, and the reformist impulse of Evangelicalism and the "Second Spring" of the Oxford Movement in Britain. It was a season of religious ferment and discontent, especially among the intellectuals Jameson knew on both sides of the Atlantic.

It would be easy to assume Jameson's indebtedness to her better-known contemporaries, such as Newman, Emerson, Ruskin, and Rossetti. But the publication dates of her work—the first three volumes of *Sacred and Legendary Art* had appeared by 1852—indicate instead that she helped shape the discussions, no doubt aided by conversations with woman friends deeply interested in religion and art, such as Lady Byron and Mary Howitt. (The private conversations of women—who were after all the majority of Victorian churchgoers—may have mattered as much as the publications of men for the religious spirit of the age.) Jameson's originality lay in combining her knowledge of church history and doctrine with her own (and others') insights into religious art, and thus producing an aesthetic that made the art of another age sacred, useful, and responsive to individual and Protestant needs. Jameson's aesthetic, moreover, moved women into prominent positions: a queenly Madonna was reintroduced into the English church by a quietly authoritative art historian.

The "foreign" elements in Jameson's Anglicanism might be explained (in a typical Victorian fashion) by her travels Abroad, particularly to Germany. There are, for example, striking similarities between Jameson's definitions of religion and those of Friedrich Schleiermacher, similarities which suggest that German Romantic theology may well have shaped her views. Schleiermacher was the first theologian to lecture publicly on the life of Jesus, in 1819, and he had a important impact on the development of nineteenth-century Christology (Schweitzer, 62). Subsequent writers on the life of Jesus included William Ellery Channing, D. F. Strauss, and Ludwig Feuerbach, whose work Jameson possibly or definitely knew; their attention to Jesus' personality and character illuminates her treatment of the Mother and Son and her religious aesthetic.

Jameson made at least seven trips to Germany, and as the author of a popular work of Shakespeare criticism, *Characteristics of Women* (1832), she was welcomed into the social circles of the learned and well-born in several German cities (Thomas, 74–81, 92–97). Her lengthy discussion of German life and art in *Visits and Sketches at Home and Abroad* (1834) "opened the breadth of Germany and its yet untrodden ways" to English writers, according to her biographer Gerardine Macpherson.[13] There is no direct evidence that Jameson met Schleiermacher (who died in 1834) or read his work, but she was familiar with others in his circle: the Shakespeare critic Tieck, and the literary critic and religion scholar August Wilhelm Schlegel. She also knew Friedrich Schlegel's work on religion and art.[14] Jameson did, however, make two references in her letters to German biblical scholarship; both pertained to W. R. Greg's *The Creed of Christendom* (1851), which George Eliot (then Marian Evans) reviewed in the *Leader.* In her review, Eliot called Greg's treatment of the New Testament an unoriginal but sound summary of Strauss, Hug, Schleiermacher, and Hennell, and she praised rationalism as represented by Strauss and Hennell. Jameson, in contrast, while pointing out that England was theologically provincial in comparison to "liberal" Germany, was uneasy about the "bold and destructive" tendencies of rationalism. She clearly had more affinity for the earlier Romantic emphasis on feeling, found in the writings of the Schlegels and Schleiermacher.[15]

The similarities between Schleiermacher and Jameson start with their understanding of God as the perfect infinite whole that all long to be part of. Schleiermacher wrote, for instance, that "piety appears as a surrender, a submission to be moved by the Whole that stands over against man."[16] Jameson, as we have seen, considered religion the human desire to be completed and perfected in God (*Commonplace Book,* 57). For both writers, moreover, the apprehension of God involved emotional rather than rational awareness; they stressed *feeling* as the essential ground of religion.[17] Schleiermacher regarded the doctrines, images, and "forms" of religion as secondary and non-binding responses to the primal experience of the divine: "It matters not what conceptions a man adheres to, he can still be pious" (*On Religion,* 93–97). Jameson similarly acknowledged the "endless variety" with which religion fashions itself, focusing primarily on religious art as temporal representations of the spiritual and eternal. She discussed at length the historical development of Christian doctrines, sharing Schleiermacher's horror at efforts, often violent, to coerce belief (*On Religion,* 51, 56). But because she still identified herself with a particular religious establishment and saw Christianity as the highest form of religion (contra *On Religion,* 251), Jameson probably would have rejected Schleiermacher's radically Protestant view that every doctrine is (and should be) subjected to the emotional scrutiny of the individual and rejected if

86   unreflective of that person's revelation of God. It is also important to note that for Jameson, forms (such as religious images) can be reflective of and also conducive to human experiences of the divine, whereas for Schleiermacher, forms seem to be only the reflection, the trace.

Schleiermacher's influence as a theologian extended beyond his redefinition of religion; his lectures on the life of Jesus marked the start of intense nineteenth-century interest in that topic. One of the dominant tendencies of the century's Christologies was a stress on the personality of Jesus. Schleiermacher himself considered Christ's unique God-consciousness more important than "the individuality of his character" (*On Religion*, 246–49); but William Ellery Channing was more typical in reversing the emphasis. Channing (1780–1842), a leader of New England Unitarianism, met Jameson during her visit to Boston in 1837, and she quoted him approvingly in her writings.[18] For Channing, Christ is imitable not because he is God but because he is a truly human savior, the Son and messenger of the Father: "Our great privilege as Christians is that we know the mind and the character of Jesus. . . . [He came] to lay open to us his soul, and thus to regenerate the human soul" (Channing, 371, 385, 994, 995). Channing claimed that Christ can be reliably known through the Gospels (306–9, 988–99). In contrast, D. F. Strauss, in his notorious *Life of Jesus* (1835–36), argued that the Gospels are *not* a reliable biography of Jesus— the historical Jesus is unattainable—but that they do contain the early Church's impression of his remarkable personality. In them we have a mythical portrait from antiquity, if not the man himself (e.g., 86–87, 757). Ludwig Feuerbach denied even the independent existence of the Son or the Father; he claimed that both, rightly seen, are just the divinized qualities of perfect human nature, which man has objectified and considered other than himself, rather than part of himself (*Essence of Christianity*, 1854). Feuerbach presented the Son as the best-loved character in a sacred fiction written by human longing. He has a definite personality—the loving, merciful, self-sacrificing God-man—and "This one personality presses on me the belief in its reality" (145–46). Rather like Pygmalion with Galatea, the early Christians (in Feuerbach's account) fell in love with the personality they had dreamed of and claimed it had come to life.[19] In reaction to Strauss and later Renan (*La Vie de Jésus*, 1865), numerous British authors, particularly after 1860, produced lives of Jesus, which, according to Daniel Pals, were efforts to harmonize an orthodox picture of Jesus with recent biblical scholarship in narratives with a popular appeal.[20]

The studies of Jesus by Schleiermacher, Channing, Strauss, and Feuerbach are a revealing context for Jameson's treatment of Jesus and Mary. Like Strauss, and his translator George Eliot, she recognized the historicized nature of the church's representation of divine personages, but her faith was not shaken because, like Schleiermacher, she saw religious feeling as leading to enduring truth. Whereas Schleiermacher characterized Christ as the divine-human mediator between God and humankind, Jameson began *Legends of the Madonna* by attributing this role to Mary (*Madonna*, xvii–xxi, xlii). Most importantly, Jameson continued and expanded the nineteenth-century emphasis on divine *personality*. As noted earlier, she defined Christianity as the response to the "personal character" of Christ, and she suggested that the essential differences in masculine and feminine "personality" mean Christianity has two divinized models of human perfection, the Son and the Mother (*Commonplace Book*, 57, 77–78, 83; *Madonna*, xx).

At the same time, Jameson worked in original ways with the theological term "personality." The corresponding concept in her discussions of religious art seems to be "portrait"; she responded to religious paintings as *portraits* of divine or holy personages. For example, she said of her favorite *Sistine Madonna*:

> Some of Correggio's and Guido's virgins—the virgin of Murillo at the Leuchtenberg palace—have more beauty, in the common meaning of the word; but every other female face, however lovely, however majestic, would, I am convinced, appear either trite or exaggerated, if brought into immediate comparison with this divine countenance. There is such a blessed calm in every feature! and the eyes, beaming with a kind of internal light, look straight out of the picture—not at you or me—not at any thing belonging to this world,—but through and through the universe. (*Sketches of Art*, 350–51)

Jameson had this reaction to the "portrait" of Christ by Titian, also at Dresden: "—so pure from any trace of passion!—so refined, so intellectual, so benevolent! The only head of Christ I ever entirely approved" (*Sketches of Art*, 358). Jameson's treatment of paintings as portraits suggests a way of dealing with the historical challenges faced by writers of lives of Jesus. There are many portraits, but one person, and since one knows in one's heart the personality of Jesus, one can use this knowledge to evaluate the historically changing representations of him. The idea of portraits is also a way of appropriating religious art unimpeded by doctrinal differences.

88　　One responds not primarily intellectually but emotionally to the divine or holy personality who is represented, for the "portrait" reflects one's own experience of the divine and expresses one's own religious ideas. And for Jameson, as for a number of German Romantics, the art is in turn conducive to new religious experience.[21] One gazes on the image of divine countenance, and it brings one into the presence of God; one might be said to encounter the divine face to face.

Nineteenth-century Christologies provide insight into Eliot's and Fuller's work as well as Jameson's. Fuller reacted to Channing's Christology by pointing out the limitations of the heroic type of Christianity, Jesus. Greek mythology provided her with different conceptions of heroism, and Mariology a female heroic type. Eliot, like Fuller, showed her awareness that both Protestant and higher-critical images of God reflect man but not woman as divine.

In conclusion, both Jameson's Anglicanism and her religious aesthetic suggest the modifying influence of the German Romantic writers she knew, who may have included the theologian Schleiermacher. Her Mariology resembles nineteenth-century Christologies in its emphasis on divine personality, and her reading of religious art as "portrait" is an ingenious way of appropriating such art and making it true to one's own beliefs. The Church of England remained her birthright and her chosen means to God, but she did not make exclusive claims for it. For Jameson (as for Fuller), religion encompasses all the historical churches and cannot be confined to one, as the divine cannot be contained in any symbol. It is possible that for Jameson Anglicanism itself worked the way religious art did: as a system of teachings and images that may sometimes be taken symbolically rather than literally, expressing her own larger understanding of the divine.

The Queen of Heaven and
the Angel in the House

Coventry Patmore gave the name "the Angel in the House" to the domestic Madonna, who is one of the most familiar icons of Victorian womanhood. She appears in the novels of Dickens, Gaskell, and Eliot, the social criticism of Ruskin, and the paintings of Ford Madox Brown. She has been discussed by Virginia Woolf (who wanted to kill her) and more recent literary critics, including Nina Auerbach, Elizabeth Langland, Tricia Lootens, and Alison Booth. Auerbach and Langland argue for the hidden power of the Angel; Langland, for example, links her capacity for sweet ordering and arrangement, as described by Ruskin, to the fearsome power of the Victorian domestic manager.[1] More often, though, critics emphasize the limitations imposed on the Angel or "doll-Madonna" by her deferential sweetness, her ignorance of the world, and the walls of the household.[2] All of these scholars note that the Angel is also called a Madonna, but they seldom explore the relation between these figures and Victorian religious beliefs.[3] Yet Patmore's Angel has strong similarities to John Henry Newman's portraits of the Virgin Mary and John Ruskin's Queen of the Garden—resemblances that are hardly surprising, given the connections among the writers. Newman was probably the most important Mariologist in Victorian Britain and helped start the Anglo-Catholic movement that provided

90   much of Jameson's readership. He was admired by Patmore, who followed him into the Catholic Church. Patmore was in turn a friend of John Ruskin, who used the poet's Angel as the basis of his feminine ideal in "Of Queens' Gardens." Through Newman and Patmore one can see the roots of this domesticated Madonna-figure in Catholic belief, specifically the Mariology of the early Church Fathers. Jameson, however, promoted a different Madonna, with feminist appeal: the powerful Queen of Heaven. She was able to do so because she knew and freely drew on a different mariological tradition, the doctrines and art of the Middle Ages.

Jameson's feminism and what we might call her freethinking or eclectic Anglicanism help explain her high claims for Mary. But Anglo-Catholicism is, interestingly, more of a negative influence, because she early distanced herself from the Oxford Movement. This movement began in July 1833 with John Keble's assize sermon "National Apostasy" and was led in the 1830s and 1840s by Keble, Newman, and E. B. Pusey. Keble was the first of the Tractarians to encourage Anglican reverence for the Virgin Mary. His highly popular cycle of devotional poems, *The Christian Year* (1827), includes "The Annunciation of the Blessed Virgin Mary," in which the Virgin is addressed as "Ave Maria! thou whose name / All but adoring love may claim." "[Such] accents," according to historian Hilda Graef, "had not been heard in the Church of England since the seventeenth century."[4] Yet Mary has a very limited role and presence in *The Christian Year;* feminine attributes are instead given to Jesus, as was common in the nineteenth century.[5]

Keble and Pusey prove less important figures than Newman for a study of English Mariology, first, because Newman's writings on Mary are more extensive and (unlike Pusey's *Eirenicon*) positive rather than negative, and second, because his conversion to Catholicism in 1845 meant that he eventually made greater doctrinal and devotional claims for Mary— her Immaculate Conception, her Assumption into heaven, her role as Intercessor—than any Anglican would have. But he was not as bold as Jameson, who emphasized the equality rather than the inferiority of the Virgin to her Son. Nowhere is the distance between the feminist and the priest shown more clearly than in their contrasting representations of Mary as the Queen of Heaven and as the shy maid of Galilee, the cloistered virgin in the house.

In his five sermons dealing with the Virgin (two written before and the rest after his 1845 conversion), Newman consistently characterizes Mary as possessing certain virtues and prerogatives: humility, faith, obedience, and purity. For example, he notes that although she was mother of the Lord on high, she "did but humbly seek her son in the daily Mass of those, who, though her ministers in heaven, were her superiors in the Church on earth."[6] Newman places greatest emphasis on Mary's purity, a term that encompasses both her sinlessness and her virginity. While an Anglican he held back from preaching the Immaculate Conception,[7] but this doctrine received full articulation in his later, Catholic sermons, where Mary is "the only spotless child of Adam's seed."[8] Newman several times states that Mary has taken a vow of virginity, and it explains her reluctance (recorded in the Bible) to seize the honor offered her by the angel at the Annunciation; she does not initially see how holy maternity—being Mother of God according to the flesh—does not require disobedience ("Our Lady," 97–98; "Fitness," 274). Newman's interpretation of Mary's role in the Incarnation (which follows the Church Fathers) is important in several ways. First, he makes Mary an active rather than a passive participant in the Incarnation: she is blessed as the body that bore Christ, the "tabernacle" where God lay, but even more blessed as the obedient soul full of grace ("Our Lady," 93–99). Her agency links her to the prophets of the Bible and preachers of the Church, whose personal holiness is essential to their sacred offices ("Fitness," 265–67). Second, Newman emphasizes the more imitable aspect of Mary's response—her obedience—over the inimitable—her divine maternity. She is not "alone of all her sex" in her righteousness (though unique in its degree), but a pattern for believers, both male and female. Third, Newman's assigning a lower place to the *physical* honor paid to Mary downplays the unique contribution the female sex makes to salvation in Christian thought, and points to his consistent denigration of the body. The spiritual life is better than the worldly, he says, as the soul is better than the body, and virginity is better than marriage or maternity. Mary's devotion to the virgin state becomes his model of the sanctified life.[9]

Newman's commitment to celibacy seems to have predated his interest in Mary. She became a symbol of beliefs he already held. In a recently reissued collection of his hymns and poems, most written before his 1845 conversion, only one poem (dated 1850) is about Mary, celebrating her as the "Queen of Seasons," while at least six texts (none mentioning the Virgin) praise the ascetic and celibate life. The most interesting of these

92   poems is "The Married and the Single (A Fragment from St. Gregory Nazianzen)," which contrasts the sweaty complacency and worldly joys (wealth, companionship, offspring, good cheer) of married men with the gaunt, grim, God-centered life of a nun-like virgin (who is properly silent, so Newman speaks for her). The description of the "glorious Celibate" (who is so far above sexuality as to be designed by the neuter pronoun "it") leaves little doubt about the superiority of the single state.[10] Newman himself believed in a celibate priesthood even before his conversion to Catholicism, and he felt "sickish" when he learned of his colleague Keble's marriage (which led to Keble's resignation of his Oxford fellowship and removal to a country parsonage).[11] A sexless life seems to have troubled Newman less than the thought of heterosexual intimacy. Newman's thought is not overtly misogynistic on this point, though: in his poems and sermons, he makes both men and women negative models of the married state, and Mary and other female figures positive representatives of the celibate and spiritual life. Yet even though he is aware that the peculiar contribution of the female sex to salvation is the physical parentage of God, he emphasizes the lowness of the idea of salvation by physical means ("Our Lady," 99). He even goes so far as to claim that Mary's "purity is a higher gift than her [maternal] relationship to God" and that "rather than relinquish her virginity, she was willing to lose Him for a Son" ("Glories," 253; "Fitness," 274). Newman thus implies that virginity is more valuable than the Incarnation itself, not least because the Incarnation is a violation of what is fitting for Godhead, requiring God, because of man's fallen state, to descend to earth in weakness rather than in power, and with the divine glory dimmed ("Glories," 259). Such mariological statements articulate a radical asceticism unusual in Victorian England. There is a characteristic (though not original) tension in Newman's thought between his orthodox presentation of Christ's two natures, a doctrine that is safeguarded by Mary's role as *Deipara* (*Theotokos*), the mother of the God-man ("Glories," 249–51; *Letter to Pusey*, 61–67), and his effort, prompted by his anti-materialism, to minimize the importance of the body even in the Incarnation. He seems to extend the Pauline condemnation of the flesh to the body itself: human beings are physical beings, but that is nothing to be proud of or content with.

    Newman's fullest statement of his Mariology is his 1866 *Letter to the Rev. E. B. Pusey*, a reply to his former colleague's critical *Eirenicon*.[12] Following the Church Fathers Justin Martyr, Tertullian, and Irenaeus (second century),

Newman here develops Mary's role as the New Eve. "It was in Adam that we fell," Newman states, because Adam rather than Eve represents the human race. "Though Eve had fallen, still, if Adam had stood, we should not have lost those supernatural privileges, which were bestowed on him as our first father" (*Letter to Pusey*, 31–32). Eve instead has a special role, as "Mother of All Living," and also a special culpability for bringing about sin—she is a "positive, active cause of it." But the three parties of Genesis 3, the man, the woman, and the serpent, meet again, and this time the man, the second Adam, is Christ, and the new Eve is Mary, whose role in the restoration of humankind can be determined from Eve's. Newman sums up the teaching of the three Fathers on this point:

> as Eve forfeited privileges by sin, so Mary earned privileges by the fruits of grace; that, as Eve was disobedient and unbelieving, so Mary was obedient and believing; that, as Eve was a cause of ruin to all, Mary was a cause of salvation to all; that as Eve made room for Adam's fall, so Mary made room for our Lord's reparation of it; and thus . . . as Eve co-operated in effecting a great evil, Mary co-operated in effecting a much greater good. (36)

Newman as a Catholic bases other important Marian doctrines—the *Theotokos*, the Immaculate Conception, Mary's intercessory power in heaven—on her role as the New Eve (46–50).

In his autobiography, *Apologia pro Vita Sua* (1864, 1890), Newman writes that even when he was an adversary of Rome, "I had a true devotion to the Blessed Virgin, in whose college [at Oxford] I lived, whose altar I served, and whose Immaculate Purity I had in one of my earliest printed Sermons made much of" (133). Newman comes to identify with Mary in numerous ways. He is, like her, an avowed virgin, and he feels he resembles her as an exemplar of patience, obedience, and self-surrender ("Fitness," 274; *Letter to Pusey*, 19). He sees Mary, as the mother of the Word, providing a model for theological creativity ("Fitness," 266–67). She is especially important as the exemplar of the sanctified life, a life spent in meditation and prayer apart from the world, in the separate sphere of the holy.[13]

What is notable about Newman's descriptions of Mary—her purity, her self-abnegation, her retired life of pious study and prayer—is that in Victorian England these were considered feminine traits and practices.

94 Newman was thus laying claim to the "separate sphere" of women as a sacred place for both sexes—but particularly for men, who were the almost exclusive focus of his pastoral energies and his writings.[14] Newman, however, ensured that when he and his male followers chose the feminine sphere *in imitatio Mariae*, they did not forfeit the superior power and privileges of their sex. He argued that "woman is inferior to man, as he to Christ," and he commended Mary for making way, "as a creature, a mother, and a woman," for her Son.[15]

Margaret Miles and Caroline Bynum have argued that medieval and Renaissance monks commonly held up Mary as a model and used feminine images for the divine, but that these practices did not register any corresponding respect for women or elevation of their status. Bynum notes the prevalent medieval stereotypes of women as less rational and more lascivious than men, and the hostility of cloistered males toward actual mothers and women (St. Bernard, for example, in his commentary on the Song of Solomon, warns against contamination by women).[16] What is unusual about Newman's *imitatio Mariae* is not his practice but the context. In Victorian ideology, women were still generally considered irrational, creatures of feeling rather than thought, but they were pure and pious, and allowed to be men's moral superiors if they (like Newman's "inquirer into heavenly truths") stayed in their domestic temples and escaped contamination by the world; woman thus reimagined deserved no monkish reproach. Newman's assertion of male superiority shows his care to ward off any undesired change in meaning (for example, the priest as a feminized figure), due to Victorian reconceptions of gender roles, when he appropriates the medieval ideal of the retired life.[17]

Throughout his writings Newman acknowledged his indebtedness to the Fathers of the early Church, whom he studied intensely from the time of his Oriel fellowship and whom he called his "ladder" into the Catholic Church.[18] His reliance on the Fathers led him to draw a Marian portrait with direct implications for Victorian women. Hilda Graef's *Mary: A History of Doctrine and Devotion* helps us make this connection; she quotes a document attributed to the Greek Fathers that had been printed among the proverbs of the Council of Nicaea (325) and preserved in Coptic:

> "A wise Virgin resembles Mary. Who could name the beauty of the Mother of our Lord, who was loved by God because of her works? . . . Mary never saw the face of a strange man, that was why she was confused when she heard the voice of the angel Gabriel. She did not eat to feed a body, but she ate because of

the necessity of her nature. . . . She withdrew all by herself into
her house, being served by her own mother. . . . She sat always
with her face turned towards the East, because she prayed con-
tinually. For her brothers wanted to see her and speak to her.
And she did not receive them. For the angels came many times
to her; they observed her singular way of life and admired her.
She slept only according to the need of sleep. . . When she put
on a garment she used to shut her eyes . . . For she did not know
many things of this life, because she remained far from the company of women. For the Lord looked upon the whole of creation
and he saw no-one to equal Mary. Therefore he chose her for
his mother. If, therefore, a girl wants to be called a virgin, she
should resemble Mary."

Graef comments on this document:

> It is interesting to note how Mary is here portrayed not as she
> appears in Scripture, but as the ideal of the fourth-century con-
> secrated virgin, who always stayed at home and prayed, meticu-
> lously guarded against any masculine society, whereas the Mary
> of the Gospels did not hesitate to visit her cousin Elizabeth,
> went up to the Temple for the feasts and generally behaved like
> a normal Jewish girl of her time. But, as we shall see again and
> again, every age unconsciously forms its image of the Virgin ac-
> cording to its own ideal; and the age of the Fathers of the Desert
> could not conceive her otherwise than as a solitary, leading a life
> of the most exemplary austerity and consorting not even with
> her own brothers but only with angels. (Graef, 1:50–51)

Graef not only points out the historicized nature of this Marian ideal
but also makes us aware of its similarities to the restrictive model for conduct imposed on Victorian women. The model virgin remains secluded at
home, praying and doing good works that show her inner beauty. Her
mother protects her against "masculine society"—not only strange men but
even her evidently rough brothers—and she is kept innocent of the
worldly knowledge of women as well. She has no appetites, physical or
sexual. She refuses to look on her own naked body. Her lack of sleep must
give her the pale and interesting looks of an invalid. There are indeed
intimations of the Virgin in the House, the Victorian domestic Madonna!

And Newman draws them out. His version of the Virgin's history has

96   striking similarities to the fourth-century document Graef quotes. Like the Greek Fathers, Newman uses Mary's life to show that "the highest graces of the soul may be matured in private" ("Reverence," 311). He claims Mary is reluctant as a dedicated virgin, one who is "separate from man" and "detach[ed] from creatures," to bear the Christ if that means exchanging her state for the worldly lot of ordinary wives and mothers ("Glories," 254). And he places special emphasis on her proper feminine humility:

> It became her, as a creature, a mother, and a woman, to stand aside and make way for the Creator, to minister to her Son, and to win her way into the world's homage by sweet and gracious persuasion. ("Glories," 258)

> Our heart yearns towards that pure Virgin, that gentle Mother, and our congratulations follow her, as she rises from Nazareth and Ephesus, through the choirs of angels, to her throne on high, so weak, yet so strong; so delicate, yet so glorious; so modest and yet so mighty. . . . I recall the strange emotion which took by surprise men and women, young and old, when, at the Coronation of our present Queen, they gazed on the figure of one so like a child, so small, so tender, so shrinking, who had been exalted to so great an inheritance and so vast a rule, who was such a contrast in her own person to the solemn pageant which centred in her. . . . And did not the All-wise know the human heart when He took to Himself a Mother? did He not anticipate our emotion at the sight of such an exaltation in one so simple and so lowly? (*Letter to Pusey*, 85–86)

Newman here expresses the Mariology of the Fathers in quintessentially Victorian language. The Virgin Mary is the sweet lily of Eden's shade ("Fitness," 273), fragile, meek, retiring, appropriately deferential to her Son, and never seeking power for herself (unlike that harpy Queen Elizabeth or nineteenth-century feminists), but instead winning her way through her quiet influence and example. She is suitably compared to England's own dear little queen, Victoria, who ascended the throne at eighteen. Newman's work thus reveals a direct connection between the early Fathers of the Church, particularly the Greek Fathers, and the Victorian feminine ideal.

Coventry Patmore, another English Catholic writer, with connections to Newman, had an even greater influence on Victorian conceptions of ideal womanhood. Patmore converted to Catholicism (from high Anglicanism) in 1864, after he finished his long poem *The Angel in the House* (1854–62), but he had long immersed himself in works of Catholic piety. He claimed later that he found nothing in his poem incompatible with Catholic truth and feeling.[19] Patmore's Angel in the House was modeled on his first wife, Emily. Her Madonna-like qualities are suggested in the following representative passage, in which Eve, the original of woman, is the crown of creation and has many of the New Eve's virtues:

> Lo, when the Lord made North and South
> And sun and moon ordained, He,
> Forthbringing each by word of mouth
> In order of its dignity,
> Did man from the crude clay express
> By sequence, and, all else decreed,
> He formed the women; nor might less
> Than Sabbath such a work succeed.
> And still with favour singled out,
> Marr'd less than man by mortal fall,
> Her disposition is devout,
> Her countenance angelical;
> The best things that the best believe
> Are in her face so kindly writ
> The faithless, seeing her, conceive
> Not only heaven, but hope of it.[20]

The Angel is a considerably grander conception than the highly domesticated Virgin Mary of Patmore's later poem "Regina Coeli" (Queen of Heaven).[21] But the same cluster of traits is present in both works: purity, maternity, salvific queenship. It is fascinating to consider how all these poetic Madonnas point back to Emily Patmore, who was not only her husband's model but in his mind a substitute for the Virgin Mary herself. When Patmore, not long after his wife's death and his conversion, saw his children resist the new practice of praying to Our Lady, he said, "Pray to your mother, if you like that better."[22]

98   Patmore's pure Madonnas of redeeming love, the Angel and the Regina Coeli, both resemble Newman's Virgin Mary. A common source may be indicated, since Patmore, like Newman, centered his religious reading not only on the Bible but also on "ancient Catholic books of devotion" and the Church Fathers.[23] But it is instead quite possible that *The Angel in the House* and later poems were influenced by Newman's writings on Mary. Patmore's feelings for Newman were "ardent and affectionate," according to the poet's biographer, and his letters contain numerous references to the Catholic leader. He records his one meeting with Newman, in which he was struck by the latter's exact truthfulness; he notes that he sent Newman books, including one he wrote; and he seems to have tried to negotiate with the Pre-Raphaelite artist Woolner about making a statue of the Cardinal.[24] Like Newman, Patmore had a special reverence for the Virgin. But the poet's three marriages (the Angel remained his saint but was replaced as wife) and his ideal of the sacred sensuousness of wedded love ("it is only through marriage-love that we can understand the love of Christ") show that on certain points they would have strongly disagreed (Champneys, 2:84).

      Patmore's *The Angel in the House* in time became a Victorian best-seller, helped by an early favorable article in the *Edinburgh Review* (January 1858) and a later notice in *Macmillan's Magazine* (1879). The long poem was admired by Carlyle, Tennyson, and Gerard Manley Hopkins (who in letters of 1883 discussed metrics with Patmore and helped him revise his poems for a new edition). Ruskin also praised the *Angel*, in a correspondence with the poet that lasted for over thirty years.[25] When Patmore was discouraged by some early slighting reviews, Ruskin was at first reluctant to write publicly about the poem, because he did not wish to draw attention to his own unhappy and unconsummated marriage, which had very recently been annulled (July 1854).[26] But in 1860 Ruskin responded to an attack on the second part of the poem, *The Victories of Love*, calling Patmore's work, in a letter to *The Critic*, "a singularly perfect piece of art." Ruskin also took notice of the *Angel* in his *Elements of Drawing* ("the sweetest analysis we possess of quiet modern domestic feeling"). And he told the author that he quoted the poem, "with much applause," when he delivered his lecture "Of Queens' Gardens" at Manchester in 1864 (as well as on later occasions); eight lines are included in the later printed editions of Ruskin's lecture, with the comment "You cannot read [Patmore] too often or too carefully."[27]

      Indeed, the influence of Patmore is apparent throughout "Of Queens'

Gardens," in which the ideal woman, like Patmore's paragon, is a Madonna-   99
figure with a regal influence. Ruskin exhorts his female audience:

> And whether consciously or not, you must be, in many a heart,
> enthroned: there is no putting by that crown; queens you must
> always be: queens to your lovers; queens to your husbands and
> your sons; queens of higher mystery to the world beyond, which
> bows itself, and will for ever bow, before the myrtle crown and
> the stainless sceptre of womanhood. . . holding [power] straight
> in gift from the Prince of all Peace. (18:139)

Ruskin's "Of Queens' Gardens" was the most popular of all his writings;
160,000 copies had been printed by the turn of the century, and it went
through multiple editions.[28] Though Ruskin (a Protestant) was dismayed
by the news of his friend's religious conversion, thinking it would limit Patmore's "good pious" influence,[29] his championship of the poet would have
had the opposite effect; his own readers would have known, directly or indirectly, of Patmore's work. By pointing his readers toward *The Angel in the
House* and by representing women as Madonnas and household queens, as
Patmore does, Ruskin joins the poet and Newman in this argument about
the indebtedness of the Victorian feminine ideal to English Catholicism
and directly or indirectly to the Church Fathers.[30]

In contrast to Newman, Patmore, and Ruskin, Jameson makes claims
for Mary that do not domesticate but instead liberate and empower
women. She does so by closing the covers on the Church Fathers and
focusing on Marian doctrines of the late Middle Ages, particularly as expressed in art. Jameson does not accept many Marian doctrines literally.
But they inspire her and give her license to advance her own religious and
feminist beliefs, confident that they are historically grounded in Christian
tradition and consistent with the spirit of Christianity.

Jameson has a strong preference for medieval art, especially by Italian
painters. She is quite specific about the period: the twelfth through fifteen
centuries. In a long passage from *Legends of the Madonna*, she argues that art
developed progressively during this period, with "the spiritual for some
time in advance of the material influences; the moral idea emanating as it
were *from* the soul, and the influences of external nature flowing *into* it"

100   (xxiv–xxv, xxx). Jameson's favorite painter, Raphael, is the culmination of this late-medieval tradition. After him came the fall of religious art (i.e., the Renaissance). In the "learned, half-pagan" sixteenth century and the "polished" seventeenth, religious images became offensively materialistic, in Jameson's view, and even the Counter-Reformation did not mark a return to the spirituality of the Middle Ages. Art instead became theological, carefully controlled and used by the Catholic Church to assert the doctrines under attack by the Reformers (183–84, xxxii–xxxviii). Jameson's reactions probably reflect a tolerant Anglican's sense that medieval art was still true to the teachings of the early Church and thus part of her own tradition. Post-Tridentine art, in contrast, was no longer "hers," because it promoted doctrines (e.g., of the papacy and the Mass) that the Church of England, sometimes claiming to represent a "purified Catholicism," defined itself against during the sixteenth and seventeenth centuries.[31]

Jameson's account of the development of Western art lists the Marian subjects that were introduced during the Middle Ages. She notes that in the eleventh and twelfth centuries (as a consequence of the pilgrimages and crusades to the Holy Land), the legends of Mary's parents Joachim and Anna, and the death, Assumption, and Coronation of the Virgin began to appear in art. In the thirteenth and fourteenth centuries, Mary's countenance was given a new sympathetic expressiveness: "Compared with the spectral rigidity, the hard monotony, of the conventional Byzantines, the more animated eyes, the little touch of sweetness in the still, mild face, must have been like a smile out of heaven" (*Madonna*, xxv). Mary was also first represented as Our Lady (a title drawn from chivalry), the Queen of Heaven, and the Mother of Mercy at this time. In the late fifteenth century, there were new scenes showing the Holy Family, and the first portrait Madonnas (xxv–xxxiii, 26–34). In Jameson's view, virtually every subject added to the Marian "repertoire" in the late Middle Ages augmented the power and status of the Virgin; the art historian could describe the Madonnas of this period not just as "contemplative," "chaste," and "serene," but also as "powerful," "beneficent," and "divine." Such figures were moving and authoritative illustrations of her claim that Mary, as the divinized representative of women and the representation of woman as divine, shows woman's fundamental equality with man. In the sweep of European history that Jameson covered, the late-medieval period was the apex of Marian art and Marian power, and she privileged the images and doctrines of this period as she constructed her own Mariology.

While Jameson's expertise was sometimes slighted by contemporaries like Ruskin, the accuracy of her account can be confirmed by Emile Mâle, the historian of religious art, and Jaroslav Pelikan, an equally authoritative source for the doctrinal development of the late Middle Ages.[32] Pelikan underlines the differences between late-medieval Marian innovations (e.g., Mary as the Queen of Mercy), which Jameson stresses, and patristic Mariology (Mary as the New Eve, the *Theotokos*, and "the woman clothed with the sun"), on which Newman bases his theology (*Christian Tradition*, 4:38–50). While Pelikan, like Newman, argues for a necessary qualitative distinction between Jesus and Mary, he points out that in the later Middle Ages "various titles, prerogatives, functions, and scriptural passages that had originally belonged to Christ were now by extension being 'transferred' to Mary." For example, all mercy was said to be granted through Mary's mediation, and as Queen of Heaven she was even accorded "maternal authority over God" (4:40–44). Newman was long unfamiliar with such images of a godlike Mary, and when Pusey confronted him with them, he recoiled: "Sentiments such as these . . . seem to me like a bad dream. I know not to what authority to go for them, to Scriptures, or to the Fathers, or to the decrees of Councils" (*Letter to Pusey*, 113–15). The gap in the theologian's knowledge contrasts sharply with the self-taught art historian's extensive writings on these late-medieval beliefs and images, which she made central to her feminist aesthetic.

This extended comparison of Jameson, Newman, and other Victorian writers demonstrates that the Madonna of nineteenth-century England had numerous faces. The differences between important representations of her—Newman's Virgin of the House, Patmore's Angel, and Ruskin's Queen of the Garden, versus Jameson's Glorious Queen—can be explained not only by the four writers' differing religious beliefs and attitudes toward feminism but also by the articulated or implicit historical groundings of their Mariologies. Newman's Mary is the handmaid of the Church Fathers. Jameson's Madonna, in contrast, is regnant, not retiring. She is maternal as much as virginal. She is the Madonna of Mercy, actively involved in the salvation of humankind. She is the beneficent, pure, and powerful goddess of Christianity, the feminine face of the divine. And she is a figure familiar from the art and doctrines of the late Middle Ages. Jameson managed to construct a feminist Mariology because her starting point was a Mary seen and defined not in patristic but in late-medieval terms.

Queenship and the Politics of Mary

CHAPTER FIVE

A common element of Jameson's disparate works is her praise of *female* heroes: the Queen of Heaven, certain earthly queens, saints, abbesses, actresses, Shakespearean heroines, and nine-teenth-century reformers. Her books thus reply to the con-temporaneous celebrations of male heroes by Goethe, Carlyle, Emerson, and others.[1] For example, Jameson in *Legends of the Monastic Orders* (1850), like Carlyle in *Past and Present* (1843), values medieval religious houses for the possibilities of commu-nity that nineteenth-century England has lost. She is primarily concerned, though, with what these religious communities of-fered to women: refuge, education, opportunities for leader-ship. She and Carlyle both show interest in the religious heroes of British history, such as the martyred St. Edmund (ninth century). But her lists of heroes do not include Carlyle's John Knox or Oliver Cromwell (*On Heroes*, 1840–41; see also Johnston, 189). Instead, she writes about St. Hilda, Abbess of Whitby, renowned for her learning, piety, and leadership (sev-enth century); her contemporary St. Ethelreda, the miracle-working founder and abbess of Ely; and St. Bridget of Ireland (fifth century), converted by St. Patrick and devoted to the service and instruction of the poor, especially women. Brid-get's female disciples at Kildare watched her heavenly lamp "with as much devotion as the Vestal Virgins of old the sacred fire."[2] It is clear that Jameson was committed to the Victorian project of reconstructing a proud medieval past for England,

but she differed from Carlyle, as well as from Sir Walter Scott, Ruskin, and   103
the Pre-Raphaelites, in her focus on eminent women's achievements and
her related concern for the condition of contemporary women.

Jameson herself had a place in a "heroic tradition" of female authorship, first described by Elaine Showalter (3–36, 100–112) and Ellen Moers
(13–66, 187–88). As an established literary critic and art historian, she was
a figure of sometimes frightening celebrity to ambitious younger women,
such as the Langham Place feminists Barbara Bodichon and Bessie Parkes,
who hoped similarly to combine a career with feminist activism, and to
Margaret Fuller, George Eliot, and the American sculptor Harriet Hosmer,
who sought to rival men as intellectuals and artists. All this emulation
raises the question whether Jameson had any direct influence on women as
artists as well as authors. Bodichon and Parkes were indeed dedicated amateur artists, but they painted in one of the "feminine" genres, landscape
(other approved genres for women were still life and portrait), and they
did not mention Jameson in connection with their art. Jameson's writings
instead would have encouraged the production of religious art and the
"masculine" genre of history painting and sculpture ("masculine," in large
part, because few women could receive the necessary instruction in drawing from the nude).[3]

Jameson did, however, become an artistic mentor to one of the professionals in her circle: the American Harriet Hosmer (1830–1908). A
neoclassical sculptor based in Rome, Hosmer was one of the first women
to challenge the masculine domination of her field. Jameson published several books on secular and spiritual queens—*Celebrated Female Sovereigns*
(1831), *Characteristics of Women* (1832), and *Legends of the Madonna*—and Hosmer relied on the older woman's writings and advice for her sculpture *Zenobia in Chains* (showing the third-century Palmyran queen; see figure 8) and
probably also for her *Queen Isabella of Castile* (figure 9).[4] *Zenobia* was seen by
thousands and highly praised at the 1862 London International Exhibition
and on tour in the States. *Isabella* was commissioned by a Chicago suffragist group for the World's Columbian Exposition of 1893 (see photos 8 and
9). Hosmer was enthusiastic about queens as subjects for sculpture, as symbols of artistic achievement, and as political leaders—this during the period of struggle for Italian unification and a constitutional government.
Jameson, in contrast, was rather dubious about either male or female exercise of sovereign power and advocated spiritual rather than secular queenship as a model for women. A comparison of these two women allows us

to examine the conflicting attitudes toward queenship among nineteenth-century Anglo-American feminists and women of achievement.

Harriet Hosmer is a good example of the links that could exist in the nineteenth century between bourgeois feminism and queenship—queenship considered as both a political reality and a metaphor for female achievement. Although nineteenth-century neoclassical sculptors often chose the queens of mythology and ancient history as subjects for their work (e.g., William Wetmore Story represented Semiramis), Hosmer is notable for her progress from female victims (Tennyson's deserted shepherdess Oenone, and Daphne) to women who rebel against patriarchy (such as the parricide Beatrice Cenci) and queens who shape history.[5] The queens include Zenobia, the ruler of Palmyra, who challenged the imperial power of Rome and lost. Hosmer's 1859 sculpture represents her walking in chains in Emperor Aurelian's triumph at Rome (Sherwood, 231–32; cf. Jameson, *Celebrated Female Sovereigns*, 1:46). In contrast to Hosmer's noble women, many of her male subjects for sculpture—Puck, the Will-o'-the-Wisp, and the Fauns—are sexually well endowed but subhuman.

Hosmer's queens—Zenobia, Maria Sophia the Queen of Naples (seen as a modern Zenobia), and Isabella of Castile—were often read as ideal representations of modern woman: powerful, beautiful, and brave. Zenobia and Isabella were also linked to the issue of women's rights, as a notice of *Zenobia* in the December 1864 *Atlantic Monthly* indicates:

> A captive Queen, compelled to grace the triumph of her conqueror, forced to deck herself in her royal robes, and to move at another's will, a Queen who has proved her right to her throne by grand statesmanlike qualities, both moral and intellectual. . . . [P]ride and sorrow struggle in the knotted brow, the level eyelids, contracted nostrils, and scornfully curled lip. (Carr, 363–64)

In this interpretation, Woman, like Zenobia, has proven her moral and intellectual right to her throne, but she is still forced to wear the chains of patriarchy.

As Zenobia was read as modern woman, so Harriet Hosmer, the female artist, was in turn read as a queen. In a burst of Yankee pride, Hosmer was called "the Queen of the West," who brought the Queen of the East to march "in this, *our* [American] triumph" (Carr, 192, 367). But Hosmer

was also called "prince" or "knight." Her friend Lydia Maria Child, for 105
example, wrote to her at the time of *Zenobia*'s tour: "You have fairly won
your spurs in the field of art. 'Arise, Sir Harriet Hosmer!'" (Carr, 145). "Sir
Hosmer" is a fitting form of address, given the artist's boyish, we might say
butch, appearance and mannerisms: she had short hair and dressed like a
boy above the waist, as Hawthorne said; she had men as chums rather than
beaux, and women as romantic friends; she rode her horse at daredevil
speed across the Roman Campagna. But the tension between "queen" and
"knight" as honorifics for Hosmer also points to interesting midcentury debates about women and artistic power. The Irish writer Frances Power
Cobbe, sometimes part of Hosmer's international circle in Italy, argues in
Frazer's Magazine (November 1862) that the natural genius of women is not
for sweetness and softness, as they have been told. Instead, the best female
artists (Cobbe named Elizabeth Barrett Browning, the French painter Rosa
Bonheur, and Hosmer) are known, as the best male artists are, for the
"power, force, and grandeur" of their work.[6] For Cobbe, artistic power has
no sex. The queens of art do not differ from the kings.

But more often nineteenth-century artists and critics regarded power
as masculine, and thought women did not have it. The Rome-based sculptor William Wetmore Story, with whom Hosmer later competed for commissions and prizes, said of her during her apprenticeship: "It is one thing
to copy & another to create. She may or may not have inventive powers as
an artist. If she have, will she not be the first woman who ever had?" (11
Feb. 1853, in Sherwood, 63). Hosmer proved him wrong with her nine-
foot bronze sculpture of Thomas Hart Benton, the late Missouri senator
(1868) (she had to wear "Zouave costume," shortened skirts, to work on it
lest she fall off the high scaffolding) and her *Pompeian Sentinel* (1878). As
Hosmer hoped, these sculptures of male figures plus *Zenobia* earned her
praise not only for her "manly" power as an artist but also for her ability to
represent or reproduce masculinity. The last thought—her ability to reproduce masculinity—seems to have been unsettling, for some of the same
reasons Marjorie Garber describes in her essay "Spare Parts," on female-to-
male transsexuals: only males, not females, ought to be capable of con-
structing manhood, of becoming men. Unsurprisingly, then, Hosmer, like
other women sculptors of the nineteenth century, had to defend herself
several times against charges that a man (her teacher John Gibson, or a studio artisan) did her work for her.[7]

Hosmer's celebration of power extended beyond her sculpture to her
politics. Although she was a democrat at home in America, competing for

Figure 8. Harriet Hosmer, *Zenobia in Chains* (1859). Courtesy of the Schlesinger Library, Radcliffe Institute, Harvard University.

Figure 9. Harriet Hosmer, *Queen Isabella of Castile* (1893). This sculpture was shown at the World's Columbian Exposition in Chicago. Courtesy of the Schlesinger Library, Radcliffe Institute, Harvard University.

108   commissions for monuments to Lincoln and the freed slaves after the Civil War and advocating women's suffrage, she was a monarchist abroad. "The romance of [her] life," she says, was with Maria Sophia, the Queen of Naples and the Two Sicilies, who with her husband Francis II lost their kingdom to republican forces in 1861 and took refuge in Rome. Hosmer made a statue of the heroic queen as she appeared during the siege. Hosmer also sided with Pope Pius IX against the forces that wanted to unite Italy and end his temporal rule of the papal states. She left Rome when the pope, his supporters defeated, retreated into the Vatican and the city under the "usurper" Victor Emmanuel II started becoming drearily egalitarian, like the United States.[8]

It is revealing to compare Hosmer's political positions with those of Margaret Fuller, who covered the 1848 Roman revolution for the *New-York Tribune* and sided with the revolutionaries, even having a child—a junior rebel, as she thought—with one of them. Fuller read the Roman revolution in the terms of the American revolution, as a freedom struggle against tyranny and state-supported priestcraft. The impending loss of Pius IX's kingdom in 1870 would make Hosmer weep; but Fuller, two decades earlier, called this pope a blind and weak leader, the betrayer of his own people. An even greater villain for Fuller was the father-in-law of the queen of Naples, Ferdinand II, nicknamed King Bomba in 1848 for bombing his own subjects (Fuller, *"These Sad But Glorious Days,"* 23, 229–32, 244).

This comparison of Fuller and Hosmer shows that democratic principles were sometimes used to interpret the tumultuous events in nineteenth-century Europe—but Hosmer chose not to use them. If one discounts Hosmer's democratic (and opportunistic) gestures at home in America, she is a figure of alarming consistency. Hosmer's queens expressed her own sense of belonging to an artistic elite and her support of a political elite, the monarchs and aristocrats (such as the Prince of Wales, later Edward VII, the Queen of Naples, Lady Marian Alford, and Louisa Lady Ashburton) who bought her work and welcomed her to their homes. But Hosmer's attitude toward queenship was not unique among Americans (or Britons). The suffragists in the Queen Isabella Association who commissioned her work for the 1893 Columbian Exposition in Chicago took Queen Isabella as a role model because of her assumed co-equal part in discovering America. Isabella paid for Columbus's voyage with her jewels; Hosmer represented her holding them out to him. The commissioning of this statue suggests that many (though not all) nineteenth-century bourgeois feminists, including Susan B. Anthony and Elizabeth Cady Stanton, could readily accommodate imperialism. The Chicago suffragists, despite criticisms of Isabella as a religious fanatic and founder of the Inquisition (Weimann, 39), had no qualms about choosing a symbol of female achievement who exacerbated ethnic, religious, and class divisions among American women that dated from the time of Columbus.[9]

Hosmer's treatment of queenship is a useful introduction to the more complex attitudes of Anna Jameson. Jameson celebrated Mary as the faultless Mother of God and Queen of Heaven, and stressed the Virgin Mother's equality or near-equality with her Son, in order to advance an agenda of her own: her feminist and religious belief in the fundamental equality of men and women. But Jameson's praise of the Queen of Heaven did not always extend to *earthly* queens. She, at least early in her career, was dubious about women's exercise of sovereign power. In *Celebrated Female Sovereigns* she sharply criticized the formidable Semiramis and Zenobia and the gorgeous Cleopatra for precisely the violent and self-serving actions that helped them keep their thrones and kingdoms: their elimination of rivals, including family members; their empire-building wars; their adornment of their cities, palaces, and royal selves; and their sexual intrigues. Jameson advised Hosmer on her representation of Zenobia, but her own reading of that Queen was quite different.

Jameson's favorite queens included Mary Queen of Scots, whom she considered a courageous martyr, the victim of others' treachery, and Isabella of Castile, whom she characterized as a pious, generous, and just queen, appropriately deferential to her husband except where the rights of Castile were involved. Jameson told the story of Queen Isabella's jewels, but, in contrast to the later American feminists, she said that Columbus's voyages do not properly belong in Isabella's history, since the Queen was more concerned with domestic crises than with "the conquest of kingdoms or the discovery of worlds" (*Celebrated Female Sovereigns*, 1:152, 154). Isabella's virtues, according to Jameson, were her own, and her vices those of her age. Jameson went too far in trying to dissociate her favorites from the evil events of their reigns—such as the mysterious death of a husband, or the Inquisition and the enslavement of Indians in the New World. But more importantly, Jameson, in contrast to Hosmer, here celebrated only the queens who exercised power for a limited time or in limited ways; it is Isabella's husband who is said to make the unfortunate decisions and wage the wars in Spain. Sovereign power, because of its history of oppressive uses,

110   seemed to Jameson incompatible with female virtue. Her "good queens,"
with their pious instincts yet limited ability to act, seem to have marked
the start of her search for an alternative model of power, *spiritual* power.

Jameson's and Hosmer's work on queens raises the question of their attitudes toward Queen Victoria, who figured prominently in contemporaneous discussions of women's roles and has been the subject of much
recent work in literary and cultural studies. Adrienne Munich, in her far-
reaching work *Queen Victoria's Secrets*, reveals Victoria's hold on the British
imagination by analyzing her image as the legitimizer of the monarchy
through public spectacles; as the deliberately dowdy little wife and inconsolable widow; and as a monumental figure synonymous with Empire.
While the clear tendency of studies like Munich's has been to demonstrate
Queen Victoria's multivalence as a symbol, critics have found common
ground in their attention to two issues: the nature and extent of Victoria's
power, and her function as a role model. Munich and Margaret Homans
stress the tensions between Victoria's position and her sex: as a monarch,
she exercised considerable power, yet as a woman she was considered unfit
to rule.[10] Elizabeth Langland, Sharon Weltman, Deborah Cherry, and Alison Booth all discuss Victoria as a queenly role model who they think generally elevated the position of middle-class women. Weltman and
Langland pay particular attention to John Ruskin's "Of Queens' Gardens,"
arguing that his richly ambiguous imagery empowered women as social activists and philanthropists and expanded their sphere beyond the household "garden."[11] But neither Ruskin nor the monarch on whom he partly
modeled his queens supported feminism; Ruskin's ideal woman was instead
a figure of "real but nonpolitical potency."[12]

It is not surprising, then, that British and American feminists had
mixed feelings about Queen Victoria. To be sure, Emily Faithfull, the
British founder of the Victoria Press (which trained women in the printing
trades) and the publisher of the *Victoria Magazine* (which succeeded the
feminist *English Woman's Journal*), regularly suggested parallels between herself and the Queen, as Maria Frawley has pointed out.[13] And John Stuart
Mill, Harriet Martineau, Elizabeth Cady Stanton, and Susan B. Anthony,
among others, used the British monarch to argue for women's fitness to exercise political power and participate in public debate.[14] Yet they realized
the limitations of the bourgeois image that Victoria assiduously cultivated

(the queen as wife, mother, and "Albert's relict"). Stanton and Anthony valued the kind of domestic competence they saw the queen as demonstrating, but one of the sparks that led to the Seneca Falls revolution was Stanton's fury at her confinement to domestic roles.[15] Moreover, Fuller, Stanton, and other feminists frequently criticized Victoria's exercise of the power and wealth she did have, such as her decision to build more memorials to Albert rather than to provide adequate homes and schools for her people.[16] Anthony, in an 1899 interview, bitterly noted the queen's silence on all legislation relating to women: "Take for instance the three great movements in England—the abolition of the Contagious Diseases Act, the obtaining of property rights for wives and of suffrage for women—the Queen has appeared wholly oblivious when a word from her would have turned the scales" (Harper, 3:1157). Recent literary scholarship has, in my view, tended to obscure our understanding of female power by defining it variously as agency, ideology, domestic authority, grandeur, and political might. But as Anthony's comment indicates, nineteenth-century feminist activists knew what power meant to them: the possession of the same rights and privileges then enjoyed by free men, including property rights, access to higher education and the professions, and the right to participate in representative government, symbolized by the vote. And few saw Queen Victoria as a friend to the Cause.

Victoria is conspicuously absent from both Hosmer's and Jameson's work on queens, and while the negative reactions of feminists to the monarch certainly suggest an explanation, there seem to be additional reasons. Hosmer, as a neoclassical sculptor and an American living in Rome, naturally looked to the past and to Italy rather than to Britain for her queens, although viewers likely saw parallels between her Zenobia and Queen Victoria (Sherwood, 236). Moreover, it might have been tactless for her to do a sculpture of the queen, since her customers included the Prince of Wales, who resented his long exclusion from royal power (196). But it is also the case that Hosmer and her contemporaries increasingly differentiated truly talented women (like Hosmer herself) from women who owed their eminence only to birth or marriage. For example, at the World's Columbian Exposition in 1893, the celebrated queens were Isabella of Castile and Bertha (Mrs. Potter) Palmer, the formidable president of the Board of Lady Managers,[17] and Queen Victoria unfortunately forfeited her privilege of staying distantly regal by submitting samples of her own handiwork: the watercolor of a fox terrier that could not have been identified

112   without the label, and a white-and-green excrescence of a hat made with
       the royal hands (see Weimann, 270–71). By allowing herself to be unfa-
       vorably compared to true women of achievement, such as Hosmer and
       Mary Cassatt, the British queen revealed the mediocrity of royalty.[18]

       Jameson's situation is somewhat different from Hosmer's, because she
       wrote her books on female sovereigns and Shakespeare's queens before
       Victoria's accession to the throne in 1837, and she avoided overt political
       references in her later series *Sacred and Legendary Art.* However, her letters
       from the 1830s through the 1850s show that she (like Harriet Martineau,
       a feminist of her generation) had some British pride in the queen but usu-
       ally represented her as very young, with a good heart but limited power,
       and she never called her bright.[19] In addition, Jameson's positions on Irish
       issues seem to have led her to give another queen precedence over Victo-
       ria. Jameson would have been aware of the Virgin Mary's current role in
       secular politics on the Continent, where she was used by popes, monarchs,
       and political conservatives to support the ancien regimes. In Ireland, how-
       ever, the Madonna functioned as a symbol of Irish Catholic resistance to
       British rule, especially at the 1840s independence rallies led by the Irish
       Catholic M.P. Daniel O'Connell. O'Connell, for instance, scheduled his
       Monster Meeting at Tara for the Feast Day of the Assumption of the Vir-
       gin Mary, 15 August 1843, and Mass was said at six altars there through-
       out the morning. When O'Connell was arrested (as too great a political
       threat to the British government), his followers often prayed for him in
       public by saying the Rosary. The Irish leader attributed his release from
       prison to the Novena held throughout the country for the Nativity of the
       Virgin (8 September 1844).[20] Margaret Fuller refers to this event in *Woman
       in the Nineteenth Century* (1845), noting the close association the Irish made
       between the Virgin Mary and the cause of liberty (*WNC,* 340–41). And
       Anna Jameson, though an Anglican living near London, was born red-haired
       Anna Murphy in Dublin; her father, who had been a member of the revo-
       lutionary United Irishmen, left Ireland for professional reasons in 1798 and
       thus escaped involvement in the rebellions of that year and 1803.[21] Jame-
       son embraced her Irish identity, particularly when she was under duress.[22]
       She visited her "native land" in 1848 and was horribly distressed by the
       famine there,[23] and she took liberal positions on Irish politics, opposing
       the Irish Coercion Bill of the mid-1840s and wanting Ireland to be rid
       of "that pest, the Irish Church" (i.e., the Anglican Church in Ireland).[24]
       Although Jameson thought Ireland should stay in the union with Great
       Britain, in an 1848 letter she highly praised O'Connell and the Irish
       people involved in his Repeal movement and sympathized with their de-

mands for more freedom and better treatment by the British government.[25]   113
Jameson's Queen of Heaven thus seems to have had a politics; she stood
for resistance to the abuses of imperial power and symbolized the hope for
reconciliation of the opposing sides (see, e.g., *Letters*, 20 Feb. [1846] and 4
April 1846, 156–57). The criticisms of Victoria by Stanton and Anthony
extended to her opposition to Irish home rule; Jameson's support of
O'Connell and *his* queen, earlier in the century, may similarly have precluded her positive use of Victoria, since the policies that O'Connell was
protesting were those of Her Majesty's government.

The near-absence of Victoria from Jameson's work is one of the indications that her thinking about power underwent a shift in the 1830s and
1840s, after the publication of *Celebrated Female Sovereigns*. Even though England once again had a female monarch, Jameson no longer used secular
queenship as a model for women's power. One reason seems to have been
her growing awareness of the problems of British imperialism. In her travel
book *Winter Studies and Summer Rambles in Canada* (1838), Jameson still could
state her belief in the superiority of Western civilization and Christianity
to native American cultures, and accordingly support the missions to the
Indians that had begun when Isabella funded Columbus's voyage long ago.
Yet she also described the Indians' corruption by European settlers, particularly those selling alcohol, and the Indian women's loss of status resulting
from their shift to purchasing rather than producing certain necessary
goods. She sadly concluded that the Indians had to keep moving west in
order to escape the degrading and deadly "advance" of European civilization. A few years after her return to England, Jameson met Lucretia Mott
and the young Elizabeth Cady Stanton at the 1840 World Anti-Slavery
Convention in London, at which the female delegates (including Mott)
were not allowed to take their seats; eight years later, Mott and Stanton
joined forces at Seneca Falls. The 1840 outrage may also have triggered
Jameson's involvement in public affairs on behalf of women and other oppressed groups. During the famine years in Ireland, she sought out Anglo-
Irish leaders concerned with relief measures—for example, Maziere Brady,
the lord chancellor of Ireland, Richard Whateley, archbishop of Dublin,
and Maria Edgeworth, the novelist and author of a book on the potato—
and discussed policy proposals. She also took advantage of an earlier introduction to Prime Minister Robert Peel (she had described his art
collection in one of her handbooks), to write him an impassioned letter
about the Irish catastrophe (Thomas, 183–86; Erskine, 250–61).

114   In the 1850s, Jameson took part in the campaign for married women's property rights and also delivered two public lectures for the feminist cause, *Sisters of Charity* and *The Communion of Labor*. These lectures indicate some wariness about joining rather than remaking a patriarchal system (and thus show Jameson's affinities with the tradition of radical or separatist feminism represented by Charlotte Perkins Gilman [*Herland*] and Adrienne Rich). In *Sisters of Charity*, Jameson proposed that Anglican sisterhoods be established in England in imitation of the Catholic Sisters of Charity on the Continent. The Anglican sisterhoods would not have what Jameson considered the most objectionable elements of nunneries: enclosure (which Victorian women already experienced too much of) and binding vows. Her medieval model was, significantly, the lay order of the Beguines, not the Benedictines. The sisterhoods would provide women with valuable work to do, the necessary training, and a home and emotional companionship. In a world where men were often not dependable, Jameson envisioned worlds in which women could live without men.[26]

Jameson's changing views on power, and women's use of power, are reflected in her works on queens. In *Celebrated Female Sovereigns*, she saw a conflict between female sovereignty and female piety, and she chose piety, praising a Mary Queen of Scots over an Elizabeth or a Semiramis (see also Johnston, 56–66). This choice seems to be in tension with her later advocacy of women's rights, and one explanation is that Jameson herself became more radical. But it is important to note her continued belief that monarchs, both male and female, and governments had never exercised their sovereign power justly. Passive piety merely dodged the problem, and Queen Victoria (an opponent of "this mad wicked folly of 'Women's Rights'") failed to inspire her (Weltman, 119). Therefore, in *Legends of the Madonna* (1852), Jameson turned away from secular queenship and instead proposed the Virgin Mary as a model of queenship—queenship that is spiritual (perhaps adumbrated by Mary Queen of Scots), yet empowered, since the heavenly queen, especially in Jameson's analysis, is an active and authoritative figure. She thus became a model of action for women like Jameson.

It could be said that when Jameson said women should imitate Mary, she merely softened the rule of men and kept the class structure intact. An example of the latter is bourgeois women's demonstrating the Marian virtues of beneficence, piety, and purity to women of the lower classes. But in nineteenth-century Britain and America, women saw their religious commitments as legitimizing their activism, including their protests of the

rule of governments and of men. Examples include the Grimké sisters, who
spoke publicly in support of abolitionism and women's rights, and the
Seneca Falls feminists (see Rossi, 418–20; later, though, some of these
women left their religious traditions). Jameson, in Britain, also based her activism on her religious beliefs, and she gave the feminist movement a queen
as a symbol of them. She saw spiritual queenship as authorizing women's
claims of gender equality and their reform efforts, and as marking their resistance to the unjust government of society, which they would renovate
according to what she considered higher, religious values. Spiritual queenship became Jameson's most important contribution to the nineteenth-
century feminist discussion of queenship as politics and metaphor.

While Jameson's arguments do have their tensions, it is important to
note that by calling into question the appropriateness of secular as opposed to spiritual queenship as a model for women's (especially bourgeois
women's) power, she manages to break some of the links between feminism
and imperialism. Indeed, the comparison of Jameson and Hosmer may
point to a significant change in feminist discussions of power during the
nineteenth century. Feminists like Jameson and Eliot, writing in the half-
century after Wollstonecraft, warned against female tyranny in the household (Rosamond Vincy comes to mind) and the state; past queens
prompted the fear that if women suddenly gained equal power, especially
without adequate education, they might wield it like men.[27] The two writers also emphasized a distinctive feminine sensibility rather than equal
power when they discussed women as artists. For example, Jameson was
horrified that a *woman*, Artemisia Gentileschi (seventeenth century), could
paint a particularly graphic *Judith and Holofernes*. In contrast, feminists later
in the century, such as Hosmer, Frances Power Cobbe, and the Queen Isabella Association, all focusing on men's and women's sameness in their arguments for equality, considered "power" a term of praise for female
achievement. Women artists and women rulers were for them queens
worth celebrating. But the elitist values of "queenship" accommodated imperialism and exacerbated the religious, class, and ethnic differences
among women. When these feminist "queens" claimed equality with the
"kings" of various realms, the cost was female solidarity.

One, finally, could object that the "spiritual power" Jameson advocated is not really power. The problem here is the vagueness of the term,
which could refer merely to domestic piety. In Jameson's understanding,
spiritual power describes the force and activities that come from an individual's religious commitments. Jameson insisted that women possessing

116 spiritual power should protest injustice and promote peace in the world, in imitation of Mary.[28] Although her early *Sovereigns* was a rather ladylike protest against unjust rule, she later became more outspoken about the marital oppression of women in all cultures, women's right to education and employment, single-sex religious communities as alternatives to marriage, the often sexualized violence that created female martyrs and saints, and the reconception of God (or the human ideal of goodness) in the image of women. As Gloria Steinem says, women become more radical with age.

These chapters on Jameson have demonstrated that her *Legends of the Madonna* is both an impressive work of art history and the basis of the author's feminist Mariology. Jameson saw Mary's high place in Christianity as an important sign of male-female equality—an acknowledgment that female nature is represented by the blessed Virgin Mother rather than by the fallen Eve, and that female as well as male nature can be made radiant, perfect, divine. God, in her argument, has a feminine as well as a masculine face. Mary's roles show, moreover, that woman's destiny is not merely to be a man's dependant and a mother devoted only to her own family. She is also Queen of Heaven and "Mother of All Humanity," and as the solitary, self-sufficient Virgin she is "complete in her own perfections." Statements like these reflect Jameson's painstaking art-historical scholarship, but they are hardly disinterested. They instead mirror the author's own feminist and religious beliefs.

Jameson identified herself as a Protestant and an Anglican, and this self-designation seems to have precluded her literal acceptance of certain Roman Catholic teachings about Mary, such as the Immaculate Conception. But Jameson was emotionally open to the powerful images of a goddess-figure not found in the Church of England. She was, moreover, intellectually able to defend her responses, because, like many Romantic writers, including the German theologian Schleiermacher, she considered feeling the ground of religion, and she found that religious images allowed experiences of the divine quite apart from the historicized doctrines they expressed. For Jameson, as for Fuller, the enduring spirit of Christianity transcended the changing forms, just as religion was larger than any institutional structure, even her own.

Although Jameson had obvious interests in the revival of religious art and liturgy fostered by the Anglican Oxford Movement and the Camden

Society, she was distanced by her feminism from the Tractarian leaders, Keble, Pusey, and Newman. The cloistered Virgin of Newman's descriptions, indebted to his constant study of the Church Fathers, helped foster the Victorian feminine ideal of the Angel in the House, made famous by another Catholic convert, Patmore. Jameson, in contrast, had a strong preference for the Marian art and doctrine of the late Middle Ages. And she found there a Madonna—the mighty Queen of Heaven—whom she made expressive of a feminist ideal.

Jameson's Madonnas and Jameson herself were, moreover, central to the female hero-worship that was pervasive in nineteenth-century women's art and writings and an answer to the veneration of male heroes proposed by Goethe, Carlyle, Emerson, and others. The art historian had an impact on feminist art production in this period: she and a protégée, the sculptor Harriet Hosmer, were known for their representations of queens. But Jameson profoundly differed from Hosmer in advocating the spiritual queenship of Mary, rather than secular queenship, as a model for women's activity. Yet spiritual power does not mean disengagement: the Queen of Heaven took on a liberatory role in Irish Catholic political activism, which Jameson supported, and became a model for her own feminist activities. A comparison of the spiritual and secular queens associated with Jameson and Hosmer indicates the complex and changing value of queenship in both nationalist and feminist politics during the age of Victoria.

Finally, Jameson's historical guidebooks, which provide a clear map of Marian art and doctrine, are useful preparation for an analysis of Margaret Fuller's more allusive and lyrical *Woman in the Nineteenth Century*. For Fuller, like the older writer, reread testimony from the past and present (by mystics, poets, and the feminist Anna Jameson) in order to find intimations of woman's glorious, even divine potential. Fuller's realization that the goddess of Christians could serve as the goddess of feminism may have influenced Jameson's interpretations of Mary, since *Woman in the Nineteenth Century* predates *Legends of the Madonna*. Both Jameson and Fuller condemned women's confinement to domestic roles and their subordination to their husbands, and for this reason, they resisted use of the domestic Madonna. Jameson's Marian alternative is primarily the heavenly Queen, but Fuller's is a reconceptualized Virgin Mother, who is central to her discussions of female creativity. This Virgin Mother is Fuller's most important contribution to mariological feminism, a figure who then reappears in Eliot's fiction.

"Would [Woman] But Assume Her Inheritance, Mary Would Not Be the Only Virgin Mother"

CHAPTER SIX

Margaret Fuller, like her contemporaries Anna Jameson and George Eliot, found the Madonna a rich and empowering symbol for herself and for other women. Throughout her work she used the Virgin Mother to represent and analyze her own experience as a freethinking Protestant, feminist intellectual, and political radical, as well as the generalized experiences of other women (maidens, wives, and mothers) in the nineteenth century.[1]

To be sure, Fuller as a religious thinker never completely abandoned her father's religion (Unitarianism) or its paternal terms for God, but in her religious thought, as in Jameson's, the figure of the Madonna registered the limitations of even gender-neutral terms for God, which for Fuller helped guarantee the spiritual equality of men and women but could not express her sense of the divine within woman, of woman's capacity for perfection. In her feminist writings, notably *Woman in the Nineteenth Century*, Fuller, like Jameson and Eliot, used the Madonna to link her Enlightenment-liberal arguments for women's equality (which were based on men's and women's equality as souls) and her essentialist arguments about women's nature and roles. Her ideal for woman is thus not, as many have thought, the solitary and self-reliant goddess-figures of *Woman in the Nineteenth Century* but instead the Madonna, who, as both a virgin and a wife and mother, both an independent self and a companion to man, represents the perfect balance of the self-reliant and relational aspects of female identity.

As these points suggest, while Fuller obviously redefined

Figure 10. Margaret Fuller during the 1848 revolution in Rome (portrait by Thomas Hicks). Her unusually thin face and swollen body suggest that she was pregnant or had recently become a mother. By permission of the Houghton Library, Harvard University (shelf mark bMS Am 1086 box 1).

120　the Madonna of Christian traditions, she drew on these traditions to show how the Madonna's glory reflects on women and to make men reconsider the misogynistic stories they have told about womankind as Eve. With the Virgin Mary, she also called into question the domination of the Father and Son as Christian representatives of divinity. In addition, Fuller made significant use of the Madonna throughout her writings to explore issues of female creativity. The female writer is represented as a powerful virgin mother, creating by a kind of parthenogenesis—though in the process, she may have to choose between literal and literary motherhood and may experience the limitations of both. The Madonna was, finally, a personal symbol for Fuller, as she compared her lot as an unmarried intellectual in New England and New York to that of the ideal "virgin wife" she described in *Woman in the Nineteenth Century*, and later, when, as a writer living in Catholic Italy, she became not only "Signora Ossoli" but a "virgin mother" herself.

Seen in this light, the Madonna's religious, literary, and artistic importance for Margaret Fuller has revisionist implications. First, Fuller's Protestant and feminist appropriation of the Madonna qualifies a view held by many feminist scholars, that the Madonna, defined by a patriarchal church as the exceptional woman who shows the inferiority of all other women, has oppressed rather than empowered women.[2] Second, this study questions the tendency of feminist historians and literary critics to associate the Madonna only with the Angel in the House as an enfeebling icon of "True Womanhood."[3] Fuller's Madonna is, in fact, a powerful figure set in opposition to the True Woman. Third, the study suggests that critics of Fuller's feminist writings have focused too exclusively on the figures of Minerva and the Muse, Isis and Leila, and Ceres and Proserpine in preference to the goddess-figure of Christianity, the Virgin Mary.[4] Finally, Fuller's use of the Madonna constitutes a key element in a more integrative portrait of the author, one that differs from the representations of her biographers, who make determinative of this woman's character either her "feminist" roles as unmarried writer and intellectual,[5] or her "feminine" roles as daughter, "whetstone" of male genius, and lover, wife, and mother.[6] Fuller, in fact, sought to harmonize the roles of "Virgin" and "Wife/Mother" in her writings as well as in her life. The dynamic nature of her engagement with Boston Unitarianism, which is a determining context for her use of the Madonna figure, also benefits from a more detailed examination, especially since biographers have tended to sum Fuller up as orthodox or

heterodox without giving the development of her religious views the   121
attention that her friends' ideas (notably Emerson's) have received.[7]

With Fuller, as with Jameson and Eliot, it is necessary to understand
her religious views to comprehend her innovative treatment of the
Madonna. A good starting point is her mystical "conversion experience" of
1831, when she was twenty-one. She obeyed her father by attending a
dispiriting Thanksgiving service at the Unitarian church and hurried away
afterward into the solitary woods and fields, there at last to receive a vision of the divine: "Suddenly the sun shone out with that transparent
sweetness, like the last smile of a dying lover. . . . And, even then, passed
into my thought a beam from its true sun" (*Essential Fuller*, 11). In the first of
her two accounts of the event, the divine message was solitude:

> I saw . . . that more extended personal relations would only have
> given me pleasures which then seemed not worth my care, and
> which would surely have dimmed my sense of the spiritual
> meaning of all which had passed. I felt how true it was that
> nothing in any being which was fit for me, could long be kept
> from me. (*Letters*, 21 Oct. 1838, 1:347)

In the second account, though, the divine message seemed a demand for
self-transcendence:

> I saw how long it must be before the soul can learn to act under
> these limitations of time and space, and human nature, but I saw,
> also, that it MUST do it. . . . I saw there was no self; that selfish-
> ness was all folly, and the result of circumstance; that it was only
> because I thought self real that I suffered; that I had only to live
> in the idea of the ALL, and all was mine. This truth came to me,
> and I received it unhesitatingly; so that I was for that hour taken
> up into God. In that true ray all the relations of earth seemed
> mere film, phenomena. (1840, *Essential Fuller*, 10–12)

In the first account of the vision, Fuller accepted solitude, and with it spiritual and intellectual independence. In the second, she learned what it
meant to "live first for God's sake" (*WNC*, 346): a transcendence of the

122   limitations of the self, including the need for recognition and for external rather than internal indications of achievement. As Fuller's two interpretations suggest, the depressed daughter and lonely young woman was coming to reject definitions of self in terms of others and so was entering into what she would later call the "virgin's" state—virginity being a term she would rescue from its association with mere spinsterhood and use to designate spiritual self-reliance. We see here, too, a recurrent element in Fuller's religious experience: the desire to be enfolded by God, serene, still, and silent, all striving brought to an end by the sense of completion in God, "all vehemence, all eccentricity purged by [the] streams of divine light" (*Letters*, Sept. 1840, 2:158–60). Such a desire could be in part a psychological response to feelings of despair, loss, and disgust with the world (Fuller's two expressions of her desire to withdraw into God coincided with the 1840 marriage of two people she was in love with, Samuel Ward and Anna Barker, and with the last days of the 1848 Roman revolution). Yet these moments of feeling "exalted and exhausted" by the Infinite were also for Fuller the highest points of her religious life.[8]

At nightfall on that Thanksgiving Day in 1831, Fuller wandered into the churchyard and had another vision, which moved her to prayer: "May my life be a church, full of devout thoughts, and solemn music" (*Letters*, 1:348). This prayer was expanded in a subsequent journal entry:

> What is done here at home in my heart is my religion. . . . Let others choose their way, I feel that mine is to keep my equipoise as steadfastly as I may, to see, to think a faithful sceptic, to reject nothing but accept nothing till it is affirmed in the due order of mine own nature. I belong nowhere. I have pledged myself to nothing. God and the soul and nature are all my creed, subdivisions are unimportant.— . . . I have my church where I am by turns priest & lay man. (Habich, 336)

Fuller's Thanksgiving-Day visions, then, marked the start of her journey away from her father's house. Her spiritual journey ended with her becoming her own church: religion was re-housed in her woman's heart.

Fuller's mystical insights led not only to changes in the locus of her religion but also to analogous changes in her conception of God. Throughout her letters and journals she stated her lack of confidence in God as a father and her disbelief in his providence. One impetus for such statements was intellectual; another, psychological. As a young adult Fuller undertook a reexamination of Unitarian beliefs, especially as articulated by Dr. William Ellery Channing, the leading Unitarian minister of her day and an admired friend. Channing emphasized the joyous sufficiency of God's role as Father as a corollary of the oneness of God. (For instance, he called God the "Universal Parent," benevolent and merciful, "in whom our weaknesses, imperfections, and sorrows may find resource" [*Works*, 400].) Fuller in an early letter sharply criticized such beliefs as the refuge of "loving or feeble natures": "I do not ask or wish consolation,—I wish to know and feel my pain, to investigate its nature and its source; I will not have my thoughts diverted, or my feelings soothed." She did, however, admit that some day, weary of spiritual self-reliance, she might find herself wishing to "lean on something above" (*Letters*, 1:158–59; see also 1:223–24).

Fuller's attitude toward the heavenly Father was psychologically complicated by her association, even conflation, of him with earthly father-figures—Timothy Fuller, and later Pius IX, "papa" of the Roman people—who left her, betrayed her, and proved too weak to protect her and those she cared about. For example, she wrote in her journal at the time of her father's death (1835): "Grant, Oh Father, that neither the joys and sorrows of this past season shall have visited my heart in vain. . . . My father's image follows me constantly, whenever I am in my room; he seems to open the door and look on me with a complacent tender smile" (*Essential Fuller*, 2). Both the earthly and the heavenly father seem present here, comforting her for her loss. In later letters to her suitor James Nathan, she once again linked the two fathers, but now by inverting their places: she described God as a comforting parent, taking the place of her late father and her absent mother, and she placed her father in heaven, blessing her relationship with Nathan. But her father was remote, unseeing, unknowing—because his daughter had closed his eyes, lest he see and weep at "the sad sights of this world." The daughter had become the protective parent, shielding her father from her own harsh adult knowledge.[9]

Fuller later, and probably more consciously, associated the pope with God the Father, and allowed the strength and reliability of the Roman "papa" to determine her confidence in the heavenly one: "A kind of chastened libertine I rove, pensively, always, in deep sadness, often O God help me; is all my cry. Yet I have very little faith in the paternal love, I need; the government of the earth does seem so ruthless or so negligent" (*Letters*, 10 Mar. 1849, 5:205). Indeed, in her analysis of the Roman revolution, the pope lost his legitimacy as a ruler, even before he fled Rome, when he allowed the priest in him to triumph over the reformer, thereby betraying

124 his paternal responsibilities. His place would be taken by his politically maturing people, in a process replicating Fuller's own disempowerment and displacement of Timothy Fuller.[10] Maturity (psychological, political, religious) seems to have been in opposition to reliance on any father.

References to God as "Father" never completely disappear from Fuller's writing. For example, in "Darkness Visible" (a public credal statement published in the *New-York Tribune*, 4 Mar. 1846), she wrote, "[Man] is born capable both of good and evil, and the Holy Spirit in working on him only quickens the soul already there to know its Father" (*Essays*, 339). But she increasingly used gender-neutral and depersonalized terms for God and placed the emphasis on God within rather than God without. An 1841 private credal statement from her journal illustrates both these tendencies:

> There is a spirit uncontainable and uncontained. Within it all manifestation is contained, whether of good (accomplishment) or evil (obstruction). . . . By living it seeks to know itself. Thus evolving plants, animals, men, suns, stars, angels, and, it is to be presumed an infinity of forms not yet visible in the horizon of this being who now writes. . . . The moment we have broken through an obstruction, not accidentally but by the aid of Faith we begin to see why any was permitted. We begin to interpret the Universe and deeper depths are opened with each soul that is convinced. For it would seem that the Divine expressed his meaning to himself more distinctly in man than in the other forms of our sphere. (*Essential Fuller,* 21–22)

The Father-God and Holy Spirit of Unitarianism are here transformed into "a spirit uncontainable and uncontained," who is both within and without the human being. As in Unitarianism, the essence of religion is said to be human growth, which involves overcoming obstructions (evil is a test of human beings rather than the essential mark of human nature), and achieving increased awareness of and conformity to the spirit within (see Channing, 367–408; Hutchison, 1–21). But here the human being also seems to be *God's* teacher: the spirit knows itself through the forms it evolves, and knows itself best in us. Revelation is not said to lead human beings to God; instead, human beings are a revelation to God.

This Transcendentalist reconception of God—as the creative force within both men and women, who makes the individual the source of divine authority, rather than as the Father of revelation, who is made in the image of men—in turn underlies Fuller's feminist arguments in *Woman in the* *Nineteenth Century*. Like Wollstonecraft and Jameson, she based her claims for the equality of men and women on their equality as souls rather than as citizens, and like Eliot later, she called for women's equal freedom to develop their God-given capacities, not first of all for equal rights. While describing the legal, social, and cultural disadvantages of women, she claimed that these are the consequence of a misunderstanding of woman's nature: that she is made for man, to be ruled and formed by him, rather than possessing like him an immortal soul (*WNC*, 260–61, 268). Changes in woman's temporal condition, Fuller said, would follow from acknowledgment of this fundamental truth (258).

But the equality of men's and women's souls did not imply their identicality. Fuller's Enlightenment-liberal arguments in *Woman in the Nineteenth Century* and her *Tribune* essays, which (as above) emphasized women's rights as individuals to the same freedoms and privileges as men, were intertwined with arguments based on the presumed essential differences between men and women and the complementary relation of the sexes. This kind of mixed argument is characteristic of Jameson, Eliot, and Victorian feminism generally, but Fuller had her own contribution to make. Although she argued in *Woman in the Nineteenth Century* that a man and a woman each have "masculine" and "feminine" qualities ("Man partakes of the feminine in the Apollo, women of the masculine as Minerva"), and each may have propensities for tasks delegated to the other sex, she saw a Muse-like "feminine" nature (intuitive, "electric," inspiring rather than creative, and more fundamentally open to influxes of the divine) as predominant in women (309–10, 280). She also assumed that women would continue in their roles as wives, mothers, and homemakers, even arguing in her *Tribune* essays (more conservative on gender issues than *Woman in the Nineteenth Century*) that these roles were natural and best.[11] What makes Fuller's essentialist statements feminist rather than "true-womanish" is their place in her arguments for women's spiritual equality, intellectual freedom, educational and vocational opportunities, and protection from oppression. The whole human race, men as well as women, would benefit, Fuller claimed, if the "idea of Woman" were more fully "brought out" (252, 260). The complementary "masculine" and "feminine" qualities in each individual were matched in her thought by the complementarity of men and women, whom she called the two halves of the same thought, the two chambers of the same heart.[12]

The "idea of Woman" is brought out in *Woman in the Nineteenth Century*

126 and other writings by Fuller's goddess-figures: the virgin goddesses Diana, Minerva, and Vesta, representing nature, wisdom, and home, "unlike in the expression of their beauty, but alike in this,—that each was self-sufficing"; and the "great goddesses" Ceres and her daughter Proserpine (269). In Fuller's poetry and essays we also encounter Leila, Isis, and Hecate, goddesses of the night and the moon with dark penetrating eyes and dark robes from which flashes of light, or insight, gleam. Robert D. Richardson Jr. says of Fuller's use of mythological divinities: "Like Emerson, Thoreau, Parker, and other thinkers of the time, she was interested in the idea that humanity has the seeds of divinity within itself, that what is best in human beings is divine—in short, that men and women can become as gods and goddesses" (170–71). But these goddess-figures also need to be related to Fuller's God-schema. Fuller "depersonalized" but did not "repersonalize" the God of Christianity: she did not substitute goddess-figures (God as Mother, God as Virgin) for God the Father, instead speaking of God without as the "Creator Spirit." We may see the influence of Unitarianism here: it "subtracts" rather than "adds" persons to Godhead. The goddesses instead represent God within: woman's potential perfection, the divine within woman. The presence of these goddesses also suggests the limitations for Fuller of even gender-neutral terms for God, which may promote the spiritual equality of men and women but could not express her sense of the grandeur of woman's special nature. It is thus Fuller's essentialism, suspect to some feminists, that has the more radical implications for her religious thought.

Fuller's Greco-Roman and Egyptian goddesses are solitary, powerful, commanding, frightening, uncontrolled—in the case of Leila, unbounded—figures. Among them, the "Christian goddess," the Virgin Mary, seems an anomalous figure, and critics have tended to dismiss her.[13] But the Virgin Mary is probably the most important of Fuller's goddesses, first, because she is a "socialized" and "bounded" goddess; second, because of her place in Christian tradition; and third, because of her personal relevance for Fuller as she struggled to define her roles as a virgin and writer, and later as a wife and mother.

In *Woman in the Nineteenth Century*, Fuller contended that women are not achieving full development because they are not independent beings; they are instead being fully defined and absorbed by their roles as wives and mothers. An example early in the text is the trader's wife, whose husband (a spokesperson for the nineteenth-century cult of True Womanhood)

expects her to be the unthinking "heart" of the marriage: "too judicious to wish to step beyond the sphere of her sex" and subject to her "head" in everything (255–56). In a ringing criticism of such marriages, Fuller declared, "Union is only possible to those who are units." Therefore she argued for *"celibacy* as the great fact of the time" (312, emphasis added). She urged women to withdraw themselves for a time from men's instruction and from the contaminations of modern society in order to become "virgins" (her term primarily indicating women who are celibate in spirit rather than in body: self-reliant, self-taught, self-fulfilled beings).

As this point suggests, chastity is a component of Fuller's idea of virginity, but a small component, because for this idealist the body was less important than the mind or spirit. Rather, virginity is primarily a matter of self-intactness; the virgin state is "self-subsistence in its two forms of self-reliance and self-impulse," and self-centeredness of the sort that allows woman to live first for God's sake, not for man's (346–47). The corollary of self-intactness is self-expansion: woman as virgin can make her life beautiful, powerful, and complete, achieving the perfection God requires of every species and every soul.[14]

Fuller's representatives of the virgin state include the great goddesses and "the Indian girl betrothed to the sun," who, dedicated to this light of truth, "go[es] no where if his beams [do] not make clear the path," and lives apart in her own wigwam, "sustained by her own exertions" (312, 300–301). The image of the Indian girl was borrowed, with acknowledgment, from Anna Jameson, but considerably radicalized. (Jameson had used this celibate Chippewa woman, whom she called the sun's *wife*, to show the tolerance of foolish lifestyles by American Indians, in contrast to Europeans, who might have burnt her at the stake and thus started a cult [*WSSR*, 2:149–50].) One of Fuller's less exalted examples of the virgin state is Miranda, an independent thinker sometimes identified with Fuller herself. "Fortunate" in her plainness to live free from suitors and offers of marriage, Miranda has relations with both men and women that are "noble, affectionate without passion, intellectual without coldness" (*WNC*, 262).

Despite this praise of the celibate life, Fuller did not intend women to become permanently "virgin." Her ideal is rather the Virgin Mother, the *Madonna*, who represents the perfect balance of the independent and relational aspects of female identity. As Fuller wrote:

> A profound thinker has said, "No married woman can represent the female world, for she belongs to her husband. The idea of Woman must be represented by a virgin."

But that is the very fault of marriage, and of the present relation between the sexes, that the woman *does* belong to the man, instead of forming a whole with him. Were it otherwise, there would be no such limitation to the thought.

Woman, self-centered, would never be absorbed by any relation; it would be only an experience to her as to man. . . . Would she but assume her inheritance, Mary would not be the only virgin mother. (*WNC*, 347)

The Madonna is Fuller's symbol of the woman who is complete—not only a virgin but also a wife and mother, both an independent self and a companion to man. With this figure Fuller claimed for all women, married as well as single, the right to the full intellectual and spiritual self-development that men enjoyed, without giving up the satisfactions of marriage and motherhood which, as Miranda shows, are often the price of female self-reliance. Fuller's Madonna is thus set in opposition to the True Woman, who, pious, pure, domestic, and submissive, is the exemplar of nineteenth-century bourgeois femininity (see Barbara Welter, 151–74, and the discussion below of Fuller in American context).

This empowering redefinition of the Madonna's role calls into question previous critical devaluations of this figure. Indeed, only Jeffrey Steele and John Gatta have noted the pre-eminence of the Madonna-like woman among the goddess-figures in *Woman in the Nineteenth Century*.[15] In contrast, Paula Blanchard criticizes some of Fuller's female role models, including the Virgin Mary and Miranda, as passionless and asexual exemplars of "sublime passivity," and Marie Urbanski claims that Fuller looks beyond "Judeo-Christian patriarchy" to classical mythology for her prototypical mythic woman.[16] But Fuller in fact saw the Madonna as Christianity's multivalent version of the Greco-Roman goddess-figures. The Madonna does differ from the other goddess-figures in *Woman in the Nineteenth Century* in being "bounded": as a wife she is defined in relation to men, rather than being wholly (and threateningly) self-defined. But her boundedness makes her all the more useful when Fuller turned from visionary to practical arguments, and showed the domestic and social benefits for both sexes of allowing woman unrestricted self-development. It would be hard to persuade a male reader that he should want Minerva or Hecate around the house. But the Madonna, even with the independent Virgin's role Fuller gives her, is a more amenable feminine ideal.

Yet Fuller's Madonna, "bounded" and "socialized" as she is, is a protean

figure, easily joining the company of the Greco-Roman virgin goddesses. 129
It was only in the public texts with a large readership (*Woman in the Nine-teenth Century* and the *Tribune* essays) that Fuller emphasized Mary's role as wife.[17] In her private writings (her letters, journals, and poetry),[18] Fuller's attitude seems to have been "Joseph who?"; she focused almost entirely on Mary's roles and relationships that exclude her husband. As Virgin Mother, Mary not only gives birth without a husband but seems part of an unbreak-able dyad with her "holy child," who bears *her* image (e.g., *Letters*, 4:132). The Madonna is the wise educator of the young child or genius (e.g., *Letters*, 2:91–92); here her role touches that of Ceres, who could teach even the "rudest churl" (*WNC*, 345). Fuller's friendship with Caroline Sturgis is several times described as an "Elizabeth and Mary" relationship—a word-less physical and spiritual communion, later confirmed by a ring, a bond that was renewed when they, like their biblical counterparts, both became mothers.[19] Mary, then, in the greater part of Fuller's writings, is virgin, mother, but hardly ever wife. "The woman clothed with the sun," mother of the Son, maintains her kinship with "the Indian girl betrothed to the sun," one of Fuller's most striking examples of the intellectually and spiri-tually self-reliant virgin. The Madonna also seems to function in Fuller's thought in dynamic opposition to the goddess-figure Leila, or "night," whom Fuller identifies as her second self and associates with passion, cre-ativity, and self-transcendence; she is woman without restraints.[20] The Christian goddess-figure Mary and the Romantic goddess-figure Leila, who is the subject of Jeffrey Steele's recent work,[21] may prove to be a more im-portant pairing in Fuller's work than the more frequently analyzed Muse and Minerva of *Woman in the Nineteenth Century*.

The Madonna's usefulness for Fuller the feminist writer was due in large part to this figure's functioning in a religious language and a Christ-ian mythology known to the majority of her readers.[22] In *Woman in the Nine-teenth Century*, her appreciation of this familiar language is readily apparent. She reiterated many traditions about Mary, frequently citing those linking her with Eve, in order to put a corrective emphasis on one of the "truths" they contain: a recognition of woman's divine origins and holy work.

> The severe nation which taught that the happiness of the race
> was forfeited through the fault of a woman, and showed its
> thought of what sort of regard man owed her, by making him

accuse her on the first question to his God . . . even they greeted, with solemn rapture, all great and holy women as heroines, prophetesses, judges in Israel, and if they made Eve listen to the serpent gave Mary as a bride to the Holy Spirit. (266)

Fuller took care to attribute these traditions to particular groups, never herself endorsing the degrading characterizations of woman as Eve. Although the accounts are presented as part of her own and her audience's cultural inheritance, their recurrence suggests that she wished men to reread, with a more open and "spiritual" mind, the stories they had written about women.

Like other Unitarians turned Transcendentalist, Fuller regarded the Scriptures and creeds of Christianity as less important than individual experience for knowledge of God. Like Anna Jameson, she felt that these "forms" could easily become confining and dead unless they were vivified by spirit (e.g., *Letters*, 2:172–73). And like Emerson and Theodore Parker, she extended this Transcendentalist critique of religious forms to that of the persons of Christianity, notably Jesus. Indeed, Fuller said she loved Jesus because she could do without him—meaning that he was a teacher rather than a compulsory Savior. He was unnecessary as a mediator because she could go directly to the Creator Spirit, and the revelation he brought could be found in her own soul (Chevigny, 170 [1842 Credo]; *Letters*, 4:288). Furthermore, Fuller considered Jesus a limited figure, not the only spiritual messenger or "Messiah" needed by humanity. Jesus for her represented holy love and purity, nonviolence, martyrdom for the sake of truth (in a Carlylean phrase, "he never could say what he did not mean"), and sympathy that endures through suffering and is unquenched by death.[23] But she thought that such a figure, for all that, left out much of human experience—that represented by the Greek gods, for example, with their calm rather than martyred beauty and poetic and playful rather than pointed meanings.[24]

To a degree, Fuller's arguments paralleled those of both Parker and Emerson.[25] Her notable differences from Emerson had to do with his masculine characterization of Jesus. Although Emerson said that the teachings rather than the person of Jesus should be emphasized, this son of Unitarianism nonetheless seemed to feel some special kinship with the Son of God. Emerson in his sermons, for instance, called Jesus' true disciples a band of brothers who came to resemble him in manliness (Sermon 62,

Complete Sermons, 2:120, 122). Similarly, fraternal ties between the minister and his Lord proved stronger even than sacramental obligations; when Emerson resigned his ministry ostensibly over the requirement that he celebrate the Lord's Supper, he claimed that Jesus would not want him to continue a religious observance that was not meaningful to him (Sermon 162, *Complete Sermons*, 4:192). Throughout his writings Emerson patterned himself after Jesus—or Jesus after himself. Jesus seems to have been his model of pulpit eloquence.[26] As Joel Porte points out, in *Nature* Emerson spoke as an angry prophet, "assimilat[ing] his voice to that of Jesus"; in later writing he identified with Jesus as Messiah, Preacher, Poet, and Man of Beauty (Porte, *Representative Man*, 76, 115). Emerson, like Fuller, called Jesus an incomplete image of human nature, yet Jesus was also Emerson's true hero, the missing Representative Man whose story would have been the whole.[27]

It is not surprising that Fuller during her New England years, excluded from the college and divinity school that trained her male friends in rhetoric and hermeneutics, and from the pulpits and lecterns they occupied afterward, was not drawn toward the Unitarian Savior who reflected this experience, but rather toward the Virgin Mother of the broader Christian tradition. The spirit still came before the forms for her, the message before persons: when she worked with the biblical and legendary stories about Jesus and Mary, she was not primarily interested in updating interpretations of Scripture and altering Christian teachings, but rather in considering the symbolic value of the biblical figures and using them to revise prevailing views of men's and women's natures and roles. Yet she managed to appropriate for Mary two roles associated with the Father and Son of Christianity. Citing "the mystics," she noted that as Mother and Virgin, Mary can be seen as both a Creator and a Redeemer:

> If it be true . . . that humanity withers through a fault committed by and a curse laid upon woman, through her pure child, or influence, shall the new Adam, the redemption, arise. Innocence is to be replaced by virtue, dependence by a willing submission, in the heart of the Virgin Mother of the new race. (*WNC*, 301)

The Virgin Mother, like God the Father, here creates both an "Adam," a new race, and a child who redeems Adam. The child, as "influence," is the mother's messenger, as the Son bears the Father's Gospel in the New Testament; both call humanity to a life of virtue and conformity to the divine

132 parent's will. Fuller, then, not only glorified woman through the figure of the Virgin Mary but also, in a kind of back-formation, raised Mary, as a Creator and a Redeemer, to the level of the masculine representatives of the divine.

Fuller's most common metaphors for female creativity are maternal. For example, in her *Autobiographical Romance* (dated 1840 or 1841), she described her mother's garden as the womb-like ground of her own creative being: "Within the house everything was socially utilitarian; my books told of a proud world [that of ancient Rome], but in another temper were the teachings of the little garden. There my thoughts could lie fallow in the nest and only be fed and kept warm, not called to fly before the time" (*Essential Fuller*, 32). Note, however, that in this account the daughter spends time with her mother's flowers rather than with the mother herself, who is busy caring for the numerous younger children and for the household (27–28). The father seems to have been the dominant parent in Fuller's upbringing, in particular directing her education, and when he died, she (at age twenty-five) rather than her mother became head of the family. Probably for all these reasons, Fuller throughout her letters and journals more often spoke of herself as a mother than as a child being mothered. And when she used maternal metaphors in her explorations of female creativity, she usually put herself in the mother's role.

What links Fuller's use of maternal metaphors to her other feminist writings is the recurrent presence of the Madonna-figure; the creative mother is in almost every case a Virgin Mother. Because Fuller associated artistic creativity with maternal procreativity, the Virgin Mother rather than the Virgin alone is her figure for the female artist. The roles of virgin and mother counterbalance each other, in fact. Without the opportunities for solitude, self-reliance, and self-education that the virgin's state affords, women would be absorbed in their relations with others, as wives and mothers (*WNC*, 347). But the virgin's state was not a creative one for Fuller,[28] as shown by her description of her aunt Mary Rotch: "She has known peace and assurance, but not energy, not rapture. She is unacquainted with the passions and with genius. She is strong and simple, a vestal mind, transmitting the oracle in purity, but not the parent of new born angels" (*Letters*, 23 June 1842, 3:70). For Fuller the Virgin could be oracular (like Cassandra). But "rapture," "passions," and "genius" (all terms indicating an emotional and creative fullness of being, which is analogous to

sexual fulfillment) are necessary for the propagation of "angels" or "children."
Such offspring (in contrast to the oracles transmitted unchanged by a
"vestal mind") are beings non-identical with the original, experience transformed by erotic energy into something new.

Fuller sometimes saw the roles of author and mother in tension. In a
famous statement—taken as representative by Adrienne Rich and Bell Gale
Chevigny—she claimed that she preferred the children of the muse to
those of actual motherhood, because they rested more lightly on the
bosom (*Essential Fuller*, 7). Here she presented herself as an intellectual
struggling with the dilemma common to women of our era interested in
having both families and careers, and she chose to deny literal motherhood. But this statement should not receive undue emphasis, because
Fuller in fact placed a high value on actual motherhood, even sometimes
(particularly after she became a mother herself) valuing it more than literary achievement:

> They [wives and mothers like Lidian Emerson] dont see the
> whole truth about one like me, if they did they would under-
> stand why the brow of Muse or Priestess must wear a shade of
> sadness. . . . They have so much that I have not, I can't conceive
> of their wishing for what I have (*enjoying* is not the word: these I
> know are too generous for that). But when Waldo's wife, & the
> mother of that child that is gone [little Waldo, dead at five]
> thinks me the most privileged of women . . . it does seem a little
> too insulting at first blush. (1842)

> You speak of my being happy; all the solid happiness I have
> known has been at times when he [her baby Angelino] went to
> sleep in my arms. . . . If I had a little money I should go with
> him into strict retirement for a year or two and live for him
> alone. This I cannot do; all life that has been or could be natural
> to me is invariably denied. (1869)[29]

While it would be wrong to resurrect the view of earlier biographers that
Fuller fulfilled her feminine destiny through marriage and motherhood,[30]
we should also question recent feminist readings of Fuller either as re-
nouncing conventional female roles for the sake of her career[31] or as psychologically working through her maternal longings and eventually
accepting for herself the role of Minerva, the childless figure of wisdom.[32]

134   Meditations on the competing values of literal and literary motherhood occur throughout Fuller's writings, and she seems never to have made a firm choice. Rather, as the figure of the Virgin Mother in particular suggests, she attempted to reconcile the two callings.

More unexpected than Fuller's inner debates are her misgivings regarding both kinds of "maternity," because of the limitations each imposed on her. In a letter to George Davis, her unrequited love when she was in her late teens, she wrote:

> You must then bring your children as you promised and show me. I love to know these new lives in which my friends bloom again.—I feel the darkest hue on my own lot is that I have neither child, nor am yet the parent of beautiful works by which the thought of my life might be represented to another generation. Yet even this is not dark to me, though it sometimes makes me pensive. I have not lived my own life, neither loved my own love, my strength, my sympathies have been given to others, their lives are my aims. If here I could call nothing my own, it has led me to penetrate deeper into the thought which pervades all. I have not been led to limit my thoughts to a person, nor fix my affections with undue order on some one set of objects. So all things are equalized at last.— (*Letters*, 17 Dec. 1842, 3:105)

Motherhood—both literal and literary—would bring fulfillment, but it would also limit the woman to a particular object—this baby, this book— instead of letting her thoughts range freely and lead her, like the unbounded goddess-figure Leila, to unity with the All.[33] There was a worse option for Fuller, though, than either of these kinds of "limitation": a life spent living for others, without a self-chosen object for one's energies or an opportunity for leaving part of oneself to the next generation.

Fuller's metaphorical association of female creativity with virginal motherhood made the mother wholly "author" of her "child," in contrast to the (medieval) views of maternity she criticized in *Woman in the Nineteenth Century*, according to which the father gave the soul to the child, and the mother merely the body (270–71). But why, then, given this empowered female figure, was the "child" in Fuller's work usually a son? Fuller might simply have been conforming to the biblical source of her metaphor: the Virgin Mary had a son, not a daughter. But another reason might have been that "sons" and not "daughters" or "mothers" had access to public roles. That was perhaps why Fuller referred to her planned publications as

her "son" in a letter to her friend Caroline Sturgis, written a number of 135
years before she had a child:

> The life that flows in upon me from so many quarters is too
> beautiful to be checked. I would not check a single pulsation. It
> all ought to be;—if caused by any apparition of the Divine in
> me I could bless myself like the holy Mother. But like her I long
> to be virgin. I would fly from the land of my birth. I would hide
> myself in night and poverty. Does a star point out the spot. The
> gifts I must receive, yet for my child, not me. I have not words,
> wait till he is of age, then hear *him*.[34]

Here Fuller's authorial "mother," in contrast to Emerson's persona, the "ora-
tor," seems to have registered the constraints on women's presence in public discourse by suggesting that the mother's book was her necessary male
surrogate. She might speak, but only indirectly.[35]

By using the Virgin Mother to represent female creativity and authorship,
and by suggesting links between her and Minerva, Fuller calls attention to
the Madonna's possibilities as a figure of Wisdom. It seems surprising at
first that she is the only one of the female intellectuals of this study to do
so. Jameson has a few references in *Legends of the Madonna* to "the most wise
Virgin," but she never expatiates upon a role or attribute for Mary if she is
not fond of the art that contains it, and she notes that Mary as Divine Wisdom appears more often in the "theological art" of the sixteenth and seventeenth centuries (notably in paintings of the Immaculate Conception)
than in Jameson's favorite "Old Italians."[36] Of Eliot's heroines, only Romola
is an intellectual, and she rejects the scholar's life (which is negatively associated with Minerva, the goddess of Wisdom, and with virginal solitude
and self-denial) to become instead an exemplar of maternal or Madonna-
like leadership (see chapter 8).

It could be said that Eliot and Jameson are failing to take advantage of
an available image, but in fact they are closer than Fuller is to the Marian
tradition, because Holy Wisdom is not a central role for Mary in the Western church.[37] The Wisdom literature of the Hebrew Bible and Apocrypha
does contain the female figure of Holy Wisdom, or *Sophia*, who is associated with the presence of God. But Jesus rather than Mary is the primary
representative of Wisdom in Christianity, an identification reinforced by
the replacement of the feminine term *Sophia* with the masculine *Logos* in the
New Testament and early Christian writings.[38] (Some feminist theologians

136   read the Christian use of *Logos* as the deliberate suppression of the feminine aspects of God.)[39] The concept of *Sophia* was integral to Christian Gnostic literature, but Gnosticism was not a context for Victorian studies of the Madonna, since it was known mainly indirectly, through the comments of critics, before the discovery of the Nag Hammadi scrolls in 1945–46.[40] It is also the case that the Virgin Mary's closest affinities are to ancient mother-goddesses such as Ishtar, Isis, and Demeter, rather than to the wisdom-goddess Athena (Minerva).[41] Fuller's attention to Minerva in her writings on the Madonna is thus one of the frequent indications that she is inventing her own mythological parallels rather than following established links.

It is interesting, then, given Fuller's departures from Marian tradition, that her figure for female authorship seems to replicate certain limitations of that tradition. In Jameson's brief discussion of Mary as Wisdom in *Legends of the Madonna*, the examples usually show her seated on a throne and holding a book and the infant Christ (9–10, 69–70). She is here Mother of the Word, meaning Mother of Christ; the holy book testifies to the identity of the baby on her lap. She might be saying: "The gifts I must receive, yet for my child, not me. I have not words, wait till he is of age, then hear *him*." One can thus see why Jameson, Fuller, and Eliot generally found more possibilities in representations of Mary as a solitary, powerful figure (her independence including her right to think for herself, as Fuller said) rather than specifically as Holy Wisdom.

Fuller left New England in 1844 to work for Horace Greeley's reformist *New-York Tribune*, first as a New York–based reviewer and reporter and later as a European correspondent. In her New York articles, Fuller spoke positively of Catholics in order to goad her readers, whom she regarded as the spiritually slovenly and materialistic heirs of the Puritans, to undertake certain individual and social reforms. For example, she pointed out that the "rival" religion, Catholicism, promoted courtesy as well as charity toward the poor. With its "holy family" (Joseph, the Madonna, and the Christ Child), Catholicism had a high ideal of family relations. And it offered Americans a model for their own "national liturgy," in which the American holy-days (Thanksgiving, Christmas, the Fourth of July) would become occasions for spiritual meditation and renewed commitment to national ideals, such as devoted citizenship and freedom and justice for all races.[42]

Fuller's attitude toward things Catholic radically changed, however,   137
when she moved to Italy and was caught up in the 1848 Roman revolution
(during which the papal states were briefly transformed into a republic,
until French forces defeated their opponents and with Austrian help
restored the temporal rule of the pope). The Madonna, an important feminist symbol for Fuller when she was in America, became an almost unusable
symbol when the writer finally encountered her in a Catholic country, in a
sociopolitical (rather than an artistic or literary) context, in which she was
used as a repressive tool by conservative forces.[43] Fuller's experience in Italy
transformed her into a socialist and a radical supporter of the revolution[44]—
she no longer considered herself primarily a feminist—and in her last writings *Jesus*, not Mary, was the answer:

> *The work is done;* the revolution in Italy is now radical, nor can it
> stop till Italy become independent and united as a republic.
> Protestant she already is. The memory of saints and martyrs may
> continue to be revered, the ideal of Woman to be adored under
> the name of Maria.—Christ will now become to be a little
> thought of; *his* idea was already kept carefully out of sight under
> the old regime; all the worship was for Madonna and Saints,
> who were to be well paid for interceding for sinners. An example
> which might make men cease to be [sinners] was no way to be
> coveted. Now the New Testament has been translated into Ital-
> ian; copies are already dispersed far and wide; men calling them-
> selves Christians will no longer be left entirely ignorant of the
> precepts and life of Jesus. (*Dispatches*, 278–79)

Fuller, evidently shocked into Puritanism by her experiences on the Continent, now associated political and social progress with Protestant rather
than Catholic versions of Christianity. Jesus was rehabilitated in her
thought; she sometimes identified the revolutionary leader Mazzini with
Jesus. Women's roles, however, were reduced: they became merely mothers of the revolutionaries.[45]

The irony of Fuller's near-abandonment of the Madonna as a feminist symbol (the Madonna survived in original form only in letters to old friends,
such as Caroline Sturgis) was that in Italy the writer at last became herself
a "Virgin Mother." A sketch of Fuller's use of the Madonna as a personal
symbol makes this point clear. Fuller's never-achieved ideal during her

138 years in America was the Virgin Wife of *Woman in the Nineteenth Century:* a
woman who managed to balance her commitment to her husband and her
commitment to herself, who enjoyed an intimate relationship with him but
was unconsumed by it, remaining a "virgin" capable of independent intellectual growth. The evidence for this point includes Fuller's analysis of the
Emersons' marriage, which she saw as affording wonderful opportunities
for "virginal" intellectual growth but not for wifely happiness, because of
Waldo's emotional coldness. As she put it:

> In our walk and during our ride this morn[in]g L[ydian Emerson]
> talked so fully that I felt reassured except that I think she will al-
> ways have these pains, because she has always a lurking hope
> that Waldo's character will alter, and that he will be capable of
> an intimate union; now I feel convinced that it will never be
> more perfect between them two. . . . Yet in reply to all L. said, I
> would not but own that I thought it was the only way, to take
> him for what he is, as he wishes to be taken, and though my ex-
> perience of him has been, for that very reason, so precious to
> me, I don't know that I could have fortitude for it in a more inti-
> mate relation. Yet nothing could be nobler, nor more consoling
> than to be his wife, if one's mind were only thoroughly made up
> to the truth. (Habich, 331–32)

The ideal of the "Virgin Wife" is also suggested by Fuller's romantic friendships. Her strong intellectual attachments (which were also romantic attachments in the cases of George Davis, Samuel Ward, and James Nathan)
were to men rather than to women, few of whom she regarded as her intellectual equals.[46] Fuller also had romantic feelings for women (notably
Caroline Sturgis and Anna Barker), but after Sturgis refused her invitation
to spend the winter with her in Providence in 1837, she never again proposed to share a household with a female friend.[47] A "Boston marriage"
seems not to have been an option for her. Nor was utopian communal life,
another nineteenth-century alternative to traditional marriage. Although
Fuller was a frequent visitor to Brook Farm, she never became a resident
and expressed misgivings about the experiment (Blanchard, 188–89).
Fuller, then, seems not to have given up hopes of romantic companionship
in heterosexual marriage, but the perfect balance between the roles of "virgin" and "wife" remained elusive, as did a willing mate.

Finally, in Rome, Fuller met and eventually became the wife of Gio-   139
vanni Angelo Ossoli, an Italian aristocrat who fought for the republican
cause (on Fuller's presumed marriage, see Deiss, 291–92). They had a son,
Angelino, born in September 1848. With marriage and motherhood "my
heart is bound to earth as never before," Fuller said, referring to her moth-
erly fears about her sickly child's welfare and her new experiences with a
household and a family of her own (*Letters*, 5:257, 280). But the phrase
"bound to earth" also points to her association of Boston with the mind and
art, and Rome and Rieti (the "aboriginal village" where Angelino was born
and nursed) with the body. The marriage of "Boston" and "Rome," of Fuller
and Ossoli, was for her the union of mind and body. The marriage unified
Fuller as well; she had long spoken of herself as "earthy" and had felt "all
Italy glowing beneath the Saxon crust" (*Letters*, 2:202). Fuller's view of marriage now contained a frank acknowledgment of human sexuality that was
missing from former descriptions of a desirable marriage as a "brother-
sister" relationship (*Essays*, 260).

Woman in the Nineteenth Century provides a context for this earlier "fraternal" view of marriage. Fuller was interested in virginity primarily as a spiritual rather than a sexual state; she told wives as well as single women to
become virgins, self-reliant thinkers who are uncontaminated by social
mores and live always in awareness of the divine (312, 346–47). But toward
the end of the book she did consider purity in courtship and marriage, an
issue that brought together her earlier concern with freedom from social
contamination and a new emphasis on women's sexual as well as spiritual
well-being. Fuller, like Jameson (whom she cited) and Eliot later, saw contemporary relations between men and women as too often marked by "sensual and mental pollutions" (331). Men were not expected to restrain their
sexual passions, nor women to know or care if they waltzed with "Satyrs"
or become the brides of men "incapable of pure marriage" (320–22, 331).
Fuller boldly argued that prostitution was the consequence of current
courtship and marriage practices. She considered fallen women the physical and spiritual victims not only of men who were enslaved by their own
"brute natures" but also of so-called respectable women, whose fine dress
and flirtatious ways were imitated by poorer women at such a cost.[48]

Against marriage *à la mode*, that state of sensuality and inequality, Fuller
proposed what she considered ideal forms of marriage: intellectual companionship (the partners would be like "brother" and "sister"), and the still-
higher religious union, in which the partners were pilgrims journeying

140 toward a common shrine (282–89). Fuller reiterated these ideas in a *New-York Tribune* essay ("Christmas," 21 Dec. 1844), holding up the Joseph-Mary relationship as a marital ideal:

> Does [man] see in [woman] a holy mother, worthy to guard the infancy of an immortal soul? Then she assumes in his eyes those traits which the Romish Church loves to revere in Mary. Frivolity, base appetite, contempt are exorcised; and men and women appear again in unprofaned connexion, as brother and sister, the children and the servants of the one Divine love, and pilgrims to a common aim. (*Essays*, 260)

The problem with Fuller's alternatives to "profaned connexion" is, of course, that they are desexualized. Rhetorical excess is not the explanation. Fuller was long ambivalent about the place of passion in human relationships. She wrote, for example, in *Woman in the Nineteenth Century*:

> [L]et every woman . . . [see] whether she would not desire for her son a virtue which aimed at a fitness for a divine life, and involved, if not asceticism, that degree of power over the lower self, which shall "not exterminate the passions, but keep them chained at the feet of reason." The passions, like fire, are a bad master; but confine them to the hearth and the altar, and they give life to the social economy, and make each sacrifice meet for heaven. (333)

Fuller here expressed two conflicting views: a Romantic recognition of passion as the energy necessary for marital and social relationships; and a Platonic sense of our "brute nature" as needing to be kept on a leash and made to trot at Reason's heels.[49]

It was perhaps Fuller's friend Adam Mickiewicz, the Polish poet and nationalist, who helped her finally to act on her Romantic views. Mickiewicz told her, soon after they met in Paris in 1847: "For you, the first step in your delivery and in the delivery of your sex (of a certain class) is to know if it is permitted to you to remain virgin. Thou must bear to the new world the fruit furnished by the ages, the animating fruit."[50] That fall in Rome, Fuller began her sexual relationship with Ossoli, at first extramaritally, a previously self-forbidden way. She achieved a new sense of the in-

tegration of herself and her experience; "Boston" and "Rome" within her
now embraced.

But the transformation was not complete. Fuller's writings showed a
continued idealist valuation of mind over body, and a sometimes deroga-
tory bourgeois association of the body with earthiness, sensuality, and the
anti-intellectual lower classes of America[51] and Italy. For example, she proclaimed:

> My poor Italian brothers, they bleed! I do not love them much,
> —the women not at all; they are too low for me; it will be cen-
> turies before they emerge from a merely animal life.
>
> The men too, though their sentiment is real, are in thought
> too much the fanfaron. Except Mazzini, dearest, reverend friend,
> my first Italian friend, still infinitely my most prized,—a great
> and solid man.[52]

Fuller's values were a divisive element in her marriage to Ossoli, a well-
born but poorly educated Italian. There was always a sense of incompat-
ibles joined, which was made explicit in her letters to family and friends,
where she expressed her love for her husband but called their union one of
unequals (*Letters*, 5:248, 260–61); it might be compared to George Eliot's
late marriage to John Walter Cross. Marrying "Rome" and bearing "Rieti"
made Fuller a "madonna," an ordinary wife and mother of Italy. But the intellectual distance she saw between herself, a professional "Boston" writer,
and her husband meant that she was not the Virgin Wife of *Woman in the
Nineteenth Century*, involved in the kind of mentally and emotionally intimate relationship that was her enduring marital ideal.

Fuller claimed that marriage brought her contentment; but "the great
novelty, the immense gain to me is my relation with my child" (*Letters*,
5:292). Her attitude toward her son differed from her attitude toward her
husband in that she saw Angelino, who was nursed and for his first year
raised by Italians, as "part of them" but also "part of me," responsive to his
mother above all. Ossoli's absence from Rieti during Fuller's pregnancy and
the first months of the baby's life would have strengthened the mother-
child bond, while his decision—reluctantly acceded to by Fuller—to leave
the baby behind when they returned to Rome may have made her resent
him as a father, since Rome came under siege during this time, but the baby
proved to be in greater danger at Rieti, where his nursemaid starved him.[53]

142   Shortly after the French occupied Rome in 1849, the Ossolis were
forced to leave the city, and the whole family was reunited in Florence.
One of Fuller's letters from this time, written to an unnamed friend
(perhaps Sarah Shaw, whose children were often a topic of conversation),
indicated the strength of her attachment to the baby, and the growing su-
perfluity of the husband's presence:

> It is an evening of cold, statue-like moonlight, such as we have
> in New England, such as I do not remember in all my life of
> Italy. . . . Now Ossoli is gone out, and I am alone in my little
> room, beside a bright fire. I have your letter before me, and I am
> thinking how much I wish for you instead. Though your letter is
> very dear, and does me good, you are one of the persons I have
> wished so much might know about me without being told. I
> have thought a great deal about you, and things you used to tell
> me, and remembered little traits and pictures of your children
> that would surprise you. How pleasant it would be to talk over
> all these now and here; for you are quite right, it is in Italy we
> should have met. . . . It troubles me to think of going to Amer-
> ica. I fear [Ossoli] will grow melancholy-eyed and pale there,
> and indeed nothing can be more unfit and ill-fated outwardly
> than all the externals of our relation. I can only hope that true
> tenderness will soothe some of them away. I have, however, no
> regrets; we acted as seemed best at the time. If we can find a
> shelter for our little one, and tend him together, life will be very
> precious amid very uncongenial circumstances. I thought I knew
> before what is the mother's heart, I had felt so much love that
> seemed so holy and soft, that longed to purify, to protect, to sol-
> ace *infinitely*; but it was nothing to what I feel now. (*Letters*,
> 5:282–83)

This letter invites us to put Fuller's ideal of the Virgin Wife aside, as she evidently had to, and to consider anew the figure of the Virgin Mother, this
time as a distinctive role—a mother who is *not* also a wife. The Virgin
Mother, as divinely represented by Mary and Ceres, has no mate when she
bears a holy child, a child in her image who can be claimed as hers alone.
Her agony when this beloved child is lost rends the world. The Virgin
Mother is important in Fuller's thought for combining virginal independence, maternal influence and procreative power, sometimes with male-

exclusive ties to other women (see Fuller's descriptions of the Elizabeth and Mary relationship; *Essential Fuller*, 44–49). She is also a useful figure for analyzing Fuller's own experience as a wife and mother—sometimes uncannily useful, for Fuller often seemed to anticipate in her writings the form her own life would take.

Fuller after she became Signora Ossoli was still a "virgin"—an independent intellectual. She was also a loving mother, expressing hopes that her devotion to spiritual things and her pure influence would cause her child to be a holy child, a messenger of love, peace, and charity to humankind (see, e.g., *Essays*, 260). But the Christ-like child should also be a prophet of social justice and (in Angelino's case, as in Mazzini's) a savior of the suffering Italian people ("the elegant Austrian officers . . . will be driven out of Italy when Angelino is a man"; *Essays*, 362–65; *Letters*, 5:202, 305). Fuller's expectations for her son literalized those of the "authorial mother" prominent earlier in her writings, whose book was similarly her male agent in an androcentric world. Unlike the Virgin Mothers of biblical and classical mythology, however, Fuller had a husband as well as a child. But there are strong suggestions that the mother-child bond, providing a constant intimate communion—emotional, physical, perhaps eventually intellectual—would have proved more enduring than the marital bond (which she came to describe as "unfit" and "ill-fated," *Letters*, 5:282–83). Fuller was usually critical, sometimes disillusioned, about the relations between adult men and women. The mother-child relationship was the one she never stopped romanticizing.

As a mother Fuller exchanged her solitude for a family and an even larger community: her letters reveal not only the unbreakable and all-sufficient dyad of mother and child, but also the warm, strong, communicative, and husbandless bonds between her and other mothers, such as her unnamed correspondent and Caroline Sturgis Tappan. One senses in the affectionate message cited above, which was written most likely to another woman while the baby slept, the truly radical potential of the figure of the Virgin Mother. "Ossoli is gone out, . . . [and] I wish for you instead" seems Fuller's prediction of what might have awaited her in America (*Letters*, 5:282–83); she would remain the Virgin Mother but not, perhaps, Wife. One wonders whether Fuller's next move might have been beyond marriage altogether, to an informal version of a Herland like Charlotte Perkins Gilman's, a society based on the principle of motherhood and comprised of mothers and their offspring. In her marriage, then, Fuller did not achieve her earlier ideal of the Virgin *Wife*. But her last letters leave us,

144   significantly, with the image of her and Angelino as Madonna and Child, a family portrait in which her aristocratic Roman Joseph does not appear. In the months remaining to Fuller before her death, with her family, at sea, she seems to have developed her final version of the Madonna's role: she herself became the by now alternative ideal of the Virgin *Mother.*

Fuller is famous as a wide-ranging reader, and she drew on numerous ancient and modern European writers (Homer, Ovid, Christian mystics, Dante, Goethe, Manzoni, Sand, Swedenborg, Fourier) to construct her arguments about the Madonna. But though she first saw the figure of the Virgin in literature from Catholic Europe, the definitive philosophical and ideological contexts for her arguments were American ones: Boston Unitarianism and the Anglo-American cult of True Womanhood.

Fuller redefined Boston Unitarianism when she, like other Transcendentalists, reconceptualized God the Father as a depersonalized Spirit, and then moved beyond such gender-neutral ideas to use ancient goddesses, especially the Madonna, as a symbol of the divine within woman. She retold biblical and legendary stories, most importantly those of Eve and Mary, to make us alter our debased conceptions of the idea of woman. In particular, the Madonna's role in mystical thought as Creator and Redeemer gloriously intimated for her the ways woman could transform man and nature when she had "the rights of an immortal soul." Fuller's reexamination of Christian tradition and her interest in challenging, and in some ways redefining, her own religious tradition are among her strongest similarities to Jameson, who was established earlier as a writer but turned her attention to the Madonna later than Fuller did. Fuller's placement of the Christian Virgin in the company of the ancient great goddesses and her contrast of the Christian and the Greek ethos had their parallels in both Jameson and Eliot.

It is because Fuller was a "liberal Christian" (one of the Unitarians' preferred terms for themselves) and a freethinking Protestant that she could borrow creatively from Catholic writers without doctrinal or institutional constraints, and could freely celebrate rather than veil the Virgin Mary's likeness to earlier goddesses. Fuller's ability to make the Madonna an empowering symbol for women was thus a function of her distance from Catholicism. Some modern feminist scholars, such as Marina Warner and Barbara C. Pope, have argued that the Madonna has historically been a male-controlled symbol used to the detriment of women—her perfect

purity exposing all other women's carnal inferiority, her silence and submissive maternity made a model for their own conduct.[54] Fuller herself expressed similarly negative readings of the Madonna, but only when she
moved beyond Continental literature to experience Catholicism directly
as a social and political force, particularly in the papal states, where the
Virgin Mother glorified by the poets and adored by the common people
was manipulated by kings and priests to uphold the old regime. But even
then Fuller's earlier categories for the Madonna, in her private writings if
not in her journalism, survived. (Eliot's writing will exhibit similar shifts in
its "politics of Mary.")

As a feminist thinker, Fuller's most radical moves were, first, to split
apart the roles of virgin, wife, and mother (so that each could be reevalu-
ated and redefined), and then to combine these roles in new ways: as the
Virgin Wife, or the Virgin Mother. Both of these moves show Fuller's
responsiveness to the Anglo-American cult of True Womanhood, that
nineteenth-century code of conduct for the worthy bourgeois female. The
True Woman, according to Barbara Welter (151–74), was pious, the moral
center of her household. She was pure, a maiden before marriage and a
faithful wife thereafter (no matter what her husband did). She was devoted
to her domestic duties—whether that meant, as in Mrs. Sarah Ellis's popular advice book *The Women of England* (1838), that as the "least engaged
member of [the family]" she spent her time sweetly arranging the breakfast
table, greeting everyone with a smile, seeing off the travelers, thriftily ordering the dinner, and nursing the sick child (21–22); or whether, as in
Paula Blanchard's description of Fuller's mother in Groton, she did the
cooking, scrubbing, laundering, ironing, sewing, gardening, and child-
tending of the gentleman farmer's wife (77–80). The True Woman was, finally, submissive to men, and that extended not just to her daily manners
but even to her education. According to Ruskin (an extremist on this
issue), "A man ought to know any language or science he learns, thoroughly
—while a woman ought to know the same language, or science, only so far
as may enable her to sympathise in her husband's pleasures, and in those
of his best friends" ("Of Queens' Gardens," 8:128).

In opposition to the True Wife—who is well exemplified by the
trader's wife in *Woman in the Nineteenth Century*—Fuller proposed the Virgin,
that self-reliant being of pure expansive mind, and especially the Virgin
Wife, exemplified by the Madonna, whose commitment to her own self-
development prevents her from being absorbed by her relationships with
her husband and children. There is also the Virgin Mother, who does not

146   depend on a man at all. Sometimes the virginal qualities of this figure are stressed: the divine Virgin Mothers, Mary and Ceres, reproduce partheno-genetically. Sometimes maternal qualities are brought out: the ordinary mother, like the Madonna, can have an unbreakable and all-sufficient bond with her child, who is made a "holy child" by her spiritual influence.

Fuller's radical redefinitions of the Virgin Mother resonate in Eliot's work; indeed, she might be called the Muse to the novelist, throwing off quicksilver suggestions that the other massively developed. Jameson, too, was a feminist interpreter of Mary in *Legends of the Madonna*, but she was somewhat limited by the conservative design of the project; she focused on the Virgin Mary as she has appeared in the art and legends of the church. But she joined Fuller in her appreciation for the Virgin as a figure particularly important for nineteenth-century women as they struggled for intellectual self-reliance and economic and social independence. And the art historian's comments, as an unhappily married woman, on the hus-bandless groupings of Madonna and Child suggest that she, too, had thoughts on the reconfiguration of the family.[55]

The Madonnas of all three writers were, of course, defined in large part against the Victorian feminine ideal. True Womanhood helped deter-mine which new roles for women Fuller explored. She did not character-ize the Madonna or other goddess-figures simply as powerful mothers, for example, because full-time maternity with its domestic responsibilities was what nineteenth-century women needed to escape from. Fuller might have praised virginity in order to improve the spinster's status as an unchosen, threadbare, and superfluous woman (Fuller herself was in her thirties, with-out marriage prospects, when she wrote her feminist texts). But her main focus was not on the spinster herself but on the spiritual and intellectual freedom of the single state. The fact that the "Virgin Wife" had no male equivalent, and that a woman was forced to leave her household and live in solitude to rediscover what it meant to belong to herself, shows how un-conducive nineteenth-century married life usually was for women's—as opposed to men's—mental development and creative activity.

Fuller, furthermore, has a place in a larger company of women, beyond Jameson and Eliot. In *Woman in the Nineteenth Century*, she responded to the ideas of an earlier and equally brilliant feminist, Mary Wollstonecraft, par-ticularly to Wollstonecraft's melancholy concern for female self-sufficiency. Wollstonecraft in *A Vindication of the Rights of Woman* (1792) tells the fic-tional story of a woman who has developed her natural capacities and has become rational, virtuous, and physically strong. She thus remains the respected friend of her husband when his ardent affection for her dies, as is inevitable in marriage. In time, the woman is widowed, and when the pangs of loss subside, she heroically devotes herself to her children, anxious to provide for them and be both mother and father to them. Wollstonecraft concludes:

> I think I see her surrounded by her children, reaping the reward of her care. The intelligent eye meets hers, whilst health and innocence smile on their chubby cheeks, and as they grow up the cares of life are lessened by their grateful attention. She lives to see the virtues which she endeavoured to plant on principles, fixed into habits, to see her children attain a strength of character sufficient to enable them to endure adversity without forgetting their mother's example. (138–39)

According to Wollstonecraft, female self-development and self-reliance are necessary for a husband's respect, for a woman's own dignity, and for her survival, since romantic love and even the marital bond are the most fragile of human ties. It is the mother-child relationship that endures. In Wollstonecraft we seem to see Fuller's Virgin Wife and Virgin Mother in solitude and mourning, while in Charlotte Perkins Gilman the Virgin Mother reappears in the joyful community of other women, mothers and daughters. Fuller with her flexible intellectual reach seems to stretch backward and forward in time, and welcome the other mothers of feminism into her embrace.

Significantly, it is the Christian and Romantic writers Fuller cited (e.g., the Christian mystics, Dante, and Manzoni) who allowed her to conceive the Virgin Mother and Virgin Wife, exemplified above all by the Madonna, as a glorious figure. But the definitive contexts for her work were closer to home. This writer's dynamic reactions to Unitarianism and the cult of True Womanhood are what gave her Madonna her practical power, as a model of the intellectually self-reliant, relationally fulfilled woman Fuller wanted her contemporaries to become.

Sinking by Her Material Weight below Godhead

Adam Bede

CHAPTER SEVEN

The biggest difference between Eliot and her predecessors Anna Jameson and Margaret Fuller is simultaneously a point of similarity: her work seems the most marked by her awareness of the other writers. The Madonna of Eliot's *Adam Bede*, for instance, resembles the biblical Virgin described by Jameson and is responsive to two divergent theories of the "human form divine"—Ludwig Feuerbach's treatment of feminized Godhead, and Fuller's redefinition of the Virgin Mother. In *Romola* and *Middlemarch*, the novelist, like Fuller and Jameson, considers the relation between ordinary women's lives and the images and legends of the Madonna and the saints, which express, as the earlier writers claim, an ennobling "idea of Woman." Eliot's interest in the Madonna has been discussed by a number of important critics, among them Margaret Homans, Gillian Beer, and Nancy Paxton. But these studies have examined the Madonna in just a few novels and generally in relation to a larger topic, such as female authorship. Yet the Virgin Mother was a continuing presence in Eliot's work, and her treatment by the novelist reflected the changing contexts in which she was seen: art, history, and evolutionary theory.

When Eliot was writing *Adam Bede*, she encountered the Madonna most memorably in art, extracting her for use as a feminist symbol. The novelist follows Fuller in considering the Madonna as Virgin and Mother and making her a symbol of what woman might gloriously become if all her powers

could develop unchecked. In *Romola*, similarly, Eliot represents the 149
Madonna as a divine Mother, powerful and merciful, who is associated
with the ancient great goddesses. The heroine Romola emerges as a
Madonna-figure and a model of female leadership for both the fifteenth and
the nineteenth centuries. In *Romola*, religious art, Victorian feminism, and
Renaissance history all come together in a grand narrative unity. In Eliot's
subsequent works, though, the Madonna starts to function negatively and

Figure 11. George Eliot, 1872 (drawing by Lowes
Cato Dickinson). Courtesy of the National Portrait Gallery, London.

150   in more limited ways in the author's feminist arguments, even as she becomes central to the meditations on religious differences and religious inheritance. *Middlemarch* continues the emphasis on visual representation found in *Romola*, but the Madonna has a greatly diminished role, because she is largely absent from the consciousness of the Protestant Middlemarchers, who live in a modern world without awareness of the divine. The Madonna in this novel primarily functions in descriptions of the male gaze—the connoisseur's gaze (which assesses female beauty in terms of European art) and the iconizing gaze (which sees a virtuous woman in terms of the Virgin Mary but contains her in the passive roles most serviceable to men).

In mid-career Eliot grew interested in the fifteenth-century Mediterranean world, the setting of *Romola* and the dramatic poem *The Spanish Gypsy*, and as a result the Madonnas in her works became grounded in history and in particular Catholic cultures. In the early novels, the narrators reach beyond the experience of the male and female characters to suggest new possibilities in the Madonnas found in art. But in the later works, the characters themselves define the usage of this figure, and she becomes a less versatile though more historically resonant symbol. For example, *The Spanish Gypsy* and *Daniel Deronda* deal with conflicts between people of different faiths—Jews, Christians, Muslims, and Gypsies—and in neither work does the Madonna become, or remain, a model for the female protagonist. In *The Spanish Gypsy* the Christian Virgin is associated with the persecutors of the Gypsies and Moors, and in *Daniel Deronda* the Jewish heroine Mirah is deliberately not made a "Miriam," readable as the Old Testament type of Mary. The marginalization of the Madonna in these late works indicates the severity of Eliot's criticisms of Christians for their lives of "spiritual inanition" and the centuries of cruelty they have shown toward adherents of other faiths. In *Romola*, the Madonna is the divine Mother and the Blessed Lady from over the sea, and in *Middlemarch*, she becomes *his* lady, the possession of one chivalrous man. In Eliot's last works, the Lady nearly vanishes.

As this overview suggests, Eliot's Madonnas cannot be understood apart from her feminist beliefs and religious views. Her feminism, which is representative of the period, is marked not only by a commitment to male-female equality in crucial areas but also by an acceptance of certain essential physical and psychological differences between the sexes. The first strand in Eliot's feminism emphasizes women's rights, the second, the benefits to society of women's contributions. In Victorian Britain, where gender

differences were the fundamental binary opposition organizing knowledge   151
and institutions, as Mary Poovey points out (*Uneven Developments*, 1–23), the
Virgin Mother of Catholicism, a revered and empowered representation of
female nature, a sign that man is not alone divine, is possibly the most effective gendered symbol that could be used in feminist arguments, as Eliot
clearly realizes.

Eliot's treatment of religion, though most frequently analyzed in relation to the nineteenth-century philosophers Strauss, Feuerbach, and
Comte, reveals three additional and recurrent concerns. First, there is
Eliot's interest, shared by art critics like Jameson and Ruskin, in the relation between the sacred image and religious belief. In several works the author presents sacred images, especially those of the Madonna, as
expressions of the greatest human needs and aspirations and as the de-
mocratizing determinant of religious beliefs. She also suggests that the il-
legibility of religious images is one of the signs, in modern society, of the
loss of the unifying concept of God. Second, there is the question of Eliot's
own religious beliefs, which may be characterized as agnostic rather than
atheistic, since she may have retained some kind of belief in the divine.
Third, there is Eliot's constant interest in what might be called the materialist basis of religion (religion as grounded in the body and in physical and
emotional "hungers"), which eventually develops into a Lamarckian theory
of religion as a racial or physical inheritance. This understanding of religious inheritance informs her late works *The Spanish Gypsy* and *Daniel
Deronda*. The influence of Lamarckian ideas on Eliot's religious views has
not been explored by previous critics dealing with her evolutionary
thought.[1] While a unified theory of Eliot's religious views is beyond the
scope of this study, her enduring concerns, shared with many intellectuals
in the eighteenth and nineteenth centuries, will be addressed: the origin of
religion, the status of the image, the transmission of religious inheritance,
and the nature of the Divine Mystery.

Marilyn Massey, in her book *Feminine Soul* (1985), argues that the eigh-
teenth- and nineteenth-century idea of a feminine soul, or woman's unique
spiritual qualities, was not necessarily detrimental to women, as many feminists today suppose. Massey shows that for certain German and Swiss
writers (Novalis, J. H. Pestalozzi, and Friedrich Froebel) the idea of a feminine soul led to "a reconceptualization of the deity itself as female and
powerful" and seems to have encouraged women to seek "a more powerful

152   role within the family, a rebellion against the family and marriage itself, a freedom to write, and a demand for participation in social and political institutions" (23–25).[2]

Massey's insights elucidate Eliot's early fiction, particularly *Adam Bede* (1859). Eliot's treatment of the Madonna in this novel shows the influence of several works: Feuerbach's *The Essence of Christianity* (translated by Eliot in 1854), Jameson's *Legends of the Madonna* (1852), and Fuller's *Woman in the Nineteenth Century* (reviewed by Eliot in 1855). The novel contains two representatives of the feminized divine: a Feuerbachian Christ-figure (Adam Bede), and a Jamesonian Madonna-figure (Dinah Morris). The impact of Fuller's work is suggested by Dinah's radically independent role as body-denying Virgin. Yet, more importantly, *Adam Bede* demonstrates how Eliot, along with Feuerbach, Jameson, and Fuller, transforms a central nineteenth-century religious symbol. Feuerbach's version of feminine Godhead (ultimately, the feminized *Son* rather than the Mother) yields in Jameson to a celebration of the *Madonna* as divinized woman. Fuller and Eliot, in turn, make the Virgin Mother a representation of earthly women's desirable perfection and completion and—as in Jameson—a figure in a critique of the social oppression of women. While the four writers have differing understandings of God,[3] all four associate feminine qualities with the idea of perfection and progress and use the Madonna or feminine God as a symbol of completion. Feuerbach says, "Man needs a whole God" (65); for these writers, our image of God is insufficient, or our views of society and human nature are diminished, if feminine qualities are excluded. The idea of the Madonna or divinized female nature therefore functions as a symbol or a means of completion (of God, of society, of woman herself) and is central to all the writers' visions of human perfection and human progress: moral, social, intellectual.

Feuerbach, however, differs from Eliot, Jameson, and Fuller in a crucial respect: he attributes a female nature to God but separates feminine qualities, which are worthy of Godhead, from actual women, who seem not to be; he thus impoverishes women, leaving them no portion in Godhead. In contrast, Eliot, like Jameson and Fuller, makes Mary a central figure in arguments for the inclusion of women in the divine, in society, and in visions of progress. She insists that female experience and actual women be acknowledged as part of the ideals, work, and destiny of the human race. The Madonna thus serves, particularly in her early work, as in Jameson's and Fuller's, as an empowering symbol for women, a symbol of what they, freed from social restraints, might become. However, given the actual status

of women in nineteenth-century England and America, the Madonna is an
as-yet unrealized ideal for women and thus also serves as the basis of a feminist social critique.

Feuerbach's importance for Eliot has been well established, but in studies that mostly predate the rise of feminist literary criticism and are not engaged with the central issues of sex and gender in his philosophy—specifically, the masculine and feminine qualities attributed to God.[4] In *The Essence of Christianity*, Feuerbach claims that God is a projection of perfect, unlimited human nature, revered as a distinct being (14). The human being's consciousness of God is in fact self-consciousness, consciousness of his or her own nature as freed from individual limitations (12, 31). The attributes of God, infinite in number and changing as human culture develops, are human attributes, expressions of the most precious human thoughts and feelings (20–22). Human beings deny to themselves what they attribute to God; for example, monks dispense with real women and make the Virgin Mary, an ideal woman, an object of love (26). "What man withdraws from himself, what he renounces in himself," Feuerbach writes, "he only enjoys in an incomparably higher and fuller measure in God" (26).

Feuerbach considers Christ rather than God the Father to be "the real God of Christians," because "on him alone are heaped all the joys of the imagination, and all the sufferings of the heart" (147–48). Christ is also Feuerbach's primary representative of the feminine qualities of Godhead. He calls God the Father the "I" and the understanding, and God the Son the "thou" and the heart; Father and Son are united by their love for each other (65–73). Interestingly, the third person of the Trinity for Feuerbach is not the Holy Spirit but the Virgin Mother, needed to complete this holy family (70). But the Mother seems a redundant presence, because the Son already represents the feminine principle of Godhead:

> The Son is the mild, gentle, forgiving, conciliating being—the womanly sentiment of God. God, as the Father, is the generator, the active, the principle of masculine spontaneity; but the Son is begotten without himself begetting, *Deus genitus*, the passive, suffering, receptive being; he receives his existence from the Father . . . . The Son is thus the feminine feeling of dependence in the Godhead. (71)

154   The Mother herself is needed only to represent the first beloved of the Son
and the inconsolable mourner for the lost Son.[5] She is important in relation to the Son, but not, it seems, in herself.

   Feuerbach's thought in *The Essence of Christianity* is thus essentially binary (Father and Son; "I" and "Thou"; masculine and feminine; Judaism and
Christianity; divine and human; etc.). He even says, shortly before his
analysis of the Mother's participation in Godhead, that two Persons are
sufficient for the Trinity, because "two is the idea of multiplicity, and can
therefore stand as its complete substitute" (68). God-as-three, then, is a
discordant element in Feuerbach's text, and three soon yields to two: the
Mother disappears.[6] Moreover, the Son is called the feminine principle *in
abstracto*, while the Mother is the feminine principle *in concreto* (71). The
"feminine" qualities given to the Son are love, gentleness, and mercy; the
body and the maternal roles it defines are what are left for the Mother.
Even though Feuerbach elsewhere argues that "corporeality and sex" do
not contradict the idea of Godhead (93), it seems to be the concreteness
of the female body that makes the Mother fall out of the Trinity.

   Feuerbach thus shows the central importance of the feminine nature of
Godhead but the nonessentiality of the woman. In his text female divinity
seems to be a projection of the *male* desire for completion by the addition
of feminine qualities. Woman, however, cannot see herself in Feuerbach's
God. Feuerbach's position has analogies to those of other nineteenth-
century religion scholars interested in humanizing Godhead (e.g., Schleiermacher and Renan, who also feminize Jesus but do not divinize God).[7] Although the author of *The Essence of Christianity* is not concerned with the
social and political impact of his religious philosophy, his images of Godhead replicate and help to reinforce the nineteenth-century woman's subordination to men and her exclusion from power, human or divine.[8]

   A second important line of argument in Feuerbach's *The Essence of Christianity* concerns his belief, shared by many of his contemporaries, in the
progress of religion.[9] Feuerbach calls religion humankind's earliest and
most indirect form of self-knowledge: the human being first sees his nature
as if out of himself, before he sees it in himself. "The historical progress of
religion consists in this: that what by an earlier religion was regarded as
objective, is now recognised as subjective; that is, what was formerly con-
templated and worshipped as God is now perceived to be something
human" (13). Feuerbach praises Christianity as the religion most responsive
to human longings, because it worships a God made in the image of the
human being (144–45). The mystery of the Incarnation is that God so

loves humankind that he is willing even to empty himself of Godhead for   155
man's sake (50–58). The Incarnate God, then, is God as Love. And love,
according to Feuerbach, is "essentially feminine in its nature" (72). Feminine Godhead thus represents the most important and progressive element
of Christianity.

But Christianity has not yet become humanism; Feuerbach's praise alternates with criticisms of this creed as otherworldly and alienating: "there
entered with Christianity the principle of unlimited, extravagant, fanatical,
supranaturalistic subjectivity; a principle intrinsically opposed to that of
science, of culture. With Christianity man lost the capability of conceiving himself as a part of Nature, of the universe" (133; see also 160–61).
Since the course of religious development for Feuerbach involves taking
more and more from God and attributing more and more to human nature
(31), religion must progress beyond the "alienating delusions" of Christianity. Feuerbach's argument proves important for George Eliot's *Adam
Bede*, in which a more humanistic, "progressive" version of Christianity triumphs over an otherworldly version.

Probably the most famous critics of Feuerbach are Marx and Engels,
who acknowledge their indebtedness to him in their formulations of dialectical materialism. But they come to see him as insufficiently materialist; Feuerbach thinks it sufficient to interpret the world, they say, when he
ought to change it.[10] The two philosophers also criticize Feuerbach for
positing a universal "essence of humanity" found in each individual, for
having a notion of man that, like his notion of God, is an abstraction, divorced from real historical conditions.[11] This critique of Feuerbach's "man"
might be extended to his "woman," since Marx and Engels note (in a review of G. F. Daumer's *The Religion of the New Age*, 1850) that the worship of
the female as divine offers no solution to the "social distress" of actual
women, particularly the way marriage and child care prevent the exercise
of women's talents.[12] George Eliot would probably agree with such criticisms, since Feuerbach's separation of feminine qualities from actual
women and his subordination of the female when he feminizes Godhead
prove contentious issues in her novel *Adam Bede*. To be sure, Eliot was not
a Marxist; like Feuerbach, she might be termed a contemplative materialist, one much more deeply engaged with the ideas of Comte, Spencer, and
Lewes than with those of Marx and Engels.[13] But like Jameson and Fuller,
Eliot experienced the social oppression of women, and *this* seems to be what
makes her text much more gender-conscious than Feuerbach's; nineteenth-
century Marxism and feminisms touch in their acknowledgment of the

156   material conditions of women. Eliot's particular interest is the impediment that the female body (both the actual body and the socially experienced body) poses for Feuerbach and for women in English society.

In *Adam Bede*, Eliot's characterizations of her Christ-figure, Adam Bede, and her Madonna-figure, Dinah Morris, are indebted to both Feuerbach and Jameson. But her argument is more engaged with Feuerbach's. The triumph of the Christ-figure over the Madonna-figure at the end of the story indicates Eliot's interest in promoting a more humanistic, "progressive" version of Christianity, as described by Feuerbach. The ending also, more importantly, signals Eliot's feminist social critique: a nineteenth-century woman cannot be wholly a Madonna-figure, at once a self-defined and self-sufficient "Virgin" and a relationally and physically defined "Mother." The integration of these two aspects of female identity is part of Eliot's transformative vision for women, as it is part of Margaret Fuller's.

Eliot's Feuerbachian Christ-figure, the protagonist Adam Bede, is first seen as a hard, self-righteous man, but he is transformed by suffering for another into a second Adam, a more "tender," "affectionate," and forgiving man, a more Christlike man.[14] Eliot here draws upon Pauline typology (the first and second Adam, who are the original man and Christ; see Romans 5) but she gives it a humanistic, specifically Feuerbachian, interpretation. Adam Bede himself becomes Christlike ("he who suffers for others is a God to men"). The transformed Adam, like Feuerbach's Christ, can be said to be a feminized figure, since Eliot's categorization of gender traits basically accords with that of Feuerbach (who identifies "mild, gentle, forgiving, conciliating" qualities with "the womanly sentiment of God").[15]

Anna Jameson's *Legends of the Madonna* also seems to be an important and previously unnoted influence on Eliot's first novel. There are, for instance, striking similarities between some of Jameson's Madonnas and Eliot's character Dinah Morris, a traveling Methodist preacher.[16] Jameson, for example, records a physical description of the Virgin Mary which is attributed to Epiphanius (fourth century) and supposedly derived from an even earlier source:

> She was of middle stature; her face oval; her eyes brilliant, and of an olive tint; her eyebrows arched and black; her hair was of a pale brown; her complexion fair as wheat. She spoke little, but she spoke freely and affably; she was not troubled in her speech,

but grave, courteous, tranquil. Her dress was without ornament, 157
and in her deportment was nothing lax or feeble. (*Madonna*, 30)

And here is Eliot's portrait of Dinah:

> [S]he seemed above the middle height, though in reality she did
> not succeed it—an effect which was due to the slimness of her
> figure and the simple line of her black dress. . . . The stranger
> was struck with surprise as he saw her approach. . . not so much
> at the feminine delicacy of her appearance, as at the total ab-
> sence of self-consciousness in her demeanour. . . . There was no
> keenness in the eyes; they seemed rather to be shedding love
> than making observations; they had the liquid look which tells
> that the mind is full of what it has to give out, rather than im-
> pressed by external objects. . . . It was a small oval face, of a uni-
> form transparent whiteness, with . . . a full but firm mouth, a
> delicate nostril, and a low perpendicular brow, surmounted by a
> rising arch of parting between smooth locks of pale reddish hair
> . . . . The eyebrows, of the same colour as the hair, were per-
> fectly horizontal and firmly pencilled. . . —nothing was left
> blurred or unfinished. (33)

Every aspect of Epiphanius's description (Mary's height, the shape of her
face, her eyes, brows, hair, dress) is reflected in Eliot's portrait of Dinah.
The differences in coloring may be attributed to Dinah's being an English
Madonna, not a Near Eastern one. But it is significant that Dinah has the
"pale reddish hair" of Raphael's *Sistine Madonna* (figure 7), a painting which
Jameson calls "inspired," "ideal," and unparalleled (*Madonna*, xliii) and
which Eliot wept over and gazed upon daily in the Dresden Gallery during her trip to Germany with Lewes in 1858, while she was writing *Adam
Bede*.[17]

Eliot's Dinah resembles Jameson's Madonnas not just physically but
also spiritually. She is a figure of "beneficence, purity, and power," possessing most of the characteristics of the Virgin that Jameson finds in the
original Marian "portrait" drawn by Luke in the Gospels. These characteristics include "decision and prudence of character" (Mary in Jameson's description, like Eliot's Dinah, journeys alone to seek aid and bring good
news); "intellectual power" (Mary composes a hymn, Dinah her sermons);
and "sublime fortitude and faith" even to the foot of the cross (in Dinah's

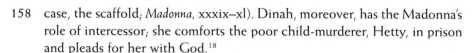

158   case, the scaffold; *Madonna*, xxxix–xl). Dinah, moreover, has the Madonna's role of intercessor; she comforts the poor child-murderer, Hetty, in prison and pleads for her with God.[18]

     In contrast to Feuerbach and Jameson, Eliot in her realist novel focuses almost exclusively on human nature rather than on the relation between the human and the divine natures. She uses the two characters, Adam and Dinah, to represent "divine" mercy and love in their community. But why does she need *two* representatives, one male and one female, of the qualities associated with feminine God? It seems that she wants to show the spread of the more loving and merciful ethic she associates with the progress of religion (*Eliot Letters*, 6:89). The original evangelist of this "feminine gospel" is Dinah; Adam, whose admiration for Dinah grows as his character is transformed, is her disciple. But then one wonders why the Christ-figure rather than the Madonna-figure becomes Eliot's triumphant representative of the "feminine" qualities of God. Adam at the end of the story is a worldly as well as a spiritual success, his community's social and moral leader. Dinah the Madonna-figure seems imprisoned and powerless —married to Adam, she is shown to be contained by a maternal body, hedged in by the household, and silenced as a preacher. It seems that Eliot's text unhappily follows Feuerbach's: the Madonna-figure is displaced by the Christ-figure and disempowered.

     A likely explanation for Adam's triumph is that he represents a version of Christianity that is more humanistic and thus more "progressive" than Dinah's Methodist beliefs, which Feuerbach would criticize as other-worldly, self-deluding, and self-alienating. Adam, for example, reads the Bible as he does the landscape of Loamshire, as the record of human activities (542), while Dinah regards the Bible as God's special message to the believer and frequently uses randomly chosen passages as divine guides for her actions. For Dinah, God is a being other than the self, all-loving, beneficent, and powerful. The believer's share of these attributes is thought to come from God; or, as Feuerbach would say, human nature is being denied to make God rich.

     Dinah's beliefs seem to be physically as well as psychologically alienating. She has almost no regard for people's material well-being; she says, "I've noticed, that in these villages where the people lead a quiet life among the green pastures and the still waters, tilling the ground and tending the cattle, there's a strange deadness to the Word, as different as can be from the great towns, like Leeds. . . . The soul gets more hungry when the body is ill at ease" (137). The most important symbol of her radical anti-

materialism is her body, or rather, bodilessness. She is physically unself-
conscious, so that others are unaware of her sex as she preaches. In her
trancelike meditations, she seems to leave her body, to become one with
the Divine Spirit (135–37). Since Eliot "everywhere agree[s]" with Feuerbach (*Eliot Letters*, 2:153), it would be problematic for her to seem to endorse in *Adam Bede* a version of the "alienating" Christianity she had in fact
rejected.

Dinah's story, however, does present a conundrum. Her bodilessness is
self-alienation, according to Feuerbach. But the female body (the biological body as well as the socially constructed female body) is equally a problem for all the female characters in the novel. Female sexuality is treated as
dangerous for men and women both, and childbirth in the Poyser family
is a painful, enfeebling, sometimes fatal event. Woman's body is, moreover,
made the basis of her social roles: she is expected to be wife and mother
only—Dinah's profession is much criticized—and her sphere of activity is
limited to the household, where she does the endless work of caring for
the needs of others' bodies (see Jean Baker Miller, 21–26). Dinah's body-
denying existence, then, allows her to escape the physical and social restraints of ordinary women's lives. Her religious self-alienation is the means
to female freedom and empowerment.

Although Dinah has physical and spiritual similarities to Jameson's
Madonnas, Eliot's problematizing of the female body helps one realize that
Dinah is, in fact, never wholly a Madonna figure, both virgin and mother.
It is the social impossibility, more than the physical impossibility, of filling
both these roles that seems to interest Eliot: Dinah is God-empowered as
body-denying virgin, but seems to sink by her material weight below Godhead to become the silenced wife and mother. The triumph of the Christ-
figure and the disempowerment of the Madonna-figure in *Adam Bede* signal
that there is not yet a free and empowered female body for Dinah to put
on—in the novel or in nineteenth-century England. Feminine qualities
here can accomplish social change only when embodied in a male, Adam.

Eliot's exploration of the problem of the female body marks an important difference between her treatment of the Madonna and those of Jameson
and Feuerbach. While Jameson presents the Madonna as the representative
of the feminine divine, her treatment of Mary as an earthly mother is positive but fairly conventional, not subject to the same searching feminist
analysis. Feuerbach, by associating highly valued feminine qualities primarily with the Son and limiting the Madonna to maternal, Son-centered
roles, effectively splits the feminine from the female and identifies woman

with the maternal body, which seems to let her slip below divinity, out of the Trinity; he is not, however, self-conscious about these aspects of his argument. Feuerbach's slippage becomes central in Eliot's much more gender-conscious text.

The female body, then, is one element of Eliot's feminist social critique. Woman can be free, it seems, only when she physically, psychically, and socially denies her own body. Another element of the critique concerns Dinah's hazardous movement from self-definition to definition by men and in terms of her relationships with men. In the final scene of the novel, Adam chooses to let the husband-centered identities of wife and mother limit Dinah; he is pleased that she has accepted the Wesleyan Conference's recently imposed restrictions on women's public activities and will no longer preach (583). The arbitrariness of these limitations is shown by the very different marriage Dinah would have had with Seth Bede, Adam's younger brother. Seth tells her early in the novel, when he proposes:

> "We both serve the same Master, and are striving after the same gifts; and I'd never be the husband to make a claim on you as could interfere with your doing the work God has fitted you for. I'd make a shift, and fend indoor and out, to give you more liberty—more than you can have now, for you've got to get your own living now, and I'm strong enough to work for us both."
> (78)

If Dinah had accepted Seth, it seems her independent identity would have been assured. Seth, moreover, opposes the new Conference restrictions and thinks he and Dinah should join a group "that puts no bonds on Christian liberty" (583). The final scene makes clear the penalties of female devotion to representative men like Adam rather than exceptional men like Seth: Dinah's self-definition is eclipsed by her definition by others, in terms of others. Eliot seems to be politicizing the situation found in Feuerbach: the Madonna loses not only some of her positive feminine qualities but also part of her self when she is defined solely in terms of the Christ-figure.

The issue of female self-definition brings us back to the divided identity of Eliot's Madonna-figure: Dinah cannot be both virgin and mother. I want to suggest that the power of defining the self, of being a self, belongs to the virgin, and furthermore, that Eliot uses the Madonna to represent her ideal conception of woman: one who is both virgin and mother, a self who is also committed to others, an independent being who is also part of a family and society. Margaret Fuller's treatment of virginity and the Madonna in *Woman in the Nineteenth Century* helps clarify Eliot's strategy here.[19] Fuller argues that Man has long had the privilege of independent self-development; now it is woman's turn, for her own good and that of the human race.[20] Therefore woman needs to become for a time "virgin," or independent from man and intellectually self-reliant. But the virgin is not a symbol of what woman should always be. Fuller instead sees the Madonna as the woman who is complete, because she is both virgin and mother, combining the youthful capacity for mental growth with mature wisdom; she is at once an autonomous self and a companion to man.

Fuller's Virgin Mother suggests how the Madonna functions in Eliot. She is Eliot's symbol of a woman who has developed her intellectual and emotional capacities, who lives for herself but also for others, as wife and mother; a woman who is independent yet also materially grounded in her own body and connected to the social body. By contrast, Dinah points toward but does not achieve true Madonna-ness, because she is independent and empowered as an ascetic virgin but dependent and silenced as a wife and mother. The Madonna in Eliot thus represents the state woman should but cannot yet achieve. She is an important part of the transformative vision that is suggested in Eliot's novels and described more directly in her nonfictional prose.

Eliot believes human efforts can contribute to the moral and social progress of the race (*Eliot Letters*, 4:472; 5:31; 6:98), and she thinks woman because of her nature has a special contribution to make.[21] For Eliot, the progress of the human race depends on the moral development of the individual, which is synonymous with the enlargement of his or her vision, emotional range, and capacity and opportunity for constructive action. Even though resignation to life's limitations is an essential part of Eliot's ethic (4:499), her letters and fiction both show that women have experienced too many limitations, too much resignation (e.g., 4:366; *The Mill on the Floss*). She therefore indicates her agreement with Fuller's "calm plea for the removal of unjust laws and artificial restrictions, so that the possibilities of [woman's] nature may have room for full development," with benefits for all (*Essays*, ed. Pinney, 200).

The important difference between Fuller's and Eliot's transforming visions for woman is the latter's sense of the intractability of material conditions. For Fuller, the idea creates the historical reality (*WNC* [1855 ed.],

162   19). For Eliot, historical reality may not be ready for the idea. In *Adam Bede* a woman escapes her material conditions only by not inhabiting the body, only by denying her physical and sexual self. Moreover, if woman's nature is defined by "possible maternity," as Eliot says (*Eliot Letters*, 4:468), then women may be strongly drawn to marriage and motherhood despite the social constraints they bring; a Dinah's fate may be nearly unavoidable. For both Eliot and Fuller, woman's self-definition and self-development are possible only in a virgin state, in singleness and social isolation or alienation. But Fuller is more optimistic about the prospect of woman's eventual return to society and self-realization there as both virgin and mother, wholly a Madonna. Eliot, in contrast, sees the Madonna state fully realized only in a mythic place and time discontinuous with present historical conditions; her novel *Romola* (1862–63), discussed in the next chapter, illustrates this point.

Critics of Eliot who discuss her treatment of the Madonna include Sandra Gilbert and Susan Gubar, who read the Madonna negatively as an asexual and powerless figure. Following Carol T. Christ, they argue that Eliot requires her heroines to be madonna-like "angels of renunciation" while she herself acts as the madwoman or "angel of destruction," taking revenge on the oppressive male characters.[22] Helena Michie similarly reads the Madonna of Christianity and the Victorian heroines made in her image as representing the valorized denial of female appetites, but fortunately Eliot's heroines can escape from this role; Dinah's blushes signal her desire for Adam and their eventual marriage (Michie, 20–30). Gillian Beer and Margaret Homans see more possibilities in the Madonna, making her a symbol of the author herself, but they conclude that this figure is empowering only in Eliot's own exceptional case (Beer, *George Eliot*, 49, 122–25; Homans, *Bearing the Word*, 156–60, 216). Beer admires Eliot, a "fallen woman" whose lover addresses her as "Madonna," for "shatter[ing] sexual stereotypes," but she is dissatisfied with Eliot's novels for failing similarly to reconcile sexual passion and vocational fulfillment. In contrast to these critics, Nina Auerbach acknowledges Victorian symbols as multivalent and thinks the Victorian Madonna and the Angel the House should be associated with independence and power as well as with enclosure and passivity (64–82).

My argument comes closest to Auerbach's. By putting Eliot's *Adam Bede* and later novels in a new context—nineteenth-century discussions of divinized woman and feminine God, notably those by Jameson and Fuller— I show that the Madonna has functioned as a positive symbol for women, most importantly through her virginity. Virginity in Fuller's work, for instance, has been inappropriately read only in sexual terms, when it should be associated primarily with self-sufficiency and self-reliance, best exemplified by the ancient virgin goddesses. Virginity in Eliot, by contrast, should be read sexually as well as psychically and socially, because of her focus on the body. Perhaps, too, it should be evaluated rather positively. In *Adam Bede*, where the virgin mother's state is shown to be nearly unattainable, Dinah's celibacy may be the next best thing, allowing her to escape women's body-defined bondage and enjoy unusual freedom and power. The irony, then, for those who value sexual freedom and fulfillment and accordingly criticize the submissive, sexually repressed household "angels" and "madonnas" they find throughout nineteenth-century literature, is that the Madonna can be a powerful figure for Eliot, Fuller, Christina Rossetti, and other writers of this period because of their radical understanding and appreciation of virginity—psychic, social, and even sexual.[23]

Romola will add a new dimension to the virgin's role. The heroine of this novel, who best represents Eliot's ideal of the Madonna, manages for a brief mythic space to be both empowered virgin and mother and honored as a heavenly queen. But the synthesis of *Romola* comes apart in *Middlemarch*, for the same English Midlanders who cannot accept a preaching virgin like Dinah reduce the Madonna-like Dorothea to a merely decorative role.

The Blessed Lady and the Decorative Virgin
Romola and *Middlemarch*

CHAPTER EIGHT

Eliot's *Romola* (1862–63) and *Middlemarch* (1871–72) are appropriately considered together, because these novels contain her fullest analyses of the Madonna in relation to European art. The *Sistine Madonna* and legends of the Virgin did inspire the earlier fiction, notably *Adam Bede*. But in the two later novels the Madonna, instead of being just a feminist symbol proposed by the narrator, is a figure familiar to characters who encounter her daily in the churches of Florence or on tours through the art galleries of Rome, and their reactions add political and religious dimensions to the discussion of this image of women. A second important change from the earlier fiction concerns which aspects of the multivalent Madonna-figure are emphasized. In *Adam Bede*, Eliot is more interested in the virgin's role, but in *Romola* the mother receives greater attention, and the Madonna comes to represent a distinctively maternal form of leadership, which is made preferable to intellectual vocations for women. The heroine Romola is, however, more than a Madonna-figure. She is also a "citizen" of Christ's kingdom who claims, like the bold Protestant and feminist women who come after her, the spiritual equality of the sexes.

 Romola is, however, largely undone in *Middlemarch*. Both novels are set at times of great political and social change, *Romola* in Medicean and Savonarolan Florence, and *Middlemarch* in England on the eve of the First Reform Bill (1831–32). But perhaps the greatest change is the religious one J. Hillis Miller has discussed: the society of *Middlemarch*, in contrast to faith-bound Florence, seems to have experienced the disappearance of God. In *Middlemarch*, Eliot considers what happens specifically to women when a society shows itself oblivious to the spiritual significance of the Virgin Mother, whose power and authority have historically benefited women, as Anna Jameson and Margaret Fuller argue. The Madonna, St. Clara, St. Barbara, and St. Theresa form a heavenly constellation beyond the comprehension of Dorothea—not to mention the Middlemarchers, who most often assess women only in terms of their ornamental value and sartorial effect. The Madonna of *Romola* is, most vividly, the Blessed Lady from beyond the sea; in *Middlemarch*, she is merely a decorative Virgin.

Eliot's *Romola* is set in Florence of the late fifteenth century. This was a transitional period in European history, the age of Ghiberti, Machiavelli, Columbus, Luther—and Savonarola, the historical figure at the center of the novel. The male characters in *Romola*—Bardo de' Bardi, the Stoic and classical scholar; his son Dino, the Dominican friar; Savonarola, the prophet-leader; and Tito, the Bacchic Greek and Renaissance man—represent various stages in the development of European culture.[1] Romola is assigned a different role by each of these characters and successively passes through them. Her father Bardo (who is blind) requires her to be a dutiful daughter, his hands and eyes but not a kindred mind, in a library that appropriately contains a headless feminine torso and the limbs of ancient statues.[2] Dino, on his deathbed, calls her to be a Christian penitent, a female religious, literally the bearer of the cross that is his legacy to her (*Romola*, 147–55). Instead Romola marries Tito, who makes her Ariadne to his Bacchus; he commissions a triptych or tabernacle showing them in these roles, enthroned together, and inside it he locks away the brother's cross, or sadness (191–92). But Romola's questioning need causes her individually to enact the historical movement (described also by Anna Jameson and Margaret Fuller) away from the Greek gods, associated here with rich, joyful, powerful nature, to the Christian god of suffering (172–73, 308–10; see also Bonaparte, 63–71, 143–76). She hangs Dino's cross around her neck and becomes, as he wished, a disciple of Savonarola and a godly citizen of the prior's purified Florence. Romola is not, however, described as a believing Christian but rather as a fellow traveler, who finds satisfaction for her "moral needs" in communion with Savonarola and the church he represents.[3]

166   Of all Romola's relationships, her ties with Savonarola prove the most important for analysis of the novel, especially the heroine's emergence as a Madonna-figure. Eliot was *au courant* in deciding to center her novel around the historical prior of San Marco, although ordinary British readers were probably mystified by her choice of subject (Bonaparte, 10; Gezari, 78). The question is, which Savonarola? There were at least four representations of him proposed in nineteenth-century religious, political, and artistic debates: the Renaissance man whose work was a blueprint for a new Italy; the superstitious medieval monk; the forerunner of the Reformation; and the reformer and purifier of art.

Historian Donald Weinstein shows that interest in Savonarola revived in Italy during the Risorgimento. A group of nineteenth-century disciples of Savonarola, calling themselves the "New Piagnoni," met at the priory of San Marco in Florence. Father Vincenzo Marchese was among their number, and his edition of materials on Savonarola was used by Pasquale Villari. Eliot read Villari's important biography of the prior (1859–61). Both Marchese and Villari saw Savonarola as the opponent of tyrannical princes and popes who threatened liberty and true religion. The prior and his Christian republic of Florence, the city where Christ was king, were proposed as models for the new Italy.[4]

Villari considered Savonarola a Renaissance man, re-Christianizing the cultural awakening that had become pagan and corrupt under patrons such as Lorenzo Medici (xxvi–xxviii). In contrast, Jacob Burckhardt identified Savonarola and the mendicant orders with the dark, superstitious Middle Ages and saw them as adversaries of all the Renaissance promised (280–96). His thesis in *The Civilization of the Renaissance in Italy* (1860) became the dominant one in Savonarola studies (Weinstein, 6–7). But Burckhardt's history, first published in Switzerland and appreciated by his colleague Nietzsche, was not well known until the late nineteenth century and thus was probably not a source for Eliot.[5]

The nineteenth-century German and English biographers of the Dominican monk proposed a third representation of Savonarola: they claimed him as a Protestant or a proto-Protestant and a martyr of the Reformation (Villari, xxxi–xxxv). Eliot owned one of these biographies, by the German scholar Karl Meier.[6] The Protestantizing of Savonarola started with Luther and his contemporaries (one of whom gave Luther, on his way to Worms, a picture of the late prior as a warning; Brecht, 1:449). Luther called Savonarola "that godly man of Florence," a true Catholic burned by a heretic—the pope ("Defense" [1518], in *Luther's Works*, 32:87–88; Fife,

578–79). He reprinted Savonarola's prison writings in 1524 and in his preface described the prior as a predecessor of himself. Both men, Luther said, attempted to purify the "slough of Rome," and both emphasized righteousness through faith (Villari, 739–41; Villari disputes Luther's second claim, that Savonarola did not also emphasize works). Savonarola is represented as one of the heralds of the Reformation on the 1868 Luther monument at Worms, where he crouches below the central figure (Grisar, 83).

A fourth categorization of Savonarola, which has not been discussed by critics of *Romola,* was offered by nineteenth-century art critics, such as A.-F. Rio, Ruskin, and Jameson. They considered him the purifier of art and the inspiration of contemporaneous and Victorian artists. The Romantic writers Friedrich Schlegel and Chateaubriand had earlier awakened interest in the art of the late Middle Ages by describing it as simple and spiritual and suggesting it was more valuable than the naturalistic and pagan art of the High Renaissance (F. Schlegel, 1–148). Rio used Schlegel to formulate his own theory of "Christian art," and his work led Jameson, Ruskin, and Eliot to an intense appreciation of the "Old Italians" (Steinberg, 3–38; Lightbown, 3–40). Rio was the first to put Savonarola into the new art-historical theory (according to the historian Ronald Steinberg), claiming that Savonarola endeavored to purify and re-Christianize art, returning it to earlier practices and thus saving it from the secularity of the Renaissance. Drawing on Vasari's *Lives of the Painters* (2nd ed. 1568), the art critic added that Savonarola's followers in this enterprise included Fra Bartolommeo and other monk-artists of the San Marco school, as well as Botticelli. Rio's argument about Savonarola influenced generations of art historians (e.g., Jameson, who discusses the prior's opposition to the secularizing "portrait Madonnas" of the Renaissance). The problem with Rio's claims, Steinberg points out, is that the prior's "followers" continued to paint in the naturalistic style of their contemporaries, and only their iconography seems indebted to him.[7]

The most interesting version of this Victorian reading of Savonarola is found in Ruskin's work. In a lecture titled "Pre-Raphaelitism" (in *Lectures on Architecture and Painting,* 1854), Ruskin contends that painting changed "about the year 1500": "Instead of the life of Christ, men had, for the most part, to paint the lives of Bacchus and Venus," and beauty of form and execution, rather than moral teaching or truth, became the first object of art (12:144–50). Although Savonarola is not mentioned here, he clearly has a place in Ruskin's theory. He was the prophetic leader of Florence in the mid-1490s, he thought artistic representations of the Virgin Mary and

Christ should everywhere replace the Medicean Hercules and Anteus (Er-langer, 175), and in Eliot's novel his opponents include the "Bacchic" Tito. Ruskin himself continues his argument against the secularization of Renais-sance art in *Ariadne Florentina* (1876) the and now discusses both Savonarola and Botticelli, having figured out what to do with the High Renaissance painter.[8]

In both *Ariadne Florentina* and the lecture on Pre-Raphaelitism, Ruskin reconfigures historical periods and blurs the distinction between Catholics and Protestants. He does so in "Pre-Raphaelitism" by eliminating the his-torical category of the Renaissance. The change that occurred in belief and art around 1500 was from "Mediaevalism" to "Modernism": "Mediaevalism began, and continued, wherever civilisation began and continued to *confess* Christ. . . . Modernism began and continues, wherever civilisation began and continues to *deny* Christ." This change took place, Ruskin says, "in the spirit of Roman Catholics and Protestants both; . . . [it] consisted in the *de-nial* of their religious belief, at least in the external and trivial affairs of life, and often in far more serious things" ("Pre-Raphaelitism," 12:139). Such ir-religious Catholics and Protestants are contrasted in *Ariadne Florentina* with four "passionate reformers": Holbein and Luther, Botticelli and Savonarola. These painters and priests were "reformers" not in the sense of "preachers of new doctrines; but witnesses against the betrayal of the old ones, which were on the lips of all men, and in the lives of none" (*Ariadne Florentina,* 22:328). Ruskin thus enrolls Catholics as well as Protestants in the Refor-mation and redefines "reformers" to include all who upheld the fundamen-tal beliefs of the Church.

Ruskin's arguments in "Pre-Raphaelitism" and *Ariadne Florentina* make him, of the nineteenth-century commentators on Savonarola, the writer closest to Eliot; these parallels have not been noted before. In "Pre-Raphaelitism," he eliminates the "Renaissance" as an operative distinction; Old Italian, Northern, sixteenth-century Florentine, and Victorian Pre-Raphaelite painters are all opponents of secular "Modernism." Ruskin thus obviates the need to ground Savonarola, a transitional figure, in a particu-lar historical period. Eliot's tactics are similar in *Romola:* her Savonarola is not definitely Villari's Renaissance Christian humanist or Burckhardt's me-dieval monk, but a prior of the late fifteenth century, a time when, as Bona-parte says, all streams of history met. Ruskin's accommodating both Catholics and Protestants in the category of "reformers" is even more im-portant for Eliot's novel. Although *Ariadne Florentina* postdates *Romola,* Eliot read and reviewed Ruskin's *Lectures on Architecture and Painting,* and one of

Lewes's letters suggests that he and Eliot were thinking about Savonarola
in Ruskinian terms: "she knows infinitely more about Savonarola than she
knew of Silas [Marner], besides having deep personal sympathies with the
old reforming priest."[9]

Eliot's "old reforming priest" is not unambiguously a Protestant, as
some *Romola* critics have suggested (e.g., Carpenter, 63, 69–71) but instead
a character whose activities resonate in both Catholic and Protestant contexts. Assuredly, Eliot generally portrays Savonarola less positively than
Ruskin does: her prior is gradually corrupted by power, party spirit, and
the self-serving belief that his prophecies are sent by God. But initially he
is presented, as in Ruskin, as a sincere renovator of the Church:

> [T]here was a man in Florence who for two years and more had
> been preaching that a scourge was at hand.[10] . . . In brilliant Fer-
> rara, seventeen years before, the contradiction between men's
> lives and their professed beliefs had pressed upon him with a
> force that had been enough to destroy his appetite for the
> world, and at the age of twenty-three had driven him into the
> cloister. He believed that God had committed to the Church the
> sacred lamp of truth for the guidance and salvation of men, and
> he saw that the Church, in its corruption, had become a sepul-
> chre to hide the lamp. . . .
>
> But the real force of demonstration for Girolamo Savonarola
> lay in his own burning indignation at the sight of wrong; in his
> fervent belief in an unseen Justice that would put an end to the
> wrong, and in an unseen Purity to which lying and uncleanness
> were an abomination. (*Romola*, 199–200)

As a reformer and a Reformer, a purifier and a Puritan, Eliot's Savonarola
looks backward to the faith and doctrine of the Middle Ages and forward
to Luther and the nineteenth century.[11]

This double aspect of Savonarola's character illuminates Romola's two
important roles in the novel. She is the Madonna made visible, a role
drawn from Catholicism. And she is a "child of Florence," a citizen of the
redeemed city where Christ is King, a role that might be called Protestant
or proto-Protestant, since Savonarola's New Jerusalem looks forward to
Calvin's theocratic Geneva and the Puritans' Boston, the "city on a hill."[12]
Romola's two roles allow Eliot's feminist beliefs and her religious views to
shape the novel. The heroine, in her capacity as a citizen of Florence,

170   assumes a number of the roles and responsibilities of men, and she articulates the spiritual equality of men and women when she justifies her rebellion against her husband and Savonarola. The claim that women are or should be men's equals, as citizens and as souls, recurs in Protestantism. It is also the backbone of Enlightenment-liberal feminist beliefs, which are part of Eliot's thought. In contrast, as a Madonna-figure, Romola shows the special maternal contributions women can make to the governing of society. Moreover, the readiness of characters such as Tessa (a peasant woman) and plague-frightened villagers to assume the noble lady is a Marian apparition suggests the human need for specifically female representations of the divine; this understanding of the Christian Goddess is found in both Jameson's and Fuller's work and will be discussed in the last part of this analysis. The social and religious respects of Madonna Romola's role point to the essentialist strand in Eliot's feminism.

This feminist interpretation of Romola's roles as Madonna and citizen is strengthened by Eliot's known links to the founders of Girton College, Barbara Leigh Smith Bodichon and Emily Davies. Eliot's gift of fifty pounds to Girton College, made by "the Author of *Romola*," may suggest that she sees Romola as a model for Girton women (Haight, 396–97; Paxton, 124–25). In letters dating from the late 1860s to Davies, Bodichon, and other friends, Eliot recommends that the students receive an education equal to men's, as Romola does, not only to allow their full mental development but also to prepare them for specifically womanly service to society.[13] Such advice accords with the novelist's essentialist-feminist views of the valuable physical and psychological differences between the sexes, though some critics have questioned whether these views are feminist at all. Romola is, however, modeled on Eliot's friend Barbara Bodichon and thus has more heroic possibilities than critics have tended to accord her. It has been noted, for instance, that Romola has Bodichon's height and pride and long reddish-gold hair, and she experiences the sexual discrimination that Bodichon campaigned against: the loss of inherited property to a husband, and the impossibility of divorce even when trust is broken.[14] But, more importantly, Romola's vocation—moral and social leadership rather than scholarship—reflects the Victorian feminist's own.

The person who calls Romola to her "Protestant" role as a "child" and a "citizen" of Florence is Savonarola (*Romola*, 340, 345). The heroine's father has died and her marriage has failed, and she decides to leave the city, disguised in religious garb; Savonarola spies her and confronts her. The prior is initially unable to make Romola submit to his religious authority ("I acknowledge no right of priests and monks to interfere with my actions" [338]). He, significantly, must go outside Catholicism to appeal to her as a pagan and an equal (since she, though a woman, comes from one of the oldest and noblest families in Florence). Even as Savonarola requires Romola to keep the marital pledge she made publicly, he tacitly acknowledges that this bond is broken by calling her to a higher obligation—her duties to Florence. Romola returns to Florence but to a new home, the city streets, where she joins Savonarola's followers, the Piagnoni ("weepers"), in caring for the needy at a time of war, sickness, and plague. In Savonarola's Florence, as in Calvin's Geneva, these everyday acts of mercy and provision by laypeople are perceived as holy work done in honor of God. Romola labors alongside other women, but she is not simply doing "women's work." We are told that she becomes interested in politics at about the same time as Savonarola and her self-serving husband Tito (223, 234, 248–50, 297–98), and she shares the priest-reformer's goal of ending economic and religious oppression and making Florence a purified city ruled by the people, a harbinger of the renovation of the world.

Romola's involvement in the life and politics of the city turns her into a protector of the Florentines; she shows mercy especially to the weakest when others, including Savonarola, require harsh justice. She comes to the aid of Tessa when some of the prior's "beardless inquisitors," his bands of boys, require her to give up her ornaments for the "bonfire of vanities." Romola points out that an involuntary gift serves no good end (406–8; Bonaparte, 209–10). The heroine protects the starving Baldassarre (the foster-father Tito has disowned) when stronger men would take the food she offers him, and she saves Savonarola himself from capture by his opponents, the Arrabbiati whom Tito serves as a double or triple agent. Finally, she tries to keep her godfather from being executed as a traitor, calling on the prior to uphold the law of appeal he has helped pass.

Romola breaks with Savonarola when he is untrue to his own principles. Indeed, she uses his arguments to justify her own rebellion:

> "Father, you yourself declare that there comes a moment when
> the soul must have no guide but the voice within it, to tell
> whether the consecrated thing has sacred virtue. And therefore I
> must speak. . . .
>
> "Do you then know so well what will further the coming of

God's Kingdom, father, that you will dare to despise the pleas of mercy—of justice—of faithfulness to your own teaching? . . . Take care, father, lest your enemies have some reason when they say, that in your visions of what will further God's Kingdom you see only what will strengthen your own party."

"And that is true!" said Savonarola, with flashing eyes. Romola's voice had seemed to him in that moment the voice of his enemies. "The cause of my party *is* the cause of God's Kingdom."

"I do not believe it!" said Romola, her whole frame shaken with passionate repugnance. "God's Kingdom is something wider—else, let me stand outside it with the beings that I love." (462, 464)

Romola can here be called a Protestant, as Felicia Bonaparte and Mary Wilson Carpenter suggest, but in a more historically specific sense than either acknowledges (Bonaparte, 203–4, 226–27; Carpenter, 63, 69–71). Like generations of Protestant women, the heroine dares to take what Eliot identifies as the principles of the Reformation and apply them to herself— a far more subversive act than any rebellion against Rome.[15] She claims that a woman's rebellion can be as sacred as her obedience. She rejects the right of any intermediary to come between her and her conscience. She makes herself the spiritual equal of men and dares to cast judgment on male leaders (*Romola*, 442, 462–64). In her spiritual boldness Romola resembles Anne Hutchinson, Ann Lee, and Eliot's Methodist aunt Elizabeth Evans, the model for Dinah. In her assertion of her equal rights as a citizen and a soul, the heroine stands in the company of Mary Wollstonecraft, the Grimké sisters, Fuller, the Seneca Falls feminists, Jameson, Bodichon, and Eliot, who all constructed feminist arguments based on the same principles. Romola's quarrel with Savonarola makes her a fictional forerunner of both Protestantism and the Enlightenment-liberal feminism it fostered.

Romola's characterization as a Madonna-figure is made clear early in the novel. She is called the "Florentine lily" and the "visible Madonna," and to people she helps, she (even more than the wonder-working icon, the Madonna of Impruneta) is the Mother of Mercy, shielding people from the harsh justice of Christ or of those who identify with him, such as the Savior of Florence, Savonarola. The heroine's role and activities as a Madonna-figure are the focus of much of the negative criticism this novel has received from recent scholars. Mary De Jong dislikes what she considers 173 Romola's traditional feminine characteristics: maternal sympathy and domesticity, submissiveness, and selflessness (79–84). Michael Wolff similarly points out that the heroine persistently identifies herself in terms of her family, as a daughter, sister, wife, and mother, and thus is "on balance more a madonna than a free woman" (209–10). Deirdre David specifically criticizes the foreclosure of a scholarly career for the unusually well-educated heroine. (Romola briefly considers joining the historic female scholar Cassandra Fedele in Venice and writing a book in honor of her late father, but she instead stays in Florence and becomes a disciple of Savonarola [David, 188–96; similarly, De Jong, 81–82].) Critics also tend to be disappointed by the ending of the novel. Alison Booth, for instance, argues that Romola, unlike her confrontational original, Barbara Bodichon, simply abandons political and personal crises and "ultimately triumphs as a long-suffering 'virgin' mother, having outgrown all personal ambition" (*Greatness Engendered*, 191). David claims that the novel fails to solve the conflict between woman's mind and man's authority, and she objects to the heroine's continued regard for Savonarola (present in the Epilogue in a portrait), who "redirected her desire for 'instructed' independence into acceptance of benevolent subjugation" (193–96). Wolff calls the ending a "fantasy-romance" with positive value only in that Romola retains some of the power and independence she gained by rejecting, or "drifting away," from a patriarchal society (209–12).[16]

Many of these negative assessments of *Romola* are based on modern feminist views that I share—for example, De Jong's understanding of a feminist as "one who rejects the ideology of separate spheres and recognizes that sexism and traditional notions of femininity and masculinity are products of socialization, not [of] nature or divine decree" (88 n. 20). But twentieth-century feminism can sometimes lead to anachronistic readings of Victorian novels. The characterization and vocation of "Madonna Romola" in fact accord with the essentialist strand of Victorian feminism, as articulated by Eliot and an important turn-of-the-century American writer, Charlotte Perkins Gilman. In addition, Romola's choice of social service and moral leadership over scholarship suggests Eliot's awareness of historical plausibility in this exhaustively researched novel, and her interest in proposing new vocations for women of her own day.

Critics' disappointment with Romola's decision not to become a scholar (like Eliot herself) may indicate our professional bias that an advanced education, particularly for a woman, should culminate in such a

174   career. But according to the historians Margaret King and Albert Rabil, "There was simply no place for the learned woman in the social environment of Renaissance Italy." Well-born, well-educated young women like Cassandra Fedele, once they were past the prodigy stage, were given the choice of marriage or the convent, and neither option proved conducive to scholarship (King and Rabil, 16, 25–26). Eliot's novel makes clear that her fifteenth-century heroine has no personal commitment to a female scholar's demanding, if usually short-lived, career. Romola's blind father seems to have forced her to become learned, because he needed an assistant—the heroine's strongest desires are instead for love and happiness—and her motive for authorship is the desire to produce a memorial to him (*Romola*, 234, 305–7). What Romola does gain from her classical studies is a "clear critical intelligence" (Bonaparte, 42), which she can turn to a number of pursuits, in the fashion of Renaissance and Victorian men similarly educated. In the Victorian period, a Fedele (or an Eliot) was still uncommon, but middle-class women with financial need and some education were pushed toward careers as teachers and novelists, even if they were not well suited for such work, because there was little else considered appropriate for them to do. In her letters about Girton College, Eliot evidently recognizes the problem of limited vocations and also clearly wishes to protect the standards in her own profession against unqualified women *and men* (*Eliot Letters*, 4:425; see also 6:49). She proposes that most Girton graduates consider new kinds of jobs, which she unfortunately describes in an offputting way as "socially unproductive labour" (4:425). The nature of this "unproductive" work is not specified, but if "social service" rather than "production of goods" is meant, the nursing or hospital reforms of Florence Nightingale, the prison reforms of Mary Carpenter, and the school-founding and feminist activism of Barbara Bodichon and Emily Davies are all possible vocations. One need not assume that this is the neighborhood charitable work of Ruskin's domestic "queen."

It is also the case that female intellectualism in *Romola* is negatively associated with the limited and distorted role of a virgin daughter. Eliot thus suggests that the conditions necessary for the free play of the mind and full scholarly development are very difficult for women to realize (as David and Booth have shown in their analyses of female intellectuals). The first female "scholar" mentioned in the novel is Minerva (Athena), who is wholly her father's child, born from Zeus's head. The virgin goddess of wisdom wears protective armor and strikes men blind if they but gaze

upon her naked body (*Romola*, 47–49), and she turns potential daughters
or disciples, like Arachne, into spiders. Modern critics see Athena as the
patriarchal antithesis of the great goddesess, focusing in particular on her
denial of the creative power associated with the mother's body (Leeming and
Page, 133–38; Rich, 109, 112, 114). Another virgin daughter mentioned
in the novel is the young Venetian scholar Fedele, whose orations were
unoriginal but considered a remarkable achievement for a woman. This
fifteenth-century woman was repeatedly described, by herself and others,
as a learned "virgin," a term carrying the connotation of "freak of nature."[17]
She represents for Romola a "solitary loveless life," far from Florence and
all the people she cares about (*Romola*, 52, 307). There is, finally, Camilla
Rucellai, a bloodthirsty prophetic "daughter" of Savonarola. Rucellai's
prophecies are not repudiated by the prior, Romola realizes, because that
might feed doubts about his own, and he in fact fulfills this woman's word
in killing Bernardo del Nero (417–21). The gray-haired Rucellai is nunlike
if technically not virginal; she divorced her husband to join the third (lay)
order of Savonarola's Dominicans, and her chamber is "arranged as much
as possible like a convent cell" (247 n., 326.) The virgins and daughters of
Romola (Athena, Fedele, and Rucellai) live derivative, solitary, and even destructive lives, and Romola rejects the vocations they represent for a more
conservative version of the one embraced by Barbara Bodichon. She leaves
the "shadows" of the library, as Bodichon did (she attended London's Bedford College), for the public spaces of the city and an unnamed village,
where she undertakes social service and becomes a moral and even, briefly,
a political leader (265). Particularly in the village, this authoritative and
merciful Madonna-figure provides a female alternative to Savonarola's
style of leadership.[18]

This passage in Romola's life begins with her godfather's death. The
despairing heroine, like Maggie Tulliver, surrenders herself to death or life
in a small boat borne across the sea. The boat takes her to a plague-
stricken village, where she organizes care for the still-living and buries the
dead. She begins by authoritatively recalling the frightened village priest
to his duty:

> "Now tell me, father, how this pestilence came, and why
> you let your people die without the Sacraments, and lie un-
> buried. For I am come over the sea to help those who are left
> alive—and you, too, will help them now. . . .

"You will fear no longer, father. . . ; you will come down
with me, and we will see who is living, and we will look for the
dead to bury them." (525)

When Romola first appears before the villagers, golden-haired and gray-
veiled and carrying an orphaned Jewish baby on her arm, she is assumed
to be not just a mother but the Madonna herself, and she remains the
Blessed Lady of their legends (518–27).

The critic Nancy Paxton has claimed that "outside the boundaries of
'civilized' Florence, Romola reconstructs a woman-centered culture and exercises her own power as a moral leader in it" (139–40). In so doing,
Madonna Romola participates in and possibly even initiates a modern feminist tradition. Indeed, Eliot's treatment of maternal government anticipates
Charlotte Perkins Gilman's feminist arguments in *The Man-Made World*
(1911) and the utopian novel *Herland* (1915).[19] Gilman claims in *The Man-
Made World* that all societies and cultures so far have been androcentric,
shaped only by the combative, competitive energies natural to men. Although in Gilman's view men and women have most traits in common
(e.g., reason and creativity), she believes women have a distinctive maternal nature. They are therefore dedicated to provision, nurturance, education, and the common good. Eliot, too, considers women maternal by
nature, and she and Gilman both feel that the essential female qualities are
badly needed in the running of the world.[20]

Gilman's chapter on law and government suggests the differences between Savonarola's Florence and the village and household where Romola
is the Madonna or matriarch. In androcentric societies, according to
Gilman, the government shows the masculine love of battle, whether in
trial by combat or in verbal contests between the champions of rival parties. The legal systems are slow, unwieldy, and biased, requiring special
"castes" to interpret and enforce them, but violations of the law, even unknowing ones, are severely punished (*Man-Made World*, 223–30). In the
Florence of Eliot's novel, three parties struggle for dominance (the Piagnoni, the Mediceans, and the Arrabbiati), and the party that gains power
tries to exile or execute its opponents. Although Savonarola begins as a reformer, he fails fully to transform the government of the city, and in time
he resembles his secular counterparts. Romola shares the prior's agenda because he emphasizes, at least initially, provision and the common good: he
organizes care for refugees and the sick and he institutes a perpetual
Lenten regime of penitential amusements and plainness in food and dress,

in recognition of the requirements of God and the poor. But Savonarola stays in power through supposed miracles, fear, and force, which is even directed against women and children. When Romola's godfather Bernardo del Nero is arrested, the prior's belief that his cause is God's and others must be sacrificed to it leads him to withhold his support for Bernardo's legal appeal (in Eliot's interpretation of historical events). To Romola's confusion and horror, the law that should apply to all does not apply to Bernardo, and he is killed. Eliot's novel thus fits Gilman's outline: androcentric government, even that of the reformer Father Girolamo, is ultimately characterized by injustice, deception, and violence in the competition for power.

According to Gilman, the government of women, as seen in the original matriarchate and its present crippled remnant, the household, is marked by common love and service, and the laws are few, clear, and obviously conducive to the public good (*Man-Made World*, 223–30). When Romola takes charge in the village, temporarily replacing the priest, she sets the example of courage ("I am used to the pestilence; I am not afraid") so that others join her in caring for the sick (*Romola*, 526). Having learned from her, the people minister to her in turn when she sinks exhausted on her bed. They take in an orphaned baby who lives among them, as she will take in children she considers her particular responsibility. Care, nurturance, provision, and education in ways to accomplish these—these are Gilman's, and Eliot's, feminist tenets of maternal good government, and they are exemplified by Romola.

Many recent *Romola* scholars link the dreamlike or mythic scenes of Romola's journey and her merciful activity in the village with the epilogue (in which she is shown at home with Monna Brigida and her new family, honoring Savonarola's portrait and teaching Tito's son). Both sets of scenes are criticized as upholding traditional feminine values and showing the heroine's continued subordination to men. But I see this mythic sequence as representing Eliot's greatest hopes for women: a vision of future fulfillment only partially realized in the confining households and public spaces of Florence.

The boat that takes Romola across the sea is "the gently-lulling cradle of a new life" (*Romola*, 519). When she disembarks, she is in an unfamiliar landscape that is haunted by the Great Mother, in all her forms: the "crescent-shaped valley" evokes Ishtar, the (untended) grain Ceres, the golden apples Eve, the cows and milk Isis (518–25). The heroine herself is taken to be the Goddess in her latest form, the Virgin Mother of Christianity, and she

178   indeed is transformed, with the power to command, rescue, and heal. As a
        virgin mother, Romola represents Eliot's ideal of woman in possession of
        her full powers. In the village, Romola is a "virgin," but no longer in the
        "Florentine" sense of virgin daughterhood. Formerly the scholar's hand-
        maid or the prior's obedient disciple, the heroine now belongs to herself
        alone (this is an older and alternative understanding of virginity, associated
        with the great goddesses), and she determines her own actions and alle-
        giances, free from involuntary ties. Romola is also no longer a wife, subject
        to masculine mastery (e.g., 274–75). Instead, she is an autonomous mother
        —a commanding figure associated with the nurturing powers and even the
        fertility of the great goddesses; as soon as she enters the village, she has a
        baby in her arms. Madonna Romola heals and re-creates a community torn
        apart by sickness, fear, and death, and her activities provide a model of a
        more just and peaceful society. She appropriately receives the homage tra-
        ditionally offered to the great goddesses, the queens of heaven: gifts of
        honey, fresh cakes, eggs, and polenta (526; Jeremiah 7:18; 44:17–19, 25).

        This reading of the ending of *Romola* builds on that of Nancy Paxton,
        who argues that the heroine, surrounded by the symbols of pre-Christian
        mother-goddesses in the woman-defined "wild zone" of the village, "dis-
        covers a sense of her own power by recognizing the 'natural authority' of
        her maternal impulses and by claiming her right to define a moral code
        that more fully honors them" (138). Yet Paxton's view of Romola as the au-
        thor of her own moral code implies that the heroine becomes a "church of
        one," rejecting the irredeemably patriarchal religious beliefs of her con-
        temporaries. It seems more accurate to regard Romola as representing a
        suppressed strand of Christian tradition still valued by the common
        people of the village and Florence (this point will be developed below).
        Paxton also incorrectly assumes that the village is a "primitive, almost pre-
        historic world," and that Romola's roles there as the Mother and the
        Blessed Lady are ancient ones, discontinuous with her earlier role as the
        visible Madonna (139–40). The villagers in fact include a Catholic priest
        and an acolyte who initially identifies Romola with the image of the
        Madonna in the local church; these rural Italians have the same religion as
        the Florentines, except that (the narrator implies) the intermingled pre-
        Christian elements have not been wholly purged (*Romola*, 522, 524–25).
        Romola's maternal power is thus not divorced from the cultural form it
        would take in fifteenth-century Italy. Eliot's novel makes more sense if it is
        placed in the context of Anna Jameson's and Margaret Fuller's interpreta-

tions of the Madonna-figure (which are based on early Christian art and documents): the Madonna is the *Christian* mother-goddess, the latest version of the Mediterranean goddesses worshipped from ancient times. When Romola emerges as the Virgin Mother of the village, she is linked to the earlier, powerful female deities, though she is not identical with them; she thus realizes the potential of her earlier role as the Madonna of Florence.

The figure of the Madonna is thus transformed rather than repudiated in the final scenes of *Romola*. Eliot, however, does alter this figure as found in her earlier fiction and in Fuller's writing by emphasizing the maternal qualities of the Virgin Mother. In *Adam Bede*, Eliot suggests that if a woman has to choose between the roles of virgin and mother, the virgin's role is preferable because it allows more freedom, both intellectual and physical. But in *Romola*, the virgin state is associated either with the unhappy partial existence of the virgin daughter or with the heroine's unbearable solitude when she has lost all of her family. Redeeming this role is obviously difficult, though Eliot quietly manages it in the village scenes; but she has another agenda in *Romola*. She focuses attention on the only role in the book that is not determined by men or mere biology; it is, unexpectedly, motherhood. Romola as a virgin mother moves outside her family and blood and legal ties to care authoritatively and mercifully for all those in need. Temporarily replacing the ineffective priest, she becomes the great mother of a fatherless village and the people learn to act in her image; she assumes an analogous role at home, where she is able to have children, even her husband's children, without being a wife. As such, *Romola* may thus be Eliot's version of the "voluntary motherhood" that was becoming part of the nineteenth- and early-twentieth-century feminist agenda and moved into parthenogenetic fantasy in Gilman's *Herland*.

To be sure, when Romola returns to Florence, she is a diminished figure. Critics have read her role as a "virgin mother"—a widow and stepparent—negatively, as private rather than public, and as largely determined by men: the heroine's late husband and her father, whose patriarchal relation to language the heroine continues as the teacher of her stepson (Homans, *Bearing the Word*, 156–60, 216). The epilogue can, however, be read more positively than this, along lines suggested by Gilman. If the village is a (temporary) matriarchy, the household, or House of Bardi, is a space where beneficent maternal rule can still be exercised. It is a dimmed but recognizable image of what was realized before. By taking the place of the male

180 members of her family, Romola shows what women can do in leadership roles, and her activity need not be seen as narrowly familial or domestic. Michael Wolff says of the novel, "[I]n the end, there is no place for a woman in . . . Florentine culture that is not defined by its family name" (209). But that is also true for all the men in Florence, except the monks (Fra Girolamo and Fra Luca, formerly Dino Bardi) and the outsider Tito. Romola, like her father and godfather before her, makes sure the house she heads provides for poor relations. But as Paxton notes, she subverts patriarchal law by taking in those with no claim either of blood or legitimacy; maternal mercy and care replace harsh "justice" (140). The house now has offspring—children, rather than Bardi's barren books. Romola also, like her godfather and the other leading men of Florence, declares her political party. She is still a Savonarolan, but with a measured appreciation of the late prior, recognizing the complex mixture of high ideals and human failings in all human affairs (*Romola*, e.g., 420–21). If she is not more actively involved in the affairs of Florence, that is probably due to historical conditions—her sex and the prohibitions against Savonarola's party in the years after his execution.

Despite the limitations on Romola's sphere of action in Florence, there remains in the epilogue the disquieting possibility of a free community, of a world remade, at least domestically, without the domination of men, and maybe without men at all. Savonarola, Tito, and Bardo are present only in representations or as figures in stories whose meanings women control, in a reversal of the rest of the novel. (In this sense, Romola, like the artist Barbara Bodichon, is an image maker, though her more important role is as a Marian image.) The three adult women of Romola's household—the "virgin" Romola, the peasant mother Tessa, and the aged Monna Brigida—may suggest the ancient triad of maiden (Persephone), mother (Demeter), and crone (Hecate); these roles indicate a human need and a female power that cannot be vanquished.[21] In *Romola*, Eliot's myths of a powerful Virgin Mother continue to resonate though pushed outside the boundaries of her realist narratives and androcentric societies (such as Renaissance Florence), just as the mother-goddesses excluded from the biblical narratives and biblical worship sometimes emerged to disrupt the patriarchal histories. (Eliot knew well the current work in biblical studies.) Thus even as Eliot shows the illusory quality of otherworldly religious claims like Savonarola's, her narratives evoke the living power of myths of the goddess, and she imagines spaces where the dominant religious and social structures can be recast. Romola cries to Savonarola, "God's Kingdom is something wider —

else, let me stand outside it with the beings that I love" (464). If she goes beyond this paternal realm again, she may once more be transformed into the Blessed Lady from over the sea, regaining her power and her associations with the Great Mother, of whom she is the latest incarnation.

As a "Protestant" heroine, a citizen of Florence, Romola anticipates the arguments of the Reformation by claiming moral equality with men. Yet her role as a Madonna-figure is rooted in Catholic thought and experience; she is seen as the living impersonation of the Church's art, doctrines, and legends. These two roles are not wholly separable, though. For example, the heroine is engaged with the politics of Florence and is a merciful protector of the people as both a citizen and a Madonna. The two roles provide alternative ways of understanding a character living, like Savonarola, on the cusp of profound historical change. The historical analysis here parallels the feminist analysis: Romola's roles also represent the intertwined strands of Eliot's fairly typical Victorian feminism. Eliot supported women's citizenship rights to an equal education and protection under the law from all abuses of power, with female suffrage as a safeguard. But she thought the sexes have important differences in their natures, functions, and contributions to society. This belief in the equality but difference of the sexes is feminist, and one indication of that is the way Eliot (like Gilman later) makes maternal leadership rather than mere domesticity her heroine's vocation. The Madonna-figure of the mythic sequences represents the culmination of Eliot's feminist thought. This wise, authoritative, but loving virgin, with her severe maternal beauty, shows what women can achieve if they seize the opportunity to command and have the freedom to realize the full resources of their nature. Readers who share Eliot's pleasure in this vision are among those disappointed by the epilogue, where Madonna Romola rules her household but is once again immured in androcentric Florence.

The ending of *Romola* brings us back to the very beginning of this argument. The historical Savonarola's role as a religious reformer, an interpretation suggested by Ruskin, is the most appropriate nineteenth-century framework for analyzing *Romola*, as I have shown. But I want to consider briefly a related role, also found in Ruskin and nineteenth-century art criticism: Savonarola as the "purifier" of art. Savonarola authorized only certain kinds of representations of the Virgin Mary, which are described by his biographers and also reflected in Eliot's novel. But in *Romola* there is a

182   competing Marian tradition, associated with Savonarola's artist opponents, the common people, and Romola herself. The two Marian traditions are the key to Eliot's arguments in this novel about the development of religion, Euhemerism, and the religious position of women.

The historical Savonarola believed that Christ and the Virgin Mary personally authorized his role as prophetic leader of Florence. In his writings, especially the *Compendium Revelationum*,[22] he recounts visions in which he saw the Virgin Mary and Christ in heaven and received special messages from them. This heavenly Virgin, like the icon of Impruneta, is an invisible Madonna—except to him, her chosen mouthpiece (Villari, 319–22, 339, 438). Savonarola tried to control the image as well as the words of the Virgin Mary. As Ruskin and Jameson note, the prior, in his capacity as a purifier of art, proscribed portrait Madonnas as "a profanation of Divine things."[23] He also condemned paintings that represented the Virgin in richly ornamented or fashionable dress: "Do you imagine the Virgin Mary went about dressed as she is depicted? . . . I tell you, she went about dressed as a poor person. . . . You make the Virgin Mary look like a harlot."[24]

Eliot's novel reflects many of these historical details. Romola and the other Piagnoni women dress very plainly in imitation of the Virgin Mary, as Savonarola requires. And when the heroine is watching the preparations for the bonfire of the vanities, she says she approves the destruction of at least some of the objects on the pyre, the cheap jewelry and false hair and rouge (*Romola*, 398). But her old friend, the painter Piero di Cosimo, strongly disagrees with her and is angry that fellow artists aid the prior by burning their own work:

> "It's enough to fetch a cudgel over the mountains to see painters, like Lorenzo di Credi and young Baccio there [later Fra Bartolommeo] helping to burn colour out of life in this fashion . . . . *Va!* Madonna Antigone [Romola], it's a shame for a woman with your hair and shoulders to run into such nonsense—leave it to women who are not worth painting. What! the most holy Virgin herself has always been dressed well; that's the doctrine of the Church:—talk of heresy, indeed!"[25]

Romola here seems to support the prior sincerely, but almost immediately afterward she takes sides against him, helping Tessa save her silver-mounted necklace and belt from the fire. The contadina in response believes that this merciful "heavenly lady" is the Virgin herself (402–9). Romola's actions here can be said to initiate a competing Marian tradition in the novel. As a Madonna-figure, she is proud, powerful, gentle, and *visible*—and increasingly not under the prior's control.[26]

Tessa's reading of Romola as a Marian apparition is repeated by the villagers later in the novel, and it is foreshadowed by the starving refugees receiving charity at the Bardi house, who praise Madonna Romola interchangeably with the Mother of God (*Romola*, 365–66). In *Romola*, as in *Adam Bede*, Eliot is offering a Euhemeristic explanation of the origin of religious beliefs, at least among the common people: the people make gods or semidivine beings out of heroic men and women, and create legends about them.[27] Euhemeristic theories were common in the progressive religious thought of the eighteenth and nineteenth centuries (Manuel, 7–9, 103–25). Eliot contributes to the discussion by considering Euhemerism in relation to images and art. In *Romola*, the people do not wholly invent their gods. Instead, their needs and longings are given shape by the images familiar to them: the fair Madonna seen through the incense smoke in the village church, or the Florentine Madonnas, such as Fra Angelico's Virgin, whose dress was covered with gold to express the artist's love and reverence (so Ruskin), or Fra Lippo Lippi's divine Mother, who has Romola's hazel eyes.[28] The Italian landscape itself is described as haunted by myths of the Great Mother. All is waiting for the next Blessed Lady to appear (*Romola*, 518–27). According to the philosophers Vico and Herder (whose works Eliot and Lewes owned), the primitive mind first thinks in images, and these give rise to myths and language.[29] If one applies to *Romola* this theory of the priority of the image, and considers the ubiquity of religious images in Renaissance Italy, one realizes how Savonarola's words and strictures cannot limit or control the representations of the Virgin Mary, which are part of people's earliest visual memories and responsive to the impulses of piety, need, and desire.

The feminist theologians Rosemary Radford Ruether and Margaret Miles elucidate the religious phenomena that Eliot treats in her novel. Ruether argues that all Christian traditions are ultimately popular, though church hierarchies try to control forms of belief. If a symbol or a belief does not correspond to an individual's or a community's experience, she says, it is modified or passes into abeyance (*Sexism and God-Talk*, 12–13, 15). Miles claims that people need religious images that express positive aspects of their circumstances, and images that compensate for the limitations of their reality (*Image as Insight*, 149). In *Romola*, Savonarola promotes

184   the image of the Virgin as a Piagnona, an image that Piero di Cosimo considers antithetical to the art that glorifies Florence and the Church. Romola's proud bearing and beauty make her Piero's ideal of the Virgin, while humbler characters mistake her for the reality. Yet the heroine is not able to "pass" as a Piagnona or a lay religious (*Romola*, 312–13, 338, 522). In these ways, the novel suggests the limited support for the prior's version of *imitatio Mariae*. The process Ruether describes is at work; the people prefer a queenly Madonna to Our Lady of the Piagnoni, and they reshape and even discard the symbol required by the religious leader. Eliot's Savonarola is also associated with the Madonna invisible, the concealed icon of Impruneta, while the people clearly long for an immanent, powerful, and comforting Great Mother. This is the need that Romola fills; she is the apparition or image compensating for the people's reality, as Miles would say. Eliot in *Romola* is remarkably sensitive in her treatment of religious beliefs she does not personally hold. The novel contains both a thoughtful analysis of the origin of religion and a broad-minded investigation of the varieties of religious beliefs (Euhemeristic popular Catholicism, doctrinal Catholicism, and Protestantism) and the insights each affords into human life and thought.

As we have seen, in *Romola* Savonarola's Mariology is challenged aesthetically and emotionally by the popular Marian tradition represented by the heroine. Eliot even goes so far as to suggest that the prior's Mariology is partly responsible for his fall. She shows that Savonarola is brought down by his dangerous politics and by the hypocrisy that costs him his idealistic supporters. But an equally important factor is a religious regime that would drive the Virgin Mary herself out of God's Kingdom—unless she, too, reforms, and stops appearing in unauthorized ways. This was, of course, the Madonna's fate under Protestantism. The Reformers repudiated the divine Mother of Catholicism (restricting Mary to her literally interpreted biblical roles), and they eliminated the principal forms of female leadership associated with her in their dissolution of the religious orders. They also destroyed the ubiquitous Marian images that might have kept alive the belief in female vocation, equality, and authority in times when Protestants lost all sight of the "priesthood of all believers" and prohibited female evangelists and preachers.[30] While the historical Savonarola tried to restrict rather than eliminate images of the Virgin and to curtail Euhemeristic excesses, and while Eliot is generally not condemnatory in her analysis of religion in *Romola*, her critical treatment of the prior suggests her awareness of the misogynistic exclusions as well as the feminist possibilities of her own Protestant tradition.

Like Jameson and Fuller, Eliot in *Romola* associates the Virgin Mary with a central insight of ancient religions, continued in Catholicism: the human need for a female representative of the divine, and the recognition of the worth and even the divinity of woman. Eliot, like the other writers, has an essentialist-feminist belief in sexual difference that allows her to see the continuities between past and present religious experiences. She also uses the Madonna-figure in *Romola* to address assumed needs in two different eras for maternal leadership and female citizenship: the fifteenth-century need to *have* maternal leaders, and the mid-nineteenth-century female need to *be* leaders and citizens. The heroine of *Romola*, like her near contemporary Theresa of Avila, benefits from a "coherent faith and order" which informs and directs the desires of her soul (*Middlemarch*, 25). The heroine of *Middlemarch* is, famously, not so fortunate. My comparison of the two novels will suggest that Eliot, like Ruskin, is critically evaluating secular Modernism, in her case from a feminist perspective, and positing that the earlier forms of piety found in *Romola* may have held greater benefits for women.

In *Middlemarch* (1871–72), Eliot continues her use of art as a symbolic system. But now the legibility and relevance of religious images are brought into question, and the Madonna becomes almost wholly a limiting figure for women, an image no longer expressive of female self-definition but instead proposed and interpreted by men. Moreover, there is no longer any space, either inside or outside society, where the Madonna can emerge in her full grandeur. She cannot be accommodated by an increasingly secular society from which awareness of spiritual things, and even God, seem to have disappeared. Eliot, like Anna Jameson and Margaret Fuller before her, suggests an important connection between the reception of sacred images of women and the status of actual women. A world from which God is absent, she suggests, is a world especially limiting for women.

The Victorian poet Robert Browning, whose work Eliot reviewed, will serve to introduce these issues of female representation in *Middlemarch*. Browning's dramatic monologues "Porphyria's Lover," "My Last Duchess," "Fra Lippo Lippi," and "Andrea del Sarto" all present female characters who are gazed at, framed, represented, and physically controlled by male artists and collectors.[31] "Porphyria's Lover" is a psychotic reversal of the myth of Pygmalion and Galatea, with the female beloved transformed, by strangulation, into a statue, rosy, still malleable, and the lover's possession forever. "My Last Duchess" has as its speaker a Duke who prefers a portrait

186   of his Duchess to the woman herself, a beauty who was insufficiently dis-
criminating and suspiciously gracious to male guests. The Duke keeps the
portrait behind a curtain only he can open, so her bright glance and smile
are now reserved for *him*. "Fra Lippo Lippi" is the most relevant of these
dramatic monologues for *Middlemarch*, because Eliot knew it well—she
quotes a long passage in her 1856 review of *Men and Women* (*SE*, 349–57)—
and because Fra Lippo, an early Renaissance painter mentioned briefly in
Romola, raises questions of physicality and secularity that are central to the
later novel. Browning's Fra Lippo uses both the creation stories of the Bible
and his illicit experience in alleys "where sportive ladies leave their doors
ajar" to assert the emerging Renaissance aesthetic of the "value and significance of flesh," even in religious paintings, where he claims the beautifully
drawn body leads the eye and mind to God. (This is the kind of argument
of which Jameson is suspicious, preferring the "spiritual" art of the Middle
Ages to the "fleshly" religious images of the High Renaissance.) The artist-
monk also shows the effect of his aesthetic on the representation of
women. The prior of the convent, wanting art to uphold medieval and
monastic values even if he does not, thinks his "niece" might be represented as Herodias ("Who went and danced and got men's heads cut off!").
But Fra Lippo paints her instead as the angelic Saint Lucy, beckoning him
into the presence of the heavenly Madonna, since "he made and devised
you, after all" (lines 5–6, 195–98, 345–89).

    Fra Lippo Lippi is the least misogynistic speaker in these poems by
Browning, perhaps because he is so attracted to women, or perhaps because his lot is similar to theirs: he is delivered by an aunt to a convent,
locked in a bedchamber during carnival to finish his pious work, and expected to be chaste, obedient, and humble. But Fra Lippo nonetheless usually has the male artist's privilege of deciding how female figures should be
represented. One wonders whether the prior's young mistress enjoys being
subjected to the male gaze or appreciates either of the roles proposed for
her: the murderous seductress or the saint. She has neither a name nor a
voice in the poem. These issues—the nature of the gaze and the coercive-
ness of representation, particularly representation as the Madonna—are
subtly explored in *Middlemarch*, George Eliot's "study of provincial life."

    Feminist art critics and film critics who analyze the gaze (notably
Laura Mulvey, Deborah Cherry, and Rozsika Parker and Griselda Pollock)
usually treat it as an expression of sexual power and control, though class
and race differentials also govern who is able to stare at whom. The term
"gaze" indicates the power of the viewer, who is typically male, to look at

the object of desire as he desires. The artist enjoys in addition the power
to frame and represent the object. The role of the object—typically female
—is to present herself to the male gaze and look away, lest her glance disrupt his visual pleasure in her beauty and her body.[32] Eliot's *Middlemarch*
elaborates on these theoretical constructions; there are four kinds of gazes
in the novel. They include the egoistic gaze, in which some aspect of the
self is both subject and object of the narrowly fond look, and the dismembering gaze of the male viewer. Eliot is most innovative in her presentation
of what I call the connoisseur's gaze and the iconizing gaze, which are associated with a higher, or at least a better-educated and more subtle, kind
of self-interest. All these kinds of gaze, but particularly the latter two, are
integrally related to the author's treatment of the Madonna and of art in a
secular age.

One of the trials of provincial life is being subject to the oversight (in
several senses) of one's friends and neighbors. The partial or egoistic gaze
is exemplified by Rosamond Vincy's contemplation of herself in the mirror
beside her friend Mary Garth: "Mary Garth seemed all the plainer standing at an angle between the two nymphs—the one in the glass, and the
one out of it, who looked at each other with eyes of heavenly blue" (*Middlemarch*, 139). When Mary points out with a laugh "what a brown patch"
she is, Rosamond replies, "Oh no! No one thinks of your appearance, you
are so sensible and useful, Mary. Beauty is of very little consequence in reality," as she continues to eye the graceful turn of her neck.[33]

The dismembering gaze is suggested by the young doctor Lydgate's
vision of marriage: "reclining in a paradise with sweet laughs for bird-
notes, and blue eyes for a heaven" (122, 335, 385). But the blue eyes—
whose name is Rosamond Vincy—turn out to have a mind and desires of
their own, which are not part of Lydgate's original picture. He eventually
is forced to become his wife's docile creature, as he thought she was his.[34]
Mr. Casaubon turns his dismembering gaze on Dorothea, with some difference from Lydgate in his intent; like the scholar Bardo (in *Romola*) and
John Milton (*Middlemarch*, 32, 40), he needs feminine hands and eyes to as-
sist with his great work, but until he learns that his life may be cut short
by heart disease before he finishes his scholarship, he will not acknowledge that a woman has a mind to bring to the task.

The characteristic gazes of Lydgate and Casaubon make us aware of
their "spots of commonness": their conventionally sexist notions of women
(*Middlemarch*, 179). Lydgate directs his searching intelligence to his scientific research, not to his courtship and marriage ("the primitive tissue was

188   still his fair unknown"), and when his wife makes a suggestion during their money troubles, that he be paid for his hours at the hospital, he tells her she does not understand his work and cannot judge (193, 305, 700). Mr. Casaubon compliments his wife during their Roman honeymoon (actually a research trip), saying that her society has fortunately prevented him from thinking beyond his hours of study (231). As Mary Wollstonecraft sardonically observes, "[Woman] was created to be the toy of man, his rattle, and it must jingle in his ears whenever, dismissing reason, he chooses to be amused" (118).

    The third kind of gaze in *Middlemarch*, the connoisseur's gaze, is usually associated with the contemplation of female beauty. It demonstrates the secularization of religious art in this novel (set in the industrial Midlands in the early 1830s) and the limitations on women's roles. An example of this gaze may be found in the opening paragraph of the novel, which contains a reference to the Virgin Mary—but it is a reference to clothing: "[Miss Brooke's] hand and wrist were so finely formed that she could wear sleeves not less bare of style than those in which the Blessed Virgin appeared to Italian painters" (29). The narrator subsequently compares Dorothea, with her simple silver-grey dress and "serene dignity," to Santa Barbara. This comparison again focuses on the young woman's appearance, but it also suggests a possibility—Dorothea's capacity for saintly and heroic action—that is not realized by the local men who are her dinner guests and deprecate her beauty in comparison to Rosamond Vincy's ("There should be a little filigree about a woman—something of the coquette," 114–15). Dorothea defines herself against the Rosamonds of the world, believing that the spiritual aspects of life are more important than the material and that display is unconscionable when so many are poor. But she cannot escape being judged on the same terms as Rosamond, who lives for and before her mirror; a woman's beauty and manner are considered her most, perhaps her only, important qualities. Not many in Middlemarch are familiar with European religious art (see 649–56), but the narrator's comparisons suggest the value it would generally have in this environment; it would train the eye in the appreciation and classification of female beauty and add sophistication to the male gaze.

    Anna Jameson in *Sacred and Legendary Art* criticizes the connoisseurship of Sir Joshua Reynolds and his contemporaries for detaching the images of religious art from their history and traditional interpretations. A painting of Mary Magdalene, for example, no longer represents the sinner's hope of forgiveness but instead is "about" flowing hair, correct proportions, and the brushstrokes of Titian (1:8). Similarly, the Evangelicalism and the Philistinism of the Middlemarch "connoisseurs" have a secularizing effect on Eliot's narrative. Religious images, when described at all, are "about" female beauty, and the possibility of a larger spiritual vision is denied. Jameson's aim in her art histories might be said to be "anti-connoisseurship," because she focuses on "legends *as illustrated in* the fine arts"; the image is important primarily as a summation of the holy story. But in *Middlemarch*, the comparisons of Dorothea to the Madonna or female saints make one aware that she never has a "legend," since her plans for a life of ardent and meaningful action are continually thwarted. Dorothea is an image detached from its wanted significance and assessed primarily in terms of its ornamental value.

Adolf Naumann, the German Nazarene painter whom the Casaubons meet in Rome, catches more of Dorothea with his trained connoisseur's eye than her neighbors do. When he first sees her in the Vatican galleries, he proposes to represent her as a nun or a Madonna or a "Christian Antigone—sensuous force controlled by spiritual passion."[35] But Naumann is subtly discredited as an artist and interpreter, first by his voyeurism and deception. He stares at the oblivious Dorothea in the gallery, comparing her form to that of the voluptuous marble Ariadne reclining nearby, and he is able to sketch her as Santa Clara by pretending his preferred model is Mr. Casaubon for Aquinas (*Middlemarch*, 219–23, 247–50). Naumann enjoys the male artist's power to depict Dorothea as he wishes, while she is unable to choose her own representation or "legend." Similarly, his friend Will Ladislaw, who both versifies and sketches, says to Dorothea: "You *are* a poem—and that is to be the best part of a poet—what makes up the poet's consciousness in his best moods" (256). Her role is thus to complete him; it seems to occur to neither him or Dorothea that she has a consciousness of her own or might be a poet herself. Eliot's scenes involving artists and writers and the female subjects of their art function here as they do in Robert Browning's and Christina Rossetti's poems, highlighting the power inequities in virtually all male-female relationships.[36] Will Ladislaw's criticisms of Naumann's misty historical allegories of the Church reflect Eliot's own misgivings about the Nazarene school of painters, according to Hugh Witemeyer. She felt their monumental paintings contained "too much mind and not enough nature," and they tried to renovate archaic forms and beliefs and propose a Christian "key to all mythologies" as

190   misguided as Casaubon's own (Witemeyer, 78–87). One sees here a possible explanation for Eliot's not directing Dorothea toward the Anglican
Oxford Movement, with its patristic theology and medieval aesthetic.[37] It
seems to be the only reform movement the author overlooks in a novel set
in the early 1830s.

    The final category of gaze in *Middlemarch* is the "iconizing gaze," first
indicated by the recurrent references to Will's "adoration" of Dorothea
(e.g., 250, 510–14). There is also an antithetical or parodic version of this
gaze: Lydgate's homage to his wife before her mirror, which she does not
return but accepts "as if she had been a serene and lovely image, now and
then miraculously dimpling towards her votary" (708–9). Later in the
story, Lydgate, who is inclining toward misogyny because he cannot
share his troubles with his wife, realizes all women are not like her. Falsely
suspected of criminal collaboration with his client Mr. Bulstrode and of
possible medical malpractice, he is able to confide in Dorothea, who still
believes in him and helps to clear his name. As Lydgate rides away, he
thinks: "This young creature has a heart large enough for the Virgin Mary.
She evidently thinks nothing of her own future, and would pledge away
half her income at once, as if she wanted nothing for herself but a chair to
sit in from which she can look down with those clear eyes at the poor mortals who pray to her" (826). Lydgate and Will Ladislaw feel that Dorothea
sees them largely and sees them whole (819); she is a mirror reflecting
back to them their best selves. They respond by worshiping this divine
woman so far above them and making her into an icon (it is notable that
Lydgate never thinks of her beauty [327]). Will, however, is not similarly
subject to Dorothea's iconizing gaze. She keeps a miniature of his grand-
mother Julia, who has his features, to remind her of him, and she thinks of
him as a "lunette" letting light into the prison of her marriage (308, 396,
591–92); both small images are suggestive of his moral size and function
in comparison to hers.

    George Eliot herself was not adverse to adoration; she was called
"Madonna" by Lewes and regally received admirers during afternoon re-
ceptions at the Priory, and she complacently says of Lewes's eldest son
Charles, "the worship he gives me [prepares] him, I hope for a yet more
complete devotion to some Beatrice in store for him" (*Letters*, 4:118). But
the iconizing gaze she describes in *Middlemarch* clearly has problems. First,
Lydgate sees "Madonna" Dorothea only in terms of his own needs and
assumes she has none of her own, just at the point in the book where her
passion for Will has been awakened. Second, this gaze and the correspond-

ing representation of woman keep her immobile. St. Theresa of Avila combined a contemplative life with intense activity (Attwater, 319); Dorothea, in Lydgate's vision, should never turn away her merciful eyes from worshippers or stir from her throne. It is fitting that Lydgate proposes the most important identification of Dorothea with the Virgin Mary, since he is one of the few characters in *Middlemarch* who has been to Europe and seen the art there. But he assimilates this image to his common notions of womanhood; Dorothea, like the Virgin, is considered alone among her sex in being worthy of worship. But that does not mean Lydgate imagines a life for her that is not centered on and limited by men.

The treatment of the Madonna and of art in *Middlemarch*, the limiting and even secularizing power of the male gaze, and the heroine's thwarted efforts to find a vocation larger than marriage[38] are all evidence of a larger phenomenon in the novel—what J. Hillis Miller calls the disappearance of God. In Miller's explanation, modern Western society, for various reasons (including the growth of cities and the rise of Protestantism and its merely symbolic Eucharist), has lost the links connecting God, humankind, nature, and language that characterized earlier ages. When the circle was broken, God became unreachable; God disappeared. Miller's book is centered on the "Romantic" authors (e.g., Hopkins and Emily Bronte) who cannot bear God's disappearance and try to create new ties to the divine. He excludes Eliot from this analysis because he considers her a contented atheist, akin to Marx, Feuerbach, and Sartre ("'There is no God. Therefore let us rejoice'"; Miller, *Disappearance of God*, 1–16). T. R. Wright, Diana Postelthwaite, and James Scott do, however, discuss Eliot and *Middlemarch* in this general context.[39]

My main concern is: When God disappears, what happens to women? I will show there are negative consequences for them, as for art, in *Middlemarch*, and the welfare of both is closely related. This argument will be developed with reference to Anna Jameson and Margaret Fuller, both writers attentive to the place of women in history, art, and theory. Jameson, for instance, was one of the first feminist theorists to argue that historical "progress" is not necessarily beneficial to women, and women's religious status is a measure of their social status and their welfare. In her lecture *The Communion of Labor*, Jameson states that the early and medieval Church adored the Virgin and honored exceptional women as saints. The Reformers, however, feared rather than revered women; they "had repudiated

192   angels and saints, but . . . still devoutly believed in devils and witches."
More women died as witches under the Protestants than were executed as
heretics under the Inquisition, according to Jameson; they were "hanged,
tortured, burned, drowned like mad dogs" (282–83). Similarly, Margaret
Fuller claims that the sages of biblical times helped keep alive "the idea of
woman," which modern society now needs to actualize: "[If the sages]
taught that the happiness of the race was forfeited through the fault of a
woman, . . . they greeted, with solemn rapture, all great and holy women
as heroines, prophetesses, judges in Israel, and if they made Eve listen to
the serpent[, they] gave Mary as a bride to the Holy Spirit" (*WNC,* 266).
But Fuller's statement makes clear that the sages, like Jameson's Reformers,
also promulgated negative images of women, which contribute to their
degradation.

    Does Eliot make this kind of argument in *Middlemarch?* Subtly, yes. As
Gillian Beer and others have noted, Eliot often utilized Jameson's legends
of female saints "as a vision of women coming to authority" (Beer, *George
Eliot,* 122–24). But Beer does not apply this point to *Middlemarch,* because
knowledge and imitation of the saints are always just out of reach for
Dorothea (Beer, 163–64). The heroine seems never to have heard of St.
Theresa, to whom the narrator famously compares her,[40] and as a "Puritan,"
a daughter of Calvin's Geneva, she is bewildered by the religious art of
Rome. Dorothea does seem to make some progress in reading this art (and
Naumann's imitations of it): "[she] felt that she was getting quite new notions as to the significance of Madonnas seated under inexplicable
canopied thrones with the simple country as a background, and of saints
with architectural models in their hands, or knives accidentally wedged in
their skulls" (*Middlemarch,* 246; cf. 251–52). But such knowledge seems to
be left behind, along with the picture of St. Clara she poses for, when the
heroine returns to England. Dorothea finds inadequate the Scripture-based
Protestant models of womanhood that are offered her: Sara the blessed
mother, Dorcas the charitable worker. But throughout the book she remains almost wholly unresponsive to the classical and Catholic images
that might offer her an alternative, considering this art violent and strange
and associating it with economic and social injustice. She says to her
uncle, for example: "I used to come from the village with all that dirt and
coarse ugliness like a pain within me, and the simpering pictures in the
drawing room [Correggio prints] seemed to me like a wicked attempt to
find delight in what is false, while we don't mind how hard the truth is for
the neighbours outside our walls."[41]

The Madonnas in Eliot's novels before *Middlemarch* tend to function as both a way of making the divine immanent and a way of imagining female possibility. When Romola is metamorphosed into a Madonna-figure, that occurs in a mythic space largely separable from the realistic worlds of the novels. The scene of transformation can also be analyzed in artistic terms. It is evocative of devotional paintings, in which the divine personage (Christ or the Virgin) is shown in the upper part of the painting in a circular composition, separable by blue ether (or in Eliot's fiction, by blue water) from the square space below where the earthly worshippers are gathered. Heaven and earth for an instant come together in the unity Miller describes, just as the ideal and the actual momentarily touch in Eliot's novels. The Madonna when incarnate as Romola, for example, is at once an image of the divine, an expression of the people's longing for a merciful immanent Mother in the line of the ancient nature goddesses, and a symbol for Victorian readers of the nobility and realized power of women. But in *Middlemarch*, heaven, the ideal, and the mythic space all vanish, and the heroine undergoes no divinizing transformation. The figure of the Madonna now exists only in male fantasy (the perfectly selfless, perfectly sympathetic woman) or in the sartorial imagination: Our Lady of the Plain Sleeves.

In *Middlemarch*, the male characters' acts of gazing, framing, and representing are (as art and film critics have argued) signs and instruments of male power. But such power has additional significance in this novel; it is indicative of art that has lost its religious function. Women can no longer be pictured as saints, except in Naumann's obscure and anachronistic way. But they are not Eves and devils (the alternative Jameson and Fuller describe) because even that carries religious meaning. Instead, as Jameson complains, they and the art in which they appear are valued merely as decorative collectibles. Lydgate's iconizing "portrait" of Dorothea as the Madonna is the image that comes closest to devotional art. But his expectation of *mutual* devotion ("as if she wanted nothing for herself but . . . [to] look down with those clear eyes at the poor mortals who pray to her," *Middlemarch*, 826) makes the possessive portraiture described by Christina Rossetti a more telling comparison:

> He feeds upon her face by day and night
> And she with true kind eyes looks back at him
> Fair as the moon and joyful as the light:
> Not wan with waiting, not with sorrow dim;

194   Not as she is, but was when hope shown bright;
             Not as she is, but as she fills his dream.[42]

Woman is not the Blessed Lady, but *his* lady, perhaps honored by art, but
ultimately used by it.

Hugh Witemeyer's *George Eliot and the Visual Arts* is the most important
critical discussion of art in the novels, but several recent articles have contributed to our understanding of *Middlemarch*.[43] Joseph Wiesenfarth and
Abigail Ritschin both analyze the scenes involving the sculpture of Ariadne, which was misidentified in the early nineteenth century as Cleopatra, in the Vatican Museum. They show that the story of Ariadne sheds
light on the emerging love triangle of Dorothea, Mr. Casaubon, and Will:
Ariadne (Dorothea) is abandoned by Theseus (Casaubon) and will eventually be rescued by Bacchus (Will). The sexual pleasure of this rescue,
Ritschin says, is suggested by the known earlier identification of the sculpture as Cleopatra.[44] These critics offer fairly optimistic readings of the outcome of *Middlemarch* because they see the art as signaling Dorothea's erotic
and emotional fulfillment.[45] But the figure of Ariadne has a different significance in *Romola*. Tito has his wife painted as Ariadne enthroned and
wants this new role to make her forget everything but present bliss: "I
should like to see you under that southern sun, lying among the flowers,
subdued into mere enjoyment, while I bent over you and touched the lute
and sang to you some little unconscious strain that seemed all one with the
light and the warmth"; "I should like to dip [my Romola] a little in the soft
waters of forgetfulness" (*Romola*, 172–74, 177–79, 190–92, 268–69). Physically sated, emotionally replete, Tito's Ariadne is to become mentally
numb, forgetful of her promises to her family and her growing misgivings
about her husband. If in *Middlemarch* art has only these limited dimensions
—if Dorothea can be an Ariadne or a Cleopatra but not a Madonna, erot-
ically but not intellectually or spiritually fulfilled—then there are hazards
for women. Only certain desires will be met, and these through men. The
ardent longings of Eliot's heroines will be satisfied far more easily, and ba-
nally, than we imagined. In Eliot's fiction, religious art has signified the
empowering possibility; it represents the transcendent, or the ideal, or the
nobly dreamed and desired. But by Dorothea's time (despite the best efforts of Jameson), this art has largely become illegible. The images cannot
be decoded, as Eliot shows, and the language no longer exists to suggest
what else one might know or do or be. The early Renaissance painter Fra
Lippo Lippi says, in Browning's poem, that the beauty of the physical

world, and the "value and significance of flesh," lead the eye and mind to   195
God. But Fra Lippo's later contemporary Savonarola disagrees with him
and proscribes portrait Madonnas, like the one Fra Lippo painted of his
lover Lucrezia Buti, because the divine was forgotten in the celebration of
physical beauty. *Middlemarch* shows the end of the historical process. When
the divine disappears from art, the art may signify the considerable pleasures of "flesh" and feeling, but it reduces women to their beauty and their
bodies.

In a curious way, *Romola* and *Middlemarch* are preparation for Eliot's final
novel, *Daniel Deronda*. The narrator's claim that Dorothea is a thwarted St.
Theresa makes one aware that Eliot's few heroines with realized vocations
have had religious ones: Dinah is a preacher, Romola a "Madonna" or maternal leader. The religious imagination, exemplified by Dinah, is able to
envision an alternative world (the world of the spirit, or God's presence),
act as though it existed, and work to bring it about. This is a capacity belonging to actresses—Laure in *Middlemarch*, Alcharisi in *Daniel Deronda*—
and in the last novel it is ceded to them, but with a significant shift.
Actresses raise the question of the reliability of the image and the relation
between truth and illusion. They create multiple, unstable worlds and multiple, fragmentary selves. Eliot's uses of visual art in *Romola* and *Middlemarch*
chart the disappearance of the unifying concept of the divine in human
life, and the association of the sacred image with a common ideal and a
shared, enduring truth. Dramatic art becomes the art form characteristic of
the secular and modern world.

"Our Lady" Nearly Vanishes
The Spanish Gypsy and *Daniel Deronda*

"My God! and is that all?" was the reaction of at least one nineteenth-century reader to *Middlemarch*, as the critic T. R. Wright reports (149–51). The allusions to saints' lives and the glimpses of sacred paintings in this novel seem intended, for readers who know more than Dorothea about the past, to prevent solace and closure. They are a measure of what has been lost: knowledge of the mystery, access to the divine presence. The melancholic tone of *Middlemarch* may be an indication that the author, too, feels this loss. Most Eliot scholars consider the author an atheist, but she is better termed an agnostic. She may even have had some enduring belief in an existent if not knowable God, despite her loss of orthodox Christian faith.

The following discussion will suggest a revisionist reading of Eliot's own religious beliefs, and it will also show an important change in her theories of the nature and development of religions, a change that enabled her to write her dramatic poem *The Spanish Gypsy* (1868) and her last novel, *Daniel Deronda* (1876). Eliot's arguments about the progress of religion, which stress the philosophical indefensibility of ancestral religions such as Judaism, gradually yield to a Lamarckian view of religion as racial inheritance and to an insistence on the integrity and validity of all religions. This paradigm shift leads to changes in Eliot's treatment of the Madonna: the Virgin Mother becomes an indigenous symbol, associated with Catholic cultures rather than with unfettered Womankind, and even an oppressive symbol, as Eliot focuses on the peoples historically victimized by Christianity. *Middlemarch*, which comes between *The Spanish Gypsy* and *Daniel Deronda*, makes clear that Eliot's interest in feminist issues continues and even intensifies. But the Madonna in these three works is not associated with female self-definition and does not empower women. Instead, she is controlled by men and functions in a feminist critique of the limitations imposed on women. The Madonna does, however, become central to Eliot's religious arguments, her increasingly historicized explorations of the varieties of religious belief.

Eliot's interests in religious inheritance and the science of religion have no parallel in Jameson's or Fuller's work. Both of these writers analyzed the Virgin Mary almost exclusively in relation to Christianity and the earlier Mediterranean goddess traditions. When Fuller became aware of the nineteenth-century politics of Mary—during the Roman revolution she saw the Virgin Mother claimed and controlled by the church—she curtailed her use of this figure. Eliot, in contrast, moved on from her early work to evaluate the Madonna in political and historical as well as artistic contexts and to consider the function of this figure in the conflicts between Christianity and other religions. It is significant that of the three writers, only Eliot lived in the age of Darwin and Spencer (Jameson died in 1860, Fuller in 1850). Only she was in a position to develop a science of religion and an explanation of religious inheritance in relation to the new evolutionary theories.

The starting point for these arguments about religion and the Madonna in Eliot's late works is the author's own religious views. The most interesting aspect of the beliefs Dorothea expresses in *Middlemarch* (her desire for the good, even when that good is unknown, because the desire makes one part of "the divine power," and her conviction that personal petitions to Providence are egoistic and misguided [427]) is that these beliefs are very close to the author's own. Although Eliot, an ex-Evangelical, is often considered an atheist, she was more likely an agnostic. There is, however, some evidence that she had a greatly altered yet continuing belief in the divine.

Eliot's letters provide the primary support for this revisionary reading. For instance, she wrote to her old Coventry friend Charles Bray, "The fact that in the scheme of things we see a constant and tremendous sacrifice of individuals is, it seems to me only one of the many proofs that urge upon

198   us our total inability to find in our own natures a key to the Divine Mystery. I could more readily turn Christian and worship Jesus again than embrace a Theism which professes to explain the proceedings of God."[1] To paraphrase Eliot's statement, the constant sacrifice of individuals to the selfish interests of others shows us that human nature is erring and imperfect and thus cannot give us insight into the Divine Mystery. Therefore Theism (represented in the nineteenth century by Theodore Parker and Frances Power Cobbe, among others) is inadequate as a religious philosophy. Eliot's criticisms of Pantheism in another letter are similar: Pantheism is not a practical religion, because it is an effort to look at the universe from outside our own relationship to it as human beings (*Eliot Letters*, 8 May 1869, 5:31). While these statements could be read as agnosticism (the philosophical position that God is unknowable), in her letter to Bray Eliot *does* claim to know something about the Mystery: it is "Divine." Eliot also refers to a "mystery" beyond human explanation—probably again "the Divine Mystery"—when recording her reaction to Darwin's *Origin of Species:* "To me the Development theory and all other explanations of processes by which things came to be, produce a feeble impression compared with the mystery that lies under the processes" (*Eliot Letters*, 5 Dec. 1859, 3:227). This statement might be elucidated by the views of Max Müller, a German scholar of language and religion, whom Eliot and Lewes read and admired:

> [B]eyond, behind, beneath, and within the finite, the infinite is always present to our senses. It presses upon us, it grows upon us from every side. What we call the finite in space and time, in form and word, is nothing but a veil or net which we ourselves have thrown over the infinite. The finite by itself, without the infinite, is simply inconceivable, as inconceivable as the infinite without the finite.[2]

While Eliot does not go as far as Müller, who claims sensory awareness of the infinite, she does have a strong "impression" of a mystery far greater and more compelling than the "nets" of human theories. Eliot's term "mystery" does not seem moored within agnosticism; sometimes it comes very close to an acknowledgment of a God. This writer's demonstrated knowledge of materialist religious philosophers like Comte[3] and Feuerbach does not mean her rich and subtle statements of her religious views should be assumed to be generally in agreement with theirs. Schleiermacher and Müller, for example, were also her contemporaries.

One of John Stuart Mill's points of disagreement with Comte's *Cours de Philosophie Positive* provides a helpful context for analyzing Eliot's views. Comte's theory is that the universe in all its aspects is governed by unvarying laws, which are all we know about phenomena. Mill criticizes Comte for claiming that positivism, which displaces the "theological" and "metaphysical" modes of philosophizing, has atheism as its necessary consequence. Mill says that if the universe had a beginning, that beginning is necessarily supernatural, since the laws of Nature cannot explain their own origins (*Auguste Comte and Positivism*, 1–15). Therefore he finds it compatible with positive philosophy to believe "that the universe was created, and even that it is continuously governed, by an Intelligence, provided we admit that the intelligent Governor adheres to fixed laws, which are only modified or counteracted by other laws of the same dispensation, and are never either capriciously or providentially departed from."[4] Mill's interpretation of Comte is echoed by Eliot (*Eliot Letters*, 4:367), and the general argument that Mill makes (theories about nature cannot explain what is outside nature) helps elucidate Eliot's own views, particularly her contention that human theories cannot explain what is not human (e.g., 2:403; 5:31). Her language in her letters and her fiction suggests that instead of accepting atheism, as Comte does, she may well choose the option Mill holds out of believing in an existent something that is supernatural and beyond human understanding, to which she gives Godlike names—"the Divine Mystery," "the Ineffable," "the Unspeakable" (*Romola*, 539). These names do not, however, presume the knowledge of God's nature that biblical revelation claims, with its "God the Father" and "God of Israel."

Interestingly, when Eliot reviewed R. W. Mackay's *The Progress of the Intellect* in 1851, she quoted and praised a long passage on religion and science that shows, she says, how faith is compatible with "the presence of undeviating law in the material and moral world." According to Mackay, "True faith is a belief in things probable"; it transcends but does not contradict our experience. It is a law of our nature, operating silently and intuitively to supplement the imperfections of our knowledge. Mackay here argues for the mutual dependence of science and religion and, like Mill, shows how the positivist emphases of the nineteenth century coexist with an enduring religious faith in "'things unseen'" (review in *SE*, 271–75).

Eliot's letters written in the early 1840s, at the time of her "Holy War" when she renounced Christianity, more clearly indicate a continued belief in the existence of the divine, though her religious views were likely still undergoing modification, since she mentioned the soon-to-be-familiar

200   theme of the necessity of conformity to law but used names and terms for God that do not appear in later texts. (Her language and ideas at this time probably show the influence of Emerson and Fuller; see chapter 1.) For example, Eliot wrote to her father (who was no longer speaking to her because of her refusal to go to church) of her continued wish "to obey the laws of my Creator" (*Eliot Letters*, 1:130). Similarly, she told her sympathetic neighbor Mrs. Pears of her delight in the "lovely Earth" and "the thoughts of the good and great" and expressed her desire to be "one in will and design with the Great Mind that has laid open to us these treasures" (1:133; see also 1:125). After the initial euphoria of embracing Truth set free (seen in the letter to Mrs. Pears), Eliot went through a period of hostility toward religious sects, which she described in an 1859 letter to her Swiss friend François d'Albert-Durade (3:230–32). But in the same letter she wrote, "I have no longer any antagonism towards any faith in which human sorrow and human longing for purity have expressed themselves" (3:231). And she later told another friend, "I should urge you to consider your early religious experience as a portion of valid knowledge, and to cherish its emotional results in relation to objects and ideas which are either substitutes or metamorphoses of the earlier" (27 Jan. 1875, 6:120; see also 4:64–65, 472). Eliot's position here may be compatible with a continued belief in some kind of God, whereas an atheist would be more wary of the religious delusions he or she had once accepted. For Eliot, the otherworldly deity should be replaced as the object of religious devotion by a human ideal—the Good rather than God (5:447–48)—but her aspiration to what is greater than the self continues, as does her sense of the Divine Mystery beyond all human knowledge.

Having suggested the possibility of the existence of the divine but denied the transcendent as an appropriate object of religious contemplation, Eliot offers an anthropological, even a physical, explanation of what religion is. Music rather than prayer is for her both the image and the means of losing oneself in communion with the whole, and when the "whole" is identified, it is people, not God. For example, in *The Spanish Gypsy*, Fedalma says of her spontaneous dance before the people of Bedmar, indecorous for one engaged to a Duke:

> "And all the people felt a common joy
> And shouted for the dance. A brightness soft

As of the angels moving down to see
Illumined the broad space. The joy, the life
Around, within me, were one heaven: I longed
To blend them visibly: I longed to dance
Before the people,—be as mounting flame
To all that burned within them! Nay, I danced;
There was no longing: I but did the deed
Being moved to do it. Oh, I seemed new-waked
To life in unison with a multitude,—
Feeling my soul upborne by all their souls,
Floating within their gladness! Soon I lost
All sense of separateness: Fedalma died
As a star dies, and melts into the light.
I was not, but joy was, and love and triumph."[5]

The "inward ebb and outward vast" that Fedalma united in her dance also came together when Eliot and Lewes heard religious music at Nuremberg: "Then we went to the Catholic church, the Frauenkirche, where the organ and voices were giving forth a glorious mass, and we stood with a feeling of brotherhood among the standing congregation, till the last note of the organ had died out" (Eliot Letters, 2:452; cf. Middlemarch, 90).

Eliot throughout her works uses images for religion that associate it with the body. Religion is, for example, a duty "knit up" from our feelings, so that we are tied by our "heartstrings" to others, particularly family members (this language shows Eliot consciously working with one of the presumed root meanings of the term religio, "binding").[6] Religion is also a "hunger" (e.g., "And so the poor child, with her soul's hunger. . . , began to nibble at this thick-rinded fruit of the tree of knowledge" [The Mill on the Floss, 380]). But religious inheritance is, more negatively, a growth on the body, or even a corpse:

> Errors which we once fancied were a mere incrustation have
> grown into the living body. . . and we cannot in the majority of
> cases, wrench them away without destroying vitality. (Eliot Letters,
> 1:162)

> [E]ach age and each race has had a faith and a symbolism suited
> to its need and its stage of development, and. . . for succeeding
> ages to dream of retaining the spirit along with the forms of the

past, is as futile as the embalming of the dead body in the hope
that it may one day be resumed by the living soul. (Review of
Mackay, in *SE*, 269)

These bodily images help one see the place of asceticism in Eliot's
thought. Denying the body, its physical and psychic needs and appetites,
lessens the hold of the family, society, and the past on the individual. It is
no accident that the religious enthusiasts and revolutionaries in Eliot's novels (Dinah, Maggie, Savonarola, Dorothea, Mordecai) all have ascetic tendencies. (Denying a sexually differentiated female body has feminist as
well as religious resonances, fostering revolutionary claims of moral sameness and individual rights, as the analysis of *Romola* has shown.) Physical
and emotional self-denial, which Eliot, like John Bunyan, associates with
Protestantism or "Protestantizing" currents in religious history (e.g.,
Savonarola's "purifying" regime) rather than with "fleshly" Catholicism,
helps her characters liberate themselves, at least temporarily, from an inheritance she describes in cultural, physical, and eventually racial terms.
Obviously, as one cannot leave the body entirely, one cannot be entirely
free from a religion or a past that is part of one's "bodily" inheritance. But
as Nancy Paxton points out, Eliot's thought is not strictly deterministic;
one is able to choose. The asceticism of the reformer or revolutionary indicates both a choice and the extreme difficulty of that choice, since the
past is seen as part of one's bone and marrow and perhaps cannot be torn
out, as Eliot says, without destroying life itself.

Eliot in her essays and reviews on religious subjects, most written in
the 1850s, reveals her acceptance of a dominant theory: the progress of religion from "primitive" polytheism to more advanced monotheism and
then to "philosophy" or "positivism."[7] According to this theory, every people
goes through the same stages of religious belief; a tenacious adherence to
an ancestral religion—Judaism, for example—is seen as intellectual and
cultural backwardness. But even as Eliot endorses theories of progress, the
bodily metaphors she uses suggest the difficulty of escaping the hold of
the past. Eventually in her writings the physical aspect of religion pre-
dominates over the theory of uniform and rational religious progress. This
change in paradigms primarily results from Eliot's growing interest in scientific and evolutionary thought (her relationship with Lewes was of
course a factor). By the time of *The Spanish Gypsy* (1868–69), she speaks of
religion in Lamarckian terms, as a physical or racial inheritance. The emphasis shifts from progress (though that idea is still present in evolutionary theories) to the deep-rootedness and validity of religious difference.

Jean Baptiste de Lamarck (1744–1829) argued that creatures adapt to   203
the environment and thus acquire characteristics, which are then passed
down.[8] Despite Darwin's authorship of a counter theory, he and Herbert
Spencer, along with other intellectuals during the latter part of the nineteenth century, were influenced by Lamarck's idea of the inheritance of acquired characteristics, applying it to cultural phenomena as well as to
physical traits and sometimes using it as an explanation for religion.[9]
Gertrude Himmelfarb traces the impact of Lamarck's theory on Darwin,
particularly his *Descent of Man* (1871), and shows how it affected even Darwin's formulations of religious disbelief.[10] In a passage that his wife and
daughter piously excised from his *Life and Letters*, Darwin writes:

> May not [the highest convictions and feelings] be the result of
> the connection between cause and effect which strikes us as a
> necessary one, but probably depends merely on inherited experi-
> ence? Nor must we overlook the probability of the constant in-
> culcation of a belief in God on the minds of children producing
> so strong and perhaps an inherited effect on their brains, not as
> yet fully developed, that it would be as difficult for them to
> throw off their belief in God, as for a monkey to throw off its
> instinctive fear and hatred of a snake. (Himmelfarb, 384–85)

Darwin here suggests that religious belief results from vigorous catechiz-
ing and inherited instinct (perhaps encompassing, even among humans,
the fear of the original serpent or snake).

The currency of such ideas might also be illustrated by Eliot's younger
contemporary Freud, who saw inherited religious instincts at work within
himself and used Lamarck to explain them. Peter Gay in his recent biography quotes letters in which Freud describes "dark emotional powers" and
"strange secret longings, perhaps from the heritage of my ancestors," that
kept him tied to Judaism and made him discontented with his life in the
modern world.[11] In Gay's interpretation, such intimations, though obscurely expressed, "are a concrete consequence of Freud's belief in the inheritance of acquired characteristics; in some mysterious way his
Jewishness, his identifying quality, had to be part of his phylogenetic inheritance. He never explored how his Lamarckian 'racial' endowment
worked in himself, but he was convinced it was there" (Gay, 601–2). Gay
and the religion scholar Daniel Pals also note the impact of Lamarck's
theories on *Totem and Taboo* (1913), Freud's anthropological account connecting primitive taboos with certain religious observances, the primary

204   example being parricide and communion (Gay, 333; Pals, 66–70, 80–81).
The acceptance of Lamarckian ideas by this Jewish theorist complicates
what may be our modern assumption, that such views of religious inheritance have only dangerous and racist implications.[12] Indeed, strange as it
may seem today, the idea of religion as a racial inheritance seems to have
made Eliot more rather than less tolerant, as her changing attitudes toward
Judaism show.

    During her Evangelical adolescence and even later, as the assistant edi-
tor of the *Westminster Review*, Eliot was critical of Judaism.[13] Her polemical
attitude toward "anti-modern" religious traditions clearly changed, though,
by the mid- to late 1850s,[14] and the turning point in her attitude specifically toward Judaism seems to have been her trips to Europe with Lewes.
William Baker emphasizes the importance of the meetings she and Lewes
had with learned Jews in Berlin in 1855 (though most were not observant),
and her growing first-hand knowledge of Jews and Judaism (Baker, 9–10,
30). Her visit to a Portuguese synagogue in Amsterdam (part of a Spinoza
pilgrimage) in 1866 is an instance of her experiencing what she had long
known intellectually—that Judaism is an ancient but living faith:

> . . . in the evening we went to see the worship there. Not a
> woman was present, but of devout *men* not a few, curious reversal
> of what one sees in other temples. The chanting and the sway-
> ing about of the bodies—almost a wriggling—are not beautiful
> to the sense, but I fairly cried at witnessing this faint symbolism
> of a religion of sublime far-off memories. The skulls of St. Ur-
> sula's eleven thousand virgins seem a modern suggestion com-
> pared with the Jewish Synagogue. (*Eliot Letters*, 10 Aug. 1866,
> 4:298)

    The passage begins with a tourist's sense of distance from the odd for-
eign practices but swiftly moves to sympathy. The reference to "a religion
of sublime far-off memories" may indicate memories that are not just en-
coded in the teachings of Judaism but also are a racial inheritance transmitted to Jews themselves; the statement may be evidence of Eliot's
paradigm shift. The more obvious point is that Eliot's earlier disapproval of
Judaism, fostered by Evangelicalism and theories of the progress of religion, has disappeared. By the time she visited the synagogue, she had
started *The Spanish Gypsy*, and a version of this scene appears in *Daniel*

Deronda (*Eliot Letters*, 4:165–67, 179 n., 184). In both of these texts she portrays ancestral religion as a precious inheritance that defines a people and a culture, and cannot and will not be given up.

Scholars who deal with evolution and inheritance in the fiction of Eliot and her contemporaries (e.g., Gillian Beer, George Levine, Nancy Paxton, Suzanne Graver, and Bernard Semmel) prefer to focus on Darwin and Comte and have not noticed Lamarckian influences on Eliot's views of religion and inheritance. For example, Beer in *Darwin's Plots* briefly discusses Lamarck's evolutionary theories, with their emphasis on intention, will, and accretion, but she is primarily interested in the "post-structuralist" Darwin, who, in contrast to his predecessor, writes evolutionary "narratives" that are multivalent and resistant to anthropocentrism and closure (3–26). Levine also discusses Darwin and narrative, while Paxton focuses on the relation between evolutionary theory and feminism in Spencer and Eliot. Semmel analyzes Eliot's treatment of inheritance in the context of Romantic thinkers (Burke, Herder, Scott) and Comte. All these scholars except Beer make only a few references to Lamarck or to religion.[15] A frequent assumption among Eliot critics seems to be that after she finished her translations of Strauss and Feuerbach and wrote her first two novels, she passed on in her intellectual interests from religion to science and the social sciences (though with due attention to Comte's positivist religion). Yet, as we have seen, her interest in religion in fact intensified and became synthesized with her evolutionary views.

The Spanish Gypsy (1868–69), Eliot's longest poem, is set in the Spain of Ferdinand and Isabella and draws on her research for *Romola*, which also takes place in the 1490s. The opening verses of the poem are reminiscent of that novel when they describe the light from the East; Renaissance man awakens to "[spell] the record of his long descent" and read the Greek sages and orators once again (24). But the primary emphasis of the poem is on Spain as the western frontier against the "night" of advancing Islam. The Christians there are at war against the Moors and their Gypsy allies, and even orthodox Catholics are uneasy about the "hot wind from Seville"—the Inquisition (23–26, 37).

The starting point for *The Spanish Gypsy*, according to Eliot, was an Annunciation by Titian, seen in Venice; it gave her an idea never before used by tragedians:

A young maiden, believing herself to be on the eve of the chief event of her life,—marriage,—about to share in the ordinary lot of womanhood, full of young hope, has suddenly announced to her that she is chosen to fulfil a great destiny, entailing a terribly different experience from that of ordinary womanhood. She is chosen . . . as a result of foregoing hereditary conditions . . . ; she obeys. "Behold the handmaid of the Lord."[16]

This subject symbolized to Eliot the part that "hereditary conditions, in the largest sense"—racial or national identity, family ties, even our inherited human nature—play in the human lot. These rather obscure statements are elucidated by the plot of the poem: Fedalma, foster-sister and fiancée of Silva, Duke of Bedmar, discovers the night before her wedding that she is the daughter of the gypsy king Zarca. She gives up individual happiness, and her adopted nationality and Catholic faith, in recognition of her people's claim; she becomes Queen of the Zincali. In an earlier essay on *Antigone* (1856), Eliot had defined tragedy as the conflict between two goods, one inward and individual (here, Antigone's responsibility to her dead brother and the gods) and one outward and general (the claims of the state).[17] In her notes on *The Spanish Gypsy* she built on this definition, describing tragedy in Lamarckian or Darwinian terms as "the irreparable collision between the individual and the general," the latter term being understood as hereditary conditions (15). Eliot always considered it essential to tragedy and to moral heroism that both claims are good and valid; on this ground she criticized a novel for advancing the argument that nothing renounced "for the sake of a higher principle will prove to have been worth the keeping."[18]

The Spanish Gypsy is notably Lamarckian in its treatment of religion as a physically inherited characteristic of peoples and races. Prior Isidor, the uncle of Duke Silva, says of Fedalma:

> "She bears the marks
> Of races unbaptized, that never bowed
> Before the holy signs, were never moved
> By stirrings of the sacramental gifts. . . .
> I read a record deeper than the skin.
> What! Shall the trick of nostrils and of lips
> Descend through generations, and the soul
> That moves within our frame like God in worlds—

Convulsing, urging, melting, withering—
Imprint no record, leave no documents,
Of her great history?" (79)

207

The Prior has sinister motives for this speech; he wants to subject Fedalma, that "spotless maiden with a pagan soul," to the Inquisition and thus prevent her marriage to Duke Silva, who will then remain a celibate and a single-minded defender of the faith (75–81, 112–16). Yet almost every speaker in the poem, including the narrator, agrees with the Prior on his central point, religion as an "inherited soul"; the belief is affirmed rather than invalidated in the poem. For example, the narrator says that the innkeeper Lorenzo, whose prudent father made him convert from Judaism at age ten, could never replace the infant faith he lost: "Baptism seemed to him a merry game / . . . And all religions a queer human whim / Or else a vice, according to degrees" (28–29). The full passage combines stereotypes about Jews with sympathy for Lorenzo's state of religious alienation. Later in the poem, the analysis becomes less offensive and more edged; an observant Jew, Sephardo, who is a physician and scholar, has his religion and loyalty to his persecuted people described as his "inherited rage" (161).

Fedalma has had intimations of her gypsy birth, and when she encounters the piercing gaze of the captured gypsy king and later examines the strange carving of his necklace, taken as booty, she feels the stirring of individual and ancestral memories—her "heritage of sorrow" (89, 102–3). She acknowledges this man, Zarca, as her father and readily accepts his argument that she must be the bride of her people, not of Don Silva. Zarca's language is an echo of the Prior's:

"Will you adopt a soul without its thoughts,
Or grasp a life apart from flesh and blood?
Till then you cannot wed a Spanish Duke. . . ." (133)

While the only religion of the Zincali is faithfulness to each other, the hereditary basis of this "creed" is made clear; the likeness of people to each other, according to Zarca, creates community, which is the "mother divine of customs, faith, and laws" (122–26, 206).

Don Silva denies the idea dominating the poem; claiming that "love comes to cancel all ancestral hate," he chooses Fedalma, and individual love and happiness, over *his* people and religion. But though he leaves Bedmar to join the gypsies, he cannot escape "that hereditary right / Which

208   held dim habitations in his frame," and he cannot stop seeing the faces of the Mother and Son and the comrades he has betrayed: they are "the warmly mingled lifeblood of his mind" (220, 237–38). His choice of a paradise of two over ancestral loyalties has awful consequences: the Moors and gypsies kill his boyhood companions in battle, sack Bedmar, desecrate the church, and hang the Prior; Don Silva kills Zarca in revenge (249–62). At the end of the poem, the "knight-apostate" becomes a Spaniard again, reaffirming his bond to his dead uncle (the "flesh-twin" of his father), as Fedalma chooses her father; he will atone for his betrayals by losing his life in wars for Spain (258, 275–80). The ending of *The Spanish Gypsy* is both horrifying and problematic, in large part because the poem does not work as tragedy, on Eliot's own terms. Tragedy is supposed to involve a choice between two goods, but Don Silva's choice of marriage (or individual happiness) can be hardly be a good, since he betrays his every ideal and abandons his people and kingdom to destruction by the enemy.

The role of the Madonna in *The Spanish Gypsy* is intimated by the mothers in the prologue, who include "broad-breasted Spain . . . / (A calm earth-goddess crowned with corn and vines)" and the "fond Present," mother of time.[19] The point of view here is Christian but soon yields to multiple perspectives, and the goddess *in* Spain takes various forms. The Castilian knight Don Silva adores the Virgin Mary and her likeness, the "virgin goddess" Fedalma, who is pure, prayed to, and his (87–88, 146, 215, 239). The physical descriptions of the heroine, though, suggest the inappropriateness of this role, even before her gypsy birth is known: she is a *dark* beauty (as Western Madonnas before Murillo are generally not), and when she dances she is *"sensuously* pure," a quality never associated with the Virgin Mary (65–66, emphasis added).

    In contrast to Don Silva, Zarca characterizes Fedalma, the "goddess" of the Zincali, as Queen and Mother. As Queen, Fedalma rules the gypsies by hereditary lot, and is expected to continue her father's work of making this people a nation and their law the memory of heroic deeds. At Zarca's death, she becomes their mother, subduing her grief as her children's protector (221, 223, 263–67). But she realizes her calling is futile; she cannot unite the Zincali because she lacks her father's will and the people's loyalty (271). She instead sees her role as priestess in her father's temple ("the deepest hunger of a faithful heart is faithfulness" [278]); her role is finally self-defined, but it is still subject to her father's vision.

    What is notable about Eliot's treatment of the Madonna in *The Spanish*

Gypsy is the way the qualities associated with this figure are split up: the Christians worship her as Virgin, while the Zincali see *their* goddess as Queen and Mother. The Madonna is no longer, as in *Adam Bede*, an extra-cultural symbol of female empowerment proposed by the narrator; instead, she is an indigenous figure, the goddess of the Spanish and Catholic characters, expressing their ideals, beliefs, and sense of their identity as a people. (The poem thus suggests why the Madonna in Eliot's next major work, *Middlemarch*, is not a usable figure for the English Protestant heroine or her provincial culture.) In contrast to the Spanish Catholics, the Zincali and their Moorish allies see the Madonna as Our Lady of Pain; their battle song is "Swear to hate the cruel cross," whose defenders persecute and kill those of other faiths. As Zarca tells his daughter, who escaped the Inquisition, "[They] reared you for the flames" (204, 241–43). It is unexpected to have peoples usually treated as the Other by nineteenth-century writers given voice and subjectivity. Eliot's dialogic text asserts the value of every religion, as a cultural and racial inheritance, and uses the scenes of religious bloodshed to show the need for sympathy and tolerance.

When the Prior accuses Fedalma of having "unchristian blood," Don Silva replies, "Unchristian as the Blessed Virgin's blood / Before the angel spoke the word, 'All hail!'" (79). He is ironically right. Mary is not Christian at the time of the Annunciation—the Gospels characterize her as a Jewish maiden—and Fedalma, responding to *her* father's call to be exceptional among women, remains where the Prior has situated her, outside the Church (135). *The Spanish Gypsy* is Eliot's only work in which she does not undercut the possibility of an Annunciation ("no radiant angel came across the gloom with a clear message" for Romola, and poor Dorothea is mistaken when she thinks Mr. Casaubon is Gabriel [*Romola*, 309; *Middlemarch*, 50]). The evident reason is that Fedalma's summons is not miraculous (though relying on coincidences), and it leads her *away* from Christianity. Eliot is never gentle as an intellectual, and her poem seems designed to unsettle the Christians among her readers in several ways. She suggests the Annunciation might be paralleled among other peoples and cultures, she redefines the event as a tragedy, and (at a time when faith is threatened by science) she explains religion in evolutionary terms.[20]

Daniel Deronda (1876) is a double-plotted novel, the story of Gwendolen Harleth, a proud English beauty who marries a wealthy sadist and is slowly broken by him, and the story of Daniel Deronda, who responds to

210   Gwendolen's pleas for help and also saves a young Jewish woman, Mirah Lapidoth, from killing herself in despair. Daniel's quest to find Mirah's mother and family, from whom she was torn away as a child, leads to the discovery of his own mother and the realization of his Jewish identity. In the "Jewish plot" of *Daniel Deronda*, Eliot revises her treatment of religion in *The Spanish Gypsy* by offering *two* explanations of the transmission of religion. The first explanation, familiar from *The Spanish Gypsy*, presents religion as a racial inheritance, an "ancestral yearning" transmitted through fathers. The other explanation emphasizes the acquisition of religious characteristics through maternal nurturance.

    "Inheritance" in *Daniel Deronda* indicates the possession of willed property and titles as well as the child's natural legacy from the parents. Critics have tended to stress the former kind of inheritance, represented by the trunk full of papers about Judaism that Daniel's grandfather leaves for him. Philip Fisher and Alexander Welsh, for example, argue that the "abstract heritage" of the trunk is more important than Daniel's discovery of his parentage. Welsh states:

> The search for Deronda's parents is successful—brilliantly successful—precisely in the degree that it is ambivalent. . . .
> [A]n unintended moral of *Daniel Deronda* is that the only good father is a dead grandfather, the only good mother one who ceases to interfere with her son.
> . . . The plot of the novel moves silently to throw over fathers and mothers . . . in favor of ancestry and liturgy and ultimately ideology. (322, 328; see also Fisher, 3–38, 203–27)

But Eliot in fact emphasizes a different kind of inheritance in this book, one that questions the largely Oedipal opposition Welsh has set up. For ancestry, liturgy, and ideology are precisely what are transmitted through parents in Eliot's Lamarckian view.

    Daniel Deronda is the ward—he believes the illegitimate son—of Sir Hugo Mallinger, an English baronet, and he has been raised as an English gentleman. Yet he has long had intimations that he is not of English birth. As a boy he realizes that none of the ancestors in Sir Hugo's portrait gallery looks the least bit like him, and he feels "the presence of a new guest who seemed . . . to carry dimly conjectured, dreaded revelations" (*Daniel Deronda*, 140–41). Sir Hugo proposes a singing career for the boy,

not a gentleman's vocation, and all the musicians in his narrated experience
(except the amateur Miss Arrowpoint) are Jewish. As an adult he is repeatedly taken for a Jew, and when he attends synagogue services for the first
time, in Frankfort, he feels an unexpected emotional response to the liturgy:

> The Hebrew liturgy, like others, has its transitions of litany,
> lyric, proclamation, dry statement and blessing; but this evening
> all were one for Deronda: the change of the *Chazan's* or Reader's
> grand wide-ranging voice with its passage from monotony to
> sudden cries, the outburst of sweet boys' voices from the little
> quire, the devotional swaying of men's bodies backwards and
> forwards, the very commonness of the building and shabbiness
> of the scene where a national faith, which had penetrated the
> thinking of half the world, and moulded the splendid forms of
> that world's religion, was finding a remote, obscure echo—all
> were blent for him, as one expression of a binding history, tragic
> and yet glorious. He wondered at the strength of his own feel-
> ing; it seemed beyond the occasion—what one might imagine to
> be a divine influx in the darkness, before there was any vision to
> interpret. (310)

Soon afterward, Daniel meets his mother for the first time and learns that
he is indeed a Jew. This revelation leads him to voice his belief in religion
as an "inherited yearning—the effect of brooding, passionate thoughts in
many ancestors—thoughts that seem to have been intensely present in my
grandfather." His examples are pertinent to his own life—and his mother's.
They include the longing of a stolen child (as he and Mirah are) for the
never-seen ancestral mountains, and artistic talent (like his mother's) that
troubles the soul even if it cannot be expressed (642).

Daniel is denied knowledge of his Jewish birth by his mother. She
hated Judaism and the life of "slavery" as a Jewish woman, imposed on her
by her father, and abandons them after his death, transforming herself into
Alcharisi, the renowned European singer and actress. She abandons Daniel, too, giving him to Sir Hugo to raise and thereby securing for him (she
thinks) the better life of a Gentile and a gentleman. But Daniel rejects the
birthright she chose for him (an ironic repetition of her father's resented
choosing for her) and instead will become what her father wanted: a
grandson with a "true Jewish heart." He tells his mother:

"Your will was strong, but my grandfather's trust which you accepted and did not fulfil—what you call his yoke—is the expression of something stronger, with deeper, farther-spreading roots,
knit into the foundations of sacredness for all men. You renounced me—you still banish me—as a son— . . . But that
stronger Something has determined that I shall be all the more
the grandson whom also you willed to annihilate." (568)

In *The Spanish Gypsy* no mothers are present, while in Daniel's plot the
mother is a powerful but repudiated force. But the effect initially is the
same: religion is described, primarily by the male characters, as the faith of
the fathers, transmitted to the child as an inner longing and overcoming,
in Daniel's case, the mother's effort to deny him his place as son and heir.[21]

Mirah, in contrast to Daniel, sees her religion as a gift from her
mother, and as the consequence of nurture rather than nature. She says:

"I think my life began with waking up and loving my mother's
face: it was so near to me, and her arms were round me, and she
sang to me. One hymn she sang so often, so often: and then she
taught me to sing it with her: it was the first I ever sang. They
were always Hebrew hymns she sang; and because I never knew
the meaning of the words they seemed full of nothing but our
love and happiness." (179)

Judaism, a matrilineal religion, is in Mirah's experience maternal as well: its
fundamental teaching is the pious bond of mother and daughter. Only
when Mirah is taken away by her father, on a short trip that lasts over a
decade and prevents her from ever seeing her mother again, does she learn
the law associated with the father—that Judaism is a religion of suffering,
"a long song of mourning." Mirah's father is non-observant and inclined to
ridicule Jews; she obtains prayerbooks and a Bible and attends synagogue
when she can to help reestablish the connection to her mother and her
faith, otherwise known only through memories and dreams (182–84).

Mirah's brother Mordecai, a Jewish scholar whom Daniel meets and
restores to her, demonstrates both understandings of religion—maternal
nurturance and paternal inheritance—although he privileges the second.
He repeatedly likens education in the Jewish tradition to feeding at the
mother's breast (e.g., saying that Spinoza, though not a faithful Jew, "had
sucked the life of his intellect at the breasts of Jewish tradition").[22] This

image is perhaps echoed by Mirah when she describes lying in her mother's arms, seeing everything white above her, as though she is still nursing, and hearing her mother's songs (179). Mordecai himself attempts the "maternal" transmission of Judaism, exemplified earlier by the singing mother and listening daughter. He makes the young Jacob Cohen hear and memorize—he orally "prints" on the boy—a long Hebrew poem about the past of Israel and its future hopes. But Mordecai's attempt fails because Jacob, though quick to mimic the Hebrew sounds, is an irreverent little boy who listens while walking on his hands and gabbles with a see-saw rhythm "a verse on which Mordecai had spent some of his too scanty heart's blood" (408–10). Mordecai thus looks for a different sort of son, who will "take up [his] life where it is broken" and work to realize his vision (shared with Daniel's grandfather Daniel Charisi) of a "land and polity" for the Jews.

Mordecai, like Daniel, sees Judaism as "the inborn half of memory" and "an inheritance that has never ceased to quiver in millions of human frames" (454–58). But he attributes many of his own visions and memories to a medieval soul that was born within him in boyhood, and he dies confident that his own soul will live again in Daniel (427, 643, 695). Mordecai's is a medieval and Kabbalah-influenced version of Daniel's modern views (and Eliot's in *The Spanish Gypsy*), and Daniel harmonizes the differences by pledging himself to act on his friend's and his grandfather's visions but saying that he will not believe "exactly as my fathers have believed" (620).

Mordecai, then, moves from being a "mother" to being a "father" in his search for an heir. But it is notable that he consistently regards Judaism as a patriarchal religion, as shown by his language (which is echoed by Daniel)—"the God of our fathers," "the men of Israel"—and his desire for *male* followers, despite his eventual reunion with a sister. Even as Mordecai describes learned men sucking at the breasts of Jewish tradition, actual women are curiously absent from his representations of the national history and heritage.

The two explanations of religion offered by characters in *Daniel Deronda* might be put together—by analogy with Lamarck's theory, which contains the two components of acquisition of traits and (subsequent) inheritance of them. The starting point is one of Daniel's examples of religion as an "inherited yearning": music. He describes one's "inherited frame" —one's ancestral nature—as a spell-bound instrument waiting to be played, waiting to respond to the right touch (642). Mirah's story indicates

214   that the instrument is first played by the mother's songs. The mother's role thus brings together nature and nurture, heredity and learned behavior, the inherited frame and the music that awakens the instrument. The process seems analogous to the acquisition of language; learning to speak is a natural tendency, but there seems to be a particular window in childhood when that happens, as shown by the recently publicized case of Genie, a late-twentieth-century "wild child" who was taught too late and has never mastered speech.

Mirah's account of her childhood may fill in a gap in Daniel's. Alcharisi tells her adult son that she did not have much affection for him and was glad to be free of him (536–39). But his single memory of his life before Sir Hugo is "a dim sense of having been kissed very much, and surrounded by thin, cloudy, scented drapery [which Alcharisi still wears], till his fingers caught in something hard, which hurt him, and he began to cry" (140). Could a wife and a musician in a Jewish household who loved her child enough to cover him with kisses fail to sing Hebrew songs to him, as Mirah's mother did? (And could a forgotten childhood experience contribute to Daniel's strong response to the music in the synagogue?) The son's memory suggests that Alcharisi's disavowal of love is a lie, an effort to deny loss and ward off sweet filial affection that would come too late. The effect of Alcharisi's stated rejection is to make Daniel wholly his grandfather's son and exclude his mother from his explanations of his heritage; he is Jewish, he says, because of a nature inherited from his grandfather, which she sought to annihilate. The only inheritance Alcharisi claims to value is the family fortune, which she takes care to pass on to him, along with the father's ring (543)—possibly the "something hard" in which the baby Daniel catches his fingers.

Mirah's narrative, then, may provide what is missing from Daniel's: sure memories of a mother's love and of early, musical nurturance in the mother's religion. It may thus allow a more sympathetic reading of Alcharisi, as a mother who gave up a *loved* son to ensure him (she thought) a privileged life free from religious superstition and the effects of anti-Semitic prejudice. It is not at all clear, as critics such as Bonnie Zimmerman, Gillian Beer, Nancy Paxton, and Catherine Gallagher have argued, that Alcharisi represents the dilemma of the woman artist in having to choose between her career and motherhood, and daring, as few have, to sacrifice her child to her artistic calling.[23] When Sir Hugo adopts Daniel at age two, Alcharisi's career is well established; neither marriage nor motherhood, but only the late father's opposition, seems to have impeded it. Moreover, her husband is now dead, and there is no obvious risk of more pregnancies and children. It is quite possible then, despite Alcharisi's cold speeches, that the son's better life as an English gentleman rather than the mother's career was the primary motive for her actions, and his loss is still felt.

But even if Mirah's early experience of a loving mother is *not* Daniel's, the stories of these two characters, when combined, enable Eliot to continue but complicate the explanation of religious inheritance found in *The Spanish Gypsy*. In *Daniel Deronda*, Eliot emphasizes the process of acquisition as well as the characteristics inherited—nurture as confirming nature. She also emphasizes the mother's role, to which Daniel may, ironically, owe all of his Jewishness. For Alcharisi is the only living parent, as well as the only parent, who can confirm Daniel's birth (since in Judaism descent is traced through the mother), and she may have first tuned his ear to the mother tongue of that heritage. Eliot thus rewrites accounts of the past (including her own in *The Spanish Gypsy*) to restore to history the mother and her essential cultural and religious role.

As noted earlier (in the analysis of the "Annunciation" scene of *The Spanish Gypsy*), Eliot defines tragedy as the conflict of two goods—the internal and individual good; and the outward and general, or hereditary, good. The final, intriguing complication of the encounter between Daniel and Alcharisi is that their life choices, which tragically conflict, are justified on the *same* ground. Daniel, like Fedalma in *The Spanish Gypsy*, chooses a life of struggle to help his "hereditary people" over a life of easeful happiness in the circle of an adoptive family (*Daniel Deronda*, 566). But Alcharisi, when explaining her decision to be an artist rather than a traditional Jewish woman, claims that she, too, chose the hereditary good: "My nature gave me a charter" (570). Daniel agrees with her in this scene and probably again later, when he compares the "ancestral yearning" to inborn artistic talent that troubles the soul (642). Daniel also here likens the human being to a "frame" and an "instrument" waiting for the right music, and his language is a perhaps unconscious echo of his mother's. She says earlier of the father she defied: "I tell you, he never thought of his daughter except as an *instrument*. Because I had wants outside of his purpose, I was to be put in a *frame* and tortured" (567, emphasis added). The same language gives opposing views of Jewish heritage. Alcharisi claims that because she is female, her father denied her the human freedom Daniel assumes as his right, that of not being owned or controlled by another. The father, for selfish reasons rather than the general good, made her into a

216   commodity, valued only for the religious heritage that passes through her (it is thus unsurprising that she prizes material commodities like jewels over this heritage). Life as a Jewish woman, she says, was a form of enslavement because it was contrary to her own inherited nature (541). Eliot here provides what for her is the strongest possible argument for the woman artist, especially in the context of Daniel's grievance: Alcharisi was not choosing an individual good but a hereditary good, since the creative impulse is part of her nature, akin to the longing for God.

The debate between mother and son is also between opposing factions in nineteenth-century Judaism. Daniel's is the voice of committed, proto-Zionist Judaism, while Alcharisi's is the voice of assimilationist Judaism, represented in Eliot's experience by the accomplished Jewish women (all converts to Christianity) whom she had met in the salons of Berlin in the 1850s: Rahel Varnhagen, Henriette Mendelssohn Herz, Dorothea Mendelssohn Schlegel (Laqueur, *Zionism*, 3–39; Haight, 169–75). Daniel himself agrees with the assimilationist position before he becomes a follower of Mordecai and his late grandfather (*Daniel Deronda*, 176, 306). Eliot does not clearly choose sides between religious observance and secular assimilationism; her own complicated position of respect for the religious heritage *she* rejected is obviously a factor. Instead, she gives weight to both sides by having the mother and the son make the *same* kind of argument, based on hereditary good rather than individual good. And she complicates the discussion by introducing gender issues, showing how a religious heritage may be freedom or slavery, depending on whether it is viewed by the son or the daughter.

Eliot's sympathetic focus on Jewish questions contrasts with her treatment of Christianity in *Daniel Deronda*. The march of the Christian victors through English history is suggested by the chronicles of Sir Hugo Mallinger's family, marked by conquest and dispossession: the family crest is three Saracens, who were vanquished (along with many Jews) in the Crusades, and the Mallinger estate is a former Benedictine abbey, a gift from Henry VIII at the time of the dissolution of the monasteries (140, 350–51). The monks' refectory is now Sir Hugo's drawing room, and the chapel, ruined by Cromwell's troops as an insult to the images of "Ashtoreth" (the Virgin Mary), is given over to the horses. These stables have a strange, exquisite beauty: "Each finely-arched chapel was turned into a stall, where in the dusty glazing of the windows there still gleamed patches of crimson, orange, blue, and palest violet; . . . a soft light fell from the upper windows on sleek brown or grey flanks and haunches, on mild equine faces looking out." But the scene is also evocative of Swift: certainly these Houyhnhnms are creatures superior to reptilian Englishmen like Grandcourt, Sir Hugo's heir, who, when Daniel stands bare-headed in recognition of a once-holy place, sneers, "Do you take off your hat to the horses?" (359–60).

The "bare ruined choirs" of Abbot's and King's Topping may indicate that Christianity has taken up its abode elsewhere—for example, in a smart new Gothic chapel in Mayfair. But the speeches of Sir Hugo and Mr. Gascoigne, the guardians of Daniel and Gwendolen, point instead to the spiritual barrenness of the English gentry. Mr. Gascoigne, a rector and Gwendolen's uncle, sees no difference between "Providence" and social expedience. He tells Gwendolen it is her duty and responsibility to marry Grandcourt because of his wealth and rank, despite her evident lack of affection for the man and his own suspicion that Grandcourt may have a mistress (117–20). When Daniel is first offered his Jewish heritage in the Frankfort synagogue—a friend of his grandfather curiously approaches him and inquires his name—he coldly replies, "I am an Englishman." But the essence of that identity, as defined by Sir Hugo, is intellectual narrowness, an "English cut" in tailoring, and high standards for tobacco. The English Christian thus seems to be signs without soul—most perfectly, a Grandcourt. No wonder Daniel is drawn to the music in the synagogue, which (as elsewhere in Eliot) puts the listener into harmony with present and past generations and lifts him to communion with the "all Good" or God (155–56, 310–11).

The names of characters in *Daniel Deronda* are one of Eliot's most important indications of the comparative status of Christianity and Judaism. Gwendolen's name comes from Arthurian legend (it is akin to "Guinevere"), and she is repeatedly described as a Greco-Roman goddess (Artemis, "the Leubronn Diana"), though she is the prey, not the huntress, in her marriage to Grandcourt (*Daniel Deronda*, 57–59, 272). The male characters in the Jewish plot are named for biblical prophets of the Exile. Mordecai Cohen explains to Daniel that he was formerly known by his first name, Ezra, and was ready to sail to Palestine, on the mission he now urges on Daniel, when he received a frantic letter from his mother saying his father had disappeared with Mirah. He turned his back on Palestine and went to comfort his mother, back into exile in Europe (the land of the Diaspora). Because he could not be another Ezra, a restorer of Israel, he

218   began to call himself Mordecai (an exilic figure, the uncle of Esther). Daniel, Mordecai insists, "will take up my life where it was broken" (461–63). Daniel will thus become both Ezra and "Cohen" (i.e., a priest who recalls his people to their ancestral faith). Daniel seems ready for these roles because, like the biblical Daniel, he is a man of purity and faith, detesting the sexual crassness of his aristocratic relatives and all "moral stupidity." This Daniel, as Mordecai's heir, will also be a visionary of the courses of history and will help restore the nation of Israel.

One might expect the sister of Mordecai to be an "Esther," the faithful defender of her people. Eliot, however, does not call her Jewish heroine "Esther," perhaps because this is the name of numerous fallen women in fiction by Balzac, Gaskell, Hawthorne, and Eliot herself (*Adam Bede*).[24] But it also seems significant that a character says of Mirah, "She wants to be no one but herself," and she receives a name with no obvious religious or literary resonances: "Mirah" is Slavonic, meaning "peace."[25] "Mirah" is, however, close to the biblical "Miriam"; Eliot's publisher John Blackwood, in fact, once misread it as such (*Eliot Letters*, 6:145). As a "Miriam" Eliot's character would be associated with both Moses' sister, a musician and prophetess, and with Naomi in the book of Ruth, who returns from exile as a childless widow and calls herself "Mara," or "bitter." "Miriam" is also, significantly, the name of Jesus' mother in the New Testament. The absence of a "Miriam" in *Daniel Deronda* could indicate that Eliot misses her chance to create a Jewish Virgin Mother, the type of the powerful, salvific Madonna-figure of Christianity and an alternative to the submissive Jewish woman that Alcharisi criticizes. But the author evidently had second thoughts about the system of typological signification she had used in *Adam Bede*, since it would make the Old Testament merely the foreshadowing of the New and would reflect the conventional assumption that "the Chosen People . . . [were] a people chosen for the sake of somebody else" (*Daniel Deronda*, 306). Eliot's insistence on a "Mirah" consequently helps ensure that Judaism (like the Jewish heroine) is read in terms of itself, as a living religion and not as the archaic predecessor of other faiths.[26]

Eliot's decision not to make Mirah a Mary-figure illuminates Alcharisi's role as well. Both *The Spanish Gypsy* and *Daniel Deronda* are centered around the tragic conflict between individual and hereditary good, but the later work cannot be said to have an Annunciation scene coherently based on the Christian model. In the encounters between Alcharisi and her son, *Daniel* is in Mary's place, called to a new destiny, whereas the *woman* is the father's messenger (ironically so, since she repudiated the ancestral faith).

Alcharisi in fact has none of the characteristics of the biblical Virgin Mary. She refused motherhood, although she may have given up her son out of maternal love. And in some obvious and less-than-obvious ways, she is not a virgin. Catherine Gallagher has brilliantly shown that actresses like Alcharisi were linked not only to prostitutes but also to moneylending in the nineteenth century (Gallagher, esp. 47, 53–59). The linkage I want to explore is the association of actresses with the generation of inauthentic images (for the performer was seen as merely a medium for others' art). Whereas Eliot associates Mirah's virginity with singleness or purity of identity ("She wants to be no one but herself"), Alcharisi, as an actress, presents multiple selves, and changing and uncertain identities and motives. Even during the reunion with her son, she is said to be *playing* herself, and the attitudes she voices ("I was glad to be freed from you") may be the most feigned part of the whole performance (*Daniel Deronda*, 539). In *Romola*, "singleness" of identity or meaning is associated with the visual arts; the sacred image represents a shared, enduring truth—that the divine is present in human life. But in *Daniel Deronda*, the scenes between Alcharisi and Daniel are marked by collisions of beliefs and motives and the uncertain, unstable relationship between representation and reality. The "multiplicity" of dramatic art may make it, for Eliot, the art form most evocative of the modern world.

But while Alcharisi's profession allows us to consider the symbolic implications of "virginity" and "generation," "singleness" and "multiplicity," she, like Mirah, also confirms a more basic point about Eliot's treatment of religion. Eliot, with her virgin Mirah and an Annunciation scene that transgenders the biblical roles and reiterates a refusal of motherhood, signals that the earlier Christian iconography cannot be imposed on *this* novel. She thus breaks the "Mary chain" that runs all through her work. When Mirah sits in the Meyricks' house with a "cloud of witnesses," including the Madonnas of Christian art, above her on the walls, she testifies to her willingness to die for *another* faith, notwithstanding the Meyrick sisters' hope of her "normalizing" conversion (179–93). The scene illustrates the "separateness with connection" of Judaism and Christianity that is the proto-Zionist model of relations between the two religions.

But the absence of a Madonna-figure in *Daniel Deronda* also suggests the to unworthiness of Christianity to serve as a model for other religions or claim precedence over them. Irving Howe says that in her last novel, Eliot finds herself "with a vision of society astonishingly caustic, still more astonishingly deficient in positive figures or voices" (Howe, 373). The abbey

220   remains as a material inheritance, but the English gentry who live there are left without legitimate heirs, and the spirit of the monks who, as Carlyle says, "worked out their life-wrestle" in constant awareness of Eternity, is long gone (*Past and Present*, 54). Only by leaving England will Daniel and Mirah come into their religious inheritance and help the Jews of the Diaspora find a homeland with more possibilities for spiritual renewal than the Europe they left behind.

Conclusion

Meek. Mild. Pure. The lily of Eden's shade. The sweet-faced mother of a divine son. The Madonna appears again and again in this guise in nineteenth-century England and America—in Patmore, in Newman, in novels and popular iconography. The three feminist writers of this study, however, have quite different Madonnas in mind. Jameson, because of the encyclopedic nature of her art histories, presents a wider range of Marian images than the other writers do, but she clearly favors certain ones: the solitary, powerful Virgin of the earliest Christian art, and the merciful Queen of the late Middle Ages. Earthly queenship disappoints her—the Queen Victoria who becomes a bourgeois icon is still an easily led girl—and Jameson looks to the heavenly queen for proof that woman is, in strength, wisdom, and virtue, the equal of man, and that female as well as male nature is made divine. The Madonna also provides more mundane consolations. The poor working woman, the young mother, the refugee, the grief-marked dignified woman who, like Jameson, is alone in old age: all see their lives and losses given value by Mary and even recognize their faces in the Madonnas of art.[1]

Margaret Fuller, like Jameson, is drawn to the solitary Virgin, but even more to the Virgin Mother, a paradoxical figure that intrigues her subtle mind. Both writers' Madonna-figures attest to the "idea" or ideal of Woman and symbolize the complementarity and equality of the sexes. But the equality that most attracts Fuller is the right of women to have both a

222 creative and a marital life. Fuller differs from many of her male contemporaries by contrasting not creativity and femaleness, but creativity and the self-contained virgin's state. Minerva and the Muse, the Virgin and the Mother, represent for her the most fundamental if difficult of unions. For Fuller, even more than for Jameson, the Madonna is a symbol of her own life. The American writer leaves sexuality out of her early meditations on creativity (female authorship as a virgin birth) and even marriage (a model for which is the brother-sister relationship), but she finds that this tactic will not do. She describes one of her female romantic friendships as between Mary and Elizabeth, but Mary realizes she wants Joseph even more. Yet Fuller's association of sexuality with the lower or earthly nature and the uneducated classes leads to a permanent tension in her writing, as in her personal life. She never managed to find someone who was both lover and intellectual peer, and that meant the full possibility of the Madonna's roles eluded her. She became the Virgin Mother of a son, but never, it seems, Virgin and Wife.

Eliot achieved what Fuller evidently did not, the status of the Virgin Wife. She had a productive career as a novelist and an emotionally and intellectually satisfying relationship with G. H. Lewes. But he was not, of course, her legal husband, and his name for his Marian, "Madonna," is suggestive of her use of this figure to challenge sexual roles (as Bonnie Zimmerman and Gillian Beer show) as well as religious assumptions. Eliot's fictional exploration of the Madonna begins with the images of European art, made memorable by the interpretations of Jameson and Ruskin, and with Fuller's Virgin Mother. The novelist initially shows the antithesis of the independent and the relational life and gives preference to the virgin. But in *Romola* she reconciles the two roles, emphasizes the mother's, and even likens the heroine, whom she admits is a "goddess," to the Great Mother of the ancient world, whose glory now shines around the heavenly Queen. The world of *Middlemarch* has lost this sense of the divine, and the comparisons of Dorothea to the Madonnas and other holy women of art bring out little more than the heroine's decorative beauty and the presumption of her selfless devotion to the male, her role as *his* lady. Eliot's suggestion in *Romola* and *Middlemarch*, that the honor formerly paid to holy personages and their images raised the status of actual women, is a connection first made by Jameson and Fuller. In Eliot's late work *The Spanish Gypsy*, the Madonna is presented in a harsher light, as the Blessed Lady of the Christians who have persecuted adherents of other faiths. This figure does, however, draw sympathetic attention to the struggles of a Spanish

maiden forced to choose between being the Lady of the Castilian Christians and the Mother of the Gypsies. The historical panorama of this dramatic poem and *Daniel Deronda*, with their emphasis on inter-religious
conflicts and the disruptive discovery of new worlds, is one of her greatest
departures from her predecessors.

Eliot's treatment of the "politics of Mary" points to an important issue
that needs to be considered more fully: why in the last work of Fuller and
Eliot the Madonna is no longer such a bright symbol for feminists and is
generally a diminished presence. Jameson never retreated from her enthusiasm for Mary, though there is some tension between her very high
Mariology in *Legends of the Madonna* and her niece's description of *History of
Our Lord* as the crown of the undertaking. Jameson's support for Daniel
O'Connell, who enlisted the Virgin Mary in his campaigns in Ireland, sug-
gests that she saw this symbol as reconciling progressive Protestants and
Catholics, who shared both a religious heritage and a commitment to reform based on biblical values of justice, mercy, and peace. Fuller's reading
of O'Connell (and the Virgin) in Ireland indicates initial similarities
between her Marian politics and Jameson's. But she largely ceded the
Madonna to the pope during the 1848 Roman revolution (the Virgin
Mother survived as a feminist symbol primarily in private letters) and she
instead returned to the Protestant Jesus as the divine figure needed to inspire the rebels in their struggle for American-style freedom. When Eliot
in the course of her career shifted her focus from religious art to religious
inheritance, she came to see the Madonna as a figure anchored in history
and too often identified with the interests of Christian oppressors. In *The
Spanish Gypsy*, for example, the Virgin is an important religious symbol but
not a positive feminist one. Moreover, the altered role of the Madonna in
Middlemarch (she becomes a feminist measure of the limitations placed on
women) and her minor role in *Daniel Deronda* are signs that the author in
her last decade regarded the ruling classes of Gentile England as leading
lives of "spiritual inanition," marked by devotion to money and status, care-
less prejudice, and even cruelty.

When the three writers encountered the Madonna in the art, legends,
and doctrines of the Church, in the eternal present of word and image,
they saw her divinized status benefiting women, and she became a figure
consonant with an individual feminist politics. But competing ecclesiastical and national interpretations started to impinge on the writers' consciousness. Jameson's Mariology could withstand such challenges, because
(despite her accommodation of O'Connell's Mother of Ireland) she read

224 Mary primarily as a symbol of spiritual rather than secular power, and such power was to be wielded, especially by women, against the unjust governments of the world (presumably even in Rome). But late in their careers Fuller and Eliot confronted the claims of bloody Crusader and illiberal pope and as a result no longer claimed the Madonna in the same personal way. Their responses attest to this figure's continued power, which, however, had fallen into the wrong hands. Jameson, however, along with others never allowed the Madonna to be appropriated by reactionary forces; this figure remained *hers*, and other women's. And an awareness of Marian politics shaped only the last two years of Fuller's life (during which she produced no extant lengthy texts), and it affected only two of Eliot's late works (*The Spanish Gypsy* and *Daniel Deronda*) in a twenty-year career. We should therefore not unduly privilege the *finis*; what is remarkable about the three intellectuals of this study is the strength of their adherence to a particular idea. For the duration or almost the duration of their careers, they all continued to be drawn to the Madonna, and they made this figure, as found in Catholic art and thought (a figure without parallel in Protestantism), the powerful Lady of Victorian feminism.

Individual and popular interpretations of the Madonna have always existed alongside the "official" versions, as we have seen. In the fourteenth century, for example, Mary was often portrayed as the Queen of Heaven, but when Julian of Norwich was overawed by a vision of the majesty of God, she looked to the Virgin of the Annunciation for comfort, and described her as a "simple, humble girl" much like herself (*Revelations of Divine Love*, 66–67). In the nineteenth century, Bernadette's Lady of Lourdes and Eliot's Blessed Lady from across the sea both became visible to satisfy very different needs. In two respects, however, the feminist Madonnas of this study are likely to remain the property of an earlier age. First, these Madonnas reflect the essentialist as well as the Enlightenment-liberal feminist beliefs of the three writers. It seems likely that only a Madonna signifying equality-but-difference would have been meaningful in a society where sex differences were the fundamental organizing principle, but such assumptions and arrangements are routinely challenged by modern feminists. For example, in the field of religion and theology, Rosemary Radford Ruether's reinterpretation of Mary as a model of discipleship common to men and women is a figure more in keeping with current feminist ideas. Second, the Madonna is most often characterized by the three writers as Virgin and Queen, and both roles present problems for modern interpreters. Feminist scholars such as the influential Marina Warner have severely criticized the inimitable purity and asexuality of the Virgin, and analyses of rulers such as Isabella, Victoria, and the Virgin Mary herself have made us aware how "Christian Queenship" has served the cause of empire. The "redeemed" figure of Mary proposed by feminist theologians tends not to be a regal or a divinized figure, but instead a peasant woman, a refugee, even an unwed mother. The idea of queenly power seems to be of greatest interest to certain proponents of feminist spirituality, but Mary is not their focus. They instead find the Goddess outside traditions they identify as patriarchal and outside religious institutions.

This study has, I hope, contributed generally to the fields of feminist studies, cultural studies, and nineteenth-century literature by suggesting new directions for research. My final points will address three frequent assumptions in these fields. The first assumption, made by a number of modern scholars, is that the history of religious ideas and the development of an individual's religious thought are of relatively little interest anymore and can be sufficiently explained in terms of economic and class interests and of gender and racial identities. Yet what is fascinating about many nineteenth-century religious figures is their reckless disregard for self-interest. George Eliot waged a "holy war" with her father in defense of truth and unbelief, and she was driven from his house—permanently, she feared. The conversions of Newman and Hopkins to Catholicism cost them academic positions and personal and familial ties. American abolitionists regularly faced mobs for the cause of faith and freedom. Scholarly approaches that overlook cultural phenomena like these may generally disregard religion and thus falsify history. In Victorian studies, for example, scholars feel little encouragement to match the magisterial works on figures like Newman, Channing, Emerson, and Hopkins with comparable studies of female religious thinkers, and Victorian religion may continue to be defined largely by men.[2] Yet Jameson produced a feminist Mariology, probably the first of its kind, which was based on her readings of the Scriptures and church doctrines and the new Romantic emphasis on feeling as the ground of belief. She also formulated an original theory of the relationship of the religious image to divine truth. Fuller was a major contributor to liberal-Christian theology, and her breadth of literary and philosophical reference and her criticisms of patriarchal thought challenged both Unitarianism and Transcendentalism. Eliot participated to a previously unrecognized extent in the nineteenth-century religious debates on the origin of belief, the status of the image, and the nature of religious inheritance. She developed a science of religion that is engaged with evolutionary

226 theories and has suggestive similarities to thinkers other than the materialist philosophers with whom she is most frequently compared.

The second assumption is that the secular is the way of liberation. One might argue instead that modern feminism began with biblical hermeneutics. In their very different ways, Mary Wollstonecraft, Sarah and Angelina Grimké, Elizabeth Cady Stanton, and Jameson, Fuller, and Eliot realized the need to confront entrenched religious views of female inferiority, and they recognized the authority or at least the utility of the Scriptures in providing counter-arguments. The three subjects of this study struggled intellectually and emotionally to reconcile two needs, both going to the core of identity: the need for the liberation and empowerment of women, and the magnetic draw toward the divine. Even Eliot, resistant to affirmations of belief, questioned the tenability for women of a world unaware of the divine, because such awareness, she suggested, historically has fostered an ideal of female value and integrity. In a world where women were not honored and were relatively powerless, they could be treated as mere commodities sold or exchanged by others.

Finally, many today assume that freethinkers rather than religious traditionalists have historically always advanced the cause of feminism. To be sure, Jameson, Fuller, and Eliot all exhibited intellectual independence in their treatment of religion. But their achievement in their work on the Madonna is due to their regard for tradition. These three writers, like other Victorian women, found Catholicism a useful corrective to the exclusions of Protestantism. When Britons began to rediscover their medieval past, and when they and their American cousins began to become acquainted with the works of European Romanticism and to view, purchase, and imitate the great art of Europe, the stage was set for challenges to Protestant belief and culture. Protestantism might teach the spiritual equality of men and women, but the pre-Reformation church, with its Virgins and saints, its abbesses and mystics (whom the Puritans tried to erase from memory), afforded new visions of what that equality might involve and new models for female leadership and intellectual and artistic achievement. Jameson, Fuller, and Eliot rediscovered and to some extent reconstructed a religious tradition that harmonized with their feminist principles and promised the elevation and empowerment of women. The figure they used most often to represent these hopes was the Virgin Mother of Christianity, who became their Lady of Victorian Feminism.

Notes

Introduction

1. When this project was close to completion, I found recent studies suggesting that Elizabeth Barrett Browning and Christina Rossetti might be added to this grouping (see Mermin, 112; Cunneen, 257–58; and the discussions below). Other nineteenth-century writers who focus on the Madonna include Eliza Farnham (*Woman and Her Era*, 1864), Margaret Oliphant (*Madonna Mary*, 1867), and Harriet Beecher Stowe (*The Minister's Wooing*, 1859). Their works postdate the main texts of this study, however, and raise the question of influence (Helsinger et al., 2:195, 199, 202–6); Sally Cunneen makes clear the connection between Jameson and Stowe (259–64).

2. Stanton, *Eighty Years and More*, 156–57. Mary and Martha lived at Bethany and were the sisters of Lazarus (see Luke 10:38–42; John 11–12).

3. Trudgill, 248–76; Auerbach, 63–108, 150–84, esp. 151; Cunneen, 262–64. Cunneen says that Stowe's reading of Jameson's work prompted her to travel to Europe to see religious art, and while she was unmoved by most of it except the *Sistine Madonna*, she returned with an image of the Madonna and ideas for a novel.

4. "Charles Kingsley's *Westward Ho!*" in Eliot, *SE*, 311–12.

5. Langland, 1–61; Auerbach, 72; Gilbert and Gubar, 18–21, 468, 485, 490–501; Michie, esp. 12–29; Helsinger et al., 3:79–170; Christ, 130–40; Beer, *George Eliot*, 49, 122–25; Homans, *Bearing the Word*, 156–60, 216; Trudgill, 248–306; Warner, esp. 47, 236–54, 333–39; Johnston, 180–207.

6. For example, Warner reads Mary as Queen of Heaven, a crowned figure with tremendous power, as confirming the authority of popes and glorifying earthly queens and kings, to the exclusion of other women (103–11). Mary as Christ's "bride" is seated beside him in heaven, but Warner sees the suggestion of equality undercut by the emphasis on Mary's "feminine" qualities of submissiveness, virginity, and motherhood (121–22, 132–33). Childless women have always prayed to the miraculous Mother, but this woman-controlled rite is said merely to confirm their bondage to the maternal body (273–84). Warner does not consider the consecrated virgin's life preferable, however, because while women gain some independence and power, modeling their lives

228   on the Virgin Mary involves labeling their sex as impure and denigrating marriage and motherhood (72–77).

Warner quotes the anthropologist Mary Douglas in support of her conclusions about Marian images: "'The man who has been raised up seeks symbols of his high estate; the one who has been degraded seeks symbols of his debasement'" (Warner, 191; see also 333–39). Douglas's view that people use images to reflect and *not* to compensate for their degrading reality contrasts with Margaret Miles's theory.

7. Lootens, 53, 57–67. Trudgill and Warner are cited on these points. Lootens's brilliant treatment of the ever-fluid nineteenth-century assessments of Shakespeare's heroines, who figured in discussions of woman's nature and roles, would apply equally well to the Madonna, whom she sees primarily as a "monumental" figure from whom Shakespeare's heroines increasingly depart (77–115; one of the critics Lootens discusses is Anna Jameson).

See also Jameson's biographer Judith Johnston, who similarly uses Warner to compare the Madonna with the more interesting Magdalene (Johnston, 180–207, esp. 204–5).

8. David Blackbourn and Jenny Franchot have argued that religious phenomena usually receive minimal attention from scholars in their fields, which are, respectively, modern history and literary and cultural criticism. The main reasons, according to Franchot, are the assumption that religious faith involves intolerance and the emphasis on literary theories derived from thinkers such as Marx, Nietzsche, Freud, and Foucault (Blackbourn, xxxiii; Franchot, 834–37; see also Marsden; Van Anglen; Kramnick and Moore, Green, and Mitchell in *Academe* [Nov.–Dec. 1996]).

The "secularizing tendency" that Blackbourn and Franchot have identified might be exemplified by Elizabeth Langland's important work of literary and cultural criticism, *Nobody's Angels: Middle-Class Women and Domestic Ideology in Victorian Culture* (1995). Langland makes the compelling argument that the traditional figure of the Angel in the House (passive, submissive, not too bright, and confined to a domestic sphere wholly apart from the masculine world of warehouse, bank, and factory) serves to obfuscate the demanding and crucial work of class and gender reproduction that Victorian women actually did (1–61, esp. 1–15). But though the Victorian Angel is commonly seen as the domestic and Protestant descendant of the Madonna, Langland discusses religion only occasionally in her book, most significantly in the context of middle-class family prayers and charitable visits to lower-class households. Such practices could serve to bridge class interests, as Langland notes. But she emphasizes instead the opportunities they offered middle-class women to watch and control their social inferiors, and thus to confirm their own power and status (54–61). Yet it is the case that religious beliefs also led many nineteenth-century bourgeois women to *challenge* social and economic hierarchies, by supporting abolitionism and unionism, speaking about male sexual violence (largely based on the class and racial distinction between "pure" and "sexual" women), and pushing for married women's property and divorce rights. Langland, however, acknowledges both religion and feminism only insofar as they con-

formed to adherents' class and gender interests and allowed oppression of other groups   229
(on nineteenth-century feminism, see 208). What she says is not historically inaccurate, but it is incomplete.

9. These points are developed in subsequent chapters.

10. An example of this approach is found in the section on religion in *The Woman Question* (1983) by Elizabeth Helsinger, Robin Sheets, and William Veeder.

Some recent work on Victorian poets does reveal new uses of the Madonna or qualities associated with her, such as virginity and purity. See Diane D'Amico and Barbara Garlick on Christina Rossetti's embrace of the virgin's life; John Maynard on Coventry Patmore's *The Unknown Eros*, where, Maynard claims, "the crown jewel of sexuality" is, unexpectedly, virginity. As these studies suggest, it is attention to authors only now moving back into the Victorian canon (Rossetti, Patmore, and Barrett Browning) and to poetry rather than narratives that is responsible for critical reconsideration of Madonna-figures. The Americanist John Gatta is an exception to this statement, however, since his *American Madonna* (1997) explores the treatment of the "Divine Woman" by major authors such as Hawthorne, Fuller, and Henry Adams.

11. The pairing of the Son and the Mother is customary in large part because Christology determines Mariology. For example, the orthodox understanding of the Incarnation, that Jesus is always wholly God and wholly human, is reinforced by the later doctrine of Mary *Theotokos*.

12. Jameson declared: "I believe that neither the law of nature, nor the Gospel law, makes any difference in the amount of virtue, self-controul and purity of heart and person required from man and woman equally"; she abhorred the double standards that "introduce[d] a horrid treacherous warfare between the sexes" (Jameson, *Letters*, 234). Fuller identified Milton with "a life of spotless virtue" and "the purity of Puritanism" (*PLA*, 1:36, 38–39). Eliot considered purity a fundamental religious instinct and expressed her sympathy toward "any faith in which human sorrow and human longing for purity have expressed themselves." She later added that the purpose of religious assemblies "[is] the recognition of a binding belief or spiritual law which is to lift us into willing obedience and save us from the slavery of unregulated passion or impulse" (*Eliot Letters*, 3:231; 5:448).

13. Fidelity on the women's side, at least. It is now thought possible that Lewes was not always faithful to Eliot and she discovered the evidence after his death. Jameson supported her friend Ottilie von Goethe when she became pregnant by a lover and gave birth; the baby, named Anna, died (Thomas, 79, 92–94).

14. Fuller, e.g., *WNC*, 319–25 (the passage begins with Fuller's praise of Jameson for courageously speaking out against prostitution); Eliot, e.g., *Daniel Deronda* (the pairing of Gwendolen Harleth and Lydia Glasher); similarly, Jameson, e.g., *Letters*, 234.

15. Mermin makes Godiva—a hero to Jameson, Elizabeth Barrett Browning, and Harriet Martineau—a complex symbol of the woman writer (xvi–xvii). These three Victorian authors, plus Fuller and Eliot, also admired St. Theresa of Avila, who early committed herself to the religious life of celibacy and became the founder of her own order (and in the twentieth century a Doctor of the Church).

230   16. Given this degree of social sanction, one can understand why Jameson tried to move actresses (such as her friends the Kembles) from the category of Magdalene associates into the category of respectable women.

17. Literary and cultural critics such as Deirdre David and Elizabeth Langland have uncovered the restrictive class and gender ideologies that have shaped women's lives and have affected even movements usually associated with resistance and liberation, such as Victorian feminism. While this book assumes that feminism is primarily a liberatory ideology, it does recognize that the nineteenth-century feminist movement was dominated by middle-class women and therefore (like any political movement) defined and pursued justice and equality in ways that benefited certain groups more than others. I have also tried to draw attention to the historicized, even "dated," nature of Victorian feminism and the related issues of terminology and critical judgments. I think the views on gender held by individuals active in or supportive of the nineteenth-century women's movement (for example, the widespread belief in the "essential" differences between women and men) should generally be considered feminist even if they do not pass the litmus tests of modern feminism. These points will be discussed at length in the next chapter.

18. See also the literary critics Sandra Gilbert and Susan Gubar, Nina Auerbach, Margaret Homans, Helena Michie, and Tricia Lootens, and the historian Barbara Pope.

19. See also Maurice Hamington's discussion of the struggle among hierarchical Catholicism, popular Catholicism, and theological Catholicism to control the symbol of Mary. Hamington makes the useful observation that Catholic theologians have always included dissenters and should not be identified with the church hierarchy, but he notes that a "separate theological Catholicism," which today includes Catholic feminist theology, became possible only with the rise of universities (2, 31–52). Jameson, Fuller, and Eliot are in certain respects the predecessors of these feminist theologians, but as Protestants and as women, they necessarily did their work outside nineteenth-century institutional structures; Hamington's categories, none of which fits the three writers well, call attention to the singularity of their achievement.

20. Miles, *Image as Insight*, 149; Rodriguez applies Miles's theory to the Virgin of Guadelupe (48). Ruether, *Sexism and God-Talk*, 18–20.

Chapter 1

1. Similarly, Fuller had earlier read Jameson's *Celebrated Female Sovereigns* (*Fuller Letters*, 1:200), and it may have been her source when she referred to Queen Isabella's financing Columbus's voyage to the New World with her jewels: "The world, at large, is readier to let woman learn and manifest the capacities of her nature than it ever was before . . . . And it ought to be so; we ought to pay for Isabella's jewels" (*WNC*, 305; see also 278).

2. Jameson to Lady Byron, The Lovelace Papers, 255–56, quoted by permission of Laurence Pollinger Limited and the Earl of Lytton; Eliot's assessment was similar:

"Margaret Fuller's mind was like some regions of her own American continent, where you are constantly stepping from the sunny 'clearings' into the mysterious twilight of the tangled forest—she often passes in one breath from forcible reasoning to dreamy vagueness" ("Margaret Fuller and Mary Wollstonecraft," in *SE*, 333).

3. *Commonplace Book*, 275. I have been unable to locate the source, but think it is one of Fuller's reviews.

4. Eliot published *Life of Jesus* in 1846, but it was a translation.

5. According to Mary Sibree, "[S]he said she considered Jesus Christ as the embodiment of perfect love, and seemed to be leaning slightly to the doctrines of Carlyle and Emerson when she remarked that she considered the Bible a revelation in a certain sense, as she considered herself a revelation of the mind of the Deity, etc." (*Eliot Letters*, 6 Mar. 1843, 1:162 n. 1).

6. Marian devotion in the nineteenth century was centered around the Rosary (a prayer cycle involving 150 recitations of the Hail Mary), the Immaculate Conception, and the Sacred Heart of Mary. The religious orders dedicated to her included the Marists and the Oblates of Mary Immaculate. See Zimdars-Swartz, 25–91; Graef, 2:78–106, 136–40; Blackbourn, xxi–41; Norman, *English Catholic Church*, e.g., 142, 184, 228–34, 347–48; Walsh, *Dictionary of Catholic Devotions*, 135–38, 219–23, 279; ODCC, 692–93, 882–83, 1221; *New Catholic Encyclopedia*, 9:368.

7. The most important of the penal laws were the Test Act (1673, 1678) and the Corporation Act (1661), which kept Catholics from holding crown or municipal offices by requiring officeholders to take an Oath of Supremacy to the British monarch adjuring the spiritual as well as the temporal authority of the pope, deny transubstantiation, and receive occasional communion according to the rite of the Church of England. Annual acts of indemnity relieved Protestant Dissenters from penalty under these acts and enabled a few to sit in Parliament.

8. The Emancipation Act did maintain certain "securities" because of fears of Catholic disloyalty (dating back at least to 1570, when Pope Pius V excommunicated Queen Elizabeth and absolved Catholics from loyalty to their Protestant sovereign). Catholic officeholders had to take a new oath requiring them to uphold the monarch's temporal authority over the pope's and not to subvert the Church of England. Certain positions remained closed to them (for example, Lord Chancellor and Lord Lieutenant of Ireland). There were restrictions on public ritual and a new, and unenforceable, ban on the religious orders. And (with O'Connell's consent) Irish forty-shilling freeholders, recently enfranchised, lost the vote to prevent a large Irish bloc in the united Parliament. Restrictions on Catholic bequests for "superstitious uses" remained. On the penal laws and Catholic emancipation, see O. Chadwick, 1:1–24; Ranelagh, 87–101; Norman, *English Catholic Church*, 29–68; Webb, 186–90, 301; ODCC, s.v. "Corporation Act (1661)," "Recusancy," "The Test Act," 349, 1164–65, 1353.

9. E.g., Norman, *English Catholic Church*, 75–81; Bossy, 332–63; O. Chadwick, 1:277–84; cf. Heimann, 1–37, esp. 4. Scholars have seen the Ultramontanists and the

232　Old Catholics and converts who comprised the "English Catholic" party as differing not only in their attitudes toward centralized ecclesiastical authority but also in their preferences in architecture and art—generally, Italianate vs. Gothic in ecclesiastical architecture, and Baroque vs. early Italian in paintings. See Haskell, 65–70; Clark, 92–107; O. Chadwick, 1:275–83; Norman, *English Catholic Church*, 234–36, 368–70.

10. Bossy, 364–83; Heimann, 70–99. Challoner's text (so popular among "English Catholics" that they became known as "Garden of the Soul" Catholics) was designed to promote the daylong awareness of God. It contains in all its nineteenth-century editions the Hail Mary, the *Ave Maris Stella*, the Litany of Loreto, and invocations of Mary and the saints (Bossy, 364–70; Heimann, 70–79). Heimann notes that Mary was also central to the most popular church-based devotions in mid-century England, the Benediction of the Blessed Sacrament and the Public Rosary (38–69). Heimann goes beyond Bossy in making the revisionist argument that the restoration of the Catholic hierarchy did not alter an idiosyncratic English devotional tradition, which included some of the practices recommended by Wiseman but was resistant to foreign innovations (such as the Forty Hours' Devotion, the Feast of the Miraculous Medal, and even Lourdes; Heimann, 42, 138–44, 167).

11. Wolffe, 16–29, 146–47; Norman, *English Catholic Church*, 15–21, 43, 186–87, 201–6; O. Chadwick, 1:7–24, 290–309.

12. E. P. Thompson, 429–40; O. Chadwick, 1:9, 20–24; Arnstein, 1–11, 62–175, 210–11; Document 17 in Norman, *Anti-Catholicism*, 212–21; Norman, *English Catholic Church*, 17, 310–11; Wolffe, 29–64; Paz, 267–96; Machin, 91–99.

13. Review of *The Poetry of Sacred and Legendary Art*, *Blackwood's* (American edition) (Feb. 1849): 175, 186, 189; review of *Legends of the Monastic Orders*, *Blackwood's* (Mar. 1851): 309; review of *Legends of the Madonna*, *Blackwood's* (July 1853): 23–38. Jameson's reviewer is identified as John Eagles in the Wellesley index. In the *Dictionary of National Biography* (1888), Eagles (1783–1855) is listed as an artist, an Anglican cleric, and a contributor to *Blackwood's* for twenty years (16:312–13). His position on medieval art might be traced back to that of Richard Hooker (1554–1600), who saw the reformed church as having continuity with the medieval one (*ODCC*, 665); my thanks to Kevin Van Anglen for making this connection. Eagles's reviews are the only ones of Jameson's works I have found where anti-Catholicism is an issue.

14. O. Chadwick, 1:9–10; Colley, 328; see also Kitson Clark, 52–55.

15. Colley, 325; Norman, *English Catholic Church*, 22; Inglis, 141–42.

16. Mr. Howitt's book appeared in 1833. In 1834 he was part of a delegation to Earl Grey requesting the separation of church and state. When Grey refused, Mr. Howitt said at least the state religion should be the faith of the majority of inhabitants, and in Ireland that meant Catholicism rather than the state-supported Anglicanism (*Mary Howitt*, 1:231–39). Late in life Mr. Howitt wrote a letter to his elder daughter still critical of the papacy as an institution (though he came to admire Leo XIII), but he was warm in his praise of ordinary Catholics, particularly women, whose holy lives and constant acts of charity were unfortunately without parallel among Protestants (2:195–96, 269).

17. Jameson, *WSSR*, 1:36; Eliot, *Adam Bede*, 409–10.

18. Anna Jameson provided Mary Howitt with letters of introduction to the
Goethe family in Germany. They both attended the World Anti-Slavery Convention
in London in 1840 and presented the petitions for married women's property rights in
the mid-1850s petition campaign (Howitt, 1:291–4, 320; 2:116–17; *Victorian Britain*, s.v.
"Married Women's Property," 478–79). George Eliot knew the Howitt family through
mutual friends, Barbara Leigh Smith Bodichon and Bessie Parkes, and read and reviewed Mary Howitt's translations of Frederika Bremer (*Eliot Letters*, 1:240, 372; 2:267;
3:343).

19. Eliot, "Ruskin's Lectures" [1854], in Wiesenfarth, ed., *Writer's Notebook*, 238;
Clark, 194–96.

20. On Jameson's trip to Ireland and letter to Robert Peel, see Macpherson,
251–60; Thomas, 183–85; Erskine, 250–53. On her support for Daniel O'Connell, see
Macpherson, 196–97. Jameson sided with O'Connell and against "Puseyism" in supporting the disestablishment of the Anglican Church in Ireland; the Catholic majority
was required to pay tithes in support of this church (see Macpherson, 226).

21. O. Chadwick, 1:9, 20–24; Arnstein, 10–11, 62–175, 210–11; Haight, 1–4,
29–31.

22. "Into whatever Fold your faith leads you, my heart will follow you. We may
not find it possible for us both to get strength for a pure and loving life by the same
means, but we have this always in common, that we believe such strength to be the
supreme good" (*Eliot Letters*, 4:131).

23. See Bernard Paris, Gordon Haight, Gillian Beer, Suzanne Graver, Nancy
Paxton, James Scott, and William Myers.

24. Harrison, 2:258–59, 268; Lootens, 51. Newton Hall was established after an
1878 split in the Positivist Society; the Chapel Street faction was led by Eliot's friend
Richard Congreve, and the Newton Hall group, which sided with Comte's French executor Pierre Lafitte, included Frederic Harrison. Eliot gave to both groups (*Eliot Letters*,
7:260 n.).

25. See, e.g., Tricia Lootens's discussion of Harrison's *New Calendar of Great Men*
(Lootens, 46–47, 50–52). Eliot's notes on Comte's calendar are in *George Eliot's* Daniel
Deronda *Notebooks*, 186–94.

26. He refuted Thomas Huxley's charge, "Why, I always thought you swung a
censer on Sundays before the altar at Chapel Street" (Harrison, 2:269–81).

27. There were also centenary celebrations of great (male) religious and political
leaders and concert performances of acceptable hymns and poems, by notable male authors plus George Eliot (Harrison, 2:276–78). The almost exclusively male objects of
devotion clearly undercut Harrison's claim that Positivism is "saturated" with ideal images of womanhood (quoted in Lootens, 50).

28. O. Chadwick, 1:66–68. Chadwick notes that *The Christian Year* sold 108,000
copies by January 1854 and 265,000 by April 1868 (1:68).

29. Newman, "The Reverence Due to the Virgin Mary" (1832), 306; "The Theory
of Developments in Religious Doctrine" (1843), 311.

30. The Tractarians also produced a *Library of the Fathers* and lives of the saints, although the series on English saints attempted in 1843–44 was criticized as too Catholic

234 and was given up. *Apologia*, 165–66, 242–54; *ODCC*, s.v. "Keble, John," 774–75; "Saints," 1228.

31. According to the art historian Kenneth Clark, "Chancels and altars, clergymen in surplices, anthems, festivals, frequent standings and kneelings—these form part of everybody's mental picture of an Anglican church. But to understand the development of the Gothic Revival we must imagine a time when all these forms were unthinkable. To a good protestant of 1830 the least suggestion of symbolism—a cross on a gable or on a prayerbook—was rank popery. All forms of ritual were equally suspect. . . . Had Anglican requirements remained unaltered, Gothic would have been abandoned as a style for churches. . . . But the Tractarians wished to revive old ritual, and to do so they required churches in which it would be accurately performed—churches with altars and deep chancels; moreover, they wished to move the imagination through symbols, and for this they required the sculpture and architecture of the church to be rich in symbolical device. In short, they wanted a true Gothic church" (153–55).

32. Clark, 95–107, 155–74; O. Chadwick, 1:212–21.

33. Clark quotes an Anglican sermon preached on Guy Fawkes Day, 1845: "as Romanism is taught *Analytically* at Oxford, it is taught *Artistically* at Cambridge,— . . . it is inculcated theoretically at one University, and it is *sculptured, painted and graven* at the other" (166–67).

34. Ahlstrom, 330–42; Hennesey, 36–48, 52–54; Maynard, *American Catholicism,* 62–73, 90–100. In Pennsylvania, Catholics throughout the colonial period could openly hold religious services, but in 1705 they lost the right to vote and hold public office (Ahlstrom, 330–42; Hennesey, 49–52). According to some historians, most American Catholics sided against the mother country of the Penal Laws during the American Revolution (Ahlstrom, 528–29; Maynard, 91–105; but cf. Hennesey, 55–63). Anti-Catholicism in the colonies (which can be found in statements by many of the Founding Fathers) reflected the political power struggles in Britain and the sectarian fears expressed and heightened by these; it was also a response to Britain's rivalries with Catholic powers in the New World—Spain, France, and France's Indian allies. In addition, many colonists were suspicious of the Jesuits, who dominated the American missions (Ahlstrom, 330–42; Hennesey, 45, 53, 91–92; Maynard, *American Catholicism,* 91–105).

35. Taves, 71, 139, 178; Kenneally, 1–2. The works of devotion included Challoner's *The Garden of the Soul, A Manual of Catholic Prayers,* and Frederick Faber's works. Challoner, as vicar apostolic of London, had his jurisdiction extend to the American colonies.

36. Taves, 21–30, 36–39. The scapular, a sign of membership in a religious confraternity, consisted of two woolen badges linked by strings and worn over the shoulders.

37. See *Summer on the Lakes,* 168, 181; *WNC,* 277–78, 340–41, 347.

38. Fuller's letters and journals, for example, never mention the burning of the Ursuline convent in nearby Charlestown, which occurred when she was twenty-four. Nor, it seems, did her family consider sending her to this prestigious school, although

other Boston Unitarian daughters were students there (Maynard, *American Catholicism*, 291–93).

39. Fuller's friend Charles Newcomb was inclined toward Catholicism, and the converts in her circle included Anna Barker Ward, Sophia Ripley (who with her husband George started Brook Farm, where Fuller sometimes stayed), and the Transcendentalists Isaac Hecker and Orestes Brownson. Hecker had lived at the utopian communities of Brook Farm and Fruitlands; he converted in 1844, became a missionary priest, and founded the Paulist order to work among American Protestants. The eccentric Brownson ended his religious pilgrimage from Presbyterianism to Universalism to atheism to Unitarianism in the Catholic Church in 1844. Brownson was an important and often cantankerous Catholic writer who supported antislavery Unionism, female education, and female subordination, praised the Virgin Mary, and criticized papal rule and the Irish in the two reviews he edited at intervals from the 1830s to the 1870s. See Hennesey, 103; Ahlstrom, 549–54, 608; Taves, 48–49, 115; Kenneally, 18–19.

40. One of Fuller's earliest references to the Irish was an 1844 journal entry, in which she notes a conversation on the arrival of Irish Catholics in Concord to work on the railroad (Berg and Perry, 100–101). See also Fuller's later sympathetic essay "The Irish Character," *New-York Tribune*, 28 June 1845, excerpted in Chevigny, 344–46.

41. "Christmas," 21 Dec. 1844, in *Essays*, 260; cf. *WNC*, 282–89.

42. Fuller speaks of the Tractarians in a letter to her friend Charles Newcomb: "the Oxford coteri . . . share your desire for an universal [probably "Catholic"] church and do not feel the force of Wordsworth's reply 'When I am a good man, then I am a Christian'" (*Fuller Letters*, 2:65, 18 Apr. 1839).

43. *Sexism and God-Talk*, 116–38, 152–58. See also Ruether's *Mary, the Feminine Face of the Church* (1977).

44. E. Johnson, "Mary and the Female Face of God," 500–26; "Marian Tradition," 120, 125; see also Hamington, 44–52, 157–79. Other representatives of this position include Marina Warner, Uta Ranke-Heinemann (340–48), and Barbara C. Pope (175, 193–96).

45. Haskell, 24; Eichner, 98–101. Honour and Lightbown point out that art critics and historians of the eighteenth and nineteenth centuries grouped together the European art preceding the High Renaissance and Baroque periods, considering it all "medieval" (Honour, 172; Lightbown, 6). I will use the term "early Renaissance" in this discussion in accordance with modern usage.

46. Haskell, 42, 106–14; Honour, 26–32, 165–72; Lightbown, 6–27.

47. The original title of Jameson's first volume in her multivolume work on religious art—*The Poetry of Sacred and Legendary Art* (1848)—is evidence of Rio's influence (Thomas, 177–82; Holcomb, "Sacred Art," 105–6; Johnston, 154–79; Johnston is particularly enlightening on the ways Victorian writers approached Italian art in terms of poetry). Rio, however, was more dogmatic than Jameson in his moral judgments of art, and the two writers differed in many of their evaluations, e.g., of Raphael's important

236   late work, the *Transfiguration* (1517–20; see Lightbown, 15–16; *History of Our Lord*, 1:341–46).

   48. Macpherson, 176; Thomas, 177–82; Holcomb, "Sacred Art," 105–6; Jameson, *Letters*, 132.

   49. See Friedrich Schlegel, "Description of Paintings in Paris and the Netherlands in the Years 1802–1804" and "Principles of Gothic Architecture," in *Aesthetic and Miscellaneous Works*, 1–199; A. W. Schlegel, *Lectures on Dramatic Art and Literature*, First Part, First Lecture, 175–86; G. H. Lewes, review of A. W. Schlegel, 160–71; Eichner, 17–102; Reed, e.g., 74–77; Jameson, e.g., *Commonplace Book*, 146–47, 278–79, 288–95; Fuller, "Modern British Poets," in *PLA*, 1:80–82; "Menzel's View of Goethe," 341–42; Eliot, e.g., "The *Antigone* and Its Moral" (1856), in *SE*, 363–66; review of Stahr, *Torso*, I, in Wiesenfarth, ed., *Writer's Notebook*, 245–46.

   50. Jameson's works on medieval and Renaissance art include *Memoirs of Early Italian Painters* (1845), originally appearing in article form, and the series *Sacred and Legendary Art* (1848–64). She wrote guidebooks to London-area public and private galleries (1840, 1844), the Queen's Garden Pavilion at Buckingham Palace (1846), and the Court of Modern Sculpture at the Crystal Palace (1854); see Thomas, 225–27. She reviewed at least one Royal Academy show, in 1838, and wrote an important biographical essay on the neoclassical sculptor John Gibson, Harriet Hosmer's teacher. Her *Sketches of Art* (1834) includes long descriptions of the early and modern painting and sculpture she saw in Germany. Jameson's popularity as a writer on art is evinced by the ready availability of American editions of her works in U.S. libraries and antiquarian bookstores.

   51. Wiesenfarth, ed., *Writer's Notebook*, 42, 245, 238–85. The Byatt edition of Eliot's essays has only the review of Ruskin's *Modern Painters*, vol. 3, and the Pinney edition has none of her writings on art.

   52. In 1862–68, for example, Eliot viewed the London International Exhibition of 1862, the historical portraits at Kensington ("It is a wonderful collection—such Gainsboroughs and Sir Joshuas!"), and the contemporary art at Leeds ("Among the figure painters Watts and old [John] Philip are supreme"); *Eliot Letters*, 4:46, 57, 362–63, 476. On Eliot and the Pre-Raphaelites, see Witemeyer, 10–11, 16, 76–78. From 1815 regular public exhibitions allowed Britons without the money to collect art or travel abroad to see European paintings. The National Gallery opened in 1824 and moved into the building in Trafalgar Square in the 1830s.

   53. "An old woman . . . eating her solitary dinner, while the noonday light, softened perhaps by a screen of leaves, falls on her mob-cap, and just touches the rim of the spinning-wheel, and her stone jug" (*AB*; critical study cited by Witemeyer, 108; see also 73–125).

   54. Fuller notes in one painting, *The Italian Shepherd Boy*, "the clouds doubly soft, the sky deeper blue, as seen shimmering through the leaves, the fyttes of golden light seen through the long glades, . . . the flutter and wild notes of the birds." She says whoever

becomes "lapt in the Elysian harmony" of the scene, as the shepherd boy does, "under- 237 stands why the observant Greek placed his departed great ones in groves" (*PLA*, 2:116–17).

55. Fuller also considered the rigid and pallid body in Allston's *The Dead Man Restored to Life on Touching the Bones of the Prophet Elisha* an inappropriate subject for art, while Jameson said, "The best part of the picture is the dead man extended in front, in whose form and expression the sickly dawn of returning life is very admirable and *fearful*." Fuller, "Washington Allston," in *PLA*, 2:111–12, 118–19; Jameson, "Washington Allston," in *Memoirs and Essays*, 162–63, 185.

56. "The Athenaeum Exhibition of Painting and Sculpture," 260–63.

57. Dall, 6–7; Blanchard, 133–34; Walker and Holcomb, 124–30. Artistic works in Fuller's time could be reproduced as woodcuts or engravings. Jameson illustrated her books with both and encouraged readers to purchase their own portfolios of engravings as illustrations of the various religious subjects she describes (*SLA*, 1:ix). But a portfolio like Samuel Ward's was expensive; Fuller found a favorite engraving of the Madonna too costly to purchase as a gift when she was in Italy.

58. Fuller, *Summer on the Lakes*, 136–37. Harold E. Wethey, in his definitive catalogue of the works of Titian, says that the original *Venus and Adonis* (1553–54), commissioned by Philip II of Spain, is in the Prado; the best replica, by Titian and his workshop, is in the National Galley of London. There are versions of the painting in the United States, in the Metropolitan Museum and the National Gallery, but Fuller could not have seen them; both were acquired by American collectors and then by the museums in the twentieth century (Wethey, 3:58–60).

Fuller does not name her source. It is not Jameson, but the art historian does include a lengthy description of the *Venus and Adonis* and the various replicas and copies in *Handbook to the Public Galleries of Art in and Near London*, a compilation of her own and others' work (63–65). The description in the *Handbook* mentions the crimson garments worn by the two figures (63–64). My thanks to Emily Sohmer Tai for providing me with a copy of this passage. See also Jameson's "Titian," which refers to the painting in the National Gallery of London, in *Memoirs of Early Italian Painters*, 247.

59. Sarah Grimké was an abolitionist speaker for a short time in the 1830s; she and her sister Angelina were the first to link the issues of slaves' rights and women's rights (G. Lerner, *Grimké Sisters*, 165–204; Ceplair, 135–41). Elizabeth Cady Stanton, also an abolitionist, helped organize the world's first women's-rights convention at Seneca Falls in 1848.

60. The antebellum Carolina Art Association in Charleston (founded 1858) and the Academy of the Fine Arts in Philadelphia (1805) seem to have been collections of American art—portraits, American history paintings, and genre scenes. The Boston Museum of Fine Arts was founded in 1870; the Athenaeum holdings were the nucleus of the collection. The Metropolitan Museum of Art in New York was founded in 1872, the Philadelphia Museum of Art in 1876 (at the time of the popular Centennial art

238 exhibition), and the National Gallery in Washington not until 1937. See *The New Encyclopaedia Britannica*, 15th ed. (Chicago, 1995), 2:404; 3:126–27; 4:780; 8:74–75, 533; Sherman, 300–301, 311–12.

61. See Jameson, *Madonna*, xli, 69–70, 134, 303–4; Pelikan, 4:38–50.

62. S. Grimké, 154, 163. On Grimké's use of Jameson, see G. Lerner, "Sarah M. Grimké's 'Sisters of Charity'" and "Comment on Lerner's 'Sarah M. Grimké's "Sisters of Charity."'"

63. *Woman's Bible*, 2:113–14; similarly, Stanton, *Eighty Years*, 230.

64. Jameson (who knew Mrs. Howitt) and Lucretia Mott were also at the anti-slavery convention (Stanton, *Eighty Years*, 80; Bacon, 91–96).

65. One of Sojourner Truth's statements in her famous "Ain't I a Woman?" speech is: "Where did your Christ come from? From God and a woman! Man had nothing to do with him" (Rossi, 428). But I have not yet found evidence that black American women writers in the nineteenth century paid much attention to the Madonna or used this figure as Jameson, Fuller, and Eliot did. Most of the texts by black women from this period are slave narratives or accounts of hard lives after the Civil War (e.g., Frances Harper's *Iola Leroy*). The writers were usually Protestant and tended to differentiate love of God from institutional religions, which upheld slavery or racial discrimination (see, e.g., Harriet Jacobs's *Incidents in the Life of a Slave Girl*, ch. 13). Because many or most black women, especially as slaves, had to struggle to become literate and did not lead privi-leged lives, they were unlikely to have had extensive exposure to European culture, and it is this kind of knowledge that distinguishes the three intellectuals of this study from most of their white middle-class countrywomen. This is not to say, however, that black women did not develop a biblical hermeneutics (see, e.g., Baker-Fletcher).

66. G. Lerner defines "feminist consciousness" as women's awareness, under patri-archal hegemony, "that they belong to a subordinate group; that they have suffered wrongs as a group; that their condition of subordination is not natural, but is societally determined; that they must join with other women to remedy these wrongs; and finally, that they must and can provide an alternate vision of societal organization in which women as well as men will enjoy autonomy and self-determination" (*Creation of Feminist Consciousness*, 14). Lerner's definition is designed to cover more ground than Offen's does: women's history from the Middle Ages to the late nineteenth century.

67. Caine, 53; Offen, 136–37. Even Mary Wollstonecraft and John Stuart Mill, who seem clear examples of "individualist" or "liberal" feminists, make mixed arguments on occasion. They question essentialist definitions of woman's nature but then let her life be determined by her capacity for motherhood, which is based on the essentialist assumption that since women bear children, they must be physically and psychologi-cally better fitted than men to raise children and also to superintend the household. Wollstonecraft wants women's education and opportunities for self-development to im-prove for women's own sake but also so that they will become more competent moth-ers, well-respected if not well-loved wives (for Wollstonecraft, romance is always a fleeting thing), and if necessary self-reliant widows (83, 138–40). Mill, although argu-

ing that women should have all the same opportunities in a society as men, thinks that when women marry (as most will), they should spend their time managing the household and raising the children; they should not be expected in addition to work outside the home. He does not consider having men share the burden of housework and child care so that women may fully participate in the work and governance of a society (*Subjection*, 164–65).

68. Cott, *Signs* (1988 forum), 203; see also Cott, *The Grounding of Modern Feminism*, 3–20, 35–50. DuBois in a later work questions this limitation of the term; see her introduction to *The Elizabeth Cady Stanton–Susan B. Anthony Reader* (xiv–xvi).

69. DuBois uses Offen's terms but makes clear her misgivings about "relational feminism," referring to the Nazis' use of such arguments and strongly contesting Offen's claim that Elizabeth Cady Stanton (whose works DuBois has edited) is in any way a relational feminist (*Signs*, 195–97). DuBois returns to this debate and the problems of defining feminism in her introduction to *Reader* (xiv–xvi).

70. See Gerda Lerner, *The Creation of Feminist Consciousness: From the Middle Ages to 1870* (1993); Dale Spender, ed., *Feminist Theorists: Three Centuries of Key Women Thinkers* (NY: Pantheon Books, 1983); Moira Ferguson, ed., *The First Feminists: British Women Writers 1578–1799* (Bloomington: Indiana University Press; Old Westbury, N.Y.: Feminist Press, 1985); Ruth Perry, *The Celebrated Mary Astell: An Early English Feminist* (Chicago: University of Chicago Press, 1986); Alice Rossi, ed., *The Feminist Papers: From Adams to de Beauvoir* (1988); Gary Kelly, *Revolutionary Feminism: The Mind and Career of Mary Wollstonecraft* (1992); Barbara Caine, *Victorian Feminists* (1992); Nancy Paxton, *George Eliot and Herbert Spencer: Feminism, Evolutionism, and the Reconstruction of Gender* (1991).

71. According to Donovan, the characteristics of Enlightenment-Liberal feminism are faith in the power of reason and education, the assumption of the ontological similarity of men and women, and a view of the individual as a rational and autonomous being (8). Cultural feminism, in her definition, emphasizes the irrational and intuitive as well as the rational powers of the human being, the differences of men and women, woman's maternal role, and the importance of the community. This feminism also sees the need for radical changes in cultural and society, including alternatives to the institutions of religion, marriage, and home (31–32). Donovan's definition of cultural feminism, particularly the emphasis on essentialism, is useful, but she tries to put too many figures in a single category; Fuller, Stanton, and Gilman have some similarities but many significant differences (31–63). I agree with DuBois that Stanton, though she does write on motherhood and matriarchy, should be classified primarily as an individualist or Enlightenment-Liberal feminist.

72. P. Levine, 13. See also Bolt, 1; Clinton, 41–72 (Clinton shows the positive uses of domestic ideology but does not here endorse "domestic feminism"); Welter, 173–74.

73. G. Lerner, *Creation of Feminist Consciousness*, 116–37. Rosemary Radford Ruether employs the term "feminism" to describe a number of movements with anti-patriarchal and egalitarian elements, such as "eschatological feminism," which dates back as far as the late first century A.D./C.E. She acknowledges several strands of nineteenth-century

240   essentialist "romantic feminism," though her own feminist theology challenges rather than appropriates such notions of "masculine" and "feminine" (*Sexism and God-Talk*, 99–115).

74. "Woman in France," in *SE*, 8–9; *Eliot Letters*, 4:468. Deirdre David, in contrast, sees "difference" rather than "sameness *and* difference" in these statements; she argues that Eliot valued education for bringing out women's essential nature, their differences from men (179–87).

75. Jameson, *WSSR* (1839); Mermin, 55–56; Killham, 109–41; Johnston, esp. 8–9, 208–35; see also Holcomb, "Sacred Art," 101–7, 113–15; Thomas, 142–43, 157–58, 208–10.

76. On Fuller's feminism, see also Steele, Blanchard, Urbanski ("The Feminist Manifesto"), and Conrad (73–82).

77. See Beer, *George Eliot*, esp. 147–99; Paxton, 3–42; and Blake.

78. Of the recent studies mentioned here, only Booth's *Greatness Engendered* has an extensive discussion of organizational feminists.

79. Marx and Engels, from the Marxist materialist standpoint, and John Stuart Mill, a bourgeois liberal, all oppose essentialist arguments. Marx and Engels criticize the German philosopher Ludwig Feuerbach for assuming there is a universal "essence of humanity"; they argue instead that human beings must instead be seen in particularized and historicized contexts ("Theses on Feuerbach," 72; *German Ideology*, 78). This critique is applied to idealized rather than historicized understandings of female nature in Marx and Engels's review of G. F. Daumer's *The Religion of the New Age* (1850; 94–96). Mill in *The Subjection of Women* demonstrates that "custom" and social conditioning rather than "nature" explain the present relations of the sexes and their differences (129–30). He argues: "What is now called the nature of women is an eminently artificial thing— the result of forced repression in some directions, unnatural stimulation in others. It may be asserted without scruple, that no other class of dependents have had their character so entirely distorted from its natural proportions by their relation with their masters" (138).

80. See Leeming and Page; Spretnak.

Chapter 2

1. Clara Thomas's 1967 biography, which before the appearance of Johnston's was the starting point for Jameson scholarship, treats the life more extensively than the writings and predates most recent scholarship on Victorian women writers, which provides a context for Jameson's work. On Jameson as an intellectual and feminist, see also Mermin, e.g., xiii–xix, 8–9, 96–98; Michie, passim; Killham, 110–41.

2. Nina Auerbach (82, 210–17, 224), Christy Desmet, Tricia Lootens (95–115), and Ann Thompson examine Jameson's Shakespeare criticism; see also the articles by Jessica Slights and Anne Russell. Jameson is sometimes classified as a Canadian writer on the basis of her travel journal; see the discussions of *WSSR* by Wayne Fraser (8–19), Helen Buss, Thomas Gerry, Bina Friewald, Leslie Monkman, and Lorraine York.

3. See Johnston, 154–207; Holcomb, "Anna Jameson on Women Artists"; "Sacred Art"; "The First Professional English Art Historian." See also H. Fraser, *The Victorians and Renaissance Italy*, 81–84, 99; Gilley; Ernstrom on Jameson's and Eliot's use of the St. Christopher legend; Kane Lew; and York. Eliot critics such as Beer (*George Eliot*) have discussed the novelist's knowledge of Jameson, but there are no extended comparisons of the two writers; instead, the art histories tend to be treated as sourcebooks for the fiction. Martha Vicinus and Gerda Lerner acknowledge Jameson's interest in female religious communities (Vicinus, 7, 15, 24–25, 46–48, 73; G. Lerner, articles on Sarah Grimké's knowledge of Jameson's *Sisters of Charity*).

4. *Sacred and Legendary Art* is the title of both the series and the first volume (which first appeared in 1848 under a longer title, *The Poetry of Sacred and Legendary Art*). The other titles are *Legends of the Monastic Orders* (1850), *Legends of the Madonna* (1852), and *History of Our Lord* (1864), completed by Elizabeth Lady Eastlake. The series was popular and went through many editions (see Thomas, 176–79).

5. Jameson mentioned issues of the *Dial* and the posthumous *Memoir* and seems to have been familiar with Fuller's reprinted essays (see *Commonplace Book*, 275). She expressed her intention to read the just-published *Woman in the Nineteenth Century* (1845; Macpherson, 214).

6. *Our Lady of Victorian Feminism* is the first extensive study of Jameson's *Legends of the Madonna* and its feminist implications. Johnston in her chapter on the art histories focuses on the first volume, *Sacred and Legendary Art*, and Jameson's revisionary treatment of the Magdalene (180–203); she reads the Madonna in Warner's dismissive terms, as a passive and domestic figure (204–6). Similarly, Holcomb, "Sacred Art"; H. Fraser, *Victorians and Renaissance Italy*, 83.

7. *Women's Theology in Nineteenth-Century Britain* (1998), ed. Julie Melnyk, and *In Our Own Voices: Four Centuries of American Women's Religious Writing* (1995), ed. Rosemary Radford Ruether and Rosemary Skinner Keller, help redress the balance. On Jameson's agenda as aesthetic rather than religious, see Johnston, 160 (Johnston does, however, discuss the political and social implications of the art histories, 184–88); Holcomb, "Professional English Art Historian," 180; H. Fraser, *Victorians and Renaissance Italy*, 81.

8. *Madonna*, xxxi–xxxviii. On Correggio, 92, 263, 324–25; on Poussin, Vandyck, and Rembrandt, 221; on Rubens, 29, 253, 326. On Jameson's preferences as representative of Romantic taste, see Witemeyer, 21–23.

9. *Madonna*, 115, 200, 275, 292–94, 240–41, 263–70. Jameson is not critical of "portrait Madonnas" in the historical scenes, apparently because Mary is not here a divinized figure. The author praises two of Rubens's paintings of the Madonna and the Holy Family in which he reproduces his own family's features (151, 253).

10. Jameson's inclusiveness in *Legends of the Madonna* significantly contrasts with her practice in the earlier *Legends of the Monastic Orders* (1850), where she proclaims in her preface that she is no Roman Catholic and describes ascetic monachism as "the apotheosis of deformity and suffering" (xiv, xviii).

11. For example, by first treating the Virgin without the Son, Jameson discusses

242   both the earliest and late (seventeenth-century) images of Mary and analyzes the solitary Queen of Heaven (the Assumption, seventh and eighth centuries) before rather than after the *Theotokos* (fifth century).

12. It was published in 1864. Eastlake carefully distinguishes her contributions from Jameson's, which are marked with the initials A. J. (*History of Our Lord*, 1:vii).

Lady Eastlake was the wife of Charles Eastlake, director of the National Gallery of London and president of the Royal Academy. Before her marriage, as Elizabeth Rigby, she famously attacked *Jane Eyre* ("an anti-Christian composition") in the influential *Quarterly Review* (Dec. 1848; see *Victorian Britain*, s.v. "Eastlake, Elizabeth Rigby," 234–35).

13. Jameson planned to begin (as she did in *Legends of the Madonna*) with ideal and devotional subjects—here, the Good Shepherd, the Lamb, and the Second Person of the Trinity—and then treat the biblical history of Jesus' life. The final section was to have been types from the Old Testament. Eastlake, in contrast, begins with the Fall of Lucifer and the Angels, the Creation, and the Fall of Adam and Eve, discusses Old Testament types (for example, Abraham, Samson, and Jonah) and prophets, and then treats the scenes of Jesus' life, from his birth and ministry to the Last Judgment (*History of Our Lord*, 1:v–xi). Her chronological organization incorporates the material Jameson had completed.

14. For example, Eastlake rejected as "spurious" and "puerile" the legendary accounts of Jesus' childhood that Jameson planned to discuss in the book, because they were represented in art (1:276).

15. Eastlake noted, for example, that Southern artists after Raphael (that is, artists of the Counter-Reformation) failed to have this aim. She also argued that the art of some German painters of the fifteenth and sixteenth centuries was debased because it predates the Reformation, which "unlock[ed] the Bible itself" (1:3, 9; 2:3–4).

16. Jameson, *Letters*, 233–34. A similar statement of beliefs appears in 1847 in Jameson's edition of the dramas of Princess Amalie of Saxony, *Social Life in Germany* (see 233 n. 1).

17. Wollstonecraft, 118; Sarah and Angelina Grimké, in Rossi, 296–322; Bodichon, *Women and Work*, in Lacey, 37–38.

18. The recurrent references to Jameson in Ruskin's *Complete Works* make clear that he knew well and relied on her art-historical research (e.g., 18:316; 24:333; 33:41, 44), though he more often than not cites it disparagingly (e.g., 3:150; 4:331). In his autobiography *Praeterita*, he describes viewing the pictures in Venice in 1845 in the company of his friend William Boxall, R. A., and Mrs. Jameson: "Mrs. Jameson was absolutely without knowledge or instinct of painting (and had no sharpness of insight even for anything else); but she was candid and industrious, with a pleasant disposition to make the best of all she saw, and to say, compliantly, that a picture was good, if anybody had ever said so before. Her peace of mind was restored in a little while, by observing that the three of us, however separate in our reasons for liking a picture, always fastened on the same pictures to like; and that she was safe, therefore, in saying that, for whatever other reason might be assigned, other people should like them also" (35:373–74).

19. Ruskin gives to the duties he prescribes a spiritual dimension: the power of man and woman "is supreme over the mind as over the person—that they not only feed and clothe, but direct and teach" ("Of Queens' Gardens," 18:139).

20. See, e.g., Kate Millet, "The Debate over Women: Ruskin vs. Mill" (1968); David, 14–16.

21. The British campaign for married women's property rights is discussed in chapter 1. In the United States, the campaigns took place on the state level. Ernestine Rose, Elizabeth Cady Stanton, and Susan B. Anthony were active in the New York campaign; acts protecting married women's property were passed in 1848 and 1860 (Schneir, 72–74, 117–27, 132–33).

22. Ruskin's "Of Queens' Gardens" has been discussed by a number of feminist scholars, some of whom have condemned his ideas about women (see Millet, 121–39; David, 14–18), while others have praised the rich possibilities of his language and have claimed that the queenly role he gives women is empowering (Auerbach, 58–62; Langland, 62–79; Weltman, 103–9). It is curious that Ruskin's essentialism is sometimes treated as less suspect than that of Victorian women like Jameson who were known to support women's-rights causes. In Ruskin's case, the need to differentiate a writer's language—which indeed may have a life of its own—from his or her activities seems particularly evident. Though he called the female sex "queens," he waspishly criticized a number of women who dared to be active in his fields of art and art criticism: Jameson, Anna Mary Howitt, Anna Blunden, Ellen Heaton (see Cherry, 187–89; Surtees). In contrast, Jameson and the Langham Place circle pressed specifically for women's entry into the male-controlled arts professions and also encouraged women artists to use their talents to promote the feminist cause.

23. *Sisters of Charity*, 49–69; *WSSR*, 301–4.

24. Jameson, *Madonna*, xxx–xxxiv, 183–84; Witemeyer, 21–23.

25. Kelly, 19–50; King, 94–101, 130–31; Wiesner, 218–33. My thanks to the Renaissance scholar Maryclaire Moroney for helping me make this point.

26. Jameson's *Commonplace Book* is a collection of discrete statements, usually by others but followed by Jameson's commentaries, that "became part of [her] individual mind" (preface, 3–5).

27. The cited passage reads in full: "[It is a mistake to believe] that there are essential masculine and feminine virtues and vices. It is not, in fact, the quality itself, but the modification of the quality, which is masculine and feminine; and on the manner or degree in which these are balanced and combined in the individual, depends the perfection of that individual character—its approximation to that of Christ. I firmly believe that as the influences of religion are extended, and as civilization advances, those qualities which are now admired as essentially *feminine* will be considered as essentially *human*, such as gentleness, purity, the more unselfish and spiritual sense of duty, and the dominance of the affections over the passions" (*Commonplace Book*, 77–78).

28. In her earlier work *Celebrated Female Sovereigns* (1831), Jameson similarly assumes that the feminine character and Christian beliefs are or ought to be allied forces for peace in the world; see her discussions of Queen Elizabeth (1:222–23); Christina of

Sweden (2:26–27), and Isabella of Castile (1:111, 120). There are interesting parallels to Jameson in Sarah Grimké's discussions of female leadership (which postdate *Celebrated Female Sovereigns*); see Grimké's *Letters on the Equality of the Sexes*, 62–67, 85–95.

Chapter 3

1. After the poor performance of *Social Life in Germany*, a translation of Princess Amalie's plays, Jameson planned what she hoped was a marketable series on art history. She was also motivated by the success of her guides to English art galleries and her articles on individual painters in the *Penny Magazine*, and her desire to travel (Macpherson, 163–78). *Legends of the Madonna* was said to "cost its writer far more thought and anxiety than either of the preceding volumes" in the series on religious art, because of the amount of material and evidently also because of concerns about the readers' reactions to the subject matter (Macpherson, 271).

2. Elaine Showalter (3–99), Mary Poovey, Deirdre David, and Alison Booth (*Greatness Engendered*) have all explored the difficult position of the Victorian "authoress" and female intellectual. See also the 1831 introduction to *Frankenstein* (1818), where Mary Shelley gives credit for her performance to her parents, husband, and friends and admits conscious artistry only in a reference to childhood "scribbling" (5–11). Another example of "writing like a lady" occurs in the introduction to *Mary Barton* (1848), where Elizabeth Gaskell claims, "I know nothing of political economy. I have tried to write truthfully," yet somehow produced this remarkable analysis of proletarian suffering in Manchester (37–38).

3. See also Jameson's niece Gerardine Macpherson: "Throughout her whole literary life Mrs. Jameson had so entirely woven in her whole personality with her work"; one example given is her *Commonplace Book* (Macpherson, 272).

4. On Jameson's Protestantism, see *Sacred and Legendary Art*, 1:6; *Sisters of Charity*, 38–39. On Jameson's Anglicanism, see *WSSR*, 2:23–24 (the Anglican Church as "our church"), *Madonna*, 252 ("our Jeremy Taylor"); *The Communion of Labor*, 285 (her use of the religious labels "Quakeress," "Roman Catholic," "Dissenter," and "Churchwoman," a common Anglican self-designation, to describe four reforming women); "A Revelation of Childhood," in *Commonplace Book*, 125–26 (a parish clerk lends the young Anna a work by Hannah More; she is taught the creeds and catechisms and given the Bible to read).

5. Holcomb, "Sacred Art," 95, 105, 111; see also Jameson's "Revelation of Childhood," *Commonplace Book*, 125–26, cited by Holcomb.

Jameson, *Commonplace Book*, 143–44 (Milton); *The Communion of Labor*, 282–83 (Reformers); Jameson, *Letters*, 19 Apr. 1851, 175, on "puseyites" and Martineau; 15 Mar. 1856, 209, on Marian Evans (George Eliot).

6. See Article 22 of the Thirty-Nine Articles. The prayerbook contains observances for New Testament Saints' Days, but the Collects are all addressed to God and do not characterize Mary or saints as intercessors. Instead, the Virgin Mary is the type of all those who hear the message of the Angel and know the Incarnation of the Lord;

St. Thomas sets the example of the doubter saved by submission to faith; and St. Peter   245
is the first bishop and the model for later church leaders.

7. Jameson describes the divine and the human contributions to Christianity in
this statement: "I incline to agree with those who think it a great mistake to consider
the present condition or conception of Christianity as complete and final: like the
human soul to which it was fitted by Divine love and wisdom, it has an immeasurable
capacity of development, and 'The Lord hath more truth yet to break forth out of his
Holy Word'" (*Commonplace Book*, 151). To paraphrase Jameson, the spirit of Christianity
is enduring (see also *Monastic Orders*, 11), yet as the human race advances God reveals
more truth, so that Christianity may be said to evolve as well.

8. Jameson, for example, after first "setting apart that which belonged to the superstition of the time," praised Benedictine monasticism as "humane, moderate, wise,
and eminently Christian in spirit" (*Monastic Orders*, 11). In contrast, she treated the extreme asceticism of the earlier Eastern monachism as a form of psychological and physical violence against the self (xviii, 2).

9. Eliot's notebooks show that she read Jameson throughout her writing career.

10. According to Jameson's younger friend Bessie Parkes (who visited Rome in
1857), the art historian could read any picture like "a plain writing": "when she looked
at it, she seemed to feel instantly for what purpose it had been wrought. . . . The
strange mystic symbolism of the early mosaics was a familiar language to her; she
would stand on the polished marble of the Lateran floor, or under the gorgeously som-
bre tribune of the Basilica of Santa Maria Maggiore, reading off the quaint emblems,
and expounding the pious thoughts of more than a thousand years ago" (Parkes, in
Macpherson, 297).

Because of the importance of art as a means to worship, particularly for the unlet-
tered, Jameson often evaluated paintings on the basis of their legibility and criticized
departures from tradition that obscured the doctrinal meaning. For example, she disliked the transformation of the medieval cherubim, represented with only heads and
wings to show they are wholly spirit, into the ridiculous and meaningless "little fat baby
heads" of later art (*SLA*, 1:46–47; 270–77). In her view, unreadable art was at best secular, and at worst irreligious.

11. See Frei, 233–44. Strauss's book truly was seen as hazardous for English readers. Numerous crises of faith in Victorian biographies and Victorian fiction were attributed to it, and even Eliot was made "Strauss-sick" (Haight, 58).

12. There are some striking similarities between Jameson's analysis of the "truth"
and "reliability" of sacred images and the theory of the Greek icon. Charles Lock explains the orthodox defense of icons in the eighth and ninth centuries in these terms:
"How but by signs, words and images, do we know anything? How can we then claim
any knowledge of the 'prototype' [that which is imaged] which would not be entirely
derived from the icon? And if our knowledge of the prototype is derived exclusively
from icons, whether pictorial or verbal, we cannot make a firm distinction between the
icon and the prototype. What are we venerating in an icon, if not all that can be known

246 by us of the prototype?" (11). Lock's analysis of the icon, though suggestive for Jameson's work, locates meaning in the nature of the sign and the "closed, determined" position of the icon, which calls forth a particular set of responses from the worshipper (16–20). Jameson, in contrast, locates meaning primarily in the viewer, and she emphasizes feeling as the means to truth. Her aesthetic has not been analyzed here in terms of the icon because, as the difference in the locus of meaning shows, her frame of reference was Romantic rather than Orthodox; she sought to explain sacred images in nineteenth-century terms.

13. Macpherson, 87–88. *Visits and Sketches at Home and Abroad* (1834) was a collected edition of Jameson's works, which included her 1826 *Diary of an Ennuyée.* I have cited Jameson's *Sketches of Art, Literature, and Character* (1834, rpt. 1875), an American edition of the travel writings on Germany. Jameson also published a translation of the plays of Princess Amalie of Saxony, *Pictures of the Social Life of Germany* (London, 2 vols., 1840). Fuller and Eliot could share in Macpherson's tribute to her aunt. While Jameson helped her readers understand and appreciate German art, these two helped introduce English-speaking audiences to Goethe. Fuller's translation of *Eckermann's Conversations with Goethe* appeared in 1839, and Eliot gave Lewes considerable help with his biography. Eliot also reviewed German authors and translated two works of German biblical scholarship.

14. On Schleiermacher's friendships from his Berlin days, ca. 1795–1801, see Eichner, 44–46. Friedrich Schlegel died in 1829; Jameson made use of his distinction between classic and romantic art and referred to his work in *Commonplace Book,* 290–95. See also Jameson, *Sketches of Art,* 345–46; Macpherson, 66–72, 80–82; Thomas, 71–97. Jameson was in Germany in 1832 when Schleiermacher, a professor at Berlin, was delivering his lectures on the life of Jesus for the fourth time. An edition of these lectures (*Leben Jesu*), based on Schleiermacher's outlines and student notes, was published in 1864, after her death. See Schweitzer, 62–67; Jack Verheyden, introduction to Schleiermacher, *The Life of Jesus,* xi–xvi, lviii–lx. One piece of highly circumstantial evidence that Jameson had some knowledge of current German religious and philosophical debates was her friendship with the family of the philosopher Arthur Schopenhauer (101–2). Since Jameson evidently did not keep a regular journal, there are gaps in our knowledge of her reading and her acquaintances that must be supplemented, when possible, from other sources (for example, Lucretia Mott and Elizabeth Cady Stanton, but not Jameson, record their 1840 meeting in London). A Schleiermacher connection for Jameson is not proven but, given her religious interests and social circle in Germany, not implausible.

15. Jameson, *Letters,* 19 Apr. 1851, 175; 16 June 1851, 177–78; Eliot, review in the *Leader* (20 Sept. 1851), reprinted in *SE,* 286–87, 289. Eliot contrasted the storm over her friend Charles Hennell's *Inquiry Concerning the Origin of Christianity,* which appeared twelve years earlier, with the "elaborate praise" elicited by Greg's derivative work: "In this *annus mirabilis* of 1851, . . . our reviewers have attained a higher standard of courage and fairness than could be ascribed to them in 1838 or even in 1845" (*SE,* 296). Eliot's account of the reception of Greg's book was quite different from Jameson's ("Another

book called the 'Creed of Christendom' has also made great noise, more than you lib-
eral Germans could imagine," Jameson, *Letters*, 175), but Eliot was undeniably biased, given her ties to Hennell and her own controversial status as the translator of Strauss and Feuerbach.

16. Schleiermacher, *On Religion: Speeches to Its Cultured Despisers* (1799), 36–37. The discussion of Schleiermacher will be based on this work, but I have also consulted his *Christmas Eve: Dialogue on the Incarnation* (*Die Weihnachtsfeier: Ein Gesprach*, 1826; Eng. trans. 1967).

17. Jameson writes, "[P]assions existed before principles; . . . principles only bind up life into a consistent whole" (*Commonplace Book*, 46). Schleiermacher, in an Emersonian moment in his text ("You lie directly on the bosom of the infinite world. In that moment, you are its soul"), makes an even finer distinction between primal religious feeling and religious consciousness or knowledge, which is the trace or recollection of that feeling (*On Religion*, 43–44).

18. Thomas, 120–24; letter to Lady Byron, The Lovelace Papers, quoted by permission of Laurence Pollinger Limited and the Earl of Lytton; *Commonplace Book*, 149–50, 173–74.

19. *Essence of Christianity*, esp. xxxiii–xliv, 140–49. See Alister McGrath, *The Making of Modern German Christology, 1750–1990*, for a detailed discussion of Schleiermacher's importance for the Hegelian School (Strauss to Feuerbach) and the liberal Christologies of the latter part of the nineteenth century (36–98).

20. Pals, *Victorian "Lives" of Jesus*, 10; Kissinger, 13–32. The British lives of Jesus include John Robert Seeley's *Ecce Homo* (1865) and F. W. Farrar's *The Life of Christ* (1874).

21. The art historian Hugh Honour gives several instances of this Romantic religious sensibility, mentioning Chateaubriand, A. W. Schlegel, and Coleridge (157–58).

Chapter 4

1. Auerbach, 72; Langland, 1–61. Langland's reconceptualized Angels could easily turn into the "domestic feminists" described by historians of the nineteenth-century women's movement. Domestic feminists argued that women's goodness and their effectiveness at home should allow them to expand their sphere and clean up society.

2. Woolf, "Professions for Women"; Booth (*Greatness Engendered*), 29–30, 52, 133, 137–38, 206–7, 229; Gilbert and Gubar, 18–21, 468, 485, 490–501; Michie, esp. 12–29; Helsinger et al., 3:79–170; Christ, 130–40; Homans, *Bearing the Word*, 156–60, 216; Trudgill, 248–306; Warner, esp. 47, 236–54, 333–39.

3. The historian Ann Douglas has identified an important nineteenth-century phenomenon, the "feminization of religion," but Protestant uses of the Madonna-figure have not been emphasized in these discussions. The term "feminization of religion" refers to a number of changes in nineteenth-century Protestantism and Catholicism: the increasingly sentimental and emotional forms of piety; the emphasis on Mary, particularly as a model for women, in Catholic countries; the Protestant characterization of Jesus as a gentle soul or a little baby; and the predominance of women at worship

248   services. Neither Douglas, who focuses on nineteenth-century America, nor David Blackbourn, who discusses nineteenth-century Germany and France, sees the feminization of religion as unambiguously improving the status of women (though Blackbourn notes some benefits), and Catholic and Protestant religious leadership remained male (Douglas; Blackbourn, 30–31, 140–41, 261–63).

4. Keble, 318; Graef, 2:106. Keble began "Ave Maria" in 1823 on the occasion of his mother's death (Graef, 2:106). As popular with Anglicans as *The Pilgrim's Progress* was with Dissenters, the book earned for its author the position of Professor of Poetry at Oxford, although Keble (unlike Newman) never had a high opinion of his verse (O. Chadwick, 1:66–68).

5. For example, in Keble's familiar "Evening" ("Sun of my soul! Thou Saviour dear"), Jesus is characterized as watching, mother-like, over his children's slumbers: "Be my last thought, how sweet to rest / For ever on my Saviour's breast" (5–8).

6. Newman, "The Glories of Mary for the Sake of Her Son" (1849), 258. See also "Our Lady in the Gospel" (1848), 96.

7. "Who can estimate the holiness and perfection of her, who was chosen to be the Mother of Christ? . . . *This contemplation runs to a higher subject, did we dare follow it*" (Newman, "The Reverence Due to the Virgin Mary" [1832], 309, emphasis added).

8. "Glories," 257; see also "On the Fitness of the Glories of Mary," 268–69.

9. "Our Lady," 99; "Glories," 254. In the first two respects—Mary's activity and her exemplary faith—Newman's reading unexpectedly resembles that of the feminist theologian Rosemary Radford Ruether. Their crucial difference is their treatment of the body; while Ruether, like Newman, deemphasizes Mary's role as physical vessel, she condemns traditional Christian devaluations of the body, especially the female body (*Sexism and God-Talk*, 139–58).

10. "The Hidden Ones" (*Hymns*, 29–31), "Wanderings" (43), "A Hermitage" (129–30), "The Two Worlds" (184–85), "Monks" (254–58), "The Married and the Single" (264–71).

11. Ker, 116, 120–21; see also *ODCC*, s.v. "Keble, John," 774–75.

12. Newman's *Letter to Pusey* appears in *Certain Difficulties Felt by Anglicans in Catholic Teaching*, Vol. 2.

13. "Observe the lesson which we gain for ourselves from the history of the Blessed Virgin; that the highest graces of the soul may be matured in private" ("Reverence," 311; see also "Developments," 311–12; "Fitness," 273; "Glories," 248).

14. Most of Newman's congregants and all of his students at Oxford were men. Almost all of his poems and hymns on saints and heroes of the faith celebrate men (Abraham, Moses, Joseph, Paul, the Greek Fathers) rather than women (see *Hymns*). And whereas his colleague E. B. Pusey was active in the Anglican effort to establish religious sisterhoods, Newman's efforts were directed toward starting a *mone*, "half College half monastery," at Littlemore, for men only (Ker, 247).

15. "Reverence," 308; "Glories," 258–59. See also *Letter to Pusey*, 31–32 (the man as representing the human race).

16. Bynum, 18–19, 136–69; Miles, "The Virgin's One Bare Breast," 206. But cf.
King, 94–101, 130–31.

17. Jameson shared the interest of Pusey and Newman in religious communities, though she was not drawn, as Newman was, to the contemplative life. In her two public lectures on women's need for education and employment, Jameson described the current work of the Sisters of Charity on the Continent and proposed reviving religious sisterhoods in England in order to train and organize her countrywomen to serve society. The leaders of the Oxford Movement had similar proposals and projects, but it is clear that their main agenda differed from Jameson's: the revitalization of the Church of England, versus jobs for women and women's self-sufficiency.

18. *Letter to Pusey*, 3, 24–25. Newman's poems also show his devotion to the Greek Fathers (see "The Greek Fathers," "St. Gregory Nazianzen," and the poems based on St. Gregory's writings, *Hymns*, 58–59, 96–97, 128–30, 264–71). According to the Newman scholar Ian Ker, Newman knew Scripture and the Fathers so much better than Aquinas and the Scholastic tradition that after his conversion, he denied he was qualified to be a Catholic theologian (*Newman the Theologian*, 41).

19. Basil Champneys was Patmore's friend as well as his biographer and obviously bases some of his statements on conversations with the poet. Emily Patmore said on her deathbed in 1862: "When I am gone, they [the Catholics] will get you; and then I shall see you no more." Champneys, 1:124–25, 211; 2:12, 49–51, 53.

20. In this passage, from "The Rose of the World," Eve is "with favour singled out" (cf. Luke 1:28, KJV: Mary is "highly favoured" among women), and though she is not free from sin ("Marr'd *less* by mortal fall"), she is clearly the moral superior of any man (*The Angel in the House*, in *Poems*, 83). Another passage, "The Tribute," describes a woman who seems clothed with the sun: "Boon Nature to the woman bows; / She walks in earth's whole glory clad" (85).

21. In this 1878 poem, Mary the "mild silent little Maid," like simple mothers everywhere, "worship[s] little baby feet" and regards her Son as God ("Regina Coeli," in *Poems*, 467).

22. Champneys also notes that the poet regarded the first Mrs. Patmore as a saint and always observed the day of her death with seclusion and prayer (1:147–48).

23. Champneys, 1:12; 2:49–50, 52.

24. Champneys, 2:18, 20, 79–80, 98, 325, 377.

25. Champneys, 1:164–77; 2:309–15, 345–55.

26. Effie Gray Ruskin soon married the painter John Millais, with whom she had eight children. See Champneys, 2:277–79; Evans, 201–2; Hilton, 117–20, 196–200.

27. Ruskin, letter to *The Critic*, 27 Oct. 1860, in *Works*, 34:488–90; *The Elements of Drawing* (1857), 15:227; "Of Queens' Gardens" (1865), 18:120; Champneys, 1:168; 2:280–85.

Since the legal basis for the annulment of Ruskin's marriage was not merely its nonconsummation but his impotence (which he later disputed), how ironic (or perhaps vengeful) is the context in which he quotes Patmore in "Of Queens' Gardens": "You

250   cannot think that the buckling on of the knight's armour by his lady's hand was a mere caprice of romantic fashion. It is the type of an eternal truth—that the soul's armour is never well set to the heart unless a woman's hand has braced it; and it is only when she braces it loosely that the honour of manhood fails" ("Of Queens' Gardens," 18:120). If manhood falls, the woman is obviously to blame.

28. It was also translated into German, French, and Italian. See Bibliographical Note, *Complete Works of John Ruskin*, 18:5–17.

29. Ruskin, *Complete Works*, 24 Dec. 1864, 36:478–79; Champneys, 2:282–83.

30. It seems legitimate to limit this discussion to *English* Catholicism, since both Newman and Patmore were resistant to the influence of Continental Catholicism. Newman even after his conversion considered Italian books of devotion and saints' lives unsuitable for English Catholics (*Letter to Pusey*, 21–23; earlier, *Apologia*, 164–66). He was unfamiliar with much Continental mariological writing from the late Middle Ages to the eighteenth century, even Alphonus Liguori's highly popular *Glories of Mary* (1786), available to Pusey in an English translation (Graef, 2:74–77, 115–18; *Letter to Pusey*, 97–118). When in his *Letter to Pusey* Newman is forced to respond to these texts, he says, "One thing, however, is clear about all these writers; that no one of them is an Englishman. . . . [T]hey are foreigners; we are not answerable for their particular devotions. . . . I suppose we owe it to the national good sense, that English Catholics have been protected from the extravagances which are elsewhere to be found. . . . If the Catholic faith spreads in England, these peculiarities will not spread with it" (98–100).

Patmore's religious reading had a narrow range and focused on early sources. He was led into the Catholic Church by "ancient Catholic books of devotion" as well as the *Summa Theologica* of Aquinas, and in later years he confined his reading almost exclusively to the Bible, the Breviary, and the Fathers of the Church (Champneys, 1:12; 2:49–50, 52). Patmore said he always loved to pray to the Virgin but disliked the Rosary and excessive Marian devotion. He could not bring himself to visit Lourdes until 1877 but then made two repeat pilgrimages (2:56).

31. Moorman, 70–79, 102–11. The positive reviews of Jameson's books suggest that a number of her Protestant readers had similar views of the periods of church history. For example, John Eagles, who has been identified by the Wellesley Index as the *Blackwood's* reviewer of several of her works—*Sacred and Legendary Art*, *Legends of the Monastic Orders*, and *Legends of the Madonna*—was probably a Calvinist and rarely missed an opportunity to castigate "popery," "Papists," and "the Romish church." Yet he generally shared Jameson's enthusiasm for religious art predating the Reformation and thought Protestants would benefit from her studies.

32. Mâle, too, observes "the faithfulness with which art reflects successive phases of Christian thought and feeling," and he notes the successive emergence in the late Middle Ages of the serene Madonna, the responsive Madonna, and the Mater Dolorosa described by his Victorian predecessor. He assigns slightly later dates to these Madonnas than Jameson does since he is focusing on France, as influenced by Italy (101).

Chapter 5

1. Jameson kept notes on Eckermann's *Conversations with Goethe* in the journal that became *Winter Studies and Summer Rambles in Canada*. She described Goethe's idea for a "*cyclus*" of twelve Scriptural figures (all but one of them male) suitable for sculpture that would represent Christianity with more individuation than Jesus and his nearly interchangeable disciples have. Goethe's *cyclus* "has made me think much," Jameson said (*WSSR*, 1:169–71), and in a subsequently published discussion of subjects for sculpture, she produced her own list of Scriptural worthies, two-thirds of them women (*Commonplace Book*, 309–17).

2. *Monastic Orders*, 58–62, 65–69, 194–97. On Jameson's negative view of Cromwell and the Reformers, see *Monastic Orders*, 39, 135; *Communion of Labor*, 282–84; on Knox's "violent" zeal and lapses of judgment, see *Celebrated Female Sovereigns*, 1:185.

Carlyle's worship of Cromwell seems to have been a particularly touchy subject for Jameson. She paid an overnight visit to the Carlyles in 1844, and in a letter she describes him "thundering away about Oliver Cromwell—of whom he thinks 'as of a man sent from God'—Even his horrible Butcheries in Ireland he called 'doing his appointed work' which he '*could not but do*'—as an instrument of Gods Justice." Carlyle evidently did not know or care that his guest was Irish-born. The next morning he defended slavery over the breakfast table. Jameson's revenge is to say of his wife Jane Carlyle: "It must be something next worse to being married to Satan himself" (Thomas, 160).

3. Jameson did campaign for women's admission to art schools. Cherry notes that Eliza Fox, who gave art classes that were attended by Bodichon, identified Jameson as a source for her painting of St. Perpetua and St. Felicitas (1861). Jameson says in *Sacred and Legendary Art* that the subject had not been worthily treated yet, and she describes Felicitas as Fox depicts her, as an African woman (Cherry, 55, 196–97; *SLA*, 2:564–65). On the genres of women's paintings in the nineteenth century, see Yeldham, 1:116–73, esp. 151; W. Chadwick, 165–90; Cherry, 124–27, 165–72.

4. Jameson met Hosmer in Florence in 1857, where they breakfasted and toured the galleries together. They had friends in common, including Robert and Elizabeth Barrett Browning, with whom Jameson stayed in Florence, and Frances Power Cobbe, a visitor from England. Jameson and Hosmer also corresponded, and Jameson visited her in her studio in Rome. Jameson's areas of expertise relevant to Hosmer's work on Zenobia included the history of the Palmyran queen, the art of the Greco-Roman world, and modern sculpture (Jameson covers the latter topics in articles and reviews). Jameson tried to supply Hosmer with casts from coins to help her depict Zenobia's face, and she admired Hosmer's plaster sketch of the queen but criticized the position of the diadem as too low. The modest Jameson also sought to limit her influence over Hosmer by telling her to take the advice of her teacher, the neoclassic sculptor John Gibson, over everyone else's, including her own. It turns out that Hosmer's Zenobia was actually modeled on a Madonna; the director of the Uffizi pointed the sculptor

252   toward a mosaic of the Virgin Mary in the Church of San Marco in Florence (Sherwood, 156–60, 178–79; Carr, 92–97, 123, 149–51).

Hosmer may have consulted Jameson's chapter on Isabella of Castile in *Celebrated Female Sovereigns* when she was working on her sculpture of the queen in the 1890s, but the Queen Isabella Association, the American suffrage organization that commissioned her work, would probably have been her primary source for materials. Eliza Allen Starr, a member of the association, published her biography *Isabella of Castile, 1492–1892* in 1889, and features on the queen appeared in the society's newspaper (Weimann, 29, 39–40, 60, 601n.). Isabella was an icon for American feminists before the Chicago World's Fair. She is mentioned, for example, in a poem on Manifest Destiny ("Westward") published in *The Revolution*, the newspaper edited by Susan B. Anthony and Elizabeth Cady Stanton (22 Jan. 1868, 1:1).

5. See Hosmer's biographer Dolly Sherwood, 128–35, 236; W. Chadwick, 201–4.

6. Cobbe, "What Shall We Do with Our Old Maids?," in Lacey, 366–69. Later in the article Cobbe called attention to the achievements of a number of women writers, beginning with Jameson (375).

7. Sherwood, 218–23, 302; on Vinnie Ream, the sculptor of Lincoln, see 288–89.

8. Carr, 271–72, 287, 289, 296; Sherwood, 294–96, 315–20.

9. Fuller also used Isabella in *Woman in the Nineteenth Century*, but she was more interested in the queen as a metaphor than as a historical figure (*WNC*, 278, 305).

10. Munich, e.g., 55–103. According to Homans, the queen's power or agency inhered in her representations, and she could rule only by giving away her authority, for example, by posing as an ordinary wife (*Royal Representations*, 55). Nicola Watson shows that Victorian writers and artists made Victoria's homely virtues the mark of her superiority to Queen Elizabeth, whose uncomfortably effective wielding of "masculine" power was seen as offset by her "feminine" vices, such as vanity and jealousy; one of Watson's sources is Jameson (Watson, 80–85).

11. Weltman, 103–9; Langland, 62–79; Cherry, 192–95 and Plate 38; Booth, "Illustrious Company," 75–77.

12. So Weltman, 117–20, 151; Auerbach, 58–62.

13. Frawley, 87–104; Munich, 217–18; see also Helsinger et al., 2:149, on Barbara Bodichon's praise of the queen as a working mother.

14. Mill, *Subjection*, 130–31; on Martineau, see David, 54 (but cf. *Autobiography*, 1:118–28, discussed below); *History of Woman Suffrage*, 4:160, 162; Weatherford, 19, 143–44.

15. Harper, 3:1156–57; Stanton, *Eighty Years*, 108–26, 136–37, 145–54; see also the Seneca Falls resolutions about woman's constricted sphere and rightful responsibilities, in Rossi, ed., 419. When Anthony died, a obituary in the York (Pennsylvania) *Dispatch* said this spinster would have benefited her country more if she had spent her life, like "Victoria the Good," bearing sons and raising *them* to have high ideals (Harper, 3:1555).

16. Stanton, *Eighty Years*, 398–99; similarly Fuller, *Dispatches*, 261, 272.

17. Jeanne Weimann, in *The Fair Women*, shows that queenship was a recurrent metaphor at the Columbian Exposition. For example, the Women's Building was decorated with medallions of Queen Isabella and Mrs. Palmer and with busts of the suffragists Susan B. Anthony, Elizabeth Cady Stanton, Lucretia Mott, and Lucy Stone. And there were the "queenly" souvenirs: the spoons, the bookmark, and the memorial quarter-dollar, featuring Isabella, Mrs. Palmer, or both (289–95, 465–86; see also 219, 221).

18. A similar situation obtained in the collective female biographies of the nineteenth century. Alison Booth notes the anomalous position of Victoria among the suffragists, authors, artists, and actresses in volumes such as James Parton's *Eminent Women* (Booth, "Illustrious Company," 72–78; Parton [1868], esp. 405–38, 566–98 [Queen Victoria and Hosmer]).

19. On Jameson, see Macpherson, e.g., 143–44, 154, 260. Martineau's reactions to Victoria are remarkably similar to Jameson's, and when combined with her criticisms of the "unreal character of the monarchy in England," they suggest why Martineau made limited symbolic use of the queen. There is only one discussion of Victoria in Martineau's autobiography, which covers seventy years (1:118–28).

20. Peter O'Dwyer, 261–62. O'Dwyer describes O'Connell as exceptionally devoted to the Virgin (259–62). O'Dwyer also connects the Rosary (which was one of the few licit expressions of Irish Catholic identity during the Penal Times) to the violent struggles against British rule in Ireland during the late nineteenth and early twentieth centuries. The Rosary was said under fire during the Easter Rebellion of 1916 and recited in unison, in Irish, by captured fighters at their cell windows and by their families at the gate of the prison (298–300).

21. The main source for this information on Jameson's father, Denis Brownell Murphy, is Gerardine Macpherson, whose biography is obviously based on family stories. (The entry on Murphy in the *Dictionary of National Biography* [1894; 39:337] adds no information on his politics and lists Macpherson as a source.) Macpherson says unsympathetically of her "patriot" grandfather that he followed the revolutionary "fashion" of the day and "escaped, by no wisdom of his own, from the network of conspiracy and betrayal in which Emmett, Lord Edward Fitzgerald, and the other leaders of the rebellion, were hurried to destruction" (1–2). Macpherson here seems to conflate the 1798 and 1803 rebellions of the United Irishmen. The unsuccessful 1798 rebellion, which was against British domination of Ireland and the Anglican Ascendancy, was led by Henry McCracken (a Protestant Belfast manufacturer), Colonel James Napper Tandy, and Wolfe Tone (a Dublin lawyer and the son of an Anglican coachmaker); Tone had managed to obtain military assistance from the French, was captured aboard a French ship, and died by his own hand in British custody. The second rebellion, which occurred two years after the union of Great Britain and Ireland, involved the remaining United Irishmen under the leadership of Robert Emmett. It also failed, and Emmett was tried and executed. See McDowell, 4:338–73; Connolly, 5:1–23, esp. 11–17; Ranelagh, 66–95; Tone.

22. In Toronto, Canada (where Jameson endured the winter of 1836–37 in a last

254   effort to save her marriage), she found the society provincial and "fourth or fifth rate," preoccupied with petty gossip and rivalries, and remarkably unfriendly to the authoress, who, possessing, as she said, quick wits and impatient affections "derived, perhaps, from my Irish blood," considered the "social frost" as painful as the winter cold (*WSSR*, 1:74, 10–11, 123–24). In reaction to these social snubs, Jameson proclaimed the superiority of the Irish to the English and the Scottish settlers in Canada, and she started on her summer travels through the Canadian wilderness as soon as the roads out of Toronto were passable (1:81, 92–98, 208–18; 2:26–30, 338–39).

    23. On Jameson's trip to Ireland, see Macpherson, 251–60; Erskine, 250–53. Her ten-day stay with the venerable Anglo-Irish author Maria Edgeworth was a cheerful one, but as she traveled through the parts of south and west Ireland stricken by the potato famine, she says she "could only feel sick at heart, viewing the horrible misery which met me at every step—large buildings, *once* mills and manufactories, all empty, idleness and desolation and starvation everywhere" (to Robert Noel, in Macpherson, 255).

    24. The Irish Coercion Bill of the mid-1840s was designed to restrict Irish protests during the potato famine; on Jameson's opposition to it "as an Irishwoman," see Macpherson, 215–16. The Anglican Church in Ireland was the wealthy established church of a very small minority, but the Catholic majority was required to support it financially. In the 1830s Daniel O'Connell had helped lead a "Tithe War" to protest the onerous tithes owed to Anglican clergy. In wanting the disestablishment of this church, Jameson felt she placed herself on the side of "freedom of mind and common sense" against "Puseyism" (letter to Robert Noel, Jan. 1845, Macpherson, 226). The leaders of the Oxford Movement (including Newman until his conversion to Catholicism in 1845) defended the power and privilege of the Established Church (including the Church of Ireland) against the state, beginning with Keble's assize sermon, "National Apostasy," in 1833.

    25. In this letter Jameson called O'Connell and his Irish followers morally courageous, generous, and the only people in Europe able to act together from high principle. And she astutely observed: "There is an old Scotch proverb which says, 'Mint at a golden gown and ye'll get the sleeve o't'—in other words, cry out 'Repeal' (or rather 'Repale') and you'll get some of that justice and redress which has been for centuries withheld from you" (to Robert Noel, 7 Dec. 1843, in Macpherson, 196–97). The historian Maurice O'Connell similarly thinks that O'Connell, a pragmatist, was probably using Repeal to win other major reforms (11–12).

    26. Anglican sisterhoods might have been an option for Jameson's own unmarried sisters, who, evidently lacking her intelligence, initiative, and self-education, did not pursue the few and ill-paid jobs available to women of the middle class and instead, like their mother and invalid father, depended on Anna to provide.

    27. Jameson cited by Holcomb, "Anna Jameson on Women Artists," 15. Eliot, "Woman in France: Madame de Sablé" (1854), and "Margaret Fuller and Mary Wollstonecraft" (1855), in *SE*, 8–9, 333–35; *Eliot Letters*, 14 May 1867, 8:402; 8 Aug. 1868, 4:468.

28. On what is sometimes called "apocalyptic feminism," see Helsinger et al.,
2:199–206.

Chapter 6

1. This discussion will draw on Fuller's *Woman in the Nineteenth Century,* her articles in the *Dial* and the *New-York Tribune,* and her letters, poems, and journals. The quite recent publication of accurate editions of her letters (edited by Robert Hudspeth) and other writings gives us a more nuanced and complete view of Fuller than was easily available to earlier scholars, and makes possible this argument about the rich and recurrent presence of the Madonna throughout Fuller's public and personal work.

2. For example, Warner, 47, 236–54, 333–39; Daly, *Gyn/ecology,* 73–105; but cf. *Beyond God the Father,* 81–97; and the feminist theorist Adrienne Rich, 103, 110, 162–63, 180.

3. For example, Gilbert and Gubar, 18–21, 468, 485, 490–501; Homans, *Bearing the Word,* 156–60, 216; and Trudgill, 257–76. See also Douglas, 80–164.

4. See Blanchard, 218–21; Chevigny, 215–23; Urbanski, *A Literary Study,* 140–43; Richardson, 169–84; Showalter, 311–12; and to some extent Steele (e.g., *Representation of the Self,* 100–133).

5. See Chevigny, Blanchard, Steele, and Capper, although his analysis of Fuller as intellectual makes her her father's rather than her mother's daughter and emphasizes her friendships with men over those with women.

6. For example, Wade and Deiss.

7. None of Fuller's modern biographers has yet spent more than fifteen pages discussing her religious views (though see Eve Kornfeld's valuable insights in *Margaret Fuller,* 14–22, 43–50), nor is there agreement on where to place her in the American religious landscape. Blanchard labels Fuller as orthodoxly Unitarian: "In actual belief she had never strayed very far from the Channingite wing of the church" (85–86); "Margaret's own religious beliefs were neither complicated nor radical; she was probably closer to James Freeman Clarke in this respect than to any of other others" (126). In contrast, Chevigny writes: "Fuller's self-nurture led her to Transcendentalism by a route which was primarily neither religious nor philosophical but literary. Though a youthful mystical experience drew her to a liberal Christianity, her faith was tentative and eclectic to the verge, for her time, of heresy. (Honesty obligated even her devoted Clarke to call her life goals only 'almost Christian.')" (146). Wade considers Fuller more comfortable in the Unitarian Church than does Capper, who characterizes her as an *avant-garde* Romantic thinker, but the two agree in reading her religious beliefs and experiences in psychological terms (Wade, 30; Capper, ix–xii, 103–4, 112–14). For a useful brief discussion of the reactions of Fuller and other Transcendentalists to Unitarianism, see Rose, 56–60, also 70–108.

8. *Letters,* 2:160; see also 5:86. Fuller's writings show how strongly she was drawn to religious mystics; it is perhaps unsurprising that her own religious experiences would take a mystical form.

9. *Letters,* 27 Apr. 1845, 4:90; 30 Sept. 1845, 4:163. Fuller's role as her father's literary

256   executor also reversed the roles of parent and child. Sorting through his papers after his death and noting how little he had accomplished of a long-planned American history, she became her father's Author, as he was hers during her childhood education.

10. *Letters*, 5:157–58, 239–40; *Dispatches*, 155, 189, 278–85, 321–23.

11. "The Wrongs of American Woman" and "Mistress of Herself," in *Essays*, 303–10, 367–70.

12. *WNC*, 252. Susan Conrad terms these views "romantic feminism"; see her discussion of Fuller in *Perish the Thought*, 73–82. See also Julie Ellison on the Romantic and ethical dimensions of Fuller's feminism (261–87).

13. For example, Blanchard, Urbanski, and Richardson. See, however, John Gatta's discussion of Fuller in *American Madonna* (1997), 33–52. Gatta's book postdates the article version of my study ("The Madonna and Margaret Fuller," *Women's Studies* 25 [1996]: 385–405).

14. *WNC*, 347. Rich's arguments about virgin goddesses and the great mother goddesses in her important book *Of Woman Born* are similar to Fuller's, although Rich cites Fuller only as a disparager of motherhood (96, 110, 253–56).

15. The context of Steele's analysis is, however, Fuller's interest in androgyny: the Madonna, he says, is her representation of the "'radiant sovereign self' balancing masculinity and femininity, Minerva and Muse" (*Essential Margaret Fuller*, xxxv–xxxvi). Gatta calls Fuller's Madonna "an example of awakened womanhood" and of "potency of spirit," and pays particular attention to her roles as "Victoria" and "Virginia" (41–52).

16. Blanchard, 218–21; Urbanski, *A Literary Study*, 140–43. Blanchard reads Fuller's concept of virginity too narrowly, as referring only to the sexually unfulfilled state of the unmarried woman, and she does not consider the implications of the virgin *mother*. See also David Robinson on Minerva and the Muse as representations of, respectively, the masculine and feminine qualities in women (90–95); Kornfeld and Marks, 47–59. Elaine Showalter considers Miranda and Cassandra as mythic personae representing the dilemmas of the feminist intellectual ("Miranda and Cassandra," 311–12); she finds references to a female Messiah in Fuller as well as Nightingale (315). On *Woman in the Nineteenth Century* as a gender-conscious work of social and political criticism, see Robinson, esp. 95–96; Blanchard, 229–31.

17. See "Christmas," *New-York Weekly Tribune*, 21 Dec. 1844, in *Essays*, 254–60.

18. Fuller's poetry has been described as a kind of verse diary. See Steele, "'Prisoned Queen,'" 137; Berg and Perry, 42–43.

19. *Letters*, 3:220; 4:132; 5:78 n. 4; Berg and Perry, 56.

20. See "Leila" and "Leila in the Arabian Zone," *Essential Fuller*, 53–58, 233.

21. Steele, *Representation of the Self*, esp. 121–26; "'Prisoned Queen,'" 137–75; Introduction to *Essential Margaret Fuller*, xi–xlix. See also Gatta, 34–41.

22. For example, the women participating in Fuller's Conversations came to her speaking "Bostonian," a language well suited to the articulation of Christian orthodoxies. In contrast, Fuller had to teach them "Greek" (i.e., Greek and Roman mythology), and even she, though unusually well educated for a woman, could read the Greek myths only in their Latin versions (*Letters*, 2:101–2; Capper, 47–48; Dall, 42; see also

Ellison [240–56] and Zwarg [161–88] on the connections between Fuller's reading and
writing practices and her self-presentation in the Conversations). Marie Urbanski and
Robert D. Richardson, Jr., in their studies of Fuller's feminist writings and activities,
claim that she valued the Greco-Roman mythology over the Christian. But there are at
least as many references to the Madonna as to Greco-Roman goddesses in her writings.
Her choice of topics for the Conversations seems to have been instead an attempt to
introduce Boston women to a new national culture and to begin to compensate for the
intellectually demanding and classical education they were denied (*Letters*, 2:86–89).

23. Chevigny, 171; *Essential Fuller*, 19; *Letters*, 5:295–96; *Dispatches*, 242–43.

24. E.g., *Letters*, 1:219; 3:67. Like Jameson and Eliot, Fuller made the kind of contrast found in German Romanticism between Greek and Christian ideals, although Jameson, who focused on the "carnal" classicism of the Renaissance, clearly preferred the austere values represented by the Christian god.

25. See Parker, "Discourse on the Transient and Permanent in Christianity," in Miller, 259–83; Emerson, Sermon 119, in *Complete Sermons*, 3:180–81; "The Divinity School Address," *Collected Works*, 1:76–93.

26. Compare Sermons 28 ("The Christian Minister") and 119, *Complete Sermons*, 1:233–37; 3:179–83.

27. Emerson, *Letters*, 3 Aug. 1835, 1:451; *Emerson in His Journals*, 513–14.

28. *Woman in the Nineteenth Century* does have figures analogous to the Mother and the Virgin: the Muse and Minerva, the representatives, respectively, of the "electric" "feminine" and intellectual "masculine" sides of woman's nature. But female creativity is not a central issue in this text. The Muse may be associated with creativity, as an inspirer of male artists, but she is not a creator herself (*WNC*, 309–11). Fuller did, however, make the statement "The Muse [will] weave anew the tapestries of Minerva" (311). The image of weaving for female creativity is not a usual one for Fuller, but it is to be expected, given the presence of Minerva/Athena. More importantly, she showed Minerva and the Muse creating together; the intellectually self-reliant Minerva starts the work, but the "feminine" Muse seems needed to inspire and finish it. Minerva and the Muse, then, while primarily used by Fuller to make arguments about female nature rather than female creativity, help reinforce the point that Fuller's female creator-figure is the Virgin Mother, rather than either the Virgin or the Mother acting independently.

29. Habich, 332; Fuller to Caroline Sturgis Tappan, *Letters*, 16 Mar. 1869, 5:209–10; see also Fuller to Elizabeth Hoar, *Letters*, [8?] Mar. 1842, 3:47.

30. See Wade, 216–27; Deiss, 54, 79, 192.

31. See Blanchard, 173, 251, 276. Chevigny (27–28) thinks that Fuller had no expectation of marriage, but this argument seems undercut by Fuller's numerous romantic attachments: to George Davis, Ward, perhaps William Clarke (see Berg and Perry, 43–51), James Nathan, and finally Giovanni Ossoli. Since Fuller refused to have an extramarital relationship with anyone before Ossoli, the only possible outcomes of these romances seem to have been marriage or the painful break-ups that occurred in all but Ossoli's case.

32. See Steele, "'Prisoned Queen,'" 155–56.

33. "Leila," *Essential Fuller,* 53–54. One can see here reasons for Fuller's preference for free-ranging conversation, for which she was famous, over writing.

34. *Letters,* 22 Oct. 1840, 2:167. See also Fuller's 10 July 1845 letter to Sturgis (which again predated the birth of Fuller's son): "I believe I am the mother of a genius, more than a genius. It seems as if I was learning every thing, that every element of beauty and power was being reproduced in my frame, but only in my son shall they appear not in me, his unknown but happy mother" (*Letters,* 4:132).

35. Female public speakers were still a rarity in 1840s America. The abolitionists Sarah and Angelina Grimké (active in the late 1830s) were among the first women to address "mixed" (male and female) audiences; they were notorious for linking slaves' rights to women's rights. The silencing of the female delegates at the World Anti-Slavery Convention in London in 1840 led Lucretia Mott and Elizabeth Cady Stanton, eight years later, to organize the first women's-rights convention at Seneca Falls. Because of the women's reluctance to chair their own convention, James Mott acted as chair. See Clinton, 68–76; Rossi, 282–96, 413–15.

36. *Madonna,* xl, 9–10, 48–51, 69–70; Warner, 247–48.

37. Mary as Wisdom is barely mentioned by Jaroslav Pelikan, Hilda Graef, or Marina Warner, who instead emphasize such Marian roles as the Second Eve, the Blessed Virgin, the Mother of God (*Theotokos*), the Mater Dolorosa, and the Queen of Heaven (Pelikan, *Mary,* esp. vi–vii, 7–21, 25, 85; Warner, vii–viii; see also Kinsley, 215–60).

38. Ruether, *Sexism and God-Talk,* 54–61, 116–26; Engelsman, 74–120; Pelikan, *Jesus,* 57–70.

39. Ruether, *Sexism and God-Talk,* 58–61, 122–26, 134–35; Engelsman, 95, 106–20; Baring and Cashford, 611–17.

40. *ODCC,* 573–74, s.v. "Gnosticism"; Baring and Cashford, 609–34; Ruether, *Sexism and God-Talk,* 59–61; Cunneen, 78–84.

41. *Madonna,* xix–xxii; *Romola,* 518–25; Hamington, 11–12; Baring and Cashford, 556–82; Gimbutas, 319.

42. See "Prevalent Idea that Politeness is too great a Luxury to be given to the Poor," "Thanksgiving," "Christmas," and "Fourth of July," in *Essays.*

43. On Fuller's knowledge of Catholicism before her time in Rome, see chapter 1.

44. On Fuller's socialism, see *Letters,* 4:271; 5:69, 295–96; *Dispatches,* 319–20; see also 204–6; but cf. Ellison (217–98) and Zwarg (189–220), who see the interplay of socialist and aesthetic ideas throughout Fuller's *Tribune* essays, including those predating her European trip.

45. *Letters,* 5:196–98, 202, 210 (on Mazzini); 5:292, 305 (mothers of the revolution, and "Mater Dolorosa").

46. See *Letters,* 2:98, 101, 118 (on the women participants in Fuller's Conversations); 1:310–14 and 4:59 (on Caroline Sturgis).

47. On Fuller's feelings for Caroline Sturgis, see *Letters,* 1:303–15; 2:92–94; 3:220; 4:132. On Fuller and Anna Barker, see *Essential Fuller,* 1–2; *Letters,* 2:92–94; Habich, 287, 290.

48. *WNC,* 319–31. Fuller's "The Great Lawsuit," the July 1843 *Dial* essay that she
later revised and expanded into the book-length *Woman in the Nineteenth Century* (1845),
contains the discussion of virginity as self-reliance but not the material on courtship,
marriage, and prostitution. Fuller seems to have added this material after visiting the
women prisoners in Sing-Sing in the fall of 1845 (Blanchard, 210–12).

49. Fuller's mixed feelings about passion not unsurprisingly confused her beau in
New York, James Nathan. She told him in her letters, "I have felt a strong attraction to
you, almost ever since we first met"; "I feel deep confidence in my friend and know that
he will lead me on in a spirit of holy love, and that all I may learn of nature and the
soul will be legitimate. . . . Are you my guardian to domesticate me in the body, and
attach it more firmly to the earth" (*Letters,* spring 1845, 4:73, 95–96). Yet when Nathan
proposed a sexual relationship, she was upset at being so misunderstood. They should
rise above their lower natures, she chided him, those base feelings which she personi-
fied as "the man of the world" and "the dame" (4:74–78). A *purified* passion was somehow to be their ideal.

50. *Letters,* 5:175–76 n. Fuller would have liked Mickiewicz to stand as godfather
of her child; see 5:125, 129.

51. Fuller described the American lower classes as doing work connected with the
body (e.g., the laundress in "The Poor Man: An Ideal Sketch," in *Essays,* 352–61; the
prostitutes seen during her visit to Sing-Sing, *Letters,* 3:236–38). She thought that
books, which she associated with middle-class women and middle-class professions
such as teaching, would raise the mental and moral level of the lower classes (*Letters,*
3:238; "The Wrongs of American Women," in *Essays,* 306–10).

52. *Letters,* Jan. 1849, 5:168. See also *Letters,* 11 July 1848, 5:86 ("The ignorance of
this [Italian] people is amazing. I am to them a divine visitant, an instructive Ceres
telling them wonderful tales of foreign customs and even legends of their own saints.
They are people I could love and live with"); 16 Mar. 1849, 5:209, on her son's care-
takers in Rieti ("it may be a happiness for him to be with these more plebian, instinc-
tive, joyous natures. I saw he was more serene, that he was not sensitive as when with
me, and slept a great deal more").

53. *Letters,* 5:102–48, esp. 122 n., 131; 209–10, 249.

54. Warner, 47, 236–54, 333–39; Pope, 173–200; see also Rich, 103, 110, 162–63,
180.

55. Jameson did, in fact, put together a family for herself after leaving her husband. She became a foster mother to her niece Gerardine Bates (later Macpherson),
who traveled with her and helped with her books. Friends were surprised to learn that
Gerardine was not actually her daughter.

Chapter 7

1. The most important of these critics—Gillian Beer, George Levine, Nancy
Paxton, and Sally Shuttleworth—focus on the relevance of Darwin and Spencer for
Eliot's theories of science and social organization and her experiments with narrative
technique.

260   2. Massey in her conclusion suggests that the empowering possibilities of feminine soul are being explored by Adrienne Rich, Mary Daly, Julia Kristeva, and Helene Cixous (163–88).

3. For Jameson, God is the transcendent and personal God of Christianity. For Feuerbach and Eliot, God is a human ideal, the projection of perfect human nature, and for Fuller, God is the universal Spirit within and without.

4. See Paris, 72–113, 128–53; Knoepflmacher, *George Eliot's Early Novels*, 89–127; see also Knoepflmacher, *Religious Humanism*, 24–71; Wiesenfarth, *George Eliot's Mythmaking*, 37–41, 77–95. See also Myers, 18–37, 103–18.

5. Feuerbach sees the loving relationship between the divine Mother and Son as a reflection of the relationship between the human mother and son. The latter are involved in a kind of Oedipal triangle: "[The son] inasmuch as he has not the full, rigorous consciousness of independence which characterises the man, . . . feels himself drawn rather to the mother than to the father. The love of the son to the mother is the first love of the masculine being for the feminine. . . . the first yearning of man towards woman" (71). Feuerbach has no trouble seeing this human mother-son relationship reflected in Godhead—"the Mother is never out of the mind and heart of the Son" (72). But when one takes the father into account, it stretches the imagination to think of this love triangle being divinized as the trinitarian relationship of Father-Son-Mother.

6. After the chapter on the Trinity, the Mother is mentioned only once, as the paradoxical symbol of Christian reverence for both virginity and maternity (Feuerbach, 136–39).

7. On Friedrich Schleiermacher, see Massey, 136–46; on Ernst Renan, see *The Life of Jesus*, 120, 123, 158–59, 175, 202–4.

8. The French feminist critic Luce Irigaray, in "Divine Women" (1987, trans. 1993), uses Feuerbach to show that man has subjectivity and avoids finiteness by creating for himself an ideal, an infinite male God. But woman, lacking a God in her image, is defined by and against man. The Virgin Mother is excluded from the male Trinity of Christianity, and "there is no *woman* God, no female trinity: mother, daughter, spirit" (61–64). This argument is highly suggestive but is based on a partial reading of Feuerbach. As I have shown, the Mother initially is included with the Father and Son in Feuerbach's Trinity, though she soon drops out, evidently because of her identification with the body. Irigaray cites but does not explain Feuerbach's statement that feminine qualities are essential to God, although his masculinist view has interesting parallels to her own feminist essentialism (69). Finally, Irigaray envisions a God defined by and for women—a God that is mother-daughter-spirit, a feminine divine who is defined in relation to the self, not others, and is not dichotomized but a body-soul—but she thinks this God is still to be discovered (57–72). My argument is that a version of this God—Mary, the Virgin Mother of feminism—has already been imagined by several of Feuerbach's contemporaries, the women writers of this study.

9. See, e.g., Auguste Comte, *Catechism of Positive Religion*; Eliot's reviews of R. W. Mackay, *The Progress of the Intellect*, and Peter Von Bohlen, *Introduction to Genesis*, in *Essays*, 27–45, 255–60; and Eliot herself, in *Eliot Letters*, 6:89.

10. See Marx, "Theses on Feuerbach," 69–72; Marx and Engels, *The German Ideology*, esp. ch. 1; *The Holy Family, or Critique of Critical Critique*; Engels, *Ludwig Feuerbach and the Outcome of Classical German Philosophy*.

11. Marx and Engels argue instead for a particularized and historicized understanding of man: "Th[e] sum of productive forces, capitals and forms of social intercourse which every individual and every generation finds already in existence is the real basis of what the philosophers imagined to be the 'substance' and 'essence of man'" (*German Ideology*, 78). Religion, too, is seen as a social product and as responding to changing historical conditions (74–75).

12. Marx and Engels, "Review of G. F. Daumer's *The Religion of the New Age*," *Neue Rheinische Zeitung*, No. 2, 1850, 94–96.

13. See the Eliot critics William Myers, *The Teaching of George Eliot*, esp. 18–37, 103–18; Bernard Paris, *Experiments in Life: George Eliot's Quest for Values*; Suzanne Graver, *George Eliot and Community*; Nancy Paxton, *George Eliot and Herbert Spencer*.

14. Feuerbachian readings of Adam Bede have been suggested by Paris (72–113, 128–53), Knoepflmacher (*George Eliot's Early Novels*, 89–127; *Religious Humanism*, 24–71), and Wiesenfarth (*George Eliot's Mythmaking*, 37–41, 77–95); see also Myers (18–37, 103–18). Feuerbach's feminization of Godhead and its implications for Eliot's Madonna-figures have not been explored, however, with the exception of Elsie Holmes's very brief discussion ("George Eliot's Wesleyan Madonna," 52–59).

15. See Eliot to Emily Davies, 8 Aug. 1868, *Eliot Letters*, 4:468; *Daniel Deronda*, 367; her review "Woman in France: Madame de Sablé" (1854), in *Essays*, ed. Pinney, 53. Feuerbach, 71.

16. Eliot and Jameson had mutual friends in London and met more than once in the mid-1850s, before Eliot wrote *Adam Bede* (e.g., *Eliot Letters*, 8:96). Neither Jameson nor Fuller has been identified as a probable source for *Adam Bede*, although the critics Gillian Beer and Joseph Wiesenfarth have noted the impact of Jameson's work, particularly *Legends of the Madonna*, on two of Eliot's later novels, *Romola* (1862–63) and *Middlemarch* (1871–72). Wiesenfarth also suggests that Eliot was reading and taking notes on Jameson's *Sacred and Legendary Art* (1848) when she was writing her second novel, *The Mill on the Floss*. See Beer, *George Eliot*, 122–24, 157, 164–67, 193; Wiesenfarth, ed., *Writer's Notebook, 1854–1859*, xxiii–xxv; 183–86.

17. Haight, 264; Witemeyer, 21. See also Lewes's enthusiastic description of the *Sistine Madonna* in his 1858 review article "Realism in Art: Recent German Fiction," 271–87. Contra Jameson, Lewes divinizes the Christ-figure but gives Mary, the "real woman," only a "divine mission" (274).

18. Jameson's list of symbols associated with the Virgin is also suggestive for analysis of *Adam Bede*, although less compelling as evidence of specific influence. The Virgin's symbols include the moon, the lily, and the bush that burns without being consumed (*Madonna*, 33–35). In chapter 15 Dinah is shown in her moonlight-flooded bedchamber (Dinah-Madonna-Diana). She is described as having a lily-like face. And she tells Mr. Irwine, the vicar, that women preachers are like the burning bush (meaning that they are regarded only for the flame of their words, 136–37).

262   19. Eliot would have been familiar with the passages I discuss from Fuller, since they surround the ones she cites (see Eliot, *Essays*, ed. Pinney, 199–206).

20. *WNC*, 1855 ed., 23–24. The edition of *WNC* cited in this chapter is the one that Eliot reviewed; see "Margaret Fuller and Mary Wollstonecroft," Pinney, ed., *Essays*, 199, 200 n. 4.

21. For example, Eliot says in a letter to Emily Davies (a founder of Girton College) that biological differences lead to differences in the functions of the sexes; specifically, woman's essential traits—"gentleness, tenderness, possible maternity, . . . affectionateness"—prepare her to have a "special moral influence" (*Eliot Letters*, Aug. 1868, 4:468). See also Eliot's review "Woman in France: Madame de Sablé" (1854): "Under every imaginable social condition, [woman] will necessarily have a class of sensations and emotions—the maternal ones—which must remain unknown to man." In Eliot's view, such psychological differences are the positive consequence of sex differences and will remain even after woman achieves complete moral and intellectual development (*Essays*, ed. Pinney, 53).

22. Gilbert and Gubar, 18–21, 468, 485, 490–501; Christ, 130–40. See also the broader and often cited discussions of the Madonna by Trudgill, 257–76, and Warner, esp. 47, 236–54, 333–39.

23. On Christina Rossetti's treatment of the Virgin Mary and virginity, see Garlick, 105–27; D'Amico, 175–91.

Chapter 8

1. On this point, see especially Felicia Bonaparte, 34–109; Mary Wilson Carpenter, 61–103; David Carroll, 167–200. Although Bardo is most closely associated with the Stoicism, and the misogynism, of the pre-Christian world, his scholarship is possible because of the revival of the Greek language and the influx of manuscripts into Italy from the mid-fifteenth century, after the fall of Constantinople (e.g., *Romola*, 270). Dino, whom Bardo feels his daughter can never replace, fled (as he says) the devil's snares of pagan literature for Christianity (*Romola*, 147–55). He represents the emotional yet austere and radically otherworldly Christianity that was preached by the new mendicant orders of the late Middle Ages, the Franciscans and the Dominicans, and was a penitential response to the losses of the Crusades and the horrors of the plague years (see Jameson, *Monastic Orders*, xxi–xxii; Eliot, entries on monasticism in Wiesenfarth, ed., *Writer's Notebook*, 69–75; Lawrence, 238–65; Mâle, 128–32, 140–63). Tito's role as a Renaissance man is made clear by his Machiavellian diplomatic talents and his response to Ghiberti's doors on the Baptistery at Florence: "These women's figures seem moulded in a different spirit from those starved and staring [Byzantine] saints I spoke of: these heads in high relief speak of a human mind within them. . . . I have heard that your Tuscan sculptors and painters have been studying the antique a little" (*Romola*, 32). But older categorizations are also suggested. Tito is repeatedly likened to Ovid's Bacchus, an appropriate designation, since he is a newcomer to Florence, a hyacinthine-

haired southern Italian of Greek ancestry, as the blue-haired Dionysos was the youngest god and seemed a foreigner in the Olympian pantheon. Tito, moreover, is a figure of Greco-Roman decadence, with a Dionysian capacity for metamorphosis or duplicity (*Romola*, 172–79, 311; Morford and Lenardon, 187, 209–10; Detienne, 4:358–61; Bonnefoy, 1:456–63; Bonaparte, 63–71, 83–85, 143–76).

2. Bardo consoles himself for his loss of sight by having Romola read him a Latin account of Teiresias's being struck blind for seeing Minerva unveiled but thereafter carrying her image in his soul. He does not, however, associate the goddess of wisdom with the tall, proud daughter standing by his chair, instead referring to "the wandering, vagrant propensity of the feminine mind" and "the feeble powers of the feminine body" (*Romola*, 45–49).

3. No assurances from a transcendent God are available to her, "no radiant angel [comes] across the gloom with a clear message," and she instead must accept the stumbling guidance of other human beings, who glimpse, but cannot be, the ideal (*Romola*, 309–10, 366–67, 419–21). Bonaparte, in contrast, calls the heroine a convert, "the bride of Christ and the daughter of the church" (Bonaparte, 178, 181, 191).

4. On Eliot's use of Villari, see Haight, 349–50; Santangelo; Bonaparte, 180–81. On Marchese and Villari's view of Savonarola, see Weinstein, 3–6; Villari, xv–xlvii; Gezari, 86.

5. L. Goldscheider, Foreword to Burckhardt, ix–xi. There are no references to Burckhardt in the *Eliot Letters*, Gordon Haight's biography, or *The George Eliot–George Henry Lewes Library*, William Baker's catalogue of a large part of their holdings.

6. Baker, *George Eliot–George Henry Lewes Library*, no. 1430; see Bonaparte, 181; Carpenter, 70; Gezari, 86.

7. Steinberg, 3–46, 58–105; Vasari, 1:224–31; 2:116–28; *Romola*, 221; Villari, 495–97. Eliot clearly was acquainted with this reading of Savonarola, since she knew Rio's and Jameson's art histories and Vasari's *Lives* (see Bonaparte, 35, 181; *Romola*, 578 n. 80; 598 n. 22). Vasari remains a basic source for information on Renaissance painters.

8. Cook, 1:182, 518–19; 2:234–36. Ruskin's earliest reference to Savonarola seems to be in *Modern Painters*, vol. 2 (1846). Ruskin here contrasts legitimate portraiture, which is idealizing, though also faithful to the model, and illegitimate portraiture, in which artists use their models improperly (a footnoted example suggests Fra Lippo Lippi's use of his mistress) or focus only on the external and even the evil features of a person. One of Ruskin's examples of idealizing portraiture is "portraiture of love," exemplified by Fra Bartolommeo's representation of Savonarola (*Complete Works*, 4:187–91). In a paragraph later deleted from this discussion, Ruskin cites Rio on illegitimate portraiture (4:189 n. 4). Neither Eliot's letters nor Haight's biography specifically mentions her having read *Modern Painters*, Vol. 2, but her 1856 review of *Modern Painters*, Vol. 3, suggests her knowledge of the earlier books, and she quotes passages about portraiture and the ideal in religious art that build on the discussion analyzed above (see *SE*, esp. 367–68, 370–73).

264   9. Eliot's review of *Lectures on Architecture and Painting*, which includes "Pre-Raphaelitism" (*Leader,* 10 June 1854), is reprinted in Wiesenfarth, ed., *Writer's Notebook,* 238–43. While Ruskin does not name Savonarola in "Pre-Raphaelitism," Eliot's knowledge of Vasari, Rio, and Savonarola biography must have made her aware how the prior belonged in Ruskin's historical argument about a change in art ca. 1500. Eliot's reading of Ruskin included his defenses of the Pre-Raphaelite painters in the *Times* (5 and 25 May 1854; see *Eliot Letters* 2:156), and she reviewed several volumes of *Modern Painters.* George Henry Lewes wrote from Florence to John Blackwood, Eliot's usual publisher, on 28 May 1861 (*Eliot Letters,* 3:420).

10. Eliot's language here evokes the descriptions of John the Baptist in the New Testament (e.g., Matthew 3; John 1) and strengthens her initial presentation of Savonarola as a man of integrity.

11. Critics who discuss Savonarola's role in *Romola* at length include Janet Gezari, Bonaparte, Mary Wilson Carpenter, and Gennaro Santangelo. Gezari agrees with neither Villari's nor Karl Meier's reading of Savonarola; she says the prior is not the "architect of Florentine liberty" nor the Protestant reformer, but "a prophet with a compelling imaginative vision of the perfected human community" (Gezari, 87). Santangelo, however, says Eliot's Savonarola is Villari's. In his view, Eliot not only uses Villari's account of Savonarola's life to structure the novel but also follows the biographer (whom Santangelo reads as a rationalist) in differentiating Savonarola's moral message from the unacceptable "medieval" mystical elements of his thought (Santangelo, 118–31). The problem with Santangelo's reading is that Villari's biography is largely a saint's life, whereas Eliot's novel is quite critical, especially in the assigning of blame for Bernardo del Nero's death. In contrast to Gezari and Santangelo, Carpenter argues that Eliot intends Savonarola to be read in Protestant terms, while Bonaparte calls him "a Protestant without knowing it" (Carpenter, 63, 69–71; Bonaparte, 203–4, 226–27). Bonaparte claims that Romola enters her "Protestant period" when she breaks with the prior, and both she and Carpenter read the heroine as the founder of a new humanist or positive church, with Carpenter stressing the feminist values of this new order (Bonaparte, 226–45; Carpenter, 61–103).

12. Burckhardt in his *Civilization of the Renaissance* notes another similarity between the "reformers" of Florence and Geneva: their intrusions into private life (Burckhardt, 294–95).

13. Eliot to Davies, 8 Aug. 1868, *Eliot Letters,* 4:467–68; Eliot to Bodichon, Mar. 1868, 4:425–26; Davies to Bodichon, 20 Nov. 1867, 8:409–10; Eliot to John Morley, 14 May 1867, 8:402–3; Eliot to Mrs. Peter Taylor, 30 May 1867, 4:366; Eliot to [Mrs. Nassau John Senior], 4 Oct. 1869, 5:58.

14. See, e.g., Hester Burton, 48–49; Herstein, 191; Booth, *Greatness Engendered,* 153–57, 191.

15. In her review of Ruskin's lectures (1854), Eliot says the great principles of Protestantism are the obligation to think for oneself, to test the value of traditional opinions, and to submit all beliefs to the test of private judgment (Wiesenfarth, ed.,

Writer's Notebook, 238). See also David Carroll on Romola's "sacred rebellion" and her role as an imitator and interpreter of Savonarola (189–200).

16. Margaret Homans, using Romola's role as Madonna to analyze the recurrent scenes of reading and interpretation, sees the heroine as representing the "faithful, literal, passive transmission" of the Word and thus enacting women's exclusion from language (*Bearing the Word*, 196–97, 205–22). Carpenter reads Romola as rebelling against patriarchy but considers the "feminine values" she represents at the end as unpromising for the future (63, 74, 101–3).

17. Fedele is typical of the Renaissance female humanists described by King and Rabil. This educated woman noted the incompatibility of scholarship and marriage in letters exchanged with Alessandra Scala (who is mentioned briefly in *Romola*), and she was herself married off when she was too old to be a girl genius. Fedele made limited use of her knowledge during the rest of her long life (King and Rabil, 21–26, 70, 126–27; David, 190–91).

18. The negative treatment of scholarly daughters in *Romola* extends in interesting ways to their fathers. Bardo de Bardi might be called childless or barren as a scholar; he loses his son Dino to the Dominicans and regrets never getting another one to be his assistant and inherit his work. He considers Romola an inadequate son-substitute, and the books he hopes will make a name for him—his library, left to Florence—are sold and dispersed by his son-in-law Tito.

19. Gilman (1860–1935) was an American writer and activist. Her feminist credentials include her prolific writings on issues of gender and social reform and her involvement in the American suffrage movement. She and Susan B. Anthony publicly supported Elizabeth Cady Stanton's notorious *Woman's Bible* at the 1896 convention of the united suffrage organizations, but the majority voted to censure this work (Nies, 127–45; Stanton, *Woman's Bible*, xx–xxix, 215–17; Gilman's name was then Stetson).

Gilman, like Eliot, was a proponent of the nineteenth-century evolutionary hypotheses. The similarities of the two writers, while outside the scope of this analysis, can be explained in part by the impact of Herbert Spencer on Eliot's and Gilman's thought and their feminist recastings of evolutionary arguments about women. Eliot's reactions to evolutionary thought are the subject of Paxton's important study *George Eliot and Herbert Spencer* and are examined also in Gillian Beer's *Darwin's Plots*.

20. *Man-Made World*, 201–16, 229. Eliot defines woman's nature somewhat differently than Gilman, emphasizing the "gentleness" and "tenderness" that are characteristics of her heroine in *Romola*; see *Eliot Letters*, 4:366, 467–68. See also Carpenter's discussion of masculine versus feminine values in *Romola* and her pessimistic conclusion (63, 74, 101–3).

21. The identification of Monna Brigida with the Crone or Moon Goddess is strengthened by the name of this goddess among the Celts: Bridget (Leeming and Page, 66–71, 151–54).

22. Eliot read many of Savonarola's writings, including the *Compendium*. See Haight, 350; Bonaparte, 180.

23. Savonarola says in a 1497 sermon on Amos and Zechariah: "[T]hese young men go about saying of this woman and that—Here is a Magdalen, here a Virgin, there a St. John; and then ye paint their faces in the churches, the which is a great profanation of Divine things. Ye painters do very ill. . . . Ye fill the churches with vain things" (Villari, 499). The quotation that follows is from a different translation of the same sermon.

24. Erlanger, 172–3. Erlanger, a modern biographer of Savonarola, suggests that such "reprehensible" paintings, along with nudes, manuscripts, and other "vanities," were consigned to the Florentine bonfires at carnival time.

25. *Romola*, 398. See also Ruskin, as quoted by Eliot in her review of *Modern Painters*, Vol. 3: "[The early religious painters] attempted to express, not the actual fact, but their own enthusiasm about the fact; they covered the Virgin's dress with gold, not with any idea of representing her as she ever was or will be seen, but with a burning desire to show their love for her" (*SE*, 372–73).

26. Karen Chase contrasts Savonarola's private visions with the "visible religion" and "visible need" emphasized in *Romola*. She argues that the visible—associated particularly with public and shared images—is valued in Eliot's novel (Chase, "The Modern Family and the Ancient Image," 312–18).

27. *Romola*, 522–27; *Adam Bede*, 124: "For in those days the keenest bucolic minds felt a whispering awe at the sight of the gentry, such as of old men felt when they stood on tiptoe to watch the gods passing by in tall human shape."

28. *Romola*, 436, 522. Ruskin's description of the Virgins of Fra Angelico and his contemporaries is found in Eliot's review of *Modern Painters*, Vol. 3; see the note above and *SE*, 372–73; Herbert, 258–59. Fra Lippo Lippi's *Madonna and Child, with Two Angels* is in the Uffizi; see *Romola*, 289 n. David Blackbourn, in a nineteenth-century analogy, shows that the familiar features of the Miraculous Medal and the Lady at Lourdes were reproduced in subsequent Marian visions (*Marpingen*, 103–30).

29. Manuel, 149–68, 283–94; Fisch and Goddard, in the introduction to Vico, 56–58, 78. Eliot and Lewes owned a French edition of Vico's works and the *Scienza Nuova* in Italian, and three books by Herder; see Baker, *George Eliot–George Henry Lewes Library*, nos. 2219–20, 1006–8.

30. See Jameson on the Reformers' persecution of unsubmissive, "heretical" women (*Communion of Labor*, 282–83) and on Puritan iconoclasm (*Legends of the Monastic Orders*, 39). Eliot probably knew the first work and definitely read the second.

31. See *Robert Browning's Poetry*, ed. James F. Loucks, 58–59, 74–75, 105–14, 184–90.

32. Mulvey, 438–48; Cherry; Parker and Pollock, 114–19. Lorraine Gamman and Margaret Marshment's collection *The Female Gaze* is an effort to expand and alter the usual male/female dichotomies; see especially the introduction, 1–7.

33. *Middlemarch*, 140; see also Dinah's confrontation of Hetty before her mirror in *Adam Bede*, ch. 15 ("The Two Bed-Chambers"). Celia Brooke, now Lady Chettam, has a similarly exclusive and infantilizing focus on her baby Arthur and is oblivious to her newly widowed sister's feelings: "'Don't be sad, Dodo; kiss baby. What are you brood-

ing over so? . . . . If he [Mr. Casaubon] has been taken away, that is a mercy, and you
ought to be grateful. *We* should not grieve, should we, baby?' said Celia confidentially
to that unconscious centre and poise of the world" (*Middlemarch*, 531, 533).

34. *Middlemarch*, 387, 641. George Eliot's review "Margaret Fuller and Mary
Wollstonecraft," written almost twenty years earlier, seems to contain an outline of this
plot; she points out that, contrary to the prevalent view, an educated wife with opinions of her own will not be as obstinate as "your unreasoning animal, . . . the most un-
manageable of creatures," which if not controlled by force will govern (*SE*, 335). The
offensive description of the wife is a prediction of Eliot's sympathy for Lydgate. For an
application of these theories to *Middlemarch*, see Patricia E. Johnson, 39–40, 46–54.

35. This reading of Dorothea's character is also suggested by the opening chapters, where she tries to spiritualize her sensual response to the bright colors of gems
and plans to give up riding, because she enjoys it too much (*Middlemarch*, 35–36, 40–41,
220–21).

36. Patricia E. Johnson uses the Roman scenes (including this one) to argue that
Eliot in *Middlemarch* challenges not only the power of the male gaze but also the ability
of Western art to represent women (47–53). Johnson's argument does not work as a
general statement of Eliot's practice, however, for the novelist often finds empowering
images of women in Western art, as I have shown. My thanks to Sally Daugherty for
this reference.

37. In Eliot's characterization, Dorothea comes to prefer a tolerant "Broad Church"
Anglicanism to other varieties (such as High Anglicanism, or the Evangelicalism she
seems to have favored when younger): "I have always been thinking of the different
ways in which Christianity is taught, and whenever I find one way that makes it a wider
blessing than any other, I cling to that as the truest—I mean that which takes in the
most good of all kinds, and brings in the most people as sharers in it. It is better to par-
don too much, than to condemn too much" (*Middlemarch*, 537–38; cf. *ODCC*, 202, s.v.
"Broad Church").

38. The quenching of Dorothea's ardor and ambition remains one of the most important topics in *Middlemarch* criticism. Some scholars have criticized Eliot or the novel
as antifeminist for denying the heroine the kind of vocation the author herself enjoyed;
see Austen (549–61) and Edwards (223–38). Others have interpreted the novel as
showing the obstacles to education, freedom, and fulfillment that Victorian women
faced in Dorothea's day and even in Eliot's, forty years later; see Beer (*George Eliot*,
147–99), Graver (in *Approaches to Teaching Eliot's Middlemarch*, ed. Kathleen Blake), and
Blake ("*Middlemarch* and the Woman Question," 49–70). More recently, Elizabeth
Langland has criticized Eliot for failing to represent the important social and domestic
work that middle-class women did perform (though it is not clear if Langland's argument should apply to Dorothea, a member of the landed gentry, whose status is given,
not earned; 183–208). Alison Booth considers the novelist's vacillation between presenting Dorothea as a selfless and anonymous heroine (the feminine norm) and making her truly exceptional and not self-effacing (*Greatness Engendered*, 130–67).

39. Wright, 138–52; Postlethwaite, 197–200. Scott shows that in the novel Eliot

268   both reproduces and questions Comte's Positivist scheme of historical progress from the "theological" and the "metaphysical" eras to the "positive" age (59–66). Miller's as well as Scott's argument can be illustrated by the changing role of the clerical characters from *Romola* to *Middlemarch*. In *Romola*, Savonarola is briefly the priestly and prophetic leader of Florence, and he transforms the city to make it, as he claims, a place where Christ is King. But in *Middlemarch*, as Scott demonstrates, the landed gentry and the clergy have been replaced as leaders in modern secular society by the capitalists and the scientists (62–76). One might add that the clergy as well as the society have been secularized. The rural Anglican clerics in the novel are distinguished from their neighbors only by their greater leisure for hunting or trout fishing, and even Mr. Farebrother, who is praised by all for his sound moral sermons, which reach the working people in his congregations (he is a proof of Eliot's belief that morality need not depend on doctrine or even belief in God), sometimes says he is in the wrong profession. One of only two clergymen (Mr. Casaubon is the other) who has an intellectual life, his passion is for entomology, not for new forms of faith and action. The Evangelicals in the book tend to be mean-spirited hypocrites, with Mr. Bulstrode capable of using his morning devotions to pray for a man's death (*Middlemarch*, 761, 763). Dorothea alone seems to have a steady regard for a God or a good greater than the deity truly worshiped by Middlemarch (money), not subject to the limits of self-centered human desires, and offering hope for a large beneficial life beyond the provincial round. But even she must make her concessions; her first act, when she agrees to marry Will, will be to learn what everything costs.

    40. See also David Carroll on *Middlemarch* (Eliot's "empiricist fable") as a secularized saint's life. Eliot's description of Dorothea as a failed St. Theresa has been discussed by a number of critics, among them Laurence Lerner (249–69), Hilary Fraser ("St. Theresa," 400–11), Kathleen Blake (*"Middlemarch* and the Woman Question," 65–69), and Franklin Court (21–25). What I find interesting, and ironic, about Eliot's comparison is that Dorothea does not fail enough. The heroine makes choices that are the opposite of Theresa's—marriage and a life of scholarly assistance—but her married life becomes a painful parody of the conventual life. Wearing garments of Carmelite white, with a wedding ring as her only ornament, Dorothea lives dead to the world, but in a "catacomb" or "tomb" instead of a religious community (*Middlemarch*, 398; cf. Jameson, *Monastic Orders*, 411–25). She takes vows of obedience and submission, but to one who checks her every impulse with fear and commands cultic belief in his "Scripture," a key to all mythologies (*Middlemarch*, 409–10, 424, 522). She frequently rises in the middle of the night, but to read from the books needed for her husband's research rather than to sing the divine offices; these literary rather than passionate wakings reinforce the impression left by references to Casaubon's "shallow rill" of feeling, that the marriage is celibate (87, 517–19). Dorothea's second marriage, to Will Ladislaw, does not significantly alter the pattern of the first. Although she always associates Will with happiness and receptivity to her ideas and feelings, her decision to marry once again determines all her other choices, as *his* decision does not. And the

minor "channels" her wifely energies run into and the "unvisited tombs" where women like her are buried visually evoke the "catacombs" of her life with Casaubon (894, 896).

41. *Middlemarch*, 50–51, 99, 238, 251–52, 424, 429. When Will tells Dorothea about his political ambitions, she replies, "When we were in Rome, I thought you only cared for poetry and art, and the things that adorn life for us who are well off. But now I know you think about the rest of the world" (586). Joseph Wiesenfarth comes to different conclusions from mine about the same evidence in *Middlemarch*. He sees Dorothea and Will as coming to a sure Ruskinian sense of what is beautiful and good in art and in life ("*Middlemarch*: The Language of Art," 363–77, esp. 370–74).

42. Christina Rossetti, "In an Artist's Studio," lines 9–14. Rossetti here describes the studio of her brother Dante Gabriel and his obsessive relationship with Elizabeth Siddal, his model and later his wife. The poem was written in 1856 but not published until 1896.

43. Hilary Fraser has found new meaning in the figure of St. Theresa by considering Bernini's famous sculpture, which shows the saint in an eroticized moment of spiritual rapture ("St. Theresa," 403–9).

44. See Wiesenfarth, "*Middlemarch*: The Language of Art," 363–77; Ritschin, 1121–32; cf. Patricia Johnson, 46–47; 51–52.

45. H. Fraser reaches similar conclusions ("St. Theresa," 403–9).

Jill Matus, in her analysis of Dorothea as a Madonna-figure, also focuses on the use of art to characterize the heroine and on the treatment of her sexuality (esp. 287, 292–3, 297). Eliot, according to Matus, is interested in the category of "madonna" as combining two or three of the following: motherhood, sexuality, and saintliness. Dorothea pays the penalty of trying to balance all three, her "high" and her "common" yearnings; she experiences sexual fulfillment and motherhood, but there are gendered restraints on her beneficial actions. Matus provides a social explanation of what I try to account for in religious terms.

Chapter 9

1. *Eliot Letters*, 15 Nov. 1857, 2:403. The context is a statement appearing in two of Bray's books (*Christianity and Infidelity* [1857] and *The Philosophy of Necessity* [1841]) that in Eliot's view makes the disregard of individuals praiseworthy.

2. On Eliot and Lewes's knowledge of Müller, see *Eliot Letters*, 4:8, 22 (1862); Haight, 465 (an 1873 meeting with Müller), 546. Müller is quoted by Capps, 70. According to Capps, the context for Müller's statement, like Eliot's, is evolutionary thought; Müller disagreed with Comte's account of the evolution of religion, particularly Comte's emphasis on original fetishism (Capps, 68–71).

3. Eliot, for example, often mentions Comte's groundbreaking *Cours de Philosophie Positive*, which Lewes wrote a book about.

4. Mill continues: "Whoever regards all events as parts of a constant order, each one being the invariable consequent of some antecedent condition, or combination of conditions, accepts fully the Positive mode of thought: whether he acknowledges or

270   not an universal antecedent on which the whole system of nature was originally consequent, and whether that universal antecedent is conceived as an Intelligence or not"
(*Auguste Comte and Positivism*, 14–15).

    5. *Spanish Gypsy*, 69, 86–87. All references to *The Spanish Gypsy* are to page num-
ber; the cited edition of the poem does not give line numbers.

    6. *Romola*, 231–32, 305; *The Mill on the Floss*, 363; *Adam Bede*, 83–84, 576.

    7. Eliot's own statements of the theory, which have fetishism preceding polythe-
ism, are Comtean (e.g., *SE*, 360). See her reviews of R. W. Mackay, *The Progress of the
Intellect;* W. R. Greg, *The Creed of Christendom;* and Peter Von Bohlen, *Introduction to Genesis,*
in *SE*, 268–96, 358–62, esp. 268–69, 288–89, 360; Manuel, e.g., 15–53, 168–83;
Comte.

    8. In Lamarck's theory, the giraffe lengthens its neck by reaching for high leaves,
and this exercise benefits its offspring. In the theory of natural selection developed by
Darwin, the giraffe does not develop and pass down a longer neck; rather, longer-
necked giraffes survive and breed. Lamarck developed but did not invent the idea of
the inheritance of acquired characteristics (Jordanova, 2, 54–55, 100; Richard W.
Burckhardt, 170–85, esp. 179).

    9. See L. J. Jordanova on the social and cultural applications of Lamarck's views,
applications that should not be attributed to Lamarck himself (100–113). Philip Smith
and Michael Helfand, in their valuable survey of Oxford intellectual life during the
1870s (the decade of *Daniel Deronda*), point out the currency of such ideas among Eliot's
peers, Ruskin and W. K. Clifford as well as Spencer (*Oscar Wilde's Oxford Notebooks*,
10–17, 27–34); I am indebted to Joseph Gardner for this reference. Smith and Helfand
mention claims for the hereditary transmission of acquired mental, moral, and cultural
traits, which included, for Ruskin, an aesthetic sense (13).

    While Spencer argued for the hereditary basis of much of culture (see Peel,
142–46; Smith and Helfand, 27–29), he was not keenly interested in religion and does
not seem to have been a source for Eliot's Lamarckian views of faith. An early biographer, J. Arthur Thomson, says that Spencer easily sloughed off his childhood Evangelicalism and therefore had no impetus to speculate on faith (217–73). If, as Thomson
suggests, religious philosophies are shaped by individual experience, Spencer would be
unlikely to argue, with Eliot, that faith is an inheritance felt in blood and bone.
Spencer's scattered statements on religion are summarized in the following works: his
theory of the Unknowable, Kennedy, 35–39; Thomson, 270–71; ancestor worship,
Kennedy, 95–100; reassessments of religious institutions, Spencer, *Autobiography*, 2:466–
71; Thomson, 274–75.

    W. K. Clifford, a young Oxford scientist, was a friend and correspondent of Eliot
and reviewed the first volume of Lewes's *Problems of Life and Mind* (Haight, 463, 524–25).
In his *Lectures and Essays*, Clifford called piety, or the reflexive tendency to put the welfare of the tribe before that of the self, an inherited trait (Clifford, 2:111–12; Smith and
Helfand, 29–32). Even Lewes, while not himself accepting a Lamarckian interpretation

of the moral sense, warned against setting limits, at such an early stage in investiga-
tions, on what is attributable to heredity (*Problems of Life and Mind*, 1:151–52).

10. Himmelfarb, 175–83, 317–27, 362–70, 433–34.

11. Born in 1855, Freud received his university and medical education in the 1870s
and early 1880s (*The Spanish Gypsy* was published in 1868, *Daniel Deronda* in 1876). Gay
cites letters from the 1920s.

12. Because we have seen religious identity used as the basis for ethnic cleansing
by the Nazis in World War II and more recently in the Balkans, we tend to cringe at
statements about the determining force of "blood" and being Jewish "by birth" (which
are made by characters in Eliot's *The Spanish Gypsy*). But these Lamarckian arguments in
fact do not have clear parallels in Hitler's thought. In his biography *The Life and Death of
Adolf Hitler*, Robert Payne quotes a 1919 letter which he says contains almost all of
Hitler's ideas about the Jews. In this letter, Hitler argues that the Jews are "a race, not
a religious community," and notes that not all Jews practice "the Mosaic religion"; in
other words, for Hitler Jewish identity was a matter of "inbreeding" and distinct from
the Jewish religion (Payne, 130–31). Historian Andrew Lees has a similar reading of
Hitler: "For Hitler, Judaism was not essential to Jewishness, inasmuch as converting
from Judaism to Christianity (as many German Jews had done and were doing during
his lifetime) did not in his eyes relieve the convert of the burden of being '*der ewige Jude*'
(the eternal Jew). In addition, I do not think of Hitler as being indebted to Lamarck.
The emphasis on the passing on of acquired characteristics tends to run counter to the
racist emphasis on the genetic deep-seatedness of racial characteristics" (personal com-
munication).

To complicate matters, the claim that one is *born* into a particular religion (as Freud
suggests) does have resonance in modern Judaism; it continues to be debated in discussions of intermarriage and conversion. The point here is that we should be careful
about reading twentieth-century religious and political alignments back into nineteenth-
century debates. Social Darwinism provides an analogous example of the political flu-
idity of evolutionary theories. Darwinian analyses of society were used by Charlotte
Perkins Gilman to advance her feminist and socialist agenda as well as by Herbert
Spencer's American followers to promote their capitalist and imperialist views (Rossi,
566–98; Hofstadter, 4–41).

13. Eliot's acceptance of the theory of the progress of religion explains statements
such as "[T]he Hebrew Scriptures . . . exhibit a progress from degrading to enlightened
views of Divine nature and government," although there is her openly bigoted
"Everything *specifically* Jewish is of a low grade." *Eliot Letters*, 6–8 Nov. 1838, 1:13; review
of Mackay, *The Progress of the Intellect* (1850), in *SE*, 283; *Eliot Letters*, [11 Feb. 1848],
1:246–47. See also Feuerbach, ch. 11 ("The Significance of the Creation in Judaism");
Eliot's stated agreement with Feuerbach has been noted.

14. See, e.g., *Eliot Letters*, 6 Dec. 1859, 3:230–31, and her sympathetic depiction of
Anglicanism and Evangelicalism in *Scenes of Clerical Life* (1856–57).

15. Paxton, 3–42, 198–227; G. Levine, 1–23, 238–72; Semmel, esp. 3–15. Similarly, Graver discusses Comte, Spencer, and Darwin, with little attention to Lamarck.

16. Eliot, "Notes on the Spanish Gypsy and Tragedy in General," from John Walter Cross, *George Eliot's Life*, reprinted in *The Spanish Gypsy*, 13–14.

17. "The *Antigone* and Its Moral," in *SE*, 363–66.

18. "Geraldine Jewsbury's *Constance Herbert*" (1855), review in *SE*, 321.

19. *Spanish Gypsy*, 21, 25. Eliot's liking for *Aurora Leigh* is made obvious by the first image. Don Silva picks up this representation of Spain as mother ("Who nourished me on her expectant breast") in his last speech, where he vows to die nobly for his country rather than take his own life (279).

20. Most critics of *The Spanish Gypsy* have shown that Eliot's discussion of Titian's *Annunciation* is central to elucidation of the poem, and most have found problems with the characterization and fate of Fedalma. See Krasner, 55–73; Redinger, 465–67; Neufeldt, 44, 47–53; Waxman, 115–26 (she argues that gypsies served as heroes to the Victorians but sees Fedalma as an ambiguous model); but cf. Marks, 186–90. Deborah Nord, however, has the only extended discussion of racial characteristics in the poem. She focuses on Charlotte and Emily Bronte as well as Eliot and shows how they made gypsies a symbol of "aberrant femininity," using them to explore their own anomalous situations as woman writers (189–93, 206–7). Nord, though, defines "race" as "ethnicity" and stresses kinship in these texts as more a matter of psychological than biological affinity (194–202). But if we instead read "race" in terms used by Eliot and other Victorians, as indicating physical *and* cultural characteristics that were thought to be inherited, we are able to see the links between her late writings and nineteenth-century Lamarckian theories.

21. Many critics of *Daniel Deronda* have debated a question first raised by Stephen Marcus (212 n.): since Daniel was a boy born into an observant family, he must have been circumcised; why, then, does he not look down and discover he is a Jew? K. M. Newton argues that at the time the novel is set, circumcision was not always a sign of Jewish identity; boys were also circumcised because of concerns about health and sexual practices (313–27, esp. 315). Mary Wilson Carpenter says, "Just as the facts of Judaism probably meant little to Deronda until reinterpreted by Mordecai, so the slightly variant appearance of his penis might have had little importance in the absence of its interpretation as a religious symbol" (149). Cynthia Chase considers the circumcision the crucial absent signifier of the test, attributing its excision to embarrassment —"For many of Eliot's contemporary readers, being a Jew, like having sexual organs, was something to which as little attention as possible should be called" (215–27).

The problem I find with this debate is that it focuses on what is missing from the text—any mention of circumcision—and not on what is there: the numerous references to Daniel's intimations of his Jewish birth. Eliot evidently wishes the emphasis to be on religious identity as determined by internal and hereditary disposition and conscious commitment rather than by external characteristics. Also, as in *The Spanish Gypsy*, the

author presents religion as a racial inheritance, and of course circumcision is not an inherited trait. It is, rather, a *sign* that one belongs to a particular community, and not the
criterion for membership. It is possible that Eliot does not mention circumcision
(though her knowledge of the Hebrew Bible and her historical research would mean
she was well aware of the practice) because that would draw attention away from her
main concern, religion as inheritance. The circumcision is neither inherited nor transmitted from father to son.

22. *Daniel Deronda*, 457; similarly, *Spanish Gypsy*, 21, 25–26, 279.

23. Zimmerman, "'The Mother's History,'" 81–94; "George Eliot and Feminism,"
231–37; Beer, *George Eliot*, 200–16; Paxton, 198–227; Gallagher, 39–62.

24. The artist Hans Meyrick goes a step farther, preferring to represent Mirah as
Berenice, the mistress of Roman leaders and the apostate betrayer of her people.
Mirah's chastity and religious commitment keep her from Hans; Berenice is wholly pos-
sessable.

25. See Hanks and Hodge, *A Dictionary of First Names* (1990), s.v. "Mira"; Yonge,
History of Christian Names (1884; rpt. 1966), 442–43.

26. The religious scholar Judith Plaskow, in her essay "Anti-Judaism in Feminist
Christian Interpretation," sees similar problems in treating Judaism as the "prologue" to
Christianity: "Insofar as Judaism continues to exist, it is only an empty relic, because
God's promises to Israel have been transferred to the church as the new elect" (Plaskow,
119; she builds on the work of Katharina von Kellenbach).

Conclusion

1. Jameson's successor as a writer on the Madonna might be said to be the historian Henry Adams, author of *Mont Saint Michel and Chartres* (1904) and "The Dynamo and
the Virgin" (from *The Education of Henry Adams*, 1907). But while Adams, like Jameson,
recognizes the power of the Virgin, he sees that power as belonging to a past age of
faith. He is inclined instead to worship the Dynamo (generator), which he sees on display at the Great Exposition of 1900 in Paris (*Education*, 361–62). In his analysis of the
cathedral at Chartres, which is dedicated to the Virgin, his aesthetic fascination and intellectual curiosity are mixed with amusement at the childishness of an earlier age (e.g.,
Chartres, 87–88). Jameson, in contrast, contemplates with religious emotion and awe the
images of Mary, assimilates them to her Anglican faith, and appropriates them for a
newer creed, feminism. One could hardly ask for better examples of the shift from
earnest Victorian belief to the skepticism and irreverence of the modern age.

2. Some scholars are, however, addressing this concern by producing the editions
that can foster such studies. See *In Our Own Voices: Four Centuries of American Women's
Religious Writing*, ed. Rosemary Radford Ruether and Rosemary Skinner Keller, and the
Schomburg edition of black women's *Spiritual Narratives*. See also the essay collection
Women's Theology in Nineteenth-Century Britain, ed. Julie Melnyk.

Bibliography

Adams, Henry. *The Education of Henry Adams* (1907). Harmondsworth, England: Penguin Classics, 1995.

————. *Mont Saint Michel and Chartres* (1904). Harmondsworth, England: Penguin Classics, 1986.

Ahlstrom, Sydney. *A Religious History of the American People.* New Haven and London: Yale University Press, 1972.

Anthony, Susan B., and Ida H. Harper, eds. *History of Woman Suffrage,* Vol. 4. New York: Arno Press and the New York Times, 1969.

Arnstein, Walter. *Protestant versus Catholic in Mid-Victorian England: Mr. Newdegate and the Nuns.* Columbia and London: University of Missouri Press, 1982.

Attwater, Donald. *The Penguin Dictionary of Saints.* Harmondsworth, England: Penguin, 1965, rpt. 1978.

Auerbach, Nina. *Woman and the Demon: The Life of a Victorian Myth.* Cambridge, Mass.: Harvard University Press, 1982.

Austen, Zelda. "Why Feminist Critics Are Angry with George Eliot." *College English* 37 (1976): 549–61.

Bacon, Margaret Hope. *Valiant Friend: The Life of Lucretia Mott.* New York: Walker, 1980.

Baker, William. *George Eliot and Judaism.* Salzburg: Institut für Englische Sprache und Literatur, Universität Salzburg, 1975.

————. *The George Eliot–George Henry Lewes Library: An Annotated Catalogue.* New York: Garland, 1977.

Baker-Fletcher, Karen. "Anna Julia Cooper and Sojourner Truth: Two Nineteenth-Century Black Feminist Interpreters of Scripture." In *Searching the Scriptures,* ed. Elisabeth Schüssler Fiorenza; vol. 1, *A Feminist Introduction,* 41–51. New York: Crossroad, 1993.

Baring, Anne, and Jules Cashford. *The Myth of the Goddess.* London: Viking Arkana, 1991.

Beer, Gillian. *Darwin's Plots.* London: Routledge and Kegan Paul, Ark Edition, 1985.

————. *George Eliot.* Bloomington: Indiana University Press, 1986.

276   Berg, Martha L., and Alice de V. Perry. "'The Impulses of Human Nature': Margaret Fuller's Journal from June through October 1844." *Proceedings of the Massachusetts Historical Society* 102 (1990): 38–126.

Blackbourn, David. *Marpingen: Apparitions of the Virgin Mary in a Nineteenth-Century German Village.* New York: Vintage, 1995.

Blake, Kathleen. "*Middlemarch* and the Woman Question." *George Eliot's Middlemarch*, ed. Harold Bloom, 49–70. Modern Critical Interpretations. New York: Chelsea House, 1987.

———, ed. *Approaches to Teaching George Eliot's Middlemarch.* New York: Modern Language Association of America, 1990.

Blanchard, Paula. *Margaret Fuller: From Transcendentalism to Revolution.* Radcliffe Biographies Series. New York: Dell; A Merloyd Lawrence Book, 1978.

Bodichon, Barbara Leigh Smith. *Women and Work* (1857). Excerpts in Candida Lacey, *Barbara Leigh Smith Bodichon and the Langham Place Group*, 36–73. Women's Source Library. New York and London: Routledge and Kegan Paul, 1987.

Bolt, Christine. *The Women's Movements in the United States and Britain from the 1790s to the 1920s.* Amherst: University of Massachusetts Press, 1993.

Bonaparte, Felicia. *The Triptych and the Cross.* New York: New York University Press, 1979.

Bonnefoy, Yves, ed. *Mythologies.* 2 vols. Chicago: University of Chicago Press, 1991.

Booth, Alison. *Greatness Engendered: George Eliot and Virginia Woolf.* Reading Women Writing series. Ithaca, N.Y.: Cornell University Press, 1992.

———. "Illustrious Company: Victoria among Other Women in Anglo-American Role Model Anthologies." In *Remaking Queen Victoria*, ed. Margaret Homans and Adrienne Munich, 59–78. Cambridge: Cambridge University Press, 1997.

Bossy, John. *The English Catholic Community 1570–1850.* New York: Oxford University Press, 1976.

Brecht, Martin. *Martin Luther: His Road to Reformation, 1483–1521.* 2 vols. Trans. James Schaaf. Philadelphia: Fortress Press, 1985.

Burckhardt, Jacob. *The Civilization of the Renaissance in Italy* (1860). Trans. L. Goldscheider. London: Phaidon Press, 1944.

Burckhardt, Richard W., Jr. *The Spirit of System: Lamarck and Evolutionary Biology.* Cambridge, Mass.: Harvard University Press, 1995.

Burton, Hester. *Barbara Bodichon.* London: John Murray, 1949.

Buss, Helen M. "Anna Jameson's *Winter Studies and Summer Rambles in Canada* as Epistolary Dijournal." In *Essays on Life Writing: From Genre to Critical Practice*, ed. Marlene Kadar. Toronto: University of Toronto Press, 1992.

Bynum, Caroline. *Jesus as Mother: Studies in the Spirituality of the High Middle Ages.* Berkeley and Los Angeles: University of California Press, 1982.

Caine, Barbara. *Victorian Feminists.* Oxford: Oxford University Press, 1992.

Capper, Charles. *Margaret Fuller: An American Romantic Life.* Vol. 1, *The Private Years.* Oxford: Oxford University Press, 1992.

Capps, Walter H. *Religious Studies: The Making of a Discipline*. Minneapolis: Fortress Press, 277 1995.

Carlyle, Thomas. *On Heroes, Hero-Worship, & the Heroic in History*. Ed. Michael K. Goldberg et al. Berkeley and Los Angeles: University of California Press, 1993.

———. *Past and Present* (1843). Ed. Richard Altick. New York: New York University Press, *The Gotham Library*, 1965.

Carpenter, Mary Wilson. *George Eliot and the Landscape of Time: Narrative Form and Protestant Apocalyptic History*. Chapel Hill: University of North Carolina Press, 1986.

Carr, Cornelia. *Harriet Hosmer: Letters and Memories*. New York: Moffat, Yard and Co., 1912.

Carroll, David. *George Eliot and the Conflict of Interpretations*. Cambridge, England: Cambridge University Press, 1992.

Chadwick, Owen. *The Victorian Church*. Part 1. New York: Oxford University Press, 1966.

Chadwick, Whitney. *Women, Art, and Society*. World of Art Series. London and New York: Thames and Hudson, Ltd., 1990.

Champneys, Basil. *Memoirs and Correspondence of Coventry Patmore*. 2 vols. London: George Bell and Sons, 1900.

Channing, William Ellery. *The Works of William Ellery Channing*. Ed. William Henry Channing. Boston: American Unitarian Association, 1896.

Chase, Cynthia. "The Decomposition of the Elephants: Double-Reading *Daniel Deronda*." *PMLA* 93 (1978): 215–27.

Chase, Karen. "The Modern Family and the Ancient Image in *Romola*." *Dickens Studies Annual* 14 (1985): 303–26.

Cherry, Deborah. *Painting Women: Victorian Women Artists*. London and New York: Routledge, 1993.

Chevigny, Bell Gale. *The Woman and the Myth: Margaret Fuller's Life and Writings*. Old Westbury, N.Y.: Feminist Press, 1976.

Christ, Carol T. "Aggression and Providential Death in George Eliot's Fiction." *Novel* 9 (winter 1976): 130–40.

Clark, Kenneth. *The Gothic Revival*. New York: Humanities Press, 1970.

Clifford, William Kingdon. *Lectures and Essays*. Ed. Leslie Stephen and Frederick Pollock. 2 vols. London: Macmillan and Co., 1879.

Clinton, Catherine. *The Other Civil War: American Women in the Nineteenth Century*. New York: Hill and Wang, 1984.

Cobbe, Frances Power. "What Shall We Do with Our Old Maids?" *Frazer's Magazine*, November 1862. In Candida Lacey, *Barbara Leigh Smith Bodichon and the Langham Place Group*, 354–77. Women's Source Library. New York and London: Routledge and Kegan Paul, 1987.

Colley, Linda. *Britons: Forging the Nation, 1707–1837*. New Haven: Yale University Press, 1992.

Comte, Auguste. *Catechism of Positive Religion*. Trans. Richard Congreve. London: Trubner, 1883.

278   Connolly, S. J. "Aftermath and Adjustment." In *A New History of Ireland*, ed. W. E. Vaughan, 5:1–23. Oxford: Clarendon Press, 1989.

Conrad, Susan. *Perish the Thought: Intellectual Women in Romantic America, 1830–1860.* New York: Oxford University Press, 1976.

Cook, E. T. *Life of John Ruskin.* 2 vols. London: George Allen, 1911.

Cott, Nancy. "A Comment on Karen Offen's 'Defining Feminism: A Comparative Historical Approach.'" *Signs* 15/1 (autumn 1989): 203–5.

———. *The Grounding of Modern Feminism.* New Haven and London: Yale University Press, 1987.

Court, Franklin. "The Image of St. Theresa in *Middlemarch* and Positive Ethics." *Victorian Newsletter* 63 (1983): 21–25.

Cross, John Walter. *George Eliot's Life as Related in Her Letters and Journals.* 1885. Reprint, New York: AMS Press, 1970.

Cunneen, Sally. *In Search of Mary: The Woman and the Symbol.* New York: Ballantine Books, 1996.

Dall, Caroline Healey. *Margaret and Her Friends.* 1895. Reprint, New York: Arno Press, 1972.

Daly, Mary. *Beyond God the Father.* Boston: Beacon Press, 1973.

———. *Gyn/ecology.* Boston: Beacon Press, 1978.

D'Amico, Diane. "Eve, Mary, and Mary Magdalene: Christina Rossetti's Feminine Triptych." In *The Achievement of Christina Rossetti*, ed. David A. Kent, 175–91. Ithaca and London: Cornell University Press, 1987.

David, Deirdre. *Intellectual Women and Victorian Patriarchy.* Ithaca, N.Y.: Cornell University Press, 1987.

Deiss, Joseph Jay. *The Roman Years of Margaret Fuller.* New York: Thomas J. Crowell Co., 1969.

De Jong, Mary. "*Romola*—A Bildungsroman for Feminists?" *South Atlantic Review* 49, no. 4 (1984): 75–90.

Desmet, Christy. "'Intercepting the Dew-Drop': Female Readers and Readings in Anna Jameson's Shakespearean Criticism." In *Women's Re-Visions of Shakespeare*, ed. Marianne Novy and Carol Neely. Urbana: University of Illinois Press, 1990.

Detienne, Marcel. "Dionysos." In *Encyclopedia of Religion*, ed. Mircea Eliade, 4:358–61. New York: Macmillan, 1987.

Donovan, Josephine. *Feminist Theory: The Intellectual Traditions of American Feminism.* New York: Continuum, 1990.

Douglas, Ann. *The Feminization of American Culture.* New York: Knopf, 1978.

DuBois, Ellen Carol. "A Comment on Karen Offen's 'Defining Feminism: A Comparative Historical Approach.'" *Signs* 15 (autumn 1989): 195–97.

DuBois, Ellen Carol, ed. *The Elizabeth Cady Stanton–Susan B. Anthony Reader.* Boston: Northeastern University Press, 1992.

Eagles, John. Review of *Legends of the Madonna. Blackwood's Edinburgh Magazine* (American edition) 74 (July 1853): 23–38.

————. Review of *Legends of the Monastic Orders. Blackwood's Edinburgh Magazine* (American 279 edition) 69 (Mar. 1851): 305–321.

————. Review of *The Poetry of Sacred and Legendary Art. Blackwood's Edinburgh Magazine* (American edition) 65 (Feb. 1849): 175–89.

Edwards, Lee. "Women, Energy, and *Middlemarch.*" *Massachusetts Review* 13 (1972): 223–38.

Eichner, Hans. *Friedrich Schlegel.* Twayne's World Authors Series, 98. New York: Twayne Publishers, Inc., 1970.

Eliot, George. *Adam Bede* (1859). Harmondsworth, England: Penguin, 1980.

————. *Daniel Deronda* (1876). New York: Oxford University Press, World's Classics, 1984.

————. *Essays of George Eliot.* Ed. Thomas Pinney. New York: Columbia University Press, 1963.

————. *The George Eliot Letters.* Ed. Gordon Haight. 9 vols. New Haven, Conn.: Yale University Press, 1954–1978.

————. *Middlemarch* (1871–72). Harmondsworth, England: Penguin, 1985.

————. *The Mill on the Floss* (1860). Harmondsworth, England: Penguin, 1979.

————. *Romola* (1862–63). New York: Oxford University Press, World's Classics, 1994.

————. *Selected Essays, Poems and Other Writings.* Ed. A. S. Byatt and Nicholas Warren. London and Harmondsworth: Penguin Classics, 1990.

————. *The Spanish Gypsy* (1868–69). In *George Eliot's Works: Miscellaneous Essays and Complete Poems.* New York: The Hovendon Co., 1885.

Ellis, Sarah Stickney. *The Women of England* (1838). Philadelphia: Herman Hooker, 1841.

Ellison, Julie. *Delicate Subjects: Romanticism, Gender, and the Ethics of Understanding.* Ithaca, N.Y.: Cornell University Press, 1990.

Emerson, Ralph Waldo. *Collected Works of Ralph Waldo Emerson.* Ed. Robert E. Spiller and Alfred R. Ferguson. Vol. 1. Cambridge, Mass: Harvard University Press, 1971.

————. *The Complete Sermons of Ralph Waldo Emerson.* Ed. Albert J. von Frank et al. Columbia: University of Missouri Press, 1989–1992. 4 vols.

————. *Emerson in His Journals.* Ed. Joel Porte. Cambridge, Mass: Harvard University Press, 1982.

————. *The Letters of Ralph Waldo Emerson.* Ed. Ralph R. Rusk and Eleanor M. Tilton. 8 vols. New York: Columbia University Press, 1939–1991.

Engels, Friedrich. *Ludwig Feuerbach and the Outcome of Classical German Philosophy.* Trans. L. Rudas. New York: International Publishers, 1934.

Engelsman, Joan Chamberlain. *The Feminine Dimension of the Divine.* Wilmette, Ill. Chiron Publications, 1987.

The English Woman's Journal, April 1860.

Erlanger, Rachel. *The Unarmed Prophet: Savonarola in Florence.* New York: McGraw-Hill Book Co., 1988.

Ernstrom, Adele M. "Anna Jameson and George Eliot." *Racar, Revue d'Art Canadienne/ Canadian Art Review* 20 (1993): 72–82.

280   Erskine, Beatrice (Mrs. Steuart), ed. *Anna Jameson: Letters & Friendships (1812–1860)*. London: T. Fisher Unwin, Ltd., 1916.

Evans, Joan. *John Ruskin*. 1952. Reprint, New York: Haskell House, 1970.

Feuerbach, Ludwig. *The Essence of Christianity* (1841). Trans. George Eliot (1854). Harper Torchbooks. New York: Harper and Row, 1957.

Fife, Robert H. *Revolt of Martin Luther*. New York: Columbia University Press, 1957.

Fisher, Philip. *Making Up Society: The Novels of George Eliot*. Pittsburgh: University of Pittsburgh Press, 1981.

Franchot, Jenny. "Invisible Domains: Religion and American Literary Studies." *American Literature* 67 (1995): 833–42.

Fraser, Hilary. "St. Theresa, St. Dorothea, and Miss Brooke in *Middlemarch*." *Nineteenth-Century Fiction* 40 (1986): 400–11.

———. *The Victorians and Renaissance Italy*. Oxford, England: Blackwell, 1992.

Fraser, Wayne. *The Dominion of Women. The Personal and Political in Canadian Women's Literature*. New York: Greenwood, 1991.

Frawley, Maria. "The Editor as Advocate: Emily Faithfull and *The Victoria Magazine*." *Victorian Periodicals Review* 31, no. 1 (1998): 87–104.

Frei, Hans. *The Eclipse of Biblical Narrative: A Study in Eighteenth and Nineteenth Century Hermeneutics*. New Haven, Conn.: Yale University Press, 1974.

Friewald, Bina. "'Femininely Speaking': Anna Jameson's *Winter Studies and Summer Rambles in Canada*." In *A Mazing Space: Writing Canadian Women Writing*, ed. Shirley Neuman and Smaro Kamboureli. Edmonton, Alberta: Longspoon, 1986.

Fuller, Margaret. "The Athenaeum Exhibition of Painting and Sculpture." *Dial* 1 (Oct. 1840): 260–63.

———. *The Essential Margaret Fuller*. Ed. Jeffrey Steele. New Brunswick, N.J.: Rutgers University Press, 1992.

———. *The Letters of Margaret Fuller*. Ed. Robert Hudspeth. 5 vols. Ithaca, N.Y.: Cornell University Press, 1983–1988.

———. *Margaret Fuller: Essays on American Life and Letters*. Ed. Joel Myerson. New Haven, Conn.: College and University Press, 1978.

———. "Menzel's View of Goethe." *Dial* 1 (Jan. 1841): 340–47.

———. *Papers on Literature and Art*. 1846. Reprint, New York: AMS Press, 1972.

———. *"These Sad But Glorious Days": Dispatches from Europe, 1846–1850*. Ed. Larry J. Reynolds and Susan Belasco Smith. New Haven, Conn: Yale University Press, 1991.

———. *Woman in the Nineteenth Century*. 1855 ed. Introduction by Bernard Rosenthal. New York: Norton, 1971.

———. *Woman in the Nineteenth Century*. 1845 ed. In *The Essential Margaret Fuller*.

Gallagher, Catherine. "George Eliot and *Daniel Deronda*: The Prostitute and the Jewish Question." In *Sex, Politics, and Science*, ed. Ruth Yeazell, 39–62. English Institute Studies 10. Baltimore: Johns Hopkins University Press, 1986.

Gamman, Lorraine, and Margaret Marshment. *The Female Gaze*. Seattle: The Real Comet Press, 1989.

Garber, Marjorie. "Spare Parts: The Surgical Construction of Gender." In *The Gay and Lesbian Studies Reader*, ed. Henry Abelove, Michele Aina Barale, and David Halperin, 321–36. New York and London: Routledge, 1993.

Garlick, Barbara. "The Frozen Fountain: Christina Rossetti, the Virgin Model, and Youthful Pre-Raphaelitism." In *Virginal Sexuality and Textuality in Victorian Literature*, ed. Lloyd Davis, 105–27. Albany: State University of New York Press, 1993.

Gaskell, Elizabeth. *Mary Barton* (1848). Harmondsworth, England: Penguin, 1982.

Gatta, John. *American Madonna: Images of the Divine Woman in Literary Culture*. New York: Oxford University Press, 1997.

Gay, Peter. *Freud: A Life for Our Time*. New York: W. W. Norton, 1988.

Gerry, Thomas. "'I Am Translated': Anna Jameson's *Sketches* and *Winter Studies and Summer Rambles in Canada*." *Journal of Canadian Studies* 25 (winter 1990–91): 34–49.

Gezari, Janet K. "*Romola* and the Myth of Apocalypse." In *George Eliot: Centenary Essays and an Unpublished Fragment*, ed. Anne Smith, 77–102. Totowa, N.J.: Barnes and Noble, 1980.

Gilbert, Sandra, and Susan Gubar. *The Madwoman in the Attic*. New Haven, Conn.: Yale University Press, 1979.

Gilley, Sheridan. "Victorian Feminism and Catholic Art: The Case of Mrs. Jameson." In *The Church and the Arts*, ed. Diana Wood, 381–91. Oxford: Blackwell, 1992.

Gilman, Charlotte Perkins. *Herland* (1915). New York: Pantheon, 1979.

———. *The Man-Made World* (1911). In *The Yellow Wallpaper and Other Writings*, ed. Lynne Sharon Schwartz, 201–40. New York: Bantam Books, 1989.

Gimbutas, Marija. *The Language of the Goddess*. San Francisco: Harper and Row, 1989.

Graef, Hilda. *Mary: A History of Doctrine and Devotion*. Reprint (2 vols. in 1), London: Sheed and Ward, 1994.

Graver, Suzanne. *George Eliot and Community*. Berkeley and Los Angeles: University of California Press, 1984.

Green, William Scott. "Religion within the Limits." *Academe* (Nov.–Dec. 1996): 24–28.

Grimké, Sarah. *Letters on the Equality of the Sexes and Other Essays*. Ed. Elizabeth Ann Bartlett. New Haven and London: Yale University Press, 1988.

Grimké, Sarah, and Angelina Grimké. *The Public Years of Sarah and Angelina Grimké: Selected Writings, 1835–1839*. Ed. Larry Ceplair. New York: Columbia University Press, 1989.

Grisar, Hartmann. *Martin Luther: His Life and Work*. Trans. Frank Eble. New York: AMS Press, 1971.

Habich, Robert D. "Margaret Fuller's Journal for October 1842." *Harvard Library Bulletin* 33 (summer 1985): 280–91.

Haight, Gordon. *George Eliot*. New York: Penguin, 1985.

Hamington, Maurice. *Hail Mary? The Struggle for Ultimate Womanhood in Catholicism*. New York: Routledge, 1995.

Handlin, Oscar. *Boston's Immigrants, 1790–1880*. Cambridge, Mass.: Harvard University Press, 1959.

Hanks, Patrick, and Flavia Hodge. *A Dictionary of First Names*. New York: Oxford University Press, 1990.

282   Harper, Ida H. *Life and Work of Susan B. Anthony*. 3 vols. Indianapolis: Hollenbeck Press, 1908.

Harrison, Frederic. *Autobiographic Memoirs*. 2 vols. London: Macmillan and Co., 1911.

Haskell, Francis. *Rediscoveries in Art: Some Aspects of Taste, Fashion, and Collecting in England and France*. Ithaca, N.Y.: Cornell University Press, 1976.

Hawthorne, Nathaniel. *The English Notebooks*. Ed. Randall Stewart. New York: Russell and Russell, 1962.

———. *The Marble Faun* (1860). Harmondsworth, England: Penguin Classics, 1990.

Heimann, Mary. *Catholic Devotion in Victorian England*. Oxford, England: Clarendon Press, 1995.

Helsinger, Elizabeth K., Robin Lauterbach Sheets, and William Veeder. *The Woman Question: Society and Literature in Britain and America, 1837–1883*. 3 vols. Chicago: University of Chicago Press, 1983.

Hennesey, John. *American Catholics: A History of the Roman Catholic Community in the United States*. New York: Oxford University Press, 1981.

Herbert, Robert, ed. *The Art Criticism of John Ruskin*. 1964. Reprint, New York: Da Capo, 1987.

Herstein, Sheila. *A Mid-Victorian Feminist: Barbara Leigh Smith Bodichon*. New Haven, Conn.: Yale University Press, 1985.

Hilton, Tim. *John Ruskin: The Early Years*. New Haven, Conn.: Yale University Press, 1985.

Himmelfarb, Gertrude. *Darwin and the Darwinian Revolution*. New York: The Norton Library, 1968.

Hofstadter, Richard. *Social Darwinism in American Thought*. Boston: Beacon Press, 1955.

Holcomb, Adele. "Anna Jameson on Women Artists." *Women's Art Journal* 8 (1987–88): 15–24.

———. "Anna Jameson (1794–1860): Sacred Art and Social Vision." In *Women as Interpreters of the Visual Arts*, ed. Claire Richter Sherman with Adele Holcomb, 93–121. Westport, Conn.: Greenwood Press, 1981.

———. "Anna Jameson: The First Professional English Art Historian." *Art History* 6 (1983): 171–87.

Holmes, Elsie. "George Eliot's Wesleyan Madonna." *The George Eliot Fellowship Review* 18 (1987): 52–59.

Homans, Margaret. *Bearing the Word: Language and Female Experience in Nineteenth-Century Women's Writing*. Chicago: University of Chicago Press, 1986, 1989.

———. *Royal Representations: Queen Victoria and British Culture, 1837–1876*. Chicago: University of Chicago Press, 1998.

Honour, Hugh. *Romanticism*. New York: Harper and Row, 1979.

Howe, Irving. "George Eliot and the Jews." *Partisan Review* 46 (1979): 359–75.

Howitt, Mary. *Mary Howitt: An Autobiography*. Ed. Margaret Howitt. Boston: Houghton Mifflin, 1889; reprint, New York: AMS Press, 1973.

Hutchison, William. *The Transcendentalist Ministers: Church Reform in the New England Renaissance*. New Haven, Conn.: Yale University Press, 1959.

Inglis, K. S. *Churches and the Working Classes in Victorian England.* London: Routledge and Kegan Paul, 1963.

Irigaray, Luce. "Divine Women." In *Sexes and Genealogies.* Trans. Gillian C. Gill. New York: Columbia University Press, 1993.

Irwin, Jane, ed. *George Eliot's Daniel Deronda Notebooks.* Cambridge: Cambridge University Press, 1996.

James, William. *The Varieties of Religious Experience* (1902). New York: Vintage Books/The Library of America, 1990.

Jameson, Anna. *Celebrated Female Sovereigns* (1831). 2 vols. Superior Printing Co., 1916.

———. *A Commonplace Book of Thought.* New York: Appleton and Co., 1855.

———. *Handbook to the Public Galleries of Art in or near London.* London: John Murray, 1845.

———. *Legends of the Madonna* (1852). 4th ed. London: Longmans, Green, and Co., 1867.

———. *Legends of the Monastic Orders* (1850). 4th ed. London: Longmans, Green, and Co., 1867.

———. *Letters of Anna Jameson to Ottilie von Goethe.* Ed. G. H. Needler. Oxford: Oxford University Press, 1939.

———. *Memoirs and Essays.* London: Richard Bentley, 1846.

———. *Memoirs of Early Italian Painters.* 1845. Revised by Estell M. Hurll. Boston and New York: Houghton, Mifflin, 1895.

———. *Sacred and Legendary Art.* 2 vols. 1848. Reprint, New York: AMS Press, 1970.

———. *Sisters of Charity and the Communion of Labor.* Boston: Ticknor and Fields, 1857; reprint, Hyperion, 1976.

———. *Sketches of Art, Literature, and Character.* Boston: James R. Osgood and Co., 1875.

———. *Winter Studies and Summer Rambles in Canada* (1838). 2 vols. New York: Wiley and Putnam, 1839.

———. "'Woman's Mission,' and Woman's Position." In *Memoirs and Essays,* 187–224. London: Richard Bentley, 1846.

———, and Elizabeth Lady Eastlake. *The History of Our Lord.* 2 vols. London: Longmans, Green, and Co., 1864.

Johnson, Elizabeth. "The Marian Tradition and the Reality of Women." *Horizons* (Villanova University) 12 (1985): 116–135.

———. "Mary and the Female Face of God." *Theological Studies* 50 (1989): 500–26.

Johnson, Patricia E. "The Gendered Politics of the Gaze: Henry James and George Eliot." *Mosaic* 30/1 (1997): 39–54.

Johnston, Judith. *Anna Jameson.* London: Ashcroft, 1997.

Jordanova, L. J. *Lamarck.* Oxford: Oxford University Press, 1984.

Julian of Norwich. *Revelations of Divine Love.* Trans. Clifton Wolters. Harmondsworth, England: Penguin, 1966.

Keble, John. *The Christian Year.* London and New York: George Routledge and Sons, 1873.

Kelly, Joan. "Did Women Have a Renaissance?" In *Women, History, and Theory,* 19–50.

Women in Culture and Society Series. Chicago: University of Chicago Press, 1984.

Kenneally, James. *The History of American Catholic Women*. New York: Crossroad, 1990.

Kennedy, James G. *Herbert Spencer*. Boston: G. K. Hall, Twayne Publishers, 1978.

Ker, Ian. *John Henry Newman. Oxford Lives*. Oxford: Oxford University Press, 1990.

————. *Newman the Theologian: A Reader*. Notre Dame, Ind. Notre Dame Press, 1990.

Killham, John. *Tennyson and "The Princess": Reflections of an Age*. London: The Athlone Press, 1958.

King, Margaret. *Women of the Renaissance*. Women in Culture and Society Series. Chicago: University of Chicago Press, 1991.

King, Margaret, and Albert Rabil, Jr. *Her Immaculate Hand: Selected Works by and about the Women Humanists of Quattrocento Italy*. Binghamton, N.Y.: Medieval and Renaissance Texts and Studies, 1983.

Kinsley, David. *The Goddesses' Mirror: Visions of the Divine from East and West*. Albany: State University of New York Press, 1989.

Kissinger, Walter. *The Lives of Jesus: A History and Bibliography*. New York: Garland Publishing, Inc., 1985.

Kitson Clark, G. *Churchmen and the Condition of England, 1832–1885*. London: Methuen and Co., 1973.

Kornfeld, Eve. *Margaret Fuller*. Boston: Bedford Books, 1997.

Kornfeld, Eve, and Melissa Marks. "Margaret Fuller: Minerva and the Muse." *Journal of American Culture* 13 (1990): 47–59.

Knoepflmacher, U. C. *George Eliot's Early Novels: The Limits of Realism*. Berkeley and Los Angeles: University of California Press, 1968.

————. *Religious Humanism in the Victorian Novel*. Princeton, N.J.: Princeton University Press, 1965.

Kramnick, Isaac, and R. Laurence Moore. "The Godless University." *Academe* (Nov.–Dec. 1996): 18–23.

Krasner, James. "'Where No Man Praised': The Retreat from Fame in George Eliot's *The Spanish Gypsy*." *Victorian Poetry* 32 (1994): 54–74.

Lacey, Candida. *Barbara Leigh Smith Bodichon and the Langham Place Group*. Women's Source Library. New York and London: Routledge and Kegan Paul, 1987.

Langland, Elizabeth. *Nobody's Angels: Middle-Class Women and Domestic Ideology in Victorian Culture*. Reading Women Writing Series. Ithaca, N.Y.: Cornell University Press, 1995.

Laqueur, Walter. *A History of Zionism*. New York: Schocken Books, 1989.

Lawrence, C. H. *Medieval Monasticism*. 2nd ed. London: Longman, 1989.

Leeming, David, and Jake Page. *Goddess: Myths of the Feminine Divine*. New York: Oxford University Press, 1994.

Lerner, Gerda. "Comment on Lerner's 'Sarah M. Grimké's "Sisters of Charity."'" *Signs* 10/4 (summer 1985): 811–15.

————. *The Creation of Feminist Consciousness: From the Middle Ages to 1870*. New York: Oxford University Press, 1993.

————. *The Grimké Sisters from South Carolina*. New York: Schocken Books, 1971.   **285**

————. "Sarah M. Grimké's 'Sisters of Charity.'" *Signs* 1 (autumn 1975): 246–56.

Lerner, Laurence. *The Truthtellers: Jane Austen, George Eliot, D. H. Lawrence*. London: Chatto and Windus, 1967

Levine, George. *Darwin and the Novelists*. Cambridge, Mass.: Harvard University Press, 1988.

Levine, Philippa. *Victorian Feminism 1850–1900*. Tallahassee: Florida State University Press, 1987.

Lew, Laurie Kane. "Cultural Anxiety in Anna Jameson's Art Criticism." *Studies in English Literature, 1500–1900* 36 (autumn 1996): 829–56.

Lewes, G. H. "Augustus William Schlegel." *Foreign Quarterly Review* 32 (Oct. 1843): 160–81.

————. *Problems of Life and Mind*. 3rd series, 2 vols. Boston: Houghton, Osgood, and Co., 1879.

————. "Realism in Art: Recent German Fiction." *Westminster Review* 70 (Oct. 1858): 271–87.

Lightbown, R. W. "The Inspiration of Christian Art." In *Influences in Victorian Art and Architecture*, ed. Sarah Macready and F. H. Thompson, 3–40. Occasional Paper (new series) 7. London: Society of Antiquaries, 1985.

Lock, Charles. "Iconic Space and the Materiality of the Sign." *Religion and the Arts* 1, no. 4 (1977): 6–22.

Lootens, Tricia. *Lost Saints: Silence, Gender, and Victorian Literary Canonization*. Victorian Literature and Culture Series. Charlottesville: University Press of Virginia, 1996.

Loucks, James F., ed. *Robert Browning's Poetry*. Norton Critical Edition. New York: W. W. Norton, 1979.

Luther, Martin. *Luther's Works*. Ed. George Forell and Helmut Lehmann. Philadelphia: Muhlenberg Press, 1955.

Machin, G. I. T. *Politics and the Churches in Great Britain, 1832–1868*. Oxford: Oxford University Press, 1977.

Macpherson, Gerardine. *Memoirs of the Life of Anna Jameson*. Boston: Roberts Brothers, 1878.

Mâle, Emile. *Religious Art from the Twelfth to the Eighteenth Century*. Princeton, N.J.: Princeton University Press, 1982.

Manuel, Frank. *The Eighteenth Century Confronts the Gods*. Cambridge, Mass.: Harvard University Press, 1959.

Marcus, Stephen. *Representations: Essays on Literature and Society*. New York: Random, 1976.

Marks, Sylvia Kasey. "A Brief Glance at George Eliot's *The Spanish Gypsy*." *Victorian Poetry* 21 (1983): 184–90.

Marsden, George. *The Soul of the American University: From Protestant Establishment to Established Nonbelief*. Oxford: Oxford University Press, 1994.

Martineau, Harriet. *Autobiography*. 2 vols. 1877. Reprint, London: Virago Press, 1983.

Marx, Karl, and Friedrich Engels. *The German Ideology* (excerpts) and "Review of G. Fr.

286   Daumer's *The Religion of the New Age.*" In *Marx and Engels on Religion*, 73–81, 90–96. New York: Schocken Books, 1974.

————. *The Holy Family, or Critique of Critical Critique.* Moscow: Foreign Languages Publishing House, 1956.

Marx, Karl. "Theses on Feuerbach." In *Marx and Engels on Religion*, 69–72. New York: Schocken Books, 1974.

Massey, Marilyn. *Feminine Soul.* Boston: Beacon Press, 1985.

Matus, Jill. "The Iconography of Motherhood: Word and Image in *Middlemarch.*" *English Studies in Canada* 17 (1991): 283–300.

Maynard, John. "Like a Virgin: Coventry Patmore's Still *Unknown Eros.*" In *Virginal Sexuality and Textuality in Victorian Literature*, ed. Lloyd Davis, 129–40. Albany: State University of New York Press, 1993.

Maynard, John. *The Story of American Catholicism.* New York: Macmillan, 1951.

McDannell, Colleen. "Catholic Domesticity, 1860–1960." In *American Catholic Women: A Historical Exploration*, ed. Karen Kennelly, 48–80. Makers of the Catholic Community. New York: Macmillan, 1989.

McDowell, R. B. "The Age of the United Irishmen: Reform and Reaction, 1789–94." In *A New History of Ireland*, ed. T. W. Moody and W. E. Vaughan, 4:289–338. Oxford: Clarendon Press, 1986.

McFadden, Maggie. "Anatomy of Difference: Toward a Classification of Feminist Theory." *Women's Studies International Forum* 7 (1984): 495–504.

McGrath, Alister. *The Making of Modern German Christology, 1750–1990.* Leicester, England: Apollos (Inter-Varsity Press), 1994.

Melnyk, Julie, ed. *Women's Theology in Nineteenth-Century Britain.* Literature and Society in Victorian Britain. New York: Garland, 1998.

Mermin, Dorothy. *Godiva's Ride.* Women of Letters Series. Bloomington and Indianapolis: Indiana University Press, 1993.

Michie, Helena. *The Flesh Made Word: Female Figures and Women's Bodies.* New York: Oxford University Press, 1987.

Miles, Margaret. *Image as Insight.* Boston: Beacon Press, 1985.

————. "The Virgin's One Bare Breast: Female Nudity and Religious Meaning in Tuscan Early Religious Culture." In *The Female Body in Western Culture*, ed. Susan Suleiman, 193–208. Cambridge, Mass.: Harvard University Press, 1985.

Mill, John Stuart. *Auguste Comte and Positivism* (1865). Ann Arbor: The University of Michigan Press, 1965.

————. *The Subjection of Women* (1869). In *On Liberty and Other Writings*, ed. Stefan Collini 117–217. Cambridge Texts in the History of Political Thought. Cambridge: Cambridge University Press, 1989.

Miller, J. Hillis. *The Disappearance of God.* Cambridge, Mass.: The Belknap Press of Harvard University Press, 1963, new ed. 1975.

Miller, Jean Baker. *Toward a New Psychology of Women.* 2nd ed. Boston: Beacon Press, 1986.

Miller, Perry, ed. *The Transcendentalists.* Cambridge, Mass.: Harvard University Press, 1960.

Millet, Kate. "The Debate over Women: Ruskin vs. Mill." In *Suffer and Be Still*, ed. Martha 287
Vicinus, 121–39. Bloomington: Indiana University Press, 1972.

Mitchell, Joshua. "Of Answers Ruled Out: Religion in Academic Life." *Academe* (Nov.–Dec. 1996): 29–32.

Moers, Ellen. *Literary Women*. New York: Oxford University Press, 1985.

Monkman, Leslie. "Primitivism and a Parasol: Anna Jameson's Indians." *Essays on Canadian Writing* 29 (summer 1984): 85–95.

Moorman, John R. H. (9th Bishop of Ripon). *The Anglican Spiritual Tradition*. Springfield, Ill.: Templegate Publishers, 1985.

Morford, Mark, and Robert Lenardon. 2nd ed. *Classical Mythology*. New York and London: Longman, 1977.

Mulvey, Laura. "Visual Pleasure and Narrative Cinema" (1975). In *Feminisms*, ed. Robyn Warhol and Diane Herndl, 438–48. New Brunswick, N.J.: Rutgers University Press, 1997.

Munich, Adrienne. *Queen Victoria's Secrets*. New York: Columbia University Press, 1996.

Myers, William. *The Teaching of George Eliot*. Totowa, N.J.: Barnes and Noble, 1984.

Myerson, Joel. "Margaret Fuller's 1842 Journal: At Concord with the Emersons." *Harvard Library Bulletin* 21 (July 1973): 320–40.

Neufeldt, Victor. "The Madonna and the Gypsy." *Studies in the Novel* 15 (1983): 44–54.

Newman, John Henry. *Apologia pro Vita Sua*. Norton Critical Editions. Ed. David deLaura. New York: W. W. Norton and Co., 1968.

———. "The Glories of Mary for the Sake of Her Son" (1849, No. 17) and "On the Fitness of the Glories of Mary" (1849, No. 18). In *Sermons and Discourses (1839–57)*, 247–76. London: Longmans, Green and Co., 1949.

———. *Hymns*. Denville, N.J.: Dimension Books, 1983.

———. *Letter to Pusey* (1866). In *Certain Difficulties Felt by Anglicans in Catholic Teaching*, 2:1–170. Westminster, Md.: Christian Classics, 1969.

———. *The New Eve*. Oxford: Newman Bookshop, 1952.

———. "Our Lady in the Gospel" (1848). In *Catholic Sermons of Cardinal Newman*, 92–104. London: Burns & Oates, 1957.

———. "The Reverence Due to the Virgin Mary" (1832). In *Parochial and Plain Sermons*, 306–13. San Francisco: Ignatius Press, 1987.

———. "The Theory of Developments in Religious Doctrine" (1843). In *Sermons, Chiefly on the Theory of Religious Belief*, 311–54. London: J. G. F. & J. Rivington, and Oxford: J. H. Parker, 1843.

Newton, K. M. "*Daniel Deronda* and Circumcision." *Essays in Criticism* 31 (1981): 313–27.

Nies, Judith. *Seven Women: Portraits from the American Radical Tradition*. New York: Viking Penguin, 1977.

Nightingale, Florence. *Cassandra* (1852). Ed. Myra Stark. New York: Feminist Press, 1979.

Nord, Deborah. "'Marks of Race': Gypsy Figures and Eccentric Femininity in Nineteenth-Century Women's Writing." *Victorian Studies* 41 (1998): 189–210.

288 Norman, Edward R. *Anti-Catholicism in Victorian England.* New York: Barnes and Noble, 1968.

———. *The English Catholic Church in the Nineteenth Century.* Oxford: Clarendon Press, 1984.

Oberman, Heiko. *Luther between God and the Devil.* Trans. Eileen Walliser-Schwarzbart. New Haven, Conn.: Yale University Press, 1989.

O'Connell, Maurice. *Daniel O'Connell: The Man and His Politics.* Dublin: Irish Academic Press, 1990.

O'Dwyer, Peter, O. Carm. *Mary: A History of Devotion in Ireland.* Dublin: Four Courts Press, 1988.

Offen, Karen. "Defining Feminism." *Signs* 14, no. 1 (1988): 119–155.

Oxford Dictionary of the Christian Church. Ed. F. L. Cross and E. A. Livingstone. Oxford: Oxford University Press, 2nd ed., rpt. 1990.

Oxford English Dictionary. Oxford: Oxford University Press, 1989.

Pals, Daniel. *Seven Theories of Religion.* New York: Oxford University Press, 1996.

———. *Victorian "Lives" of Jesus.* Trinity University Monograph Series in Religion, vol. 7. San Antonio, Tex.: Trinity University Press, 1982.

Paris, Bernard. *Experiments in Life: George Eliot's Quest for Values.* Detroit: Wayne State University Press, 1965.

Parker, Roszika, and Griselda Pollock. *Old Mistresses: Women, Art and Ideology.* New York: Pantheon, 1981.

Parkes, Bessie. *Vignettes: Twelve Biographical Sketches.* London and New York: Alexander Strahan, 1866.

Parton, James, et al. *Eminent Women of the Age.* Hartford: S. M. Betts, 1868.

Patmore, Coventry. *The Poems of Coventry Patmore.* Ed. Frederick Page. Oxford: Oxford University Press, 1949.

Paxton, Nancy. *George Eliot and Herbert Spencer.* Princeton, N.J.: Princeton University Press, 1991.

Payne, Robert. *The Life and Death of Adolf Hitler.* New York: Praeger Publishers, 1973.

Paz, D. G. *Popular Anti-Catholicism in Mid-Victorian England.* Stanford, Calif.: Stanford University Press, 1992.

Peel, J. D. Y. *Herbert Spencer.* New York: Basic Books, 1971.

Pelikan, Jaroslav. *Jesus through the Centuries.* New Haven, Conn.: Yale University Press, 1985.

———. *Mary Through the Centuries.* New Haven, Conn.: Yale University Press, 1996.

———. *Reformation of Church and Dogma (1300–1700).* Vol. 4, *The Christian Tradition.* Chicago: University of Chicago Press, 1984.

Plaskow, Judith. "Anti-Judaism in Feminist Christian Interpretation." In *Searching the Scriptures,* ed. Elisabeth Schüssler Fiorenza; vol. 1, *A Feminist Introduction,* 117–29.

Poovey, Mary. *The Proper Lady and the Woman Writer.* Women in Culture and Society. Chicago: University of Chicago Press, 1984.

———. *Uneven Developments: The Ideological Work of Gender in Mid-Victorian England.* Women in Culture and Society. Chicago: University of Chicago Press, 1988.

Pope, Barbara C. "Immaculate and Powerful: The Marian Revival in the Nineteenth 289
Century." In *Immaculate and Powerful: The Female in Sacred Image and Social Reality*, ed. C.
W. Atkinson, C. H. Buchanan, and M. R. Miles, 173–200. Boston: Beacon Press,
1985.

Porte, Joel. *Representative Man*. Oxford University Press, 1979.

Postlethwaite, Diana. "When George Eliot Reads Milton: The Muse in a Different
Voice." *ELH* 57 (1990): 197–221.

Ranelagh, John O'Beirne. *A Short History of Ireland*. 2nd ed. Cambridge: Press Syndicate
of the University of Cambridge, 1994.

Ranke-Heinemann, Uta. *Eunuchs for the Kingdom of Heaven: Women, Sexuality and the Catholic
Church*. Trans. Peter Heinegg. Harmondsworth, England: Penguin, 1990.

Redinger, Ruby. *George Eliot: The Emergent Self*. New York: Knopf, 1975.

Reed, T. J. *Schiller*. Oxford and New York: Oxford University Press, 1991.

Renan, Ernst. *The Life of Jesus*. Trans. John Haynes Holmes. New York: Random House,
1927.

Rich, Adrienne. *Of Woman Born*. New York: Bantam, 1977.

Richardson, Robert. "Margaret Fuller and Myth." *Prospects* 4 (1979): 169–184.

Rio, A. F. *The Poetry of Christian Art*. London: T. Bosworth, 1854.

Ritschin, Abigail. "Beside the Reclining Statue: Ekphrasis, Narrative, and Desire in
Middlemarch." *PMLA* 111 (1996): 1121–32.

Robinson, David M. "Margaret Fuller and the Transcendental Ethos: *Woman in the
Nineteenth Century*." *PMLA* 97 (Jan. 1982): 83–98.

Rodriguez, Jeanette. *Our Lady of Guadalupe*. Austin: University of Texas Press, 1994.

Rose, Andrea. *The Pre-Raphaelites*. London: Phaidon Press, 1992.

Rose, Anne. *Transcendentalism as a Social Movement, 1830–1850*. New Haven, Conn.: Yale
University Press, 1981.

Rossi, Alice, ed. *The Feminist Papers*. Boston: Northeastern University Press, 1988.

Ruether, Rosemary Radford. *Mary: The Feminine Face of the Church*. Philadelphia: The
Westminster Press, 1977.

———. *New Woman/New Earth*. New York: Seabury Press, 1985. 36–62.

———. *Sexism and God-Talk*. Boston: Beacon Press, 1983.

———. "Women in Utopian Movements." In *Women and Religion in America*, vol. 1, *The
Nineteenth Century*, ed. Ruether and Rosemary Skinner Keller, 46–100. New York:
Harper and Row, 1981.

Ruether, Rosemary Radford, and Rosemary Skinner Keller, eds. *In Our Own Voices: Four
Centuries of American Women's Religious Writing*. New York: Harper Collins, 1995.

Ruskin, John. *Complete Works of John Ruskin*. Ed. E. T. Cook and Alexander Wedderburn.
39 vols. London: George Allen; New York: Longmans, Green, 1903–12. (All references to Ruskin, unless otherwise indicated, are to the *Complete Works*.)

———. *Praeterita* (1885–1889). Philadelphia: University Library Association, 1885.

Russell, Anne E. "'History and Real Life': Anna Jameson, Shakespeare's Heroines and
Victorian Women." *Victorian Review: The Journal of the Victorian Studies Association of
Western Canada* 17 (winter 1991): 35–49.

290 Santangelo. Gennaro. "Villari's *Life and Times of Savonarola*: A Source for George Eliot's *Romola*." *Anglia—Zeitschrift fur Englische Philologie* 90 (1972): 118–31.

Schlegel, A. W. *Lectures on Dramatic Art and Literature*. Trans. Ralph R. Read III. In *German Romantic Criticism*, ed. A. Leslie Willson, 175–218. The German Library, vol. 21. New York: Continuum, 1982.

Schlegel, Friedrich. *Letters on Christian Art*: "Description of Paintings in Paris and the Netherlands in the Years 1802–1804" and "Principles of Gothic Architecture." In *Aesthetic and Miscellaneous Works*. Trans. E. J. Millington. London: Bohn, 1849.

Schleiermacher, Friedrich. *Christmas Eve: Dialogue on the Incarnation* (1826). Trans. Terrence N. Tice. Richmond, Va.: John Knox Press, 1967.

——. *The Life of Jesus* (1864). Trans. S. Maclean Gilmour. Ed. Jack C. Verheyden. Philadelphia: Fortress Press, 1975.

——. *On Religion: Speeches to Its Cultured Despisers* (1799). Trans. John Oman. Harper Torchbooks. New York: Harper and Brothers, 1958.

Schneir, Miriam, ed. *Feminism: The Essential Historical Writings*. New York: Vintage, 1972.

Schweitzer, Albert. *The Quest of the Historical Jesus*. Trans. W. Montgomery. New York: Macmillan, 1948.

Scott, James F. "George Eliot, Positivism, and the Social Vision of *Middlemarch*." *Victorian Studies* 16 (1972): 59–76.

Semmel, Bernard. *George Eliot and the Politics of National Inheritance*. New York: Oxford University Press, 1994.

Shelley, Mary. *Frankenstein* (1818). Oxford: Oxford University Press, World's Classics, 1992.

Sherman, Lila. *Art Museums of America: A Guide*. New York: William Morrow, 1980.

Sherwood, Dolly. *Harriet Hosmer, American Sculptor, 1830–1908*. Columbia: University of Missouri Press, 1991.

Showalter, Elaine. *A Literature of Their Own*. Princeton, N.J.: Princeton University Press, 1977.

——. "Miranda and Cassandra: The Discourse of the Feminist Intellectual." In *Tradition and the Talents of Women*, ed. Florence Howe, 313–27. Champaign: University of Illinois Press, 1991.

Slights, Jessica. "Historical Shakespeare: Anna Jameson and Womanliness." *English Studies in Canada* 19 (Dec. 1993): 387–400.

Smith, Philip E., II, and Michael S. Helfand, eds. *Oscar Wilde's Oxford Notebooks*. New York: Oxford University Press, 1989.

Smith-Rosenberg, Carroll. *Disorderly Conduct: Visions of Gender in Victorian America*. New York: Oxford University Press, 1985.

Spencer, Herbert. *An Autobiography* (1904). *Works of Herbert Spencer*. Vol. 21. Osnabruck: Otto Zeller, 1966.

Spender, Dale. *Feminist Theorists: Three Centuries of Key Women Thinkers*. New York: Pantheon Books, 1983.

Spretnak, Charlene, ed. *The Politics of Women's Spirituality*. Garden City, N.Y.: Anchor Press, 1982.

Standley, Arline. *August Comte.* Twayne's World Authors Series, No. 625. Boston: 291
Twayne, a division of G. K. Hall, 1981.

Stanton, Elizabeth Cady. *Eighty Years and More: Reminiscences 1815–1897.* Boston:
Northeastern University Press, 1993.

———. *The Woman's Bible* (1895–1898). Boston: Northeastern University Press, 1993.

Steele, Jeffrey. "Freeing the 'Prisoned Queen': The Development of Margaret Fuller's
Poetry." *Studies in the American Renaissance.* Ed. Joel Myerson. Charlottesville:
University of Virginia Press, 1992.

———. *The Representation of the Self in the American Renaissance.* Chapel Hill: University of
North Carolina Press, 1987. 100–133.

Steinberg, Ronald M. *Fra Girolamo Savonarola, Florentine Art, and Renaissance Historiography.*
Athens: Ohio University Press, 1977.

Strauss, David F. *The Life of Jesus Critically Examined* (1835–36). Trans. George Eliot
(1846). Philadelphia: Fortress Press, 1972.

Surtees, Virginia, ed. *Sublime and Instructive: Letters from John Ruskin to Louisa, Marchioness of
Waterford, Anna Blunden, and Ellen Heaton.* London: Michael Joseph, 1972.

Taves, Ann. *The Household of Faith: Roman Catholic Devotions in Mid-Nineteenth-Century
America.* Notre Dame Studies in American Catholicism. Notre Dame, Ind.:
University of Notre Dame Press, 1986.

Thomas, Clara. *Love and Work Enough: The Life of Anna Jameson.* Toronto: University of
Toronto Press, 1967.

Thompson, Ann, and Sasha Roberts, eds. *Women Reading Shakespeare, 1660–1900: An
Anthology of Criticism.* Manchester: Manchester University Press, 1997.

Thompson, E. P. *The Making of the English Working Class.* New York: Vintage, 1966.

Thomson, J. Arthur. *Herbert Spencer.* London: J. M. Dent, 1906; reprint, AMS, 1976.

Tone, Wolfe. *The Life of Theobald Wolfe Tone.* Edited by his son William Theobald Wolfe
Tone. London: Whittaker, Treacher, and Arnot, 1831.

Trudgill, Eric. *Madonnas and Magdalenes: The Origins and Development of Victorian Sexual
Attitudes.* New York: Holmes and Meier, 1976.

Urbanski, Marie O. "Margaret Fuller's *Woman in the Nineteenth Century:* The Feminist
Manifesto." In *Nineteenth-Century Women Writers of the English-Speaking World.* Ed.
Rhoda B. Nathan. Westport, Conn.: Greenwood Press, 1986.

———. *Margaret Fuller's "Woman in the Nineteenth Century": A Literary Study of Form and
Content, of Sources and Influence.* Contributions in Women's Studies No. 13. Westport,
Conn.: Greenwood Press, 1980.

Van Anglen, Kevin P. "Review Essay: The Virgin and the Dynamo in American Literary
History." *Religion and the Arts* 1 (spring 1997): 128–44.

Vasari, Giorgio. *Lives of the Painters* (2nd ed. 1568). Trans. George Bull. 2 vols.
Harmondsworth, England: Penguin, 1987.

Vicinus, Martha. *Independent Women: Work and Community for Single Women, 1850–1920.*
Women in Culture and Society. Chicago: University of Chicago Press, 1985.

Vico, Giambattista. *The Autobiography of Giambattista Vico.* Ed. and trans. Max Harold

Fisch and Thomas Goddard Bergin. Ithaca, N.Y.: Cornell University Press, 1944; reprint 1995.

Victorian Britain. Ed. Sally Mitchell. New York and London: Garland, 1988.

Villari, Pasquale. *Life and Times of Savonarola*. Trans. Linda Villari. London: T. Fisher Unwin, 1918.

Wade, Mason. *Margaret Fuller: Whetstone of Genius*. 1940. Reprint, Clifton, N.J.: Augustus M. Kelley, 1973.

Walker, Corlette, and Adele Holcomb. "Margaret Fuller (1810–1850): Her Work as an Art Critic." In *Women as Interpreters of the Visual Arts*, ed. Claire Richter Sherman with Adele Holcomb, 123–46. Westport, Conn.: Greenwood Press, 1981.

Walsh, Michael, compiler. *Dictionary of Catholic Devotions*. San Francisco: Harper San Francisco, 1993.

Warner, Marina. *Alone of All Her Sex: The Myth and Cult of the Virgin Mary*. New York: Knopf, 1976.

Watson, Nicola J. "Gloriana Victoriana: Victoria and the Cultural Memory of Elizabeth I." In *Remaking Queen Victoria*, ed. Margaret Homans and Adrienne Munich, 79–104. Cambridge: Cambridge University Press, 1997.

Waxman, Barbara. "Ethnic Heroism: Matthew Arnold's and George Eliot's Gypsies." In *Perspectives on Nineteenth-Century Heroism*, ed. Sara M. Putzell and David C. Leonard, 115–26. Madrid, Spain: Studia Humanitas, 1982.

Weatherford, Doris. *A History of the American Suffragist Movement*. Santa Barbara: ABC-Clio, 1998.

Webb, R. K. *Modern England from the Eighteenth Century to the Present*. New York: Harper and Row, 1968.

Weimann, Jeanne Madeline. *The Fair Women*. Chicago: Academy Chicago, 1981.

Weinstein, Donald. *Savonarola and Florence*. Princeton, N.J.: Princeton University Press, 1970.

Welsh, Alexander. *George Eliot and Blackmail*. Cambridge, Mass.: Harvard University Press, 1985.

Welter, Barbara. "The Cult of True Womanhood, 1820–1860." *American Quarterly* (1966): 151–74.

Weltman, Sharon Aronofsky. *Ruskin's Mythic Queen*. Athens: Ohio University Press, 1998.

Wethey, Harold E. *The Paintings of Titian*. Vol. 3, *The Mythological and Historical Paintings*. London: Phaidon, 1975.

Wiesenfarth, Joseph. *George Eliot's Mythmaking*. Heidelberg: Carl Winter Universitätsverlag, 1977.

———. "*Middlemarch*: The Language of Art." *PMLA* 97 (1982): 363–77.

———, ed. *George Eliot: A Writer's Notebook, 1854–1859*. Charlottesville: University Press of Virginia for the Bibliographical Society of the University of Virginia, 1981.

Wiesner, Merry. *Women and Gender in Early Modern Europe*. Cambridge: Cambridge University Press, 1993.

Witemeyer, Hugh. *George Eliot and the Visual Arts*. New Haven, Conn.: Yale University 293
Press, 1979.

Wolff, Michael. "Heroines Adrift: George Eliot and the Ideology of Family." In *Dickens and Other Victorians*, ed. Joanne Shattock, 202–13. New York: St. Martin's, 1988.

Wolffe, John. *The Protestant Crusade in Great Britain, 1829–1860*. Oxford: Clarendon Press, 1991.

Wollstonecraft, Mary. *A Vindication of the Rights of Woman* (1792). Ed. Miriam Brody Kramnick. Harmondsworth, England: Penguin, 1983.

Wright, T. R. "*Middlemarch* as a Religious Novel, or Life without God." In *Images of Belief in Literature*, ed. David Jasper, 138–52. New York: St. Martin's, 1984.

Yeldham, Charlotte. *Women Artists in Nineteenth-Century France and England*. 2 vols. New York: Garland Publishing Co., 1984.

Yonge, Charlotte M. *History of Christian Names*. London: Macmillan, 1884; rpt. 1966.

York, Lorraine. "'Sublime Desolation': European Art and Jameson's Perceptions of Canada." *Mosaic* 19 (spring 1986): 43–56.

Zimdars-Swartz, Sandra. *Encountering Mary*. Princeton, N.J.: Princeton University Press, 1991.

Zimmerman, Bonnie. "George Eliot and Feminism: The Case of *Daniel Deronda*." In *Nineteenth-Century Women Writers of the English-Speaking World*, ed. Rhoda B. Nathan, 231–37. Westport, Conn.: Greenwood Press, 1986.

———. "'The Mother's History' in George Eliot's Life, Literature, and Political Ideology." In *The Lost Tradition: Mothers and Daughters in Literature*, ed. Cathy N. Davidson and E. M. Broner, 81–94. New York: Ungar, 1980.

Zwarg, Christina. *Feminist Conversations: Fuller, Emerson, and the Play of Reading*. Ithaca, N.Y.: Cornell University Press, 1994.

Index